THE U.S. CONSTITUTION'S EIGHTH AMENDMENT

The U.S. Constitution's Eighth Amendment: Bail, Fines, and Punishments is an in-depth exploration of the Eighth Amendment's pivotal role in American jurisprudence. This comprehensive casebook is the very first of its kind, dedicated entirely to the Eighth Amendment, with every relevant Supreme Court precedent included to 2025.

The book delves into the intricacies of bail, fines, and punishments litigation, featuring key excerpts from landmark Supreme Court cases that have defined the Amendment over the past 200 years. This work examines the historical context and evolving interpretations of the Amendment, starting with its origin in English Law and highlighting the impact of Supreme Court jurisprudence on the wider justice system. Through expert analysis of major cases, the book reveals how the Eighth Amendment shapes debates on relevant issues, providing unique insights into cases and addressing contemporary issues like racial bias in sentencing, the vanishing applicability of the death penalty, the importance of age in sentencing and punishment, and solitary confinement.

Ideal for legal scholars, practitioners, and anyone interested in constitutional law, this is a vital resource for understanding one of the Constitution's most essential protections.

Charlie Eastaugh holds a first class honors degree (L.L.B.) in English Law and a Ph.D. in U.S. Constitutional Law. His first book, *Unconstitutional Solitude*, focusing on the legality of long-term solitary confinement was published in 2016.

THE U.S. CONSTITUTION'S EIGHTH AMENDMENT

Bail, Fines, and Punishments

Charlie Eastaugh

Routledge
Taylor & Francis Group
NEW YORK AND LONDON

Designed cover image: Archive Holdings Inc.

First published 2025
by Routledge
605 Third Avenue, New York, NY 10158

and by Routledge
4 Park Square, Milton Park, Abingdon, Oxon, OX14 4RN

Routledge is an imprint of the Taylor & Francis Group, an informa business

Library of Congress Cataloging-in-Publication Data
Names: Eastaugh, Charlie, author.
Title: The U.S. Constitution's Eighth Amendment : bail, fines, and punishments / Charlie Eastaugh.
Other titles: United States Constitution's Eighth Amendment
Description: Abingdon, Oxon [UK] ; New York, NY : Routledge, 2025. | Includes bibliographical references and index.
Identifiers: LCCN 2024036942 (print) | LCCN 2024036943 (ebook) | ISBN 9780367025991 (hardback) | ISBN 9780367026011 (paperback) | ISBN 9780429398780 (ebook)
Subjects: LCSH: United States. Constitution. 8th Amendment. | Punishment—United States. | Fines (Penalties)—United States. | Bail—United States. | Imprisonment—United States. | Criminal justice, Administration of—United States.
Classification: LCC KF4558 8th .E33 2025 (print) | LCC KF4558 8th (ebook) | DDC 345.73/0773—dc23/eng/20240814
LC record available at https://lccn.loc.gov/2024036942
LC ebook record available at https://lccn.loc.gov/2024036943

ISBN: 978-0-367-02599-1 (hbk)
ISBN: 978-0-367-02601-1 (pbk)
ISBN: 978-0-429-39878-0 (ebk)

DOI: 10.4324/9780429398780

Typeset in Sabon
by Apex CoVantage, LLC

To L.C.

CONTENTS

EXCERPTED CASES

O'Neil v. Vermont 144 U.S. 323 (1892)
Weems v. United States, 217 U.S. 349 (1910)
Trop v. Dulles, 356 U.S. 86 (1958)
Robinson v. California, 370 U.S. 660 (1962)
Stack v. Boyle, 342 U.S. 1 (1951)
United States v Salerno, 481 U.S. 739 (1987)
Browning-Ferris Industries of Vermont, Inc. v. Kelco Disposal, Inc., 492 U.S. 257 (1989)
Austin v. United States, 509 U.S. 602 (1993)
United States v. Bajakajian, 524 U.S. 321 (1998)
Timbs v. Indiana, 139 S. Ct. 682 (2019)
Furman v. Georgia, 408 U.S. 238 (1972)
Gregg v. Georgia, 428 U.S. 153 (1976)
Lockett v. Ohio, 438 U.S. 586 (1978)
Coker v. Georgia, 433 U.S. 584 (1977)
Enmund v. Florida, 458 U.S. 782 (1982)
Kennedy v. Louisiana, 554 U.S. 407 (2008)
Eddings v. Oklahoma, 455 U.S. 104 (1982)
Thompson v. Oklahoma, 487 U.S. 815 (1988)
Roper v. Simmons, 543 U.S. 551 (2005)
Ford v. Wainwright, 477 U.S. 399 (1986)
Atkins v. Virginia, 536 U.S. 304 (2002)
Wilkerson v. Utah, 99 U.S. 130 (1878)
In re Kemmler, 136 U.S. 436 (1890)
Louisiana ex rel. Francis v. Resweber, 329 U.S. 459 (1947)

Baze v. Rees, 553 U.S. 35 (2008)
Glossip v. Gross, 576 U.S. 863 (2015)
McCleskey v. Kemp, 481 U.S. 279 (1987)
Solem v. Helm, 463 U.S. 277 (1983)
Harmelin v. Michigan, 501 U.S. 957 (1991)
Ewing v. California, 538 U.S. 11 (2003)
Lockyer v. Andrade, 538 U.S. 63 (2003)
Graham v. Florida, 560 U.S. 48 (2010)
Miller v. Alabama, 567 U.S. 460 (2012)
Estelle v. Gamble, 429 U.S. 97 (1976)
Hutto v. Finney, 437 U.S. 678 (1978)
Whitley v. Albers, 475 U.S. 312 (1986)
Wilson v. Seiter, 501 U.S. 294 (1991)
Hudson v. McMillian, 503 U.S. 1 (1992)
Helling v. McKinney, 509 U.S. 25 (1993)
Farmer v. Brennan, 511 U.S. 825 (1994)
Hope v. Pelzer, 536 U.S. 730 (2002)
Brown v. Plata, 563 U.S. 493 (2011)

ACKNOWLEDGMENTS

This book is the product of over a decade of fascination with the U.S. Supreme Court. I feel privileged to have been able to author it, compiling some of the most impressive writing in the annals of constitutional law. The true credit must go to the authors of those opinions, their clerks, and the advocates who made it their business to ensure the Eighth Amendment remains unfastened to the obsolete and that it continues to be enlightened by a humane justice.

I am hugely grateful to Ellen Boyne at Routledge, who allowed me to delay this project for many years before the spark returned and I was finally able to finish the drafting. I owe a debt of gratitude to my good friends B.E.D., M.A.W., and R.B.B., for remaining on the journey, and to my parents, sister, and grandparents for their unwavering support.

Finally, to L.C., to whom this is dedicated: thank you for everything.

INTRODUCTION

As is traditional in a constitutional law text, this book focuses on judicial decision-making, primarily by the Supreme Court. Legislation, where relevant, is included as an important backdrop for judicial decision-making, often the source of a complaint and context for a particular dispute. The judgments of those nine Justices are then ultimate pronouncements of constitutional interpretation, defining the extent of protection owed to a petitioner and curtailing government power. Throughout this process, the Court is engaging in a constant refinement process, breathing meaning into the written text of the Constitution. As Moskovitz set out in his instructive work "On Writing a Casebook,"[1] in any study of constitutional law certain high court cases are "landmarks," which establish a new doctrine or trend, and all other courts are required to follow those cases. General constitutional law casebooks will therefore invariably include such critical judgments as *Marbury v. Madison*, *Brown v. Board of Education*, and *Roe v. Wade*. These cases are so prominent and so often quoted in recent cases that students must be exposed to them.

Where this book diverges from that approach, however, is by focusing almost myopically on the Eighth Amendment. The rationale for this is one of page count and practicality. It has been exceptionally challenging to reduce the number of key cases to those found within these pages, let alone with the additional luxury of reproducing a number of critical *general*

1 Moskovitz, M. (2000) 'On writing a casebook', *Seattle University Law Review*, 23, p. 1019, which was extremely helpful in setting the foundations for this work.

DOI: 10.4324/9780429398780-1

constitutional law rulings. In most law school courses, very few cases are in fact "mandatory" reading, and this book does not seek to mandate a specific selection. That said, the Eighth Amendment itself has provided for a fascinating rendition of constitutional legal principles—spanning interpretative methods, social evolution, and judicial restraint, each following the ebbs and flows of the ideological leanings of each unique setup on the Court's bench.

The cases included throughout the following chapters explain the history and reasons underlying basic rules to inform the reader of the policy reasons, sociopolitical context, and historical underpinnings of Eighth Amendment interpretation and evolution. Judgments are exclusively those of the Supreme Court, although, where appropriate, some lower court judgments (in federal circuit and state superior courts) have been signposted for further useful reading, particularly where interpretation or application of a Supreme Court ruling has diverged in the courts below.

A note on case selection and editing

Careful thought has been put into the abridgment of judgments, with lengthy facts included only where they are either (1) pertinent to the decision, that is, relevant context for a particular holding, or (2) particularly interesting or illuminating, whether in respect of the way they are written or the historical importance of the story. Dissents are occasionally also included, only where they meet one or both of those same criteria. A number of cases included here have been overruled, but they are included for their importance in the "story" of the Eighth Amendment, even where some rulings might necessarily since have been cast aside as wrongly decided, or even controversial. Chapters should therefore be taken in their totality and readers should not take a judgment in isolation of the explanatory notes in the preceding paragraphs. Nearly all of the cases included in these pages date from the 1980s onward, during which the Eighth Amendment saw its most major period of constitutional adjudication and, in the same process, something of an evolution in the extent of its curtailment of state authority. Many more recent cases are included, although for reasons that become clear in reading this book there are few of significant relevance since around 2008. Other than in a couple of special exceptions, most cases have been edited to a far reduced size, often limited to a handful of pages. Irrelevant parts such as verbose or repetitive detail, references, or lengthy quotes are edited out for the ease of the reader. All footnotes have been deleted, as have the vast majority of cross-references to other court citations. The idea is solely with a view to readability and relevance: The goal is clarity of exposition while preserving the ruling and its rationale. Where possible, just one or two key paragraphs from a concurrence are included, to convey that authoring Justice's views pithily and without using up too much of the precious page count, or distracting from the majority holding. Dissents are edited in the same way: A choice on selection or the extent of editing of any element of a case is not a value judgment on the opinion itself, but an editorial decision on both readability and substance.

This book has been structured so that, roughly speaking, each chapter can be relied on as one week's teaching or studentship. While there are few Eighth Amendments dedicated courses taught in the United States, it is hoped that work such as this will inspire current and future professors to consider teaching a new course in this area. Ideally, this book will provide a useful guide for reference and study. For the practitioner, it encompasses all critical Eighth Amendment jurisprudence currently in force (at the time of writing in October 2024), where many of the pre-1990s (certainly pre-1976) decisions are interesting historically, if not quite as relevant today. There are, naturally, major exceptions to that generalization. *Trop v. Dulles*, *Furman v. Georgia*, *Gregg v. Georgia*—to name a few—remain pervasive and important in Eighth Amendment decision-making (and scholarship) to this day. While the vast bulk of this work centers on the Punishments Clause, for reasons which will soon become clear, the book aims to do justice for the first time to the Bail and Fines clauses, with chapters dedicated to each. This is novel for a constitutional law casebook, and it is hoped that it will pave the way for more studentship and scholarship on those important provisions in future.

Reference

Moskovitz, M. (2000) 'On writing a casebook', *Seattle University Law Review*, 23, p. 1019.

1

FRAMING AND EARLY HISTORY

Founding Father James Madison's prescient warning, articulated in the Federalist No. 48, underscores the enduring vulnerability of constitutional clauses, cautioning against their erosion into mere "parchment barriers" (Madison, 1788). This chapter embarks on a historical exploration of the Eighth Amendment, tracing its evolution from the admonitions of Madison to its roots in the Glorious Revolution of 1688–1689, delving into the impact of Enlightenment principles on the American Revolution, before examining the debates surrounding its framing and early judicial interpretation.

The Eighth Amendment's English and common law roots

To understand the roots of the Eighth Amendment, it is essential to delve into the historical context surrounding the Glorious Revolution. This period, occurring a century before the ratification of the U.S. Constitution, witnessed the removal of King James II—a Catholic monarch of the Stuart dynasty—and the establishment of Protestant co-regents, William and Mary. The repercussions of this transformative event had a profound impact globally, prompting the formulation of the English Declaration of Rights, a legal document that reshaped the English legal landscape and paved the way for the enactment of the English Bill of Rights in 1689. The Declaration responded to the actions of King James II's "evil counsellors," proclaimed violations of Magna Carta and the imposition of "despotic power" and "arbitrary government." In January 1689, the Convention Parliament boldly asserted that King James II had abdicated the throne, leading to its vacancy.

DOI: 10.4324/9780429398780-2

The historic Convention Parliament, instrumental in offering the crown to William and Mary, outlined specific grievances to address abuses of power experienced during the Stuart reign—the nineteenth on this list focused on preventing excessive bail requirements, imposing excessive fines, and inflicting illegal punishments. Simultaneously, in Edinburgh, the Declaration of the Estates of the Kingdom of Scotland, aligning with the English Bill of Rights, voiced opposition to extraordinary fines, exorbitant bail, and premature disposals of fines and forfeitures. The final version of the Declaration of Rights, presented to Prince William and Princess Mary, listed 13 grievances, including the following oratory as its tenth article:

> That excessive Baile ought not to be required nor excessive Fines imposed nor cruell and unusuall Punishments inflicted.
>
> *(Prince of Orange, 1688)*

Royal Assent was granted, making the statement law on December 16, 1689, within the inaugural year of William and Mary's reign. Formally titled "An Act Declaring the Rights and Liberties of the Subject, and Settling the Succession of the Crown,"[1] the English Bill of Rights solidified the prohibition against the behavior of the Stuarts and their gratuitous Star Chamber, embedding principles of proportionate governmental power in the legal fabric of modern England.

Punishments context

The power and influence of the "Star Chamber" had grown under the Stuarts, a court utilized by King James and his son Charles I, to quash dissenters and rule often in favor of the Sovereign. The Star Chamber would impose often gruesome and disproportionate punishments, carried out publicly, to reinforce the Stuarts' rein of fear and terror (Bessler, 2019, p. 989). Unchecked tyranny imposed by the court included the famous sentencing of Scottish clergyman Dr. Alexander Leighton in 1630 to branding, flogging, pillorying, and nose slitting. Another instance in 1634 involved the punishment of William Prynne, a prominent lawyer. Prynne was landed with a £5,000 fine, lifelong imprisonment, loss of academic degrees, expulsion from professional associations, pillorying, and ear cutting, all for publishing a book denouncing dramatic productions as the Devil's work. The ramifications of the English Declaration of Rights became particularly

1 The Bill of Rights (1689). *The Glorious revolution.* Available at: http://perma.cc/G85R-DR6V

evident in the postrevolutionary era, with notable cases such as that of Titus Oates. Oates, tried for perjury in 1685 at the onset of James II's reign, had falsely claimed a "Popish Plot" to assassinate King Charles II, implicating various prominent English figures, including royals. His fabrications led to the execution of numerous Catholics, earning him the epithet "the Blackest of Villains."

Oates's sentencing, pronounced by Justice Francis Wythens, mandated that he "stand upon the Pillory, and in the Pillory, here before Westminster-hall gate on the following Monday for an hour's time between 10:00 AM and noon with a paper over his head declaring his crime [. . .] first to be paraded round about to all the Courts in Westminster-hall with that ignominious placard [and whipped] from Aldgate to Newgate," a distance of three miles (Howell, 1816). In addition, Wythens had imposed on Oates an extraordinary annual punishment. Every year on three specific dates, for as long as he lived, Oates was to stand for an hour in the pillory on each date, with his head and hands locked into a wooden frame, to be publicly shamed and abused, often pelted with rotting matter. The severity of Oates's punishment raised concerns and escalated all the way to the House of Lords, the highest judicial body in England and later the United Kingdom.[2] Oates's punishment was upheld by 35 votes to 23 of the peers who heard the case, with the minority labeling it as "barbarous, inhumane, and un-Christian." There was, they concluded, "no precedent to warrant the punishments of whipping and committing to prison for life, for the crime of perjury; which yet were but part of the punishments inflicted upon him" (Howell, 1816). While a majority had affirmed the judgment, a minority decried the punishment as contrary to the newly issued Declaration of Rights, emphasizing the prohibition of excessive punishments. The House of Commons, echoing the sentiment, invoked the "cruel and unusual" clause to justify remission, branding Oates's sentence as barbarous and an "ill Example to future Ages."

Fines, too, were prevalent throughout the development of English common law, even earlier than Magna Carta, through the system of amercement. Essentially a form of civil payment imposed by the Crown, these fines were designed to be both punitive and remedial, required by offenders who were "in the King's mercy." Amercements were unbridled and often excessive, sometimes imposed against entire town settlements for collective wrongdoing such as failing to live up to their civic duties. The use of

2 In 2005, the U.K. Supreme Court was established, superseding the House of Lords in this capacity, leaving the latter to its primary function as the second legislative chamber of the United Kingdom of Great Britain and Northern Ireland.

such a penalty was widespread, with one commentary claiming that any man in England could expect to be amerced at least annually (Pollock and Maitland, 1905, pp. 522–525). In response to the frequent, often abusive use of amercements by the King as a weapon against enemies of the Crown, Magna Carta included several provisions placing limits on the process and value of such penalties, including the first type of proportionality restriction on fines that would be reflected many centuries later in the English and then American Bills of Rights. As Chapter 4 shows, the U.S. Supreme Court's view of the Excessive Fines Clause's operation against civil (punitive) damages is a complex one, finally incorporating the clause in 2019.

By the time the Eighth Amendment was ratified in the United States, three types of forfeiture had existed in England. The first was the biblical notion of "deodand," which saw the value of an inanimate object causing the accidental death of a King's subject forfeited to the Crown. The second mode of common law forfeiture was imposed only on those convicted of a high crime or treason, where a convict would forfeit all of his belongings and land to the Crown, including forfeitures of estate. This method of punishment served to punish offenders severely, justified as a response to having breached the individual contract with society. The third English forfeiture was statutory, imposed on all objects used in violation of customs and revenue provisions. For example, the Navigation Acts, 12 Cha. 2. c. (1660) that required the forfeiture of illegal goods carried by ship. These provisions were severe and could be imposed on the Crown to seize the entire ship itself, even if the captain was unaware of the actions of the criminal seaman.

The Eighth Amendment in the early United States

As the colonists bristled under the perceived oppression of the new King George III and the British Parliament, their protests culminated in the Revolutionary War (1775–1783) and the Declaration of Independence (1776). Jefferson's proclamation in the same Declaration was that British "political bands" over American colonies must "dissolve" was inspired in part by Beccaria's European calls in for proportionate and limited punishment, in the pursuit of life, liberty, and happiness (Beccaria, 1764, pp. 10, 63). American Founders Benjamin Franklin and Benjamin Rush were influenced further by another significant Enlightenment thinker, Voltaire, with whom they were in frequent contact (Maestro, 1973, pp. 18–19). In framing a new legal order for the fledgling nation of the United States, early American lawyers sought limits on governmental power. Motivated by a desire for both structural checks on power and substantive safeguards for individual rights, the Framers of early state constitutions and the U.S. Constitution rejected England's draconian "Bloody Code" imposed under the Stuarts. That code, the Waltham Black Act 9 Geo. I c. 22 (1723), once designated over 200 crimes punishable by death, permitting the total destruction of a citizen for crimes as minor as theft of livestock. Early American leaders sought to establish a legal framework that prohibited such excesses, influenced too by Enlightenment thinkers such as Montesquieu and Cesare Beccaria, who had emphasized the importance of proportionate and necessary punishments, decrying anything beyond as "tyrannical."

Among those championing such ideals was James Madison's close associate, William Bradford Jr., whose essay in 1793, "An Enquiry How Far the Punishment of Death Is Necessary in Pennsylvania," echoed the enlightened Europeans. Even before this, in June 1789, Madison proposed the inclusion of prohibitions against excessive bail, fines, and cruel punishments in the U.S. Constitution. This proposal, later incorporated into the U.S. House of Representatives' discussions in August 1789, received considerable support. Delegates from various state conventions, including New York, North Carolina, Pennsylvania, Rhode Island, and Virginia, also sought similar prohibitions in their respective state constitutions between 1787 and 1790. George Mason, drafting the Virginia Declaration of Rights in 1776, explicitly relied on the English Bill of Rights to articulate Americans' rights. The preservation of these principles became crucial in the face of abuses reminiscent of the Stuart kings, Judge Jeffreys, the Bloody Assizes, and the infamous Titus Oates.

Despite the emphasis on protections against cruel and unusual punishments, the early years following the Eighth Amendment's ratification saw limited litigation on the subject. The lack of recorded debates has left a dearth of evidence regarding the understanding of late 18th-century Americans on the concept of cruel and unusual punishment. At the First Congress, during the critical debates surrounding the formulation of the U.S. Bill of Rights, the discussions on what would later become the Eighth Amendment were notably scarce. Only two instances stand out, shedding light on the concerns and perspectives of some delegates (Cogan, 2015). William Loughton Smith, representing South Carolina, raised an objection that revolved around the perceived ambiguity of the phrase "cruel and unusual punishments." Smith's contention was rooted in the vagueness of the import of these words, with a lack of clarity that he saw as contentious. Samuel Livermore, hailing from New Hampshire, offered a distinct perspective on the clause. While acknowledging that the provision seemed to embody a sense of humanity, Livermore expressed skepticism about its practical utility. He questioned the necessity of the clause, asserting that, despite its humane intention, it lacked concrete meaning. Who would be the arbiters in determining excessiveness, for example, and how could the perceived necessity of harsh penalties be reconciled against the prohibition against such measures on the grounds of cruelty. Livermore's probing inquiries encompassed the challenge of balancing the need for stringent measures to correct vice and deter criminal behavior against the evolving moral standards of humanity. He questioned whether the clause might hinder the imposition of necessary punishments deemed cruel by some, suggesting that the legislature should not be constrained by a declaration lacking a clear definition of what constituted cruelty. Despite these expressed concerns, it is notable that the Eighth Amendment ultimately received substantial support and was agreed upon by a considerable majority of legislators in the First Congress (Elliot, 1881).

When examining the discussions in state ratifying conventions, additional insights emerge (Madison, 1834). Patrick Henry of Virginia emphasized the sacred nature of the right against cruel punishments, attributing it to the refusal of our ancestors to tolerate tortures or cruel and barbarous punishments. George Mason, another Virginian delegate, asserted that the Amendment unequivocally prohibited torture. Abraham Holmes from Massachusetts opined that the Amendment should preclude the use of racks and gibbets. Virginia's Governor Randolph, however, took a different stance, opposing the ratification of the Amendment. He believed that legislative majorities and independent judges would suffice to prevent oppressive practices, and only corruption could lead to unduly cruel punishments. The commitment to curbing excessive bail, fines, and cruel and unusual punishments eventually found resonance in state constitutions, with variations in wording but a consistent dedication to preventing abuses reminiscent of the Stuart Kings. In the generations that came after America's founding, many lawyers or critics would give their own take on the rationale behind the framing of the Eighth. Justice Story, for example, expressed in his 1833 commentaries on the Constitution the Amendment only served to restrain the federal government and was "adopted, as an admonition to all departments of the national government, to warn them against such violent proceedings, as had taken place in England in the arbitrary reigns of some of the Stuarts" (Story, 1833, p. 750).

The Eighth lands on the Supreme Court's docket

The proscriptions on excessive punishments, fines, and bail saw little by way of judicial interpretation in the 1st century of the new America—neither federally nor in the state analogues of the Eighth Amendment. In *Wilkerson v. Utah*, 99 U.S. 130 (1878), the Supreme Court affirmed the judgment of the Supreme Court of the Territory of Utah, allowing execution by firing squad and declaring that it was not cruel and unusual punishment under the Eighth Amendment to the United States Constitution. Irrespective, the Court held, the Amendment did not apply to the states (something that, as Chapter 2 shows, was only reversed almost a century later, in 1962). Delivering the Court's opinion in *Wilkerson*, Justice Clifford felt that "[d]ifficulty would attend the effort to define with exactness the extent of the constitutional provision which provides that cruel and unusual punishments shall not be inflicted; but it is safe to affirm that punishments of torture, such as those mentioned by the commentator referred to, and all others in the same line of unnecessary cruelty, are forbidden." Extending this analysis one year later was a judgment that still finds itself cited regularly in Eighth Amendment jurisprudence today, regarding William Kemmler, whose case is outlined in detail in Chapter 8.

Shortly after the *Wilkerson* and *Kemmler* pronouncements by the Court that firing squad and electric chair execution protocols were clear to continue under state and federal constitutions alike, the Justices heard a further challenge in ***O'NEIL v. VERMONT***, 144 U.S. 323 (1892). The Court maintained that "as a federal question, it has always been ruled that the Eighth Amendment to the Constitution of the United States does not apply to the States," dismissing the Eighth Amendment element of the petitioner's claim against a lengthy punishment of confinement at hard labor in a house of correction for 19,914 days (more than 54 years) for selling intoxicating liquor without authority. The Court maintained that it was a question reserved for the state and did not exceed constitutional authority. O'Neil's lengthy sentence was calculated by multiplying his offense by hundreds of counts of illicit supply (despite being charged with one offense), converted further when he was unable to pay a fine. His sentence was thus hard labor calculated at three days per dollar owed, which he argued was gratuitous and unconstitutional on Due Process Clause and Punishments Clause grounds. While the (6–3) majority was unconvinced, Justice Field, joined by Justice Brewer, argued in dissent that, while the Eighth "is usually applied to punishments which inflict torture, such as the rack, the thumb-screw, the iron boot, the stretching of limbs, and the like, which are attended with acute pain and suffering," they would also apply that the Constitution protects petitioners from "all punishments which, by their excessive length or severity, are greatly disproportioned to the offenses charged." Justice Harlan agreed, concluding that the sentence was—in his view—contrary to principles of due process and limited punishment and proscribed by the Constitution. These words would later ring in the ears of observers of early 20th-century jurisprudence,[3] something later chapters

3 In particular, *Weems v. United States*, 217 U.S. 349 (1910), on which see Chapter 2.

show, but on the day of *O'Neil*'s judgment in 1892, he was outnumbered. No case throughout the first full century of the United States would apply the Eighth to curtail a state's prerogative in punishing its citizenry.

References

Beccaria, C. (1995) *On crimes and punishments*, Bellamy, R. (ed.). Cambridge: Cambridge University Press, pp. 10, 63, 1764.

Bessler, J. (2019) 'A century in the making: the Glorious Revolution, the American Revolution, and the origins of the U.S. Constitution's Eighth Amendment', *William & Mary Bill of Rights Journal*, 27, pp. 989–1013.

The Bill of Rights (1689) *The Glorious revolution*. Available at: http://perma.cc/G85R-DR6V

Cogan, N.H. (ed.) (2015) *The complete bill of rights: the drafts, debates, sources, and origins*. 2nd edn. New York: Oxford University Press.

Elliot, J. (ed.) (1881) *The debates in the several state conventions on the adoption of the federal constitution*. 2nd edn. Philadelphia: J.B. Lippincott Company.

Howell, T.B. (ed.) (1816) *A complete collection of state trials and proceedings for high treason and other crimes and misdemeanors from the earliest period to the year 1783*. London: T.C. Hansard.

Madison, J. (1788) 'Federalist no. 48: these departments should not be so far separated as to have no constitutional control over each other', in *The federalist papers*. The New York Packet.

Madison, J. (1834) *Annals of Congress*, Gates, J. (ed.). Washington, D.C.: Gales and Seaton.

Maestro, M. (1973) *Cesare Beccaria and the origins of penal reform*. Philadelphia: Temple University Press, pp. 18–19.

Pollock, F. and Maitland, F. (1905) *History of English law*. 2nd edn. Cambridge: Cambridge University Press, pp. 522–525.

Prince of Orange (1688) *Declaration of the Prince of Orange*, 10 October. Available at: http://perma.cc/L9JJ-54ZZ

Story, J. (1833) *Commentaries on the constitution of the United States*. Boston: Hilliard, Gray, and Company.

Cited cases

Wilkerson v. Utah, 99 U.S. 130 (1878).
In re Kemmler, 136 U.S. 436 (1890).
O'Neil v. Vermont, 144 U.S. 323 (1892).

Cited legislation

English Declaration of Rights (1689).
English Bill of Rights (1689).
Magna Carta, §20, 9 Hen. III, ch. 14, in 1 Eng. Stat. at Large 5 (1225).
Navigation Acts, 12 Cha. 2. c. (1660).
Waltham Black Act, 9 Geo. I c. 22 (1723).

O'NEIL v. VERMONT, 144 U.S. 323 (1892)

JUSTICE BLATCHFORD delivered the opinion of the court.

The statute of Vermont under which the prosecution was instituted is embodied in sections 3800 and 3802 of chapter 169 of the Revised Laws of Vermont of 1880 (pages 734, 735), in these words:

> "Section 3800. No person shall, except as otherwise especially provided, manufacture, sell, furnish, or give away, by himself, clerk, servant, or agent, spirituous or intoxicating liquor, or mixed liquor of which a part is spirituous or intoxicating, or malt liquors or lager-beer; and the phrase 'intoxicating liquors,' where it occurs in this chapter, shall be held to include such liquors and beer."

The jury found O'Neil guilty of 307 offenses "of selling intoxicating liquor without authority, and contrary to the laws of Vermont, as of a second conviction for a like offense."

The judgment of the County Court, as entered, was that O'Neil pay a fine of $6,140, and the costs of prosecution, taxed at $497.96, and stand committed until the sentence should be complied with; and that, if the said fine and costs, and costs of commitment, ascertained to be 76 cents, the whole aggregating $6,638.72, should not be paid before March 20, 1883, he should be confined at hard labor in the house of correction at Rutland for the term of 19,914 days.

The trial and conviction of O'Neil in the County Court were solely for "selling intoxicating liquor without authority." The punishment prescribed therefor by section 3802 was that, "on the second conviction, he shall forfeit for each offense twenty dollars and costs of prosecution, and shall also be imprisoned one month." The term of confinement for 19,914 days was three days for each dollar of the $6,638, under section 4366 of the Revised Laws of Vermont, which prescribes that time of imprisonment in default of payment of the fine and costs in criminal cases. It is not assigned in this Court as error, in the assignment of errors, or in the brief for O'Neil, that he was subjected to cruel and unusual punishment, in violation of the Constitution of the United States. It appears by the report of the case in 58 Vermont that he took the point in the Supreme Court of Vermont that the statute of that State was repugnant to the Eighth Amendment to the Constitution of the United States and to that of Vermont, in that it allowed "cruel and unusual punishment." That Court said in its opinion:

> "The constitutional inhibition of cruel and unusual punishments, or excessive fines or bail, has no application. The punishment imposed by

> statute for the offense with which the respondent, O'Neil, is charged cannot be said to be excessive or oppressive. If he has subjected himself to a severe penalty, it is simply because he has committed *a great many* such offenses. It would scarcely be competent for a person to assail the constitutionality of the statute prescribing a punishment for burglary on the ground that he had committed so many burglaries that, if punishment for each were inflicted on him, he might be kept in prison for life. The mere fact that cumulative punishments may be imposed for distinct offenses in the same prosecution is not material upon this question. If the penalty were unreasonably severe for a *single* offense, the constitutional question might be urged; but here, the unreasonableness is only in the number of offenses which the respondent has committed."

We forbear the consideration of this question, because, as a federal question, it is not assigned as error, nor even suggested in the brief of the plaintiff in error; and, so far as it is a question arising under the Constitution of Vermont, it is not within our province. Moreover, as a federal question, it has always been ruled that the Eighth Amendment to the Constitution of the United States does not apply to the States.

The result is that the writ of error must be dismissed.

JUSTICE FIELD, dissenting (joined by JUSTICE BREWER)

I am compelled to disagree with my associates in their disposition of this case. The act charged as an offense in the State of Vermont was, in my judgment, a lawful transaction in the State of New York.

The accusation describes only a single offense, yet, by the addition of the words "at divers times," that document is held to justify a trial and uphold a conviction for 307 distinct offenses, only one of which is set forth in the accusation, and that defectively, all the others being brought within it by use of those words.

The punishment imposed was one exceeding in severity—considering the offenses of which the defendant was convicted—anything which I have been able to find in the records of our courts for the present century. By the justice of the peace in Vermont, before whom the defendant was accused, he was convicted of 457 distinct offenses, and sentenced to pay to the treasurer of the State a fine of $9,140 and the costs of prosecution, taxed at $472.96, and be confined at hard labor in the house of correction in the county of Rutland for one month, and, in case the fine and costs should not be paid on or before the expiration of this month's imprisonment, to be confined there at hard labor for the further term of 28,836 days, to be computed from the expiration of the month's imprisonment. This was more than 79 years for selling, furnishing, and giving away, as alleged, intoxicating liquor, which took place in New York, to be delivered in Vermont. An appeal having been taken from that judgment to the County Court of Rutland County, a jury was called, and the accused pleaded "Not guilty," and, although but one charge was specified, and that defectively, in the complaint, which was the one filed before the justice of the peace, the jurors found him guilty of 307 distinct offenses of selling intoxicating liquors without authority and contrary to the laws of Vermont. He was thereupon sentenced to pay a fine of $6,140 to the Treasurer of the State, and the costs of prosecution, taxed at $497.96, and stand committed until the sentence was complied with; and, in case the fine and costs were not paid before the 20th day of March, 1883, at 3 o'clock in the afternoon of that day, to be confined at hard labor in the house of correction for the term of 19,914 days—a period of over 54 years—a reduction from the term imposed by the justice of the peace of about 25 years.

Had he been found guilty of burglary or highway robbery, he would have received less punishment than for the offenses of which he was convicted. It was six times as great as any court in Vermont could have imposed for manslaughter, forgery, or perjury. It was one which, in its severity, considering the offenses of which he was convicted, may justly be termed both "unusual and cruel."

That designation, it is true, is usually applied to punishments which inflict torture, such as the rack, the thumb-screw, the iron boot, the stretching of limbs, and the like, which are attended with acute pain and suffering. Such punishments were at one time inflicted in England, but they were rendered impossible by the declaration of rights, adopted by Parliament on the successful termination of the Revolution of 1688, and subsequently confirmed in the Bill of Rights. It was there declared that excessive bail ought not to be required, nor excessive fines imposed, nor cruel and unusual punishments inflicted. From that period, this doctrine has been the established law of England, intended as a perpetual security against the oppression of the subject from any of those causes. It is embodied in the Eighth Amendment to the Constitution of the United States, and in the constitutions of several of the States, though Mr. Justice Story states in his Commentaries on the Constitution

> "that the provision would seem to be wholly unnecessary in a free Government, since it is scarcely possible that any department of such a Government should authorize or justify such atrocious conduct."

The inhibition is directed not only against punishments of the character mentioned, but against all punishments which, by their excessive length or severity, are greatly disproportioned to the offenses charged.

The whole inhibition is against that which is excessive either in the bail required, or fine imposed, or punishment inflicted. Fifty-four years' confinement at hard labor, away from one's home and relatives, and thereby prevented from giving assistance to them or receiving comfort from them, is a punishment at the severity of which, considering the offenses, it is hard to believe that any man of right feeling and heart can refrain from shuddering. It is no matter that, by cumulative offenses, for each of which imprisonment may be lawfully imposed for a short time, the period prescribed by the sentence was reached, the punishment was greatly beyond anything required by any humane law for the offenses. The State may, indeed, make the drinking of one drop of liquor an offense to be punished by imprisonment, but it would be an unheard-of cruelty if it should count the drops in a single glass, and make thereby a thousand offenses, and thus extend the punishment for drinking the single glass of liquor to an imprisonment of almost indefinite duration. The State has the power to inflict personal chastisement by directing whipping for petty offenses—repulsive as such mode of punishment is—and should it, for each offense, inflict 20 stripes, it might not be considered, as applied to a single offense, a severe punishment, but yet, if there had been 307 offenses committed, the number of which the defendant was convicted in this case, and 6,140 stripes were to be inflicted for these accumulated offenses, the judgment of mankind would be that the punishment was not only an unusual, but a cruel, one, and a cry of horror would rise from every civilized and Christian community of the country against it. It does not alter its character as cruel and unusual that for each distinct offense there is a small punishment, if, when they are brought together, and one punishment for the whole is inflicted, it becomes one of excessive severity. And the cruelty of it, in this case, by the imprisonment at hard labor, is further increased by the offenses' being thus made infamous crimes.

[. . .]

Due process of law required a specific description of all the offenses for which the defendant was to be put on trial. Proceeding without it was not due process of law; and, in my judgment, no legislation of Vermont could make it so. And it is to me a surprising doctrine that a party can be tried for and convicted of a criminal offense not alleged against him, and afterwards, when the sentence is attempted to be enforced, can be prevented from taking the objection that no offense was charged in the accusation because no defect of that kind was urged at the trial. So far from the defect's being waived, or his being then estopped from insisting upon the objection by his previous silence, I think he could justly claim that the whole proceeding was a nullity, a mere mockery of justice.

It is the established rule of the common law which has prevailed in England and in this country since the Revolution of 1688, if not for a period anterior to it, that, in all criminal prosecutions, the accused must be informed of the nature and cause of the accusation against him. It is the law of every civilized community; and *in no case can there be, in criminal proceedings, due process of law where the accused is not thus informed*. The information which he is to receive is that which will acquaint him with the essential particulars of the offense, so that he may appear in court prepared to meet every feature of the accusation against him.

JUSTICE HARLAN, dissenting.

[. . .] there is another reason why this writ of error should not be dismissed for want of jurisdiction. The defendant contended in the court below that the judgment of the Rutland County Court inflicted upon him, in violation of the Constitution of the United States, a punishment both cruel and unusual. It is not disputed that he distinctly made this point; and the question was decided against him in the court below. It is true, the assignments of error do not, in terms, cover this point, but it is competent for this Court to consider it, because we have jurisdiction of the case upon the grounds already stated.

I fully concur with MR. JUSTICE FIELD that, since the adoption of the Fourteenth Amendment, no one of the fundamental rights of life, liberty, or property, recognized and guarantied [sic] by the Constitution of the United States, can be denied or abridged by a State in respect to any person within its jurisdiction. These rights are principally enumerated in the earlier amendments of the Constitution. They were deemed so vital to the safety and security of the people that the absence from the Constitution, adopted by the Convention of 1787, of express guaranties of them, came very near defeating the acceptance of that instrument by the requisite number of States. The Constitution was ratified in the belief, and only because of the belief, encouraged by its leading advocates, that, immediately upon the organization of the Government of the Union, articles of amendment would be submitted to the people recognizing those essential rights of life, liberty, and property which inhered in Anglo-Saxon freedom, and which our ancestors brought with them from the mother country. Among those rights is immunity from cruel and unusual punishments secured by the Eighth Amendment against federal action, and by the Fourteenth Amendment against denial or abridgment by the States. A judgment, therefore, of a state court, even if rendered pursuant to a statute, inflicting, or allowing the infliction of a cruel and unusual punishment, is inconsistent with the supreme law of the land. The judgment before us, by which the defendant is confined at hard labor in a house of correction for the term of 19,914 days, or 54 years and 204 days, inflicts punishment which, in view of the character of the offenses committed, must be deemed cruel and unusual.

Without noticing other questions, I am of opinion that upon the ground last stated the judgment should be reversed.

2

INTERPRETATION AND INCORPORATION

The U.S. Constitution does not provide clear directives for its interpretation, leaving citizens and judges to select from various theories to discern its meaning and application in specific cases. The process involves establishing first principles, based on clear and firm moral and political judgments, and then evaluating whether a theory preserves these essential points. For example, in the current societal context, any theory permitting intentional governmental discrimination based on race or sex, by design, would be deemed unacceptable and excluded from consideration. Likewise, in the context of Punishments Clause, any policy or sentencing regime that would intentionally inflict a gratuitous amount of suffering—such as those methods of torture outlined in the prior chapter and admonished by the Framers—would fail constitutional muster when interpreted by any judicial decision-maker. Moreover, a theory must align with the realities of life in the United States, from broad principles to specific cases. In a deliberative democracy such as this, popular opinion alone is insufficient justification for choosing one theory over another; decisions must, in theory, be reasoned and justified by principles. This is the role of the judge. As Justice John Marshall, the fourth Chief Justice from 1801 until his death in 1835, espoused in *Marbury v. Madison*, 5 U.S. 137 (1803): "It is emphatically the province and duty of the judicial department to say what the law is." In the federal constitutional law context, it is the primary duty of the nine lifetime-appointed Justices of the U.S. Supreme Court. It is commonly accepted that these judges operate with an underlying positioning on

DOI: 10.4324/9780429398780-3

an ideological spectrum, a phenomenon that is observable and can be measured.[1]

Constitutional history and the backdrop of incorporation

For much of U.S. history, the Bill of Rights did not extend to many criminal cases, as its primary intent was to safeguard individuals only against potential abuses by the federal government. Indeed, for the first 170 years of the Union federal prisoners were treated as the functional equivalent of noncitizens, without access to the constitutional rights of those at liberty. The picture was no better at state-level, where local courts left matters of sentencing to the legislature, and the imposition of punishment to the executive. For the federal Punishments Clause to have purpose, its incorporation and a more active approach by the courts was required. In *Barron v. Baltimore*, 32 U.S. 7 Pet. 243 (1833), Chief Justice Marshall concluded with force that the Bill of Rights "contain[s] no expression indicating an intention to apply them to the State governments." In that ruling, the Court made clear that the Constitution created only the federal government, so its limitations on state power were not intended to apply to local governments like Baltimore. As a result, the decision upheld the primacy of states' rights. Following the American Civil War, Congress sought to afford the "inalienable rights" promised by the *Declaration of Independence* to all citizens, regardless of their race, and irrespective of the form of American government ensuring those rights. This was a primary purpose of the Fourteenth Amendment.

By ratifying that Amendment in 1868—honoring the late President Lincoln who had provided the driving force behind its enactment—Congress created a new liberty, marking the beginning of a departure from traditional federalism. Appetite for such novelty in approaching the protection of citizens around the nation did not extend to the Eighth (with the decision in *Pervear v. Commonwealth*, 72 U.S. 475 (1866) noting explicitly that it applied only to the States), and faded even further following Lincoln's death. In *McElvaine v. Brush*, 142 U.S. 155 (1891) the Supreme Court rejected a direct Eighth Amendment challenge to electrocution and

1 A leading example is Martin, A. and Quinn, K. (2002), 'Dynamic ideal point estimation via Markov Chain Monte Carlo for the US Supreme Court, 1953–1999', *Political Analysis*, 10, p. 134. See also Collins, P. (2007) 'Lobbyists before the US Supreme Court', *Political Research Quarterly*, 60, p. 55. Collins uses the ideological scale predominant in political science literature and concludes that when the number of "liberal" briefs in a case rises from one to three, the Court is just 5% more likely to hand down a "liberal" decision (3.5% for the same assessment with "conservative" briefs and equivalent opinions).

solitary confinement, instead deferring to the New York legislature and maintaining strategic distance from local matters relating to sentencing and punishment. In 1896, the Court decided *Chicago, Burlington and Quincy Railroad Company v. Chicago*, 166 U.S. 226 (1897), applying the due process clauses of the Fifth and Fourteenth Amendments to the several states:[2] the first such indication of incorporation. *Chicago Railroad Co* was handed the year following *Plessy v. Ferguson*, 163 U.S. 537 (1896), a case now widely abhorred as anticanon for its sanction of racist Jim Crow regimes, another showing of judicial deference to the states. Between 1911 and 1917 seven states legislated to abolish the death penalty for all crimes, and Tennessee for all but rape. Capital abolition seemed to be accelerating and spreading nationwide, but in the wake of the Russian Revolution, progress slowed.

At the same time that the Court upheld Jim Crow in *Plessy*, President McKinley's government was engaged in war with the Spanish. The Philippine Islands, formerly a Spanish colony, were consequentially governed by the United States as an "insular area." An account of a prominent Filipino writer in 1899 remarked the hypocrisy of America's grip on the Philippines, noting that just over a century prior the United States had broken free from a similar reign. "Give us a chance," he wrote, "treat us exactly as you demanded to be treated at the hands of England" (Aguinaldo, 1899). It would be against this backdrop that the case of ***WEEMS v. UNITED STATES***, 217 U.S. 349 (1910) would arrive at the Supreme Court. Substantively, Weems challenged his sentence of *cadena temporal*, hard and painful labor while shackled in chains for at least 12 years. Given America's control over the Filipino territory in which the punishment was imposed, the Supreme Court declared jurisdiction to provide review. Writing for the majority, Justice McKenna explained that:

> [t]ime works changes, brings into existence new conditions and purposes. Therefore a principle, to be vital, must be capable of wider application than the mischief which gave it birth. This is peculiarly true of constitutions. They are not ephemeral enactments, designed to meet passing occasions." . . . "The clause of the Constitution, in the opinion of the learned commentators, may be therefore progressive, and is not fastened to the obsolete, but may acquire meaning as public opinion becomes enlightened by a humane justice.

2 The takings clause: U.S. Const. Amendment V: "nor shall private property be taken for public use, without just compensation."

Moreover, the Court held that it is "a precept of justice that punishment for crime should be graduated and proportioned to offense," holding *cadena temporal* unconstitutional. While McKenna clarified that proportionality was a fundamental principle of the Eighth, he fell short of providing an exhaustive definition of the Punishments Clause, despite lamenting its absence. Much more significant than the merits of questions in *Weems* was the willingness of the Court to engage in such paternalism over foreign territory, invoking evolutive decency, the principle later cited in *Trop* in support of limited punishments on domestic soil.

The Philippine Islands' cultural and geographic distance from the Court enabled the Justices to view the colony as part of as a "disrespected, foreign system" (Raymond, 2006). Unprepared to answer questions surrounding such an intrusion on sovereignty, they were nonetheless willing to condemn the shortcomings of the Filipino scheme. In effect, American Imperialism was judicially legitimized. The prevalent view in the early 20th century that native Filipinos were uneducated, unsophisticated, and unambitious aided such imperialist activism. Some contemporaneous commentary was even more extreme, with one example from 1901 describing the "little brown man" from the Philippines as ignorant of the "great world, a complex sphere of action" (Benjamin, 1901). Such views bolstered the *Weems* Court's call to remember that his punishment arrived from a nation with "a government of a different form and genius from ours." Given its proximity to *Lochner v. New York*, 198 U.S. 45 (1905) (striking down a state limit on working hours), the Court was wise to take the opportunity to display deference to local state jurisdictions, reacting to criticism of *Lochner* as a paternalistic encroachment on state rights. Indeed, the Justices embraced such an opportunity in *Weems* and affirmed their conviction that states were to be considered sovereign, renewing the *Barron* assumption that the federal Bill of Rights was not controlling. Incorporation of the Punishments Clause was not a consideration that was vocalized either during an oral argument or in dicta.

The *Weems* majority's willingness to listen to the will of the people, as contained in state legislation and in reports of socioeconomic data, was something expressly ignored in *Lochner* and called for by Holmes's now famous dissent in that case. Where *Weems* differed was by the deference to public opinion shown by a majority of the bench, at least in dicta. Noting that "time works changes" within the Eighth, Justice McKenna emphasized in his majority opinion that "a principle, to be vital, must be capable of wider application than the mischief which gave it birth." Clearly, the seeds of Eighth Amendment evolution had been sown, though the decision was perhaps handed down well before its time. Progress would stutter in the following decades, with no progression in the Court's Punishments Clause jurisprudence for several decades.

The era of incorporation

Mounting social tension in the 1930s was combined with the Great Depression and culminated in that decade providing the most lethal statistics of any decade: 1,667 legal executions were carried out. At the same time, a newly composed Court under Chief Justices Hughes (1930–1941) and Stone (1941–1946) took a much more active role during World War II, emerging as a progressive agent in the protection of citizens against state control. Extensive civic reprisals surrounding social inequality and a lack of civil rights for Black Americans were seen in the 1950s, including the passing of numerous federal civil rights advancements such as the Civil Rights Act of 1960 (74 Stat. 89, Pub. L. 86–449); the Civil Rights Act of 1964 (78 Stat. 241e); the Voting Rights Act of 1964 (79 Stat. 437, Pub. L. 89–110). Overdue judicial condemnation of racial segregation arrived in 1954 in the form of the Court's unanimous pronouncement in *Brown v. Board of Education*, 347 U.S. 483 (1954) that the "separate but equal" doctrine upheld in *Plessy* half a century earlier was unlawful. *Brown* is noteworthy not just for its social context but also for its role in the enhancement of progressive moral values. The ruling was an example of the Court leading societal progression through judicial interpretation in the face of contrary popular consensus.

Despite the clear opportunity to apply a similar principle to the Eighth Amendment, Chief Justice Warren, otherwise known for his progressive civil liberties jurisprudence and opposition to the death penalty as governor of California, opted to put to one side any discussion of the death penalty in ***TROP v. DULLES***, 356 U.S. 86 (1958), in which the Court ruled that it was unconstitutional to revoke citizenship as a punishment and to which this chapter will return shortly. The *Trop* dictum, reportedly deposited as a tactic to bring on board death penalty retentionist Justice Black, was successful and indicated that the extension of its ruling to the death penalty was likely to require a new bench composition, with at least five Justices willing to challenge the historic penalty. Against the backdrop established by the Warren Court's decision in *Brown*, constitutional law in the United States began to undergo significant changes. These changes gained momentum in the subsequent decade, culminating with ***ROBINSON v. CALIFORNIA***, 370 U.S. 660 (1962). Incorporating the Punishments Clause, thereby applying it to state sentencers, Justice Stewart's majority in *Robinson* relied on "contemporary human knowledge" to condemn the Californian criminalization of narcotics addiction.

While the merits questions in *Robinson* were confined to noncapital punishment issues (focusing on a statute that criminalized addiction without criminal conduct). This decision marked a significant step in expanding constitutional protections against overly harsh and disproportionate punishments imposed by states, reinforcing the principle that punishment must be proportionate to the offense committed. It is the area of law governing the boundaries of the death penalty that has provided the richest example of Eighth Amendment evolution over the past 60 years, as this book will show. The issue of incorporation of the two residual clauses—Bail and Fines—is treated in Chapters 3 and 4, respectively.

Interpreting the Eighth Amendment

In the Eighth Amendment context, as later chapters will show, interpretation was initially confined to originalism. First is textualism, where the literal meanings of the words prevail, known as narrow originalism. The next type is original intent, where the text's definition is informed by the intention of its authors. It is unsurprising that originalism has been equated to "fundamentalism" for its seemingly secular commitment to the text. In all of these approaches, fidelity is to the original meaning of "cruel and unusual punishments" as understood by the Framers. This tenet finds more favor in the 2024 Court's composition than in many recent decades, emphasizing the historical context and the intent behind the Eighth Amendment's language.

For the vast period of major Eighth Amendment case law, from the 1970s to the 2010s, a much more liberal-leaning "evolutive" approach was taken: one of "living constitutionalism." This theory, when applied to interpretation of an old text, finds that as societal values and standards evolve, so too does interpretation of constitutional protections. By considering contemporary views of decency and human dignity, such an evolutive interpretation recognizes that what constitutes cruel and unusual punishment may change over time. David Strauss provides the most prominent definition of the concept of a living Constitution (though it was coined by McBain, 1927), describing it as "one that evolves, changes over time, and adapts to new circumstances without being formally amended" (Strauss, 2010). Such an approach to interpretation was arguably endorsed during the nation's founding by Thomas Jefferson—the principal architect of the Bill of Rights—who believed that each generation of citizens and governments should be viewed as independent of the one preceding them, and that the Constitution must "keep pace with the times" (Jefferson, 1816). Broadly speaking, the polarization of "living" versus "dead" (or "original") interpretation was accepted as the dividing line in constitutional law throughout the last century. While *Weems* established that Eighth Amendment protections extend beyond physical torture to include excessive penalties, it was only after *Trop*'s announcement in 1958 that the path was laid for true judicial advancement.

"How simple would be the tasks of constitutional adjudication and of law generally," Chief Justice Warren declared in *Trop*, "if specific problems could be solved by inspection of the labels pasted on them!" Instead, to enforce the Constitution's protection of human dignity, the Justices looked to "the evolving standards of decency that mark the progress of a maturing society, recognizing that the Eighth Amendment is not fastened to the obsolete." The words of the Eighth Amendment were, he claimed, "not time-worn adages or hollow shibboleths. They are vital, living principles that authorize and limit governmental powers in our nation. They are the rules of government. When the constitutionality of an act of Congress is challenged in this Court, we must apply those rules. If we do not, the words of the Constitution become little more than good advice." In clearly announcing a principle that would pave the way for significant judicial evolution in the following decades, Chief Justice Warren committed the Eighth Amendment to a journey of living constitutionalism, as the remaining chapters of this book will show. It is through this approach that the Punishments Clause has been increasingly applied in view of societal evolution, reducing, for example, the classes of death-eligible offenders and their relevant, aggravated, individualized offenses.

Alongside principles of living constitutionalism, central to Eighth Amendment jurisprudence is the proportionality principle, which holds that punishments should be proportional to the severity of the crime committed. This principle guides courts in evaluating whether a punishment is excessive or violates constitutional standards. By reflecting on societal norms (both nationally—by assessing state consensus and public opinion—and internationally, viewing supranational human rights institutions and their standards), the Court has applied socio-moral judgments (and professional consensus). As a consequence, the Court's precedents have expanded the clause—in both capital and noncapital sentencing—in order to protect a wider range of individuals from a broader selection of punishments. Moreover, a relatively recent increase in references to collective dignity can be observed in Eighth Amendment jurisprudence, expressed when people behave and are treated in ways worthy of humans. Meltzer Henry has pointed out in an impressive study that the Supreme Court has invoked the word "dignity" in more than 900 opinions, including in connection with the First, Fourth, Fifth, Six, Eighth, Ninth, Eleventh, Fourteenth, and Fifteenth Amendments (Henry, 2011). It is clear, as much of the case law outlined in the following chapters will show, that dignitarian principles—relied on by the Court in its "evolving standards of decency" jurisprudence—have been accepted as part of the moral framework of the Punishments Clause.

As the following chapters show, since *Trop* was decided, the Court has repeatedly explained that the Eighth Amendment draws its meaning from the "evolving standards of decency that mark the progress of a maturing society." Justice Burger's dissent in *Furman v. Georgia*, 408 U.S. 238 (1972) in particular, introduced what would become the foundation of later critiques of the test's operation (1) that the test lacked "judicially manageable criteria"; (2) that it required the Court to encroach on the legislative role of determining public opinion; and (3) that these defects enabled justices to "enact [their] personal predilections into law." One of those opponents was the larger-than-life Justice Antonin Scalia, who served on the Court from 1986 until his death in 2016—many of his rulings (and dissents) make for fantastic reading and are included in this book. Over time, Justice Scalia increasingly criticized the evolving standards test, eventually labeling even its objective component as flawed jurisprudence. On many occasions, Scalia urged the Court to reconsider its reliance on evolving standards and even proposed overturning *Trop*, stating that the case had significantly harmed jurisprudence, the federal system, and society at large. Other Justices, including Justice Thomas, subsequently joined in arguing that the cruel and unusual Punishments Clause should be interpreted based on the punishments permissible during the Founding era. It is only now, on the modern Roberts Court, that these views are mainstream.

The beginning of a departure from evolutive decision-making?

A shift in Eighth Amendment doctrine marked by *Baze v. Rees*, 553 U.S. 35 (2008), revealed a significant divergence among the Justices regarding the constitutionality of lethal injection protocols. Chief Justice Roberts, supported by Justices Kennedy and Alito, departed from the established evolving standards of decency framework that had been reiterated in prior cases. Instead, he emphasized the necessity of a constitutional method for executions. While Roberts's stance did not gain unanimous support among the Justices, the rejection of evolving standards has since become a prevailing view. The *Baze* Court's approach shifted toward evaluating whether a punishment technique posed a "demonstrated risk of severe pain," departing from the deliberate indifference standard seen in previous cases. While several precedents after *Baze* continued to apply the living constitutional framework first established in *Trop* and implemented throughout the

1970s and 80s, a brief resurgence of its application was short-lived. Subsequent decisions, notably on the lethal injection (see Chapter 8) largely sidelined the evolving standards of decency framework in Eighth Amendment jurisprudence.

Three significant changes on the Court's composition between 2017 and 2022 are likely to solidify this departure: Justices Gorsuch, Kavanaugh, and Coney Barrett replaced Scalia, Kennedy, and Ginsburg, respectively. While Scalia's replacement was less significant in terms of philosophy in this regard, the swing and left-leaning seats of Kennedy and Ginsburg have been replaced by staunch originalists who have to date not engaged in evolutive interpretation. Even President Biden's single backfill—Justice Jackson for Breyer—has claimed that the Constitution is fixed in its meaning and that the original intent and public meaning of the words pose limits on her own authority to interpret. There are now a reliable six conservative votes on the Court, often couched in originalism. Today, references to the evolving standards of decency primarily appear in dissenting and concurring opinions, highlighting a shift away from its once-central role in shaping Eighth Amendment doctrine. The Court's entrenchment of originalism has been obvious, and the media has plastered headlines such as "America Gets First Taste of an Originalist Supreme Court" (Reichmann, 2022) and "Originalism Run Amok at the Supreme Court" (Waldman, 2022).

References

Aguinaldo, A. (1899) 'Aguinaldo's case against the United States', *North American Review*, September, 1.

Benjamin, A. (1901) 'Some Filipino characteristics', *Outlook*, 68, p. 1003.

Collins, P. (2007) 'Lobbyists before the US Supreme Court', *Political Research Quarterly*, 60, p. 55.

Jefferson, T. (1816) *Letter to Samuel Kercheval*, 12 June. Available at: https://tinyurl.com/o33bvrr

Martin, A. and Quinn, K. (2002) 'Dynamic ideal point estimation via Markov Chain Monte Carlo for the US Supreme Court, 1953–1999', *Political Analysis*, 10, p. 134.

McBain, H. (1927) *The living constitution*. Workers Education Bureau Press.

Meltzer Henry, L. (2011) 'The jurisprudence of dignity', *University of Pennsylvania Law Review*, 160, p. 169.

Raymond, M. (2006) ' "No fellow in American legislation": Weems v. United States and the doctrine of proportionality', *Vermont Law Review*, 30, p. 251.

Reichmann, K. (2022). 'America gets first taste of an originalist Supreme Court', *Courthouse News Service*, 1 July.

Strauss, D. (2010) *The living constitution*. Oxford University Press.

Waldman, M. (2022). 'Originalism run amok at the Supreme Court', *Brennan Center for Justice*, 28 June.

Cited cases

Barron v. Baltimore, 7 Pet. U.S. 243 (1833).
Brown v. Board of Education, 347 U.S. 483 (1954).
Chicago, Burlington *and* Quincy Railroad Company v. *Chicago*, 166 U.S. 226 (1897).
Furman v. Georgia, 408 U.S. 238 (1972).
Marbury v. Madison, 5 U.S. 137 (1803).
McElvaine v. Brush, 142 U.S. 155 (1891).
Plessy v. Ferguson, 163 U.S. 537 (1896).
Robinson v. California, 370 U.S. 660 (1962).
Trop v. Dulles, 356 U.S. 86 (1958).
Weems v. United States, 217 U.S. 349 (1910).

Cited legislation

Civil Rights Act of 1960, 74 Stat 89, Pub. L. 86–449.
Civil Rights Act of 1964, 78 Stat 241, Pub. L. 88–352.

WEEMS v. UNITED STATES, 217 U.S. 349 (1910)

JUSTICE McKENNA delivered the opinion of the Court, joined by CHIEF JUSTICE FULLER and JUSTICES HARLAN and JAY.

(4–2, with JUSTICE MOODY absent and JUSTICE LUTON not having taken his seat: JUSTICE BREWER died before the opinion was delivered).

Weems was convicted, as we have seen, for the falsification of a public and official document, by entering therein, as paid out, the sums of 208 and 408 pesos, respectively, as wages to certain employees of the lighthouse service. In other words, in entering upon his cashbook those sums as having been paid out when they were not paid out, and the "truth," to use the language of the statue, was thereby perverted "in the narration of facts."

A false entry is all that is necessary to constitute the offense. Whether an offender against the statute injures anyone by his act, or intended to injure anyone, is not material, the trial court held. The court said:

> "It is not necessary that there be any fraud, nor even the desire to defraud, nor intention of personal gain on the part of the person committing it, that a falsification of a public document be punishable; it is sufficient that the one who committed it had the intention to pervert the truth and to falsify the document, and that by it damage might result to a third party."

The court further, in the definition of the nature of the offense and the purpose of the law, said: "In public documents, the law takes into consideration not only private interests, but also the interests of the community"; and it is its endeavor (and for this, a decision of the Supreme Court of Spain, delivered in 1873, was quoted)

> "to protect the interest of society by the most strict faithfulness on the part of a public official in the administration of the office intrusted to him,"

and thereby fulfill the "responsibility of the state to the community for the official or public documents under the safeguard of the state." And this was attempted to be secured through the law in controversy. It is found in § 1 of chapter 4 of the Penal Code of Spain. The caption of the section is, "Falsification of Official and Commercial Documents and Telegraphic Despatches." Article 300 provides as follows:

> "The penalties of *cadena temporal* and a fine of from 1,250 to 12,500 pesetas shall be imposed on a public official who, taking advantage of his

authority, shall commit a falsification . . . by perverting the truth in the narration of facts. . . ."

By other provisions of the Code, we find that there are only two degrees of punishment higher in scale than *cadena temporal*,—death, and *cadena perpetua*. The punishment of *cadena temporal* is from twelve years and one day to twenty years, which "shall be served" in certain "penal institutions." And it is provided that "those sentenced to *cadena temporal* and *cadena perpetua* shall labor for the benefit of the state. They shall always carry a chain at the ankle, hanging from the wrists; they shall be employed at hard and painful labor, and shall receive no assistance whatsoever from without the institution."

These provisions are attacked as infringing that provision of the Bill of Rights of the islands which forbids the infliction of cruel and unusual punishment. It must be confessed that they, and the sentence in this case, excite wonder in minds accustomed to a more considerate adaptation of punishment to the degree of crime. In a sense, the law in controversy seems to be independent of degrees. One may be an offender against it, as we have seen, though he gain nothing and injure nobody. It has, however, some human indulgence—it is not exactly Draconian in uniformity. Though it starts with a severe penalty, between that and the maximum penalty, it yields something to extenuating circumstances. Indeed, by Article 96 of the Penal Code, the penalty is declared to be "divisible," and the legal term of its "duration is understood as distributed into three parts, forming the three degrees—that is, the minimum, medium, and maximum"—being, respectively, twelve years and one day to fourteen years and eight months; from fourteen years, eight months, and one day to seventeen years and four months; from seventeen years, four months, and one day to twenty years. The law therefore allows a range from twelve years and a day to twenty years, and the government, in its brief, ventures to say that "the sentence of fifteen years is well within the law." But the sentence is attacked, as well as the law, and what it is to be well within the law a few words will exhibit. The minimum term of imprisonment is twelve years, and that, therefore, must be imposed for "perverting the truth" in a single item of a public record, though there be no one injured, though there be no fraud or purpose of it, no gain or desire of it. Twenty years is the maximum imprisonment, and that only can be imposed for the perversion of truth in every item of an officer's accounts, whatever be the time covered and whatever fraud it conceals or tends to conceal. Between these two possible sentences, which seem to have no adaptable relation, or rather, in the difference of eight years for the lowest possible offense and the highest possible, the courts below selected three years to add to the minimum of twelve years and a day for the falsification of two items of expenditure, amounting to the sums of 408 and 204 pesos. And the fine and "accessories" must be brought into view.

The fine was 4,000 pesetas—an excess also over the minimum. The "accessories," we have already defined. We can now give graphic description of Weems' sentence and of the law under which it was imposed. Let us confine it to the minimum degree of the law, for it is with the law that we are most concerned. Its minimum degree is confinement in a penal institution for twelve years and one day, a chain at the ankle and wrist of the offender, hard and painful labor, no assistance from friend or relative, no marital authority or parental rights or rights of property, no participation even in the family council. These parts of his penalty endure for the term of imprisonment. From other parts, there is no intermission. His prison bars and chains are removed, it is true, after twelve years, but he goes from them to a perpetual limitation of his liberty. He is forever kept under the shadow of his crime, forever kept within voice and view of the criminal magistrate, not being able to change his domicil without giving notice to the "authority immediately in charge of his surveillance," and without permission in writing. He may not seek, even in other scenes and among other people, to retrieve his fall from rectitude. Even that hope is taken from him, and he is subject to tormenting regulations that, if not so tangible as iron bars and stone walls, oppress as much by their continuity, and deprive of essential liberty. No circumstance of degradation is omitted. It may be that even the cruelty of pain is not omitted. He must bear a chain night and day. He is condemned to painful as well as hard labor. What painful labor may mean, we have no exact measure. It must be something more than hard labor. It may be hard labor pressed to the point of pain. Such penalties for such offenses amaze those who have formed their conception of the relation of a state to even its offending citizens from the practice of the American commonwealths, and believe that it is a precept of justice that punishment for crime should be graduated and proportioned to offense.

Is this also a precept of the fundamental law? We say fundamental law, for the provision of the Philippine Bill of Rights prohibiting the infliction of cruel and unusual punishment was taken from the Constitution of the United States, and must have the same meaning.

What constitutes a cruel and unusual punishment has not been exactly decided. It has been said that, ordinarily, the terms imply something inhuman and barbarous—torture and the like.

No case has occurred in this court which has called for an exhaustive definition. In *Pervear v. Massachusetts*, it was decided that the clause did not apply to state but to national legislation. But we went further, and said that we perceive nothing excessive, or cruel, or unusual in a fine of $50 and imprisonment at hard labor in the house of correction for three months, which was imposed for keeping and maintaining, without a license, a tenement for the illegal sale and illegal keeping of intoxicating liquors. A decision from which no one will dissent.

In *Wilkerson v. Utah*, the clause came up again for consideration. A statute of Utah provided that "a person convicted of a capital offense should suffer death by being shot, hanged, or beheaded," as the court might direct, or he should "have his option as to the manner of his execution." The statute was sustained. The court pointed out that death was an usual punishment for murder, that it prevailed in the territory for many years, and was inflicted by shooting; also that that mode of execution was usual under military law. It was hence concluded that it was not forbidden by the Constitution of the United States as cruel or unusual.

[. . .]

Henry and those who believed as he did would take no chances. Their predominant political impulse was distrust of power, and they insisted on constitutional limitations against its abuse. But surely they intended more than to register a fear of the forms of abuse that went out of practice with the Stuarts. Surely, their jealousy of power had a saner justification than that. They were men of action, practical and sagacious, not beset with vain imagining, and it must have come to them that there could be exercises of cruelty by laws other than those which inflicted bodily pain or mutilation. With power in a legislature great, if not unlimited, to give criminal character to the actions of men, with power unlimited to fix terms of imprisonment with what accompaniments they might, what more potent instrument of cruelty could be put into the hands of power? And it was believed that power might be tempted to cruelty. This was the motive of the clause, and if we are to attribute an intelligent providence to its advocates, we cannot think that it was intended to prohibit only practices like the Stuarts', or to prevent only an exact repetition of history. We cannot think that the possibility of a coercive cruelty being exercised through other forms of punishment was overlooked. We say "coercive cruelty" because there was more to be considered than the ordinary criminal laws. Cruelty might become an instrument of tyranny; of zeal for a purpose, either honest or sinister.

Legislation, both statutory and constitutional, is enacted, it is true, from an experience of evils, but its general language should not, therefore, be necessarily confined to the form that evil had theretofore taken. Time works changes, brings into existence new conditions and purposes. Therefore a principle, to be vital, must be capable of wider application than the mischief which gave it birth. This is peculiarly true of constitutions. They are not ephemeral enactments, designed to meet passing occasions. They are, to use the words of Chief Justice Marshall, "designed to approach immortality as nearly as human institutions can approach it." The future is their care, and provision for events of good and bad tendencies of which no prophecy can be made. In the application of a constitution, therefore, our contemplation cannot be only of what has been, but of what may be. Under any other rule, a constitution would indeed be as easy of application as it would be deficient in efficacy and power. Its general principles would have little value, and be converted by precedent into impotent and lifeless formulas. Rights declared in words might be lost in reality. And this has been recognized. The meaning and vitality of the Constitution have developed against narrow and restrictive construction.

But general discussion we need not farther pursue. We may rely on the conditions which existed when the Constitution was adopted. As we have seen, it was the thought of Story, indeed, it must come to a less trained reflection than his, that government by the people, instituted by the Constitution, would no imitate the conduct of arbitrary monarchs. The abuse of power might, indeed, be apprehended, but not that it would be manifested in provisions or practices which would shock the sensibilities of men.

An extended review of the cases in the state courts, interpreting their respective constitutions, we will not make. It may be said of all of them that there was not such challenge to the import and consequence of the inhibition of cruel and unusual punishments as the law under consideration presents. It has no fellow in American legislation. Let us remember that it has come to us from a government of a different form and genius from ours. It is cruel in its excess of imprisonment and that which accompanies and follows imprisonment. It is unusual in its character. Its punishments come under the condemnation of the Bill of Rights, both on account of their degree and kind. And they would have those bad attributes even if they were found in a Federal enactment, and not taken from an alien source.

Many of the state cases which have been brought to our attention require no comment. They are based upon sentences of courts, not upon the constitutional validity of laws. The contentions in other cases vary in merit and in their justification of serious consideration. We have seen what the contention was in *Hobbs v. State*. In others, however, there was more inducement to an historical inquiry. In *Commonwealth v. Wyatt*, 6 Rand. 694, the whipping post had to be justified, and was justified. In comparison with the "barbarities of quartering, hanging in chains, castration, etc.," it was easily reduced to insignificance. The court in the latter case pronounced it "odious, but not unusual." Other cases have seen something more than odiousness in it, and have regarded it as one of the forbidden punishments. It is certainly as odious as the pillory, and the latter has been pronounced to be within the prohibitory clause.

[. . .]

The clause of the Constitution, in the opinion of the learned commentators, may be therefore progressive, and is not fastened to the obsolete, but may acquire meaning as public opinion becomes enlightened by a humane justice.

The Philippine Code unites the penalties of *cadena temporal*, principal and accessory, and it is not in our power to separate them, even if they are separable, unless their independence is such that we can say that their union was not made imperative by the legislature. This certainly cannot be said of the Philippine Code, as a Spanish enactment, and the order putting it into effect in the islands did not attempt to destroy the unity of its provisions or the effect of that unity. In other words, it was put into force as it existed, with all its provisions dependent. We cannot, therefore, declare them separable.

It follows from these views that, even if the minimum penalty of *cadena temporal* had been imposed, it would have been repugnant to the Bill of Rights. In other words, the fault is in the law; and, as we are pointed to no other under which a sentence can be imposed, the judgment must be reversed, with directions to dismiss the proceedings.

JUSTICE WHITE delivered a dissenting opinion, joined by JUSTICE HOLMES

The Philippine Bill of Rights, which is construed and applied, is identical with the cruel and unusual punishment clause of the Eighth Amendment. Because of this identity, it is now decided that it is necessary to give to the Philippine Bill of Rights the meaning properly attributable to the provision on the same subject found in the Eighth Amendment, as, in using the language of that Amendment in the statute, it is to be presumed that Congress intended to give to the words their constitutional significance. The ruling now made, therefore, is an interpretation of the Eighth Amendment, and announces the limitation which that Amendment imposes on Congress when exercising its legislative authority to define and punish crime. The great importance of the decision is hence obvious.

Of course, in every case where punishment is inflicted for the commission of crime, if the suffering of the punishment by the wrongdoer be alone regarded, the sense of compassion aroused would mislead and render the performance of judicial duty impossible. And it is to be conceded that this natural conflict between the sense of commiseration and the commands of duty is augmented when the nature of the crime defined by the Philippine law and the punishment which that law prescribes are only abstractly considered, since the impression is at once produced that the legislative authority has been severely exerted. I say only abstractly considered because the first impression produced by the merely abstract view of the subject is met by the admonition that the duty of defining and punishing crime has never, in any civilized country, been exerted upon mere abstract considerations of the inherent nature of the crime punished, but has always involved the most practical consideration of the tendency at a particular time to commit certain crimes, of the difficulty of repressing the same, and of how far it is necessary to impose stern remedies to prevent the commission of such crimes. And, of course, as these considerations involve the necessity for a familiarity with local conditions in the Philippine Islands which I do not possess, such want of knowledge at once additionally admonishes me of the wrong to arise from forming a judgment upon insufficient data, or without a knowledge of the subject matter upon which the judgment is to be exerted. Strength, indeed, is added to this last suggestion by the fact that no question concerning the subject was raised in the courts below or there considered, and therefore no opportunity was afforded those courts, presumably, at least, relatively familiar with the local conditions, to express their views as to the considerations which may have led to the prescribing of the punishment in question. Turning aside, therefore, from mere emotional tendencies, and guiding my judgment alone by the aid of the reason at my command, I am unable to agree with the ruling of the court. As, in my opinion, that ruling rests upon an interpretation of the cruel and unusual punishment clause of the Eighth Amendment, never before announced, which is repugnant to the natural import of the language employed in the clause, and which interpretation curtails the legislative power of Congress to define and punish crime by asserting a right of judicial supervision over the exertion of that power, in disregard of the distinction between the legislative and judicial department of the government, I deem it my duty to dissent and state my reasons.

To perform this duty requires at the outset a precise statement of the construction given by the ruling now made to the provision of the Eighth Amendment. My inability to do this must, however, be confessed, because I find it impossible to fix with precision the meaning which the court gives to that provision. Not for the purpose of criticizing, but solely in order to indicate my perplexity on the subject, the reasons for my doubt are briefly given. Thus, to my mind, it appears as follows: First. That the court interprets the inhibition against cruel and unusual punishment as imposing upon Congress the duty of proportioning punishment according to the nature of the crime, and casts upon the judiciary the duty of determining whether punishments have been properly apportioned in a particular statute, and if not, to decline to enforce it. This seems to me to be the case because of the reference made by the court to the harshness of the principal punishment (imprisonment), and its comments as to what it deems to be the severity, if not inhumanity, of the accessories which result from or accompany it, and the declaration in substance that these things offend against the just principle of proportioning punishment to the nature of the crime punished, stated to be a fundamental precept of justice and of American criminal law. That this is the view now upheld, it seems to me, is additionally demonstrated by the fact that the punishment for the crime in question, as imposed by the Philippine law, is compared with other Philippine punishments for crimes deemed to be less heinous, and the conclusion is deduced that this fact, in and of itself, serves to establish that the punishment imposed in this case is an exertion of unrestrained power, condemned by the cruel and unusual punishment clause.

Second. That this duty of apportionment compels not only that the law-making power should adequately apportion punishment for the crimes as to which it legislates, but also further exacts that the performance of the duty of apportionment must be discharged by taking into view the standards, whether lenient or severe, existing in other and distinct jurisdictions; and that a failure to do so authorizes the courts to consider such standards in their discretion, and judge of the validity of the law accordingly. I say this because, although the court expressly declares in the opinion, when considering a case decided by the highest court of one of the territories of the United States, that the legislative power to define and punish crime committed in a territory, for the purpose of the Eighth Amendment, is separate and distinct from the legislation of Congress, yet, in testing the validity of the punishment affixed by the law here in question, proceeds to measure it not alone by the Philippine legislation, but by the provisions of several acts of Congress punishing crime, and in substance declares such congressional laws to be a proper standard, and in effect holds that the greater proportionate punishment inflicted by the Philippine law over the more lenient punishments prescribed in the laws of Congress establishes that the Philippine law is repugnant to the Eighth Amendment.

Third. That the cruel and unusual punishment clause of the Eighth Amendment controls not only the exertion of legislative power as to modes of punishment, proportionate or otherwise, but addresses itself also to the mainspring of the legislative motives in enacting legislation punishing crime in a particular case, and therefore confers upon courts the power to refuse to enforce a particular law defining and punishing crime, if, in their opinion, such law does not manifest that the lawmaking power, in fixing the punishment, was sufficiently impelled by a purpose to effect a reformation of the criminal. This is said because of the statements contained in the opinion of the court as to the legislative duty to shape legislation not only with a view to punish, but to reform the criminal, and the inferences which I deduce that it is conceived that the failure to do so is a violation of constitutional duty.

Fourth. That the cruel and unusual punishment clause does not merely limit the legislative power to fix the punishment for crime by excepting out of that authority the right to impose bodily punishments of a cruel kind, in the strict acceptation of those terms, but limits the legislative discretion in determining to what degree of severity an appropriate and usual mode of punishment may, in a particular case, be inflicted, and therefore endows the courts with the right to supervise the exercise of legislative discretion as to the adequacy of punishment, even although resort is had only to authorized kinds of punishment, thereby endowing the courts with the power to refuse to enforce laws punishing crime, if, in the judicial judgment, the legislative branch of the government has prescribed a too severe punishment.

Not being able to assent to these, as it to me seems, in some respects conflicting, or, at all events, widely divergent, propositions, I shall consider them all as sanctioned by the interpretation now given to the prohibition of the Eighth Amendment, and with this conception in mind shall consider the subject.

[. . .]

Whatever may be the difficulty, if any, in fixing the meaning of the prohibition at its origin, it may not be doubted, and indeed is not questioned by anyone, that the cruel punishments against which the Bill of Rights provided were the atrocious, sanguinary, and inhuman punishments which had been inflicted in the past upon the persons of criminals. This being certain, the difficulty of interpretation, if any, is involved in determining what was intended by the unusual punishments referred to and which were provided against. Light, however, on this subject, is at once afforded by observing that the unusual punishments provided against were responsive to and obviously considered to be the illegal punishments complained of. These complaints were, first, that customary modes of bodily punishments, such as whipping and the pillory, had, under the exercise of judicial discretion, been applied to so unusual a degree as to cause them to be illegal; and, second, that, in some cases, an authority to sentence to perpetual imprisonment had been exerted under the assumption that power to do so resulted from the existence of judicial discretion to sentence to imprisonment when it was unusual, and therefore illegal, to inflict life imprisonment in the absence of express legislative authority. In other words, the prohibitions, although conjunctively stated, were really disjunctive, and embraced braced as follows: *a* prohibitions against a resort to the inhuman bodily punishments of the past; *b* or, where certain bodily punishments were customary, a prohibition against their infliction to such an extent as to be unusual and consequently illegal; *c* or the infliction, under the assumption of the exercise of judicial discretion, of unusual punishments not bodily, which could not be imposed except by express statute, or which were wholly beyond the jurisdiction of the court to impose.

When the origin and purpose of the Declaration and the Bill of Rights is thus fixed, it becomes clear that that Declaration is not susceptible of the meaning now attributed to the same language found in the Constitution of the United States. That in England it was nowhere deemed that any theory of proportional punishment was suggested by the Bill of Rights, or that a protest was thereby intended against the severity of punishments, speaking generally, is demonstrated by the practice which prevailed in England as to punishing crime from the time of the Bill of Rights to the time of the American Revolution.

[. . .]

But further than this, assuming, for the sake of argument, that I am wrong in my view of the Eighth Amendment, and that it endows the courts with the power to review the discretion of the lawmaking body in prescribing sentence of imprisonment for crime, I yet cannot agree with the conclusion reached in this case, that, because of the mere term of imprisonment, it is within the rule. True, the imprisonment is at hard and painful labor. But certainly the mere qualification of painful in addition to hard cannot be the basis upon which it is now decided that the legislative discretion was abused, since to understand the meaning of the term requires a knowledge of the discipline prevailing in the prisons in the Philippine Islands. The division of hard labor into classes, one more irksome, and, it may be said, more painful than the other in the sense of severity, is well known. I do not assume that the mere fact that a chain is to be carried by the prisoner causes the punishment to be repugnant to the Bill of Rights, since, while the chain may be irksome, it is evidently not intended to prevent the performance of the penalty of hard labor. Such a provision may well be part of the ordinary prison discipline, particularly in communities where the jails are insecure, and it may be a precaution applied, as it is commonly applied in this country, as a means of preventing the escape of prisoners; for instance, where the sentence imposed is to work on the roads or other work where escape might be likely. I am brought, then, to the conclusion that the accessory punishments are the basis of the ruling now made, that the legislative discretion was so abused as to cause it to be necessary to declare the law prescribing the punishment for the crime invalid. But I can see no foundation for this ruling, as, to my mind, these accessory punishments, even under the assumption, for the sake of argument, that they amounted to an abuse of legislative discretion, are clearly separable from the main punishment—imprisonment. Where a sentence is legal in one part and illegal in another, it is not open to controversy that the illegal, if separable, may be disregarded and the legal enforced. But it is said here the illegality is not merely in the sentence, but in the law which authorizes the sentence. Grant the premise. The illegal is capable of separation from the legal in the law as well as in the sentence; and because this is a criminal case, it is nonetheless subject to the rule that, where a statute is unconstitutional in part and in part not, the unconstitutional part, if separable, may be rejected and the constitutional part maintained. Of course, it is true that that can only be done provided it can be assumed that the legislature would have enacted the legal part separate from the illegal. The ruling now made must therefore rest upon the proposition that, because the law has provided an illegal in addition to a legal punishment, it must be assumed that the legislature would not have defined and punished the crime to the legal extent, because, to some extent, the legislature was mistaken as to its powers. But this I contend is to indulge in an assumption which is unwarranted, and has been directly decided to the contrary at this term in *United States v. Union Supply Co*. In that case, a corporation was proceeded against criminally for an offense punishable by imprisonment and fine. The corporation clearly could not be subjected to the imprisonment, and the contention was that the lawmaker must be presumed to have intended that both the punishments should be inflicted upon the person violating the law, and therefore it could not be intended to include a corporation within its terms. In overruling the contention, it was said:

> "And if we free our minds from the notion that criminal statutes must be construed by some artificial and conventional rule, the natural inference, when a statute prescribes two independent penalties, is that it means to inflict them so far as it can, and that if one of them is impossible, it does not mean, on that account, to let the defendant escape."

TROP v. DULLES, 356 U.S. 86 (1958)

CHIEF JUSTICE WARREN announced the judgment of the Court (5–4), joined by JUSTICES BLACK, DOUGLAS, and WHITTAKER.

The petitioner in this case, a native-born American, is declared to have lost his United States citizenship and become stateless by reason of his conviction by court-martial for wartime desertion. [. . .] the issue before us is whether this forfeiture of citizenship comports with the Constitution.

The facts are not in dispute. In 1944, petitioner was a private in the United States Army, serving in French Morocco. On May 22, he escaped from a stockade at Casablanca, where he had been confined following a previous breach of discipline. The next day, petitioner and a companion were walking along a road towards Rabat, in the general direction back to Casablanca, when an Army truck approached and stopped. A witness testified that petitioner boarded the truck willingly, and that no words were spoken. In Rabat, petitioner was turned over to military police. Thus, ended petitioner's "desertion." He had been gone less than a day, and had willingly surrendered to an officer on an Army vehicle while he was walking back towards his base. He testified that, at the time he and his companion were picked up by the Army truck, "we had decided to return to the stockade. The going was tough. We had no money to speak of, and at the time, we were on foot and we were getting cold and hungry."

A general court-martial convicted petitioner of desertion and sentenced him to three years at hard labor, forfeiture of all pay and allowances and a dishonorable discharge.

In 1952, petitioner applied for a passport. His application was denied on the ground that, under the provisions of Section 401(g) of the Nationality Act of 1940, as amended, he had lost his citizenship by reason of his conviction and dishonorable discharge for wartime desertion.

[. . .]

Citizenship is not a license that expires upon misbehavior. The duties of citizenship are numerous, and the discharge of many of these obligations is essential to the security and wellbeing of the Nation. The citizen who fails to pay his taxes or to abide by the laws safeguarding the integrity of elections deals a dangerous blow to his country. But could a citizen be deprived of his nationality for evading these basic responsibilities of citizenship? In time of war, the citizen's duties include not only the military defense of the Nation, but also full participation in the manifold activities of the civilian ranks. Failure to perform any of these obligations may cause the Nation serious injury, and, in appropriate circumstances, the punishing power is available to deal with derelictions of duty. But citizenship is not lost every time a duty of citizenship is shirked. And the deprivation of citizenship is not a weapon that the Government may use to express its displeasure at a citizen's conduct, however reprehensible that conduct may be. As long as a person does not voluntarily renounce or abandon his citizenship, and this petitioner has done neither, I believe his fundamental right of citizenship is secure. On this ground alone, the judgment in this case should be reversed.

Since a majority of the Court concluded in *Perez v. Brownell* that citizenship may be divested in the exercise of some governmental power, I deem it appropriate to state additionally why the action taken in this case exceeds constitutional limits, even under the majority's decision in *Perez*. The Court concluded in *Perez* that citizenship could be divested in the exercise of the foreign affairs power. In this case, it is urged that the war power is adequate to support the divestment of citizenship. But there is a vital difference between the two statutes that purport to implement these powers by decreeing loss of citizenship. The statute in *Perez* decreed loss of citizenship—so the majority concluded—to eliminate those international problems that were thought to arise by reason of a citizen's having voted in a foreign election. The statute in this case, however, is entirely different. Section 401(g) decrees loss of citizenship for those found guilty of the crime of desertion. It is essentially like Section 401(j) of the Nationality Act decreeing loss of citizenship for evading the draft by remaining outside the United States. This provision was also before the Court in *Perez*, but the majority declined to consider its validity. While Section 401(j) decrees loss of citizenship without providing any semblance of procedural due process whereby the guilt of the draft evader may be determined before the sanction is imposed, Section 401(g), the provision in this case, accords the accused deserter at least the safeguards of an adjudication of guilt by a court-martial.

The constitutional question posed by Section 401(g) would appear to be whether or not denationalization may be inflicted as a punishment, even assuming that citizenship may be divested pursuant to some governmental power. But the Government contends that this statute does not impose a penalty, and that constitutional limitations on the power of Congress to punish are therefore inapplicable. We are told this is so because a committee of Cabinet members, in recommending this legislation to the Congress, said it "technically is not a penal law."

How simple would be the tasks of constitutional adjudication and of law generally if specific problems could be solved by inspection of the labels pasted on them!

[. . .]

Section 401(g) is a penal law, and we must face the question whether the Constitution permits the Congress to take away citizenship as a punishment for crime. If it is assumed that the power of Congress extends to divestment of citizenship, the problem still remains as to this statute whether denationalization is a cruel and unusual punishment within the meaning of the Eighth Amendment. Since wartime desertion is punishable by death, there can be no argument that the penalty of denationalization is excessive in relation to the gravity of the crime. The question is whether this penalty subjects the individual to a fate forbidden by the principle of civilized treatment guaranteed by the Eighth Amendment.

At the outset, let us put to one side the death penalty as an index of the constitutional limit on punishment. Whatever the arguments may be against capital punishment, both on moral grounds and in terms of accomplishing the purposes of punishment—and they are forceful—the death penalty has been employed throughout our history, and, in a day when it is still widely accepted, it cannot be said to violate the constitutional concept of cruelty. But it is equally plain that the existence of the death penalty is not a license to the Government to devise any punishment short of death within the limit of its imagination.

The exact scope of the constitutional phrase "cruel and unusual" has not been detailed by this Court. But the basic policy reflected in these words is firmly established in the Anglo-American tradition of criminal justice.

This Court has had little occasion to give precise content to the Eighth Amendment, and, in an enlightened democracy such as ours, this is not surprising. But when the Court was confronted with a punishment of 12 years in irons at hard and painful labor imposed for the crime of falsifying public records, it did not hesitate to declare that the penalty was cruel in its excessiveness and unusual in its character. [In *Weems v. United States*] The Court recognized in that case that the words of the Amendment are not precise, and that their scope is not static. The Amendment must draw its meaning from the evolving standards of decency that mark the progress of a maturing society.

We believe, as did Chief Judge Clark in the court below, that use of denationalization as a punishment is barred by the Eighth Amendment. There may be involved no physical mistreatment, no primitive torture. There is, instead, the total destruction of the individual's status in organized society. It is a form of punishment more primitive than torture, for it destroys for the individual the political existence that was centuries in the development. The punishment strips the citizen of his status in the national and international political community. His very existence is at the sufferance of the country in which he happens to find himself. While any one country may accord him some rights and, presumably, as long as he remained in this country, he would enjoy the limited rights of an alien, no country need do so, because he is stateless. Furthermore, his enjoyment of even the limited rights of an alien might be subject to termination at any time by reason of deportation. In short, the expatriate has lost the right to have rights.

This punishment is offensive to cardinal principles for which the Constitution stands. It subjects the individual to a fate of ever-increasing fear and distress. He knows not what discriminations may be established against him, what proscriptions may be directed against him, and when and for what cause his existence in his native land may be terminated. He may be subject to banishment, a fate universally decried by civilized people. He is stateless, a condition deplored in the international community of democracies. It is no answer to suggest that all the disastrous consequences of this fate may not be brought to bear on a stateless person. The threat makes the punishment obnoxious.

The civilized nations of the world are in virtual unanimity that statelessness is not to be imposed as punishment for crime. It is true that several countries prescribe expatriation in the event that their nationals engage in conduct in derogation of native allegiance. Even statutes of this sort are generally applicable primarily to naturalized citizens. But use of denationalization as punishment for crime is an entirely different matter. The United Nations' survey of the nationality laws of 84 nations of the world reveals that only two countries, the Philippines and Turkey, impose denationalization as a penalty for desertion. In this country, the Eighth Amendment forbids this to be done.

In concluding, as we do, that the Eighth Amendment forbids Congress to punish by taking away citizenship, we are mindful of the gravity of the issue inevitably raised whenever the constitutionality of an Act of the National Legislature is challenged. No member of the Court believes that, in this case the statute before us can be construed to avoid the issue of constitutionality. That issue confronts us, and the task of resolving it is inescapably ours. This task requires the exercise of judgment, not the reliance upon personal preferences. Courts must not consider the wisdom of statutes, but neither can they sanction as being merely unwise that which the Constitution forbids.

We are oath-bound to defend the Constitution. This obligation requires that congressional enactments be judged by the standards of the Constitution. The Judiciary has the duty of implementing the constitutional safeguards that protect individual rights. When the Government acts to take away the fundamental right of citizenship, the safeguards of the Constitution should be examined with special diligence.

The provisions of the Constitution are not time-worn adages or hollow shibboleths. They are vital, living principles that authorize and limit governmental powers in our Nation. They are the rules of government. When the constitutionality of an Act of Congress is challenged in this Court, we must apply those rules. If we do not, the words of the Constitution become little more than good advice.

When it appears that an Act of Congress conflicts with one of these provisions, we have no choice but to enforce the paramount commands of the Constitution. We are sworn to do no less. We cannot push back the limits of the Constitution merely to accommodate challenged legislation. We must apply those limits as the Constitution prescribes them, bearing in mind both the broad scope of legislative discretion and the ultimate responsibility of constitutional adjudication. We do well to approach this task cautiously, as all our predecessors have counseled. But the ordeal of judgment cannot be shirked. In some 81 instances since this Court was established, it has determined that congressional action exceeded the bounds of the Constitution. It is so in this case.

JUSTICE BLACK filed a concurring opinion, joined by JUSTICE DOUGLAS.

[. . .] there is one additional thing that needs to be said.

Even if citizenship could be involuntarily divested, I do not believe that the power to denationalize may be placed in the hands of military authorities. If desertion or other misconduct is to be a basis for forfeiting citizenship, guilt should be determined in a civilian court of justice, where all the protections of the Bill of Rights guard the fairness of the outcome. Such forfeiture should not rest on the findings of a military tribunal. Military courts may try soldiers and punish them for military offenses, but they should not have the last word on the soldier's right to citizenship. The statute held invalid here not only makes the military's finding of desertion final, but gives military authorities discretion to choose which soldiers convicted of desertion shall be allowed to keep their citizenship and which ones shall thereafter be stateless. Nothing in the Constitution or its history lends the slightest support for such military control over the right to be an American citizen.

JUSTICE BRENNAN filed a concurring opinion.

It seems to me that nothing is solved by the uncritical reference to service in the armed forces as the "ultimate duty of American citizenship." Indeed, it is very difficult to imagine, on this theory of power, why Congress cannot impose expatriation as punishment for any crime at all—for tax evasion, for bank robbery, for narcotics offenses. As citizens, we are also called upon to pay our taxes and to obey the laws, and these duties appear to me to be fully as related to the nature of our citizenship as our military obligations. But Congress' asserted power to expatriate the deserter bears to the war powers precisely the same relation as its power to expatriate the tax evader would bear to the taxing power.

I therefore must conclude that § 401(g) is beyond the power of Congress to enact.

JUSTICE FRANKFURTER filed a dissenting opinion, joined by JUSTICES BURTON, CLARK, and HARLAN.

All power is, in Madison's phrase, "of an encroaching nature." Judicial power is not immune against this human weakness. It also must be on guard against encroaching beyond its proper bounds, and not the less so since the only restraint upon it is self-restraint. When the power of Congress to pass a statute is challenged, the function if this Court is to determine whether legislative action lies clearly outside the constitutional grant of power to which it has been, or may fairly be, referred. In making this determination, the Court sits in judgment on the action of a coordinate branch of the Government while keeping unto itself—as it must, under our constitutional system—the final determination of its own power to act. No wonder such a function is deemed "the gravest and most delicate duty that this Court is called on to perform." This is not a lip-serving platitude.

Rigorous observance of the difference between limits of power and wise exercise of power—between questions of authority and questions of prudence—requires the most alert appreciation of this decisive but subtle relationship of two concepts that too easily coalesce. No less does it require a disciplined will to adhere to the difference. It is not easy to stand aloof and allow want of wisdom to prevail, to disregard one's own strongly held view of what is wise in the conduct of affairs. But it is not the business of this Court to pronounce policy. It must observe a fastidious regard for limitations on its own power, and this precludes the Court's giving effect to its own notions of what is wise or politic. That self-restraint is of the essence in the observance of the judicial oath, for the Constitution has not authorized the judges to sit in judgment on the wisdom of what Congress and the Executive Branch do.

[. . .]

The Court today reaffirms its decisions sustaining the power of Congress to denationalize citizens who had no desire or intention to give up their citizenship. If loss of citizenship may constitutionally be made the consequence of such conduct as marrying a foreigner, and thus certainly not "cruel and unusual," it seems more than incongruous that such loss should be thought "cruel and unusual" when it is the consequence of conduct that is also a crime. In short, denationalization, when attached to the offense of wartime desertion, cannot justifiably be deemed so at variance with enlightened concepts of "humane justice," as to be beyond the power of Congress, because constituting a "cruel and unusual" punishment within the meaning of the Eighth Amendment.

Nor has Congress fallen afoul of that prohibition because a person's post-denationalization status has elements of unpredictability. Presumably a denationalized person becomes an alien *vis-a-vis* the United States. The very substantial rights and privileges that the alien in this country enjoys under the federal and state constitutions puts him in a very different condition from that of an outlaw in fifteenth-century England. He need not be in constant fear lest some dire and unforeseen fate be imposed on him by arbitrary governmental action—certainly not "while this Court sits." The multitudinous decisions of this Court protective of the rights of aliens bear weighty testimony. And the assumption that brutal treatment is the inevitable lot of denationalized persons found in other countries is a slender basis on which to strike down an Act of Congress otherwise amply sustainable.

It misguides popular understanding of the judicial function and of the limited power of this Court in our democracy to suggest that, by not invalidating an Act of Congress, we would endanger the necessary subordination of the military to civil authority. This case, no doubt, derives from the consequence of a court-martial. But we are sitting in judgment not on the military, but on Congress. The military merely carried out a responsibility with which they were charged by Congress. Should the armed forces have ceased discharging wartime deserters because Congress attached the consequence it did to their performance of that responsibility?

This legislation is the result of an exercise by Congress of the legislative power vested in it by the Constitution, and of an exercise by the President of his constitutional power in approving a bill and thereby making it "a law." To sustain it is to respect the actions of the two branches of our Government directly responsive to the will of the people and empowered under the Constitution to determine the wisdom of legislation. The awesome power of this Court to invalidate such legislation, because in practice it is bounded only by our own prudence in discerning the limits of the Court's constitutional function, must be exercised with the utmost restraint. Mr. Justice Holmes, one of the profoundest thinkers who ever sat on this Court, expressed the conviction that

> "I do not think the United States would come to an end if we lost our power to declare an Act of Congress void. I do think the Union would be imperiled if we could not make that declaration as to the laws of the several States."

He did not, of course, deny that the power existed to strike down congressional legislation, nor did he shrink from its exercise. But the whole of his work during his thirty years of service on this Court should be a constant reminder that the power to invalidate legislation must not be exercised as if, either in constitutional theory or in the art of government, it stood as the sole bulwark against unwisdom or excesses of the moment.

ROBINSON v. CALIFORNIA, 370 U.S. 660 (1962)

JUSTICE STEWART delivered the opinion of the Court, joined by CHIEF JUSTICE WARREN and JUSTICES BLACK, DOUGLAS, HARLAN, and BRENNAN. (6–2: JUSTICE FRANKFURTER took no part in the consideration or decision of this case).

A California statute makes it a criminal offense for a person to "be addicted to the use of narcotics." This appeal draws into question the constitutionality of that provision of the state law, as construed by the California courts in the present case.

The appellant was convicted after a jury trial in the Municipal Court of Los Angeles. The evidence against him was given by two Los Angeles police officers. Officer Brown testified that he had had occasion to examine the appellant's arms one evening on a street in Los Angeles some four months before the trial. The officer testified that at that time he had observed "scar tissue and discoloration on the inside" of the appellant's right arm, and "what appeared to be numerous needle marks and a scab which was approximately three inches below the crook of the elbow" on the appellant's left arm. The officer also testified that the appellant, under questioning, had admitted to the occasional use of narcotics.

Officer Lindquist testified that he had examined the appellant the follow morning in the Central Jail in Los Angeles. The officer stated that at that time he had observed discolorations and scabs on the appellant's arms, and he identified photographs which had been taken of the appellant's arms shortly after his arrest the night before. Based upon more than ten years of experience as a member of the Narcotic Division of the Los Angeles Police Department, the witness gave his opinion that "these marks and the discoloration were the result of the injection of hypodermic needles into the tissue into the vein that was not sterile." He stated that the scabs were several days old at the time of his examination, and that the appellant was neither under the influence of narcotics nor suffering withdrawal symptoms at the time he saw him. This witness also testified that the appellant had admitted using narcotics in the past.

The appellant testified in his own behalf, denying the alleged conversations with the police officers and denying that he had ever used narcotics or been addicted to their use. He explained the marks on his arms as resulting from an allergic condition contracted during his military service. His testimony was corroborated by two witnesses.

The trial judge instructed the jury that the statute made it a misdemeanor for a person "either to use narcotics, or to be addicted to the use of narcotics. . . . That portion of the statute referring to the 'use' of narcotics is based upon the 'act' of using. That portion of the statute referring to 'addicted to the use' of narcotics is based upon a condition or status. They are not identical. . . . To be addicted to the use of narcotics is said to be a status or condition, and not an act. It is a continuing offense, and differs from most other offenses in the fact that [it] is chronic, rather than acute; that it continues after it is complete, and subjects the offender to arrest at any time before he reforms. The existence of such a chronic condition may be ascertained from a single examination if the characteristic reactions of that condition be found present."

The judge further instructed the jury that the appellant could be convicted under a general verdict if the jury agreed either that he was of the "status" or had committed the "act" denounced by the statute.

> "All that the People must show is either that the defendant did use a narcotic in Los Angeles County, or that, while in the City of Los Angeles, he was addicted to the use of narcotics. . . ."

Under these instructions, the jury returned a verdict finding the appellant "guilty of the offense charged."

[. . .]

It is unlikely that any State at this moment in history would attempt to make it a criminal offense for a person to be mentally ill, or a leper, or to be afflicted with a venereal disease. A State might determine that the general health and welfare require that the victims of these and other human afflictions be dealt with by compulsory treatment, involving quarantine, confinement, or sequestration. But, in the light of contemporary human knowledge, a law which made a criminal offense of such a disease would doubtless be universally thought to be an infliction of cruel and unusual punishment in violation of the Eighth and Fourteenth Amendments.

We cannot but consider the statute before us as of the same category. In this Court, counsel for the State recognized that narcotic addiction is an illness. Indeed, it is apparently an illness which may be contracted innocently or involuntarily. We hold that a state law which imprisons a person thus afflicted as a criminal, even though he has never touched any narcotic drug within the State or been guilty of any irregular behavior there, inflicts a cruel and unusual punishment in violation of the Fourteenth Amendment. To be sure, imprisonment for ninety days is not, in the abstract, a punishment which is either cruel or unusual. But the question cannot be considered in the abstract. Even one day in prison would be a cruel and unusual punishment for the "crime" of having a common cold.

We are not unmindful that the vicious evils of the narcotics traffic have occasioned the grave concern of government. There are, as we have said, countless fronts on which those evils may be legitimately attacked. We deal in this case only with an individual provision of a particularized local law as it has so far been interpreted by the California courts.

JUSTICE DOUGLAS filed a concurring opinion.

JUSTICE HARLAN filed a concurring opinion.

JUSTICE CLARK filed a dissenting opinion.

JUSTICE WHITE filed a dissenting opinion.

The Court has not merely tidied up California's law by removing some irritating vestige of an outmoded approach to the control of narcotics. At the very least, it has effectively removed California's power to deal effectively with the recurring case under the statute where there is ample evidence of use but no evidence of the precise location of use. Beyond this, it has cast serious doubt upon the power of any State to forbid the use of narcotics under threat of criminal punishment. I cannot believe that the Court would forbid the application of the criminal laws to the use of narcotics under any circumstances. But the States, as well as the Federal Government, are now on notice. They will have to await a final answer in another case.

[. . .]

Finally, I deem this application of "cruel and unusual punishment" so novel that I suspect the Court was hard put to find a way to ascribe to the Framers of the Constitution the result reached today rather than to its own notions of ordered liberty. If this case involved economic regulation, the present Court's allergy to substantive due process would surely save the statute and prevent the Court from imposing its own philosophical predilections upon state legislatures or Congress. I fail to see why the Court deems it more appropriate to write into the Constitution its own abstract notions of how best to handle the narcotics problem, for it obviously cannot match either the States or Congress in expert understanding.

3

EXCESSIVE BAIL

Like posttrial punishment, the roots of the bail system in the United States trace back to medieval England. During that period, individuals accused of crimes, subject to varying conditions and numbers, were permitted to stay free until their trial, often delayed by the sporadic visits of traveling judges. Initially, a simple promise from the accused or an approved surety to appear at trial sufficed. With time, the system evolved, eventually allowing release upon the pledge of money by a surety, which would be forfeited if the accused failed to appear. One of the grievances enumerated in the 1689 Bill of Rights against James II—outlined in detail in Chapter 1—was the demand for disproportionate amounts of bail to be paid by individuals in order to secure their release before criminal trials, undermining the laws enacted for the liberty of the subjects. The constitutional response to this issue was the establishment of a safeguard against "excessive bail" within Article 10. While the practical impact on reducing pretrial detentions was limited, especially in places like Newgate and other English jails, the acknowledgment of the right, at least in principle, was significant.

Both the federal government and states had significant flexibility in designing their bail systems. They generally adopted a hands-off approach, allowing the market to thrive, with commercial bail bondsmen stepping in for private sureties. In exchange for a nonrefundable monetary premium, these companies ensured a defendant's appearance at trial. If the defendant absconded, the bondsmen would forfeit their bonds, with potential reimbursement from the defendant or their relatives through indemnification contracts. This system involved a notable delegation of criminal justice authority to outsourced private entities, a practice unparalleled in scale

DOI: 10.4324/9780429398780-4

beyond the borders of the United States. A 2018 study into early state constitutions revealed that 9 of the original 12 (from 1776 to 1791) included a right to be free from demands for excessive bail by their state government, with 36 of 37 state constitutions containing that clause by the time the Fourteenth Amendment was ratified in 1868 (Calabresi *et al.*, 2018). In 2024, only Florida and Illinois contain no Bail Clause in their Bill of Rights: The remaining 48—representing 96% of the states and 89.7% of the U.S. population—provide expressly for such protection alongside their curtailment of cruel and unusual punishments, or other familiar constructions.

Incorporation of the Bail Clause

Despite such widespread adoption by the separate state constitutions, the U.S. Constitution's original (federal) proscription of excessive bail is the only clause not to have been incorporated expressly by the Supreme Court. This chapter is therefore limited both in terms of its extent and in terms of its substance, with the vast majority of constitutional litigation left in the state systems. The practical result of this caveat to the incorporation of the Eighth is that the Excessive Bail Clause only provides a national constitutional limitation on federal pretrial detention. That is, incarceration of suspects (in arraignment, pending plea, and so on) in advance of the hand down of any criminal judgment or sentence. Constitutional minima for post-sentencing detention (conditions, duration, and so on) move from the Bail Clause to the Punishments Clause—the latter taking up the vast majority of this book.

In *Schilb v. Kuebel*, 404 U.S. 357 (1971) the Supreme Court, reviewing the Illinois bail system, held in favor of the state in finding that the scheme did not violate the Equal Protection Clause of the U.S. Constitution. While the opinion did not consider the substance of an excessive bail claim, instead focusing on the Fourteenth Amendment claim (affirming the lower decision by the Illinois Supreme Court), Justice Harry Blackmun's 4–3 majority opinion suggested in dicta that the Bail Clause was an incorporated part of the U.S. Constitution irrespective of that state's lack of similar clause in its own Bill of Rights. Implying therefore that this national protection extends to claimants in state courts, Blackmun wrote: "Bail, of course, is basic to our system of law, and the Eighth Amendment's proscription of excessive bail has been assumed to have application to the States through the Fourteenth Amendment."

This assertion was cited and given more recent credence by the Court in *McDonald v. City of Chicago*, 561 U.S. 742 (2010), a landmark Second Amendment case that incorporated the right to "keep and bear arms" as enforceable against the states through the Fourteenth Amendment. While the text of such a decision is worth reading outside these pages and the substance is fundamental to the constitutional development of the Bill of Rights, it is not included in full as immaterial to the question of excessive bail. Writing for a 5–4 plurality divided by multiple concurrence, Justice Alito claimed that "The Court eventually incorporated almost all of the provisions of the Bill of Rights," citing *Schilb* at footnote 12 as having incorporated the prohibition against excessive bail, alongside a long list of other cases—many of which are widely considered to have done the same in other constitutional law contexts (indeed, the same footnote cites *Robinson v. California*, 370 U.S. 660 (1962), for its express incorporation of the Punishments Clause, outlined in detail in Chapter 2).

Bail before the Court

As already noted, bail has been a fundamental aspect of the Anglo-American criminal justice system for centuries. While the Constitution did not explicitly grant a right to bail, the Eighth Amendment prohibited only that which was "excessive." States, following a long-standing tradition, permitted pretrial release with financial conditions. Judges required defendants to secure personal surety, typically backed by property, as a guarantee for their appearance in court. Initially based on personal relationships, the bail system evolved into a commercialized practice, with defendants increasingly relying on commercial bail bondsmen instead of personal acquaintances. The Excessive Bail Clause, owing in part to its unsettled incorporation status, has hardly ever found itself in the annals of Supreme Court history, with the two primary cases of ***STACK v. BOYLE***, 342 U.S. 1 (1951) and ***UNITED STATES v. SALERNO***, 481 U.S. 739 (1987) representing the sum of its substantive national jurisprudence: Litigation is largely left to the states, which this book does not address in any depth.

First in *Stack*, the Court declared clearly in 1951—with an 8–0 majority voice—that any bail imposed above "necessity" is unconstitutional under the Excessive Bail Clause. The case revolved around the arrest and bail conditions imposed on the petitioner, Loretta Stack. Stack was one of twelve members of the Community Party in California, arrested in her capacity as organizational secretary and accused of inciting women to take up arms against the United States in support of leftist or communist ideologies. Stack was arrested in 1951 during the height of the Cold War, a period marked by heightened tensions between the United States and the Soviet Union. Stack's charge was under the Alien Registration Act, Pub. L. 76-670 (1940) (or the "Smith Act"), passed in the context of increased scrutiny and suspicion of individuals supporting communism in order to overthrow the U.S. Government. Against this backdrop, Stack's arrest and the subsequent legal challenges represented a moment in which political ideologies and concerns about national security intersected with constitutional questions regarding individual rights, including the right to reasonable bail under the Eighth Amendment. The case became a part of the broader legal and political dynamics of the post–World War II era, characterized by anti-communist sentiments and the perceived threat of subversion.

Upon her arrest, Stack and her codefendants sought bail, but the trial judge set amounts of between $2,500 and $100,000 (equivalent to around 10× those figures in 2024), which they could not afford. Subsequently, the District Court fixed bail pending trial at $50,000 per petitioner, remaining extraordinarily high in the context of usual bail values. Stack and her 11 co-petitioners brought collective proceedings through the federal courts, citing the Eighth Amendment's Excessive Bail Clause. On review by the Supreme Court, Chief Justice Fred Vinson found 8–0 that bail had not been set by adequate procedural methods and offended the U.S. Constitution. The Court declared that "The fixing of bail before trial for any individual defendant must be based upon standards relevant to the purpose of assuring the presence of that defendant," and that "Bail set at a figure higher than an amount reasonably calculated to fulfill this purpose is excessive under the Eighth Amendment." The Court emphasized that any amount of bail that is greater than usual requires specific evidence, before a hearing, to consider justifications for such action on a case-by-case basis. Summing up, Chief Justice Vinson declared:

> It is not denied that bail for each petitioner has been fixed in a sum much higher than that usually imposed for offenses with like penalties, and yet there has been no factual showing to justify such action in this case. The Government asks the courts to depart from the norm by assuming, without the introduction of evidence, that each petitioner is a pawn in a conspiracy and will, in obedience to a superior, flee the jurisdiction. To infer from the fact of indictment alone a need for bail in an unusually high amount is an arbitrary act. Such conduct would inject into our own system of government the very principles of totalitarianism which Congress was seeking to guard against in passing the statute under which petitioners have been indicted.

Stack's emphasis in 1951 was therefore on a "traditional right to freedom before conviction [which] permits the unhampered preparation of a defense, and serves to prevent the infliction of punishment prior to conviction," emphasizing that defendants facing noncapital charges had an absolute right to be admitted to bail granted by statute. Throughout the

1950s and 1960s the commercial bondsman system faced increasing criticism for its perceived failure to effectively incentivize defendants to attend trial. Numerous state jurisdictions passed new bail statutes in the 1960s, led by the federal government with its overhaul of the historical status quo in the Bail Reform Act, Pub. L. 89–465 (1966). The 1966 Act established that all defendants in noncapital proceedings (those charged with offenses not punishable by death) should be released on their own "recognizance," a promise to return to face trial in court when required, narrowing any bail's purpose to securing a defendant's trial attendance, with no provision for assessing dangerousness.

The Bail Reform Act was passed against the backdrop of broader criminal justice reform efforts during the 1960s: a transformative era marked by the civil rights movement, anti-war protests, and increased activism. The existing bail system had been criticized for perceived inequities, leaving many individuals—particularly those from marginalized communities—unable to afford bail and languishing in pretrial detention for extended periods. This raised concerns about the fairness and constitutionality of the system. In response, the 1966 Act reflected a broader societal and political emphasis on due process and fairness within the criminal justice system. Several landmark cases during this period shaped the legal landscape and influenced the context in which the federal statute was enacted, including a series of decisions that expanded constitutional protections and addressed issues related to civil rights, due process, and criminal justice.[1] Chief Justice Earl Warren played a crucial role in the Court's decisions during this period, as Chief from 1953 to 1969, advocating for civil rights and criminal justice reforms (although relative silence for the Eighth Amendment—but for the vital incorporation of the Punishments Clause in *Robinson*, on which see Chapter 2).

The backdrop of the 1960s Warren Court and 1966 Bail Reform Act was marked by broader societal shifts and initiatives like (1963–1969) President Lyndon B. Johnson's "War on Poverty" addressing systemic inequalities. Policymakers sought to address issues related to pretrial detention that disproportionately affected certain groups, including introducing through the 1966 Act a presumption of release on personal recognizance or an unsecured

1 See, for example, *Gideon v. Wainwright* 372 U.S. 335 (1963), establishing the constitutional right to legal counsel under the Sixth Amendment even if a defendant could not afford their own, and *Miranda v. Arizona*, 384 U.S. 436 (1966), requiring under the Fifth Amendment that individuals in police custody must be informed of their constitutional rights before being subjected to interrogation (including the right to remain silent and the right to an attorney, with any failure of such "*Miranda* warning" provision resulting in the inadmissibility of any statements obtained during the interrogation in subsequent legal proceedings).

bond for noncapital offenses, emphasizing that pretrial release should be the norm rather than the exception. When determining bail conditions, the Act outlined factors that courts should consider, including the nature and circumstances of the offense, the weight of the evidence, the defendant's character, family ties, employment, financial resources, and length of residence in the community. The Bail Reform Act of 1966 thus marked a pivotal moment in the evolution of pretrial procedures in the federal criminal justice system, within an important shift within all branches of the federal government toward broad and deep individual protection. The Act laid the foundation for ongoing discussions about the balance between ensuring public safety and protecting the rights of the accused during the pretrial phase.

Fast-forward two decades and the 1980s were proving pivotal in reforming federal legislation around sentencing and detention, and this extended to pretrial bail reform. With the context of the heightened focus on the "War on Drugs," policymaking in this sphere centered on the impact of drug-related crimes and sought legislative measures to address the issue: with it, curtailing individual rights and returning authority to the state. Amending the 1966 Act, the 1984 Bail Reform Act, Pub. L. No. 98–473, 98 Stat. 1976 (codified as amended at 18 U.S.C. §§ 3141–3150) significantly altered the federal bail landscape. The Act closed the loophole for dangerous, non-flight risk offenders and equipped judges with the ability to factor in both flight risks and dangerousness into detention decision-making. The Act established a presumption of release in most cases, narrowing the types of offenses that qualify for detention, with § 3142(f) outlining five categories of charged offenses that make a defendant eligible for a detention hearing (including most drug and gun crimes, offenses involving a minor victim, crimes of violence and terrorism, offenses with a maximum penalty of life in prison or death, and specific instances of reoffending). The government faced the burden of showing dangerousness by "clear and convincing evidence" (a lower standard than the criminal conviction "proof beyond a reasonable doubt," but higher than the usual pretrial "preponderance of evidence" standard). Numerous challenges to the Act followed, with Anthony Salerno's being the first to reach the Supreme Court.

Known as "Fat Tony," Salerno was a reputed member of the Genovese crime family and had been indicted in multiple cases, including at age 74, on charges related to racketeering, conspiracy, and extortion. These charges, tried in 1986, stemmed from his alleged involvement in American Mafia organized crime activities, including bid rigging in the construction industry. The federal government, citing the 1984 Bail Reform Act, sought to detain Salerno before trial with no presumption of release—unlike his usual experience of paying significant multimillion-dollar sureties in exchange for his release. The federal government argued that he posed a danger to the community and relied on their new statutory authority to detain him before trial without any bail rights—due to the seriousness of his alleged offending. The case against Salerno argued that a judge had lawfully determined that no conditions of release would reasonably assure the safety of others and the community, and thus his presumption of release was trumped by the new Act. Salerno challenged the constitutionality of this provision, arguing that it violated his Fifth and Eighth Amendment rights. He contended that this permitted preventive detention based on future dangerousness, rather than addressing the traditional purpose of bail to ensure a defendant's appearance at trial. The case presented a constitutional challenge to the government's authority to detain individuals before trial based on the perceived threat they posed to the community.

Writing for a 6–3 majority in *Salerno*, Chief Justice William Rehnquist held that the Act—and its imposition against Salerno and his codefendant—was constitutional under the Fifth Amendment's Due Process Clause and the Eighth Amendment's Excessive Bail Clause. The only federal constitutional limitation, the Court found, is "excessive" conditions of release, taking into account the "perceived evil." *Salerno* is notable for establishing the "no set of circumstances" test. When individuals mount a facial challenge against a statute, they argue that the statute is "void on its face" and, therefore, should be deemed unconstitutional. This presents a significant burden on the defendant, as the challenger of any statute must demonstrate that there are no circumstances whatsoever under which the statute could be considered valid. The Court's judgment affirmed the facial constitutionality of the Act, holding that it permits only limited exceptions to the normal practice of pretrial release and concluded that pretrial detention is more "regulatory" in nature than it is punitive, justifying less stringent safeguards for a defendant's liberty compared to those mandated at trial. Balancing these safeguards with the government's legitimate interest in public safety is, the Court held, constitutionally afforded to defendants by a detention hearing as provided for in the Act.

One major question the Court did leave unanswered was that of flight risk, omitting to provide any clear evidentiary threshold for proving such a risk. Nor does the 1984 Act specify one, providing only at § 3142(f) that a finding of dangerousness at the detention hearing "shall be supported by clear and convincing evidence," but nothing for flight risk. It has been noted that, in the absence of an explicit standard for adjudicating over an offender's possible risk of fleeing, a consensus of federal circuit courts across the country has instead read in a "preponderance of the evidence" standard to *Salerno*, a lower threshold than many constitutional protections that apply the "clear and convincing evidence threshold" (Lessnick, 2022, pp. 1245–1256).

Over time, pretrial detention, which was considered an exception prior to the 1980s, has become the norm where the public has come to view preventative detention as unexceptional. Congress had painted with a broad brush in 1984, including any federal narcotics charge within their categorization of "dangerousness" and thus removing the presumption of pretrial release from a vast class of defendants targeted by the War on Drugs, a trend that would continue well into the 1990s. This was followed by the early 2000s widespread utility of immigration detention tools on material witness warrants, in the wake of 9/11, often carrying with them lengthy pretrial detention through their attachment to counterterrorism investigations. Writing in 2005, a federal prosecutor noted that "by cutting imprisonment loose from its criminal law moorings, *United States v. Salerno* has played a pivotal role in turning what many thought to be a bedrock constitutional right into a matter of legislative or even executive policy. Even one who embraces the recognition of the state's fundamental power to protect its citizens from harm can be unsettled by this new world of few certainties" (Richman, 2005).

References

Calabresi, S.G., Lindgren, J.T., Begley, H.M., Dore, K.L. and Agudo, S.E. (2018) 'Individual rights under state constitutions in 2018: what rights are deeply rooted in a modern-day consensus of the states?' *Notre Dame Law Review*, 94(1), pp. 49–153.

Lessnick, J.M. (2022). 'Pretrial detention by a preponderance: the constitutional and interpretive shortcomings of the flight-risk standard', *University of Chicago Law Review*, 89(5), pp. 1245–1256.

Richman, D.C. (2005). 'The story of United States v. Salerno: the constitutionality of regulatory detention', *Fordham Legal Studies Research Paper*, 82, pp. 1–38.

Cited cases

Gideon v. Wainwright, 372 U.S. 335 (1963).
McDonald v. Chicago, 561 U.S. 742 (2010).
Miranda v. Arizona, 384 U.S. 436 (1966).
Robinson v. California, 370 U.S. 660 (1962).
Schilb v. Kuebel, 404 U.S. 357 (1971).
Stack v. Boyle, 342 U.S. 1 (1951).
United States v. Salerno, 481 U.S. 739 (1987).

Cited legislation

Alien Registration Act, Pub. L. 76–670 (1940).
Bail Reform Act, Pub. L. 89–465 (1966).
Bail Reform Act, Pub. L. No. 98–473, 98 Stat. 1976 (1984).

STACK v. BOYLE, 342 U.S. 1 (1951)

CHIEF JUSTICE VINSON delivered the opinion of the Court (joined by JUSTICES BLACK, REED, FRANKFURTER, DOUGLAS, JACKSIN, BURTON, and CLARK).

Indictments have been returned in the Southern District of California charging the twelve petitioners with conspiring to violate the Smith Act, 18 U.S.C. (Supp. IV) §§ 371, 2385. Upon their arrest, bail was fixed for each petitioner in the widely varying amounts of $2,500, $7,500, $75,000 and $100,000. On motion of petitioner Schneiderman following arrest in the Southern District of New York, his bail was reduced to $50,000 before his removal to California. On motion of the Government to increase bail in the case of other petitioners, and after several intermediate procedural steps not material to the issues presented here, bail was fixed in the District Court for the Southern District of California in the uniform amount of $50,000 for each petitioner.

Petitioners moved to reduce bail on the ground that bail as fixed was excessive under the Eighth Amendment. In support of their motion, petitioners submitted statements as to their financial resources, family relationships, health, prior criminal records, and other information. The only evidence offered by the Government was a certified record showing that four persons previously convicted under the Smith Act in the Southern District of New York had forfeited bail. No evidence was produced relating those four persons to the petitioners in this case. At a hearing on the motion, petitioners were examined by the District Judge and cross-examined by an attorney for the Government. Petitioners' factual statements stand uncontroverted.

After their motion to reduce bail was denied, petitioners filed applications for habeas corpus in the same District Court. Upon consideration of the record on the motion to reduce bail, the writs were denied. The Court of Appeals for the Ninth Circuit affirmed.

The petition for certiorari and the full record are now before the Court, and, since the questions presented by the petition have been fully briefed and argued, we consider it appropriate to dispose of the petition for certiorari at this time. Accordingly, the petition for certiorari is granted for review of questions important to the administration of criminal justice.

First. From the passage of the Judiciary Act of 1789, 1 Stat. 73, 91, to the present Federal Rules of Criminal Procedure, Rule 46(a)(1), federal law has unequivocally provided that a person arrested for a noncapital offense shall be admitted to bail. This traditional right to freedom before conviction permits the unhampered preparation of a defense, and serves to prevent the infliction of punishment prior to conviction. Unless this right to bail before trial is preserved, the presumption of innocence, secured only after centuries of struggle, would lose its meaning. The right to release before trial is conditioned upon the accused's giving adequate assurance that he will stand trial and submit to sentence if found guilty.

Like the ancient practice of securing the oaths of responsible persons to stand as sureties for the accused, the modern practice of requiring a bail bond or the deposit of a sum of money subject to forfeiture serves as additional assurance of the presence of an accused. Bail set at a figure higher than an amount reasonably calculated to fulfill this purpose is "excessive" under the Eighth Amendment.

Since the function of bail is limited, the fixing of bail for any individual defendant must be based upon standards relevant to the purpose of assuring the presence of that defendant. The traditional standards, as expressed in the Federal Rules of Criminal Procedure, are to be applied in each case to each defendant. In this case, petitioners are charged with offenses under the Smith Act, and, if found guilty, their convictions are subject to review with the scrupulous care demanded by our Constitution.

Upon final judgment of conviction, petitioners face imprisonment of not more than five years and a fine of not more than $10,000. It is not denied that bail for each petitioner has been fixed in a sum much higher than that usually imposed for offenses with like penalties, and yet there has been no factual showing to justify such action in this case. The Government asks the courts to depart from the norm by assuming, without the introduction of evidence, that each petitioner is a pawn in a conspiracy and will, in obedience to a superior, flee the jurisdiction. To infer from the fact of indictment alone a need for bail in an unusually high amount is an arbitrary act. Such conduct would inject into our own system of government the very principles of totalitarianism which Congress was seeking to guard against in passing the statute under which petitioners have been indicted.

If bail in an amount greater than that usually fixed for serious charges of crimes is required in the case of any of the petitioners, that is a matter to which evidence should be directed in a hearing so that the constitutional rights of each petitioner may be preserved. In the absence of such a showing, we are of the opinion that the fixing of bail before trial in these cases cannot be squared with the statutory and constitutional standards for admission to bail.

Second. The proper procedure for challenging bail as unlawfully fixed is by motion for reduction of bail and appeal to the Court of Appeals from an order denying such motion. Petitioners' motion to reduce bail did not merely invoke the discretion of the District Court setting bail within a zone of reasonableness, but challenged the bail as violating statutory and constitutional standards. As there is no discretion to refuse to reduce excessive bail, the order denying the motion to reduce bail is appealable as a "final decision" of the District Court. While habeas corpus is an appropriate remedy for one held in custody in violation of the Constitution, the District Court should withhold relief in this collateral habeas corpus action where an adequate remedy available in the criminal proceeding has not been exhausted.

The Court concludes that bail has not been fixed by proper methods in this case, and that petitioners' remedy is by motion to reduce bail, with right of appeal to the Court of Appeals. Accordingly, the judgment of the Court of Appeals is vacated, and the case is remanded to the District Court with directions to vacate its order denying petitioners' applications for writs of habeas corpus and to dismiss the applications without prejudice. Petitioners may move for reduction of bail in the criminal proceeding so that a hearing may be held for the purpose of fixing reasonable bail for each petitioner.

JUSTICE JACKSON wrote a concurrence, joined by JUSTICE FRANKFURTER.

JUSTICE MINTON took no part in the consideration or decision of this case.

UNITED STATES v. SALERNO, 481 U.S. 739 (1987)

CHIEF JUSTICE REHNQUIST delivered the opinion of the Court (joined by JUSTICES WHITE, BLACKMUN, POWELL, O'CONNOR, and SCALIA).

The Bail Reform Act of 1984 (Act) allows a federal court to detain an arrestee pending trial if the Government demonstrates by clear and convincing evidence after an adversary hearing that no release conditions "will reasonably assure . . . the safety of any other person and the community." The United States Court of Appeals for the Second Circuit struck down this provision of the Act as facially unconstitutional, because, in that court's words, this type of pretrial detention violates "substantive due process." We granted certiorari because of a conflict among the Courts of Appeals regarding the validity of the Act. We hold that, as against the facial attack mounted by these respondents, the Act fully comports with constitutional requirements. We therefore reverse.

Responding to "the alarming problem of crimes committed by persons on release," Congress formulated the Bail Reform Act of 1984, as the solution to a bail crisis in the federal courts. The Act represents the National Legislature's considered response to numerous perceived deficiencies in the federal bail process. By providing for sweeping changes in both the way federal courts consider bail applications and the circumstances under which bail is granted, Congress hoped to "give the courts adequate authority to make release decisions that give appropriate recognition to the danger a person may pose to others if released."

To this end, § 3141(a) of the Act requires a judicial officer to determine whether an arrestee shall be detained. Section 3142(e) provides that

> "[i]f, after a hearing pursuant to the provisions of subsection (f), the judicial officer finds that no condition or combination of conditions will reasonably assure the appearance of the person as required and the safety of any other person and the community, he shall order the detention of the person prior to trial."

Section 3142(f) provides the arrestee with a number of procedural safeguards. He may request the presence of counsel at the detention hearing, he may testify and present witnesses in his behalf, as well as proffer evidence, and he may cross-examine other witnesses appearing at the hearing. If the judicial officer finds that no conditions of pretrial release can reasonably assure the safety of other persons and the community, he must state his findings of fact in writing, § 3142(i), and support his conclusion with "clear and convincing evidence," § 3142(f).

The judicial officer is not given unbridled discretion in making the detention determination. Congress has specified the considerations relevant to that decision. These factors include the nature and seriousness of the charges, the substantiality of the Government's evidence against the arrestee, the arrestee's background and characteristics, and the nature and seriousness of the danger posed by the suspect's release. § 3142(g). Should a judicial officer order detention, the detainee is entitled to expedited appellate review of the detention order. §§ 3145(b), (c).

Respondents Anthony Salerno and Vincent Cafaro were arrested on March 21, 1986, after being charged in a 29-count indictment alleging various Racketeer Influenced and Corrupt Organizations Act (RICO) violations, mail and wire fraud offenses, extortion, and various criminal gambling violations. The RICO counts alleged 35 acts of racketeering activity, including fraud, extortion, gambling, and conspiracy to commit murder. At respondents' arraignment, the Government moved to have Salerno and Cafaro detained pursuant to § 3142(e), on the ground that no condition of release would assure the safety of the community or any person. The District Court held a hearing at which the Government made a detailed proffer of evidence. The Government's case showed that Salerno was the "boss" of the Genovese crime family of La Cosa Nostra, and that Cafaro was a "captain" in the Genovese family. According to the Government's proffer, based in large part on conversations intercepted by a court-ordered wiretap, the two respondents had participated in wide-ranging conspiracies to aid their illegitimate enterprises through violent means. The Government also offered the testimony of two of its trial witnesses, who would assert that Salerno personally participated in two murder conspiracies. Salerno opposed the motion for detention, challenging the credibility of the Government's witnesses. He offered the testimony of several character witnesses, as well as a letter from his doctor stating that he was suffering from a serious medical condition. Cafaro presented no evidence at the hearing, but instead characterized the wiretap conversations as merely "tough talk."

The District Court granted the Government's detention motion, concluding that the Government had established by clear and convincing evidence that no condition or combination of conditions of release would ensure the safety of the community or any person:

> "The activities of a criminal organization such as the Genovese Family do not cease with the arrest of its principals and their release on even the most stringent of bail conditions. The illegal businesses, in place for many years, require constant attention and protection, or they will fail. Under these circumstances, this court recognizes a strong incentive on the part of its leadership to continue business as usual. When business

> as usual involves threats, beatings, and murder, the present danger such people pose in the community is self-evident."

Respondents appealed, contending that, to the extent that the Bail Reform Act permits pretrial detention on the ground that the arrestee is likely to commit future crimes, it is unconstitutional on its face. Over a dissent, the United States Court of Appeals for the Second Circuit agreed.

The court concluded that the Government could not, consistent with due process, detain persons who had not been accused of any crime merely because they were thought to present a danger to the community. It reasoned that our criminal law system holds persons accountable for past actions, not anticipated future actions. Although a court could detain an arrestee who threatened to flee before trial, such detention would be permissible because it would serve the basic objective of a criminal system—bringing the accused to trial.

A facial challenge to a legislative Act is, of course, the most difficult challenge to mount successfully, since the challenger must establish that no set of circumstances exists under which the Act would be valid. The fact that the Bail Reform Act might operate unconstitutionally under some conceivable set of circumstances is insufficient to render it wholly invalid, since we have not recognized an "overbreadth" doctrine outside the limited context of the First Amendment. We think respondents have failed to shoulder their heavy burden to demonstrate that the Act is "facially" unconstitutional.

Respondents present two grounds for invalidating the Bail Reform Act's provisions permitting pretrial detention on the basis of future dangerousness. First, they rely upon the Court of Appeals' conclusion that the Act exceeds the limitations placed upon the Federal Government by the Due Process Clause of the Fifth Amendment. Second, they contend that the Act contravenes the Eighth Amendment's proscription against excessive bail. We treat these contentions in turn.

Given the legitimate and compelling regulatory purpose of the Act and the procedural protections it offers, we conclude that the Act is not facially invalid under the Due Process Clause of the Fifth Amendment.

Respondents also contend that the Bail Reform Act violates the Excessive Bail Clause of the Eighth Amendment. The Court of Appeals did not address this issue, because it found that the Act violates the Due Process Clause. We think that the Act survives a challenge founded upon the Eighth Amendment.

The Eighth Amendment addresses pretrial release by providing merely that "[e]xcessive bail shall not be required." This Clause, of course, says nothing about whether bail shall be available at all. Respondents nevertheless contend that this Clause grants them a right to bail calculated solely upon considerations of flight. They rely on *Stack v. Boyle*, in which the Court stated that "[b]ail set at a figure higher than an amount reasonably calculated [to ensure the defendant's presence at trial] is 'excessive' under the Eighth Amendment."

In respondents' view, since the Bail Reform Act allows a court essentially to set bail at an infinite amount for reasons not related to the risk of flight, it violates the Excessive Bail Clause. Respondents concede that the right to bail they have discovered in the Eighth Amendment is not absolute. A court may, for example, refuse bail in capital cases. And, as the Court of Appeals noted and respondents admit, a court may refuse bail when the defendant presents a threat to the judicial process by intimidating witnesses.

Respondents characterize these exceptions as consistent with what they claim to be the sole purpose of bail—to ensure the integrity of the judicial process.

While we agree that a primary function of bail is to safeguard the courts' role in adjudicating the guilt or innocence of defendants, we reject the proposition that the Eighth Amendment categorically prohibits the government from pursuing other admittedly compelling interests through regulation of pretrial release. The above-quoted dictum in *Stack v. Boyle* is far too slender a reed on which to rest this argument. The Court in *Stack* had no occasion to consider whether the Excessive Bail Clause requires courts to admit all defendants to bail, because the statute before the Court in that case in fact allowed the defendants to be bailed. Thus, the Court had to determine only whether bail, admittedly available in that case, was excessive if set at a sum greater than that necessary to ensure the arrestees' presence at trial.

The holding of *Stack* is illuminated by the Court's holding just four months later in *Carlson v. Landon*. In that case, remarkably similar to the present action, the detainees had been arrested and held without bail pending a determination of deportability. The Attorney General refused to release the individuals,

> "on the ground that there was reasonable cause to believe that [their] release would be prejudicial to the public interest and would endanger the welfare and safety of the United States."

The detainees brought the same challenge that respondents bring to us today: the Eighth Amendment required them to be admitted to bail. The Court squarely rejected this proposition:

> "The bail clause was lifted with slight changes from the English Bill of Rights Act. In England, that clause has never been thought to accord a

right to bail in all cases, but merely to provide that bail shall not be excessive in those cases where it is proper to grant bail. When this clause was carried over into our Bill of Rights, nothing was said that indicated any different concept. The Eighth Amendment has not prevented Congress from defining the classes of cases in which bail shall be allowed in this country. Thus, in criminal cases, bail is not compulsory where the punishment may be death. Indeed, the very language of the Amendment fails to say all arrests must be bailable."

Carlson v. Landon was a civil case, and we need not decide today whether the Excessive Bail Clause speaks at all to Congress' power to define the classes of criminal arrestees who shall be admitted to bail. For even if we were to conclude that the Eighth Amendment imposes some substantive limitations on the National Legislature's powers in this area, we would still hold that the Bail Reform Act is valid. Nothing in the text of the Bail Clause limits permissible Government considerations solely to questions of flight. The only arguable substantive limitation of the Bail Clause is that the Government's proposed conditions of release or detention not be "excessive" in light of the perceived evil. Of course, to determine whether the Government's response is excessive, we must compare that response against the interest the Government seeks to protect by means of that response. Thus, when the Government has admitted that its only interest is in preventing flight, bail must be set by a court at a sum designed to ensure that goal, and no more. We believe that, when Congress has mandated detention on the basis of a compelling interest other than prevention of flight, as it has here, the Eighth Amendment does not require release on bail.

In our society, liberty is the norm, and detention prior to trial or without trial is the carefully limited exception. We hold that the provisions for pretrial detention in the Bail Reform Act of 1984 fall within that carefully limited exception. The Act authorizes the detention prior to trial of arrestees charged with serious felonies who are found after an adversary hearing to pose a threat to the safety of individuals or to the community which no condition of release can dispel. The numerous procedural safeguards detailed above must attend this adversary hearing. We are unwilling to say that this congressional determination, based as it is upon that primary concern of every government—a concern for the safety and indeed the lives of its citizens—on its face violates either the Due Process Clause of the Fifth Amendment or the Excessive Bail Clause of the Eighth Amendment.

The judgment of the Court of Appeals is therefore reversed.

JUSTICES MARSHALL, BRENNAN, and STEVENS dissented.

4

FINES

While unnecessary to repeat the historical overview of the Eighth Amendment's drafting and early interpretation already outlined in Chapter 1, it is worth recalling that the Excessive Fines Clause traces its lineage back to at least 1215. At Runnymede in England, Magna Carta guaranteed that a "Free-man shall not be amerced for a small fault, but after the manner of the fault; and for a great fault after the greatness thereof, saving to him his contenement." Or, in modern parlance, "amercements" (medieval predecessors of fines) should be proportioned to the offense and that they should not deprive a wrongdoer of his "contenement" (livelihood). In December 1791, the Eighth Amendment was ratified, taking the clause verbatim from the Virginia Declaration of Rights of 1776, which mirrored a provision of the English Bill of Rights of 1689 and stated: ". . . nor excessive fines imposed . . ." alongside the proscriptions on excessive bail and on cruel and unusual punishments. Ten states out of the 12 to write new constitutions between 1776 and 1791 had similarly banned excessive fines, with 35 of 37 recognizing the right in 1868 (when the Fourteenth Amendment was ratified). At the time of writing in 2024, all 50 states have a constitutional provision prohibiting the imposition of excessive fines, either directly or by requiring proportionality provisions. Various formulations are present and most copy the Eighth verbatim, with others more varied, such as Vermont's: "all fines shall be proportioned to the offences."

History of the Fines Clause

Despite such widespread state adoption, the federal Fines Clause in the Eighth had also been left behind in the project of incorporation of rights

DOI: 10.4324/9780429398780-5

to the states throughout the mid-century. Earlier in 1909, the Court had remained steadfast in its tradition of non-incorporation, refusing to apply the Eighth to an excessive fines challenge. In *Waters-Pierce Oil Co. v. Texas*, 212 U.S. 86 (1909) the Court found that, even where a statute sets a range of possible civil damages that may be awarded to a private litigant, the Due Process Clause forbids damages awards that are "grossly excessive" (but refusing to engage the Eighth Amendment question presented). In that ruling, the Court declared:

> It is not contended in this connection that the prohibition of the Eighth Amendment to the federal Constitution against excessive fines operates to control the legislation of the states. The fixing of punishment for crime or penalties for unlawful acts against its laws is within the police power of the state. We can only interfere with such legislation and judicial action of the states enforcing it if the fines imposed are so grossly excessive as to amount to a deprivation of property without due process of law.

Thereby setting out that the (federal) government cannot confiscate large amounts of property without following a proportionality consideration scheme set out formally in legislation. During the same period the Court was considering the Bail Clause in the 1980s (against the backdrop of pretrial detention becoming the norm) the broader sociopolitical context was marked by heightened concerns about the War on Drugs, crime rates, and the government's efforts to combat drug trafficking and related criminal activities. With a growing public and political concern about the social and economic impact of illegal drugs, civil forfeiture became an increasingly utilized tool in the government's strategy against drug-related offenses. Law enforcement agencies were empowered to seize assets, including property and funds, believed to be linked to criminal activities. This approach was seen as a way to disrupt criminal enterprises and deprive them of resources. Critics argued that the process lacked adequate safeguards and could lead to abuse, including the seizure of property from innocent owners. It was against this backdrop that *United States v. Halper*, 490 U.S. 435 (1989) arrived at the Court, where the Justices considered the potential double jeopardy of imposing civil and criminal fines for the same conduct. Applying the Fifth Amendment, a unanimous Court held that that imposing both criminal and civil penalties for the same conduct may violate the Double Jeopardy Clause's intended protection if the civil penalty is deemed punitive or excessive (though the judgment did not apply the Eighth).

1980s and 1990s review

In the same term as *Halper* the Court handed down ***BROWNING-FERRIS INDUSTRIES OF VERMONT, INC. v. KELCO DISPOSAL***, 492 U.S. 257 (1989), the first of three crucial rulings that would break the silence in respect of Fines Clause jurisprudence and rescuing the clause from obscurity. *Browning-Ferris* was an Eighth Amendment proportionality challenge to a $6 million award of punitive damages. Writing for a divided Court (9–0 on a Fourteenth Amendment question), Justice Blackmun's majority ruled (7–2) that the Fines Clause does not extend to punitive damages awarded in private disputes, where the government has no stake. The Framers, Blackmun wrote, were primarily concerned with preventing government abuse of prosecutorial power, rather than regulating the scope or purposes of civil damages. Nor, he concluded, does English history indicate that the clause was underpinned by any common law intended to govern damages in private party disputes. The Court cited Magna Carta as having intended to curb royal power excesses, a purpose irrelevant in cases such as this one—where one private party is awarded exemplary damages from another, and the government has no stake in the recovery. Blackmun wrote that "[w]hile our opinion in *Halper* implies that punitive damages awarded to the Government in a civil action may raise Eighth Amendment concerns, that case is materially different from this one, because there the Government was exacting punishment in a civil action, whereas here the damages were awarded to a private party."[1] The Court refused to review directly the punitive damages award for excessiveness under federal common law, noting that it is a question for a jury, as guided by statute. "Prudence dictates," they wrote, "that we allow the lower courts to consider that question."

A lengthy dissent from Justice O'Connor (joined by Justice Stevens) in *Browning-Ferris* argued that they saw "no reason to distinguish one Clause of the Eighth Amendment from another for purposes of incorporation" and that "if a corporation is protected by the Due Process Clause from overbearing and oppressive monetary sanctions, it is also protected from such penalties by the Excessive Fines Clause." O'Connor's opinion tracked the history of the clause, citing *Kennedy v. Mendoza-Martinez*, 372 U. S. 144 (1963) as instructive in determining whether a sanction is penal, quoting:

> the Court has generally looked to several factors: (1) whether it involves an affirmative disability; (2) whether it has historically been regarded

1 See *Browning-Ferris*, Footnote 21, not included in the reproduction of the case's text in this chapter.

> as punishment; (3) whether it comes into play on a finding of scienter; (4) whether its operation will promote retribution and deterrence; (5) whether the behavior to which it applies is already a crime; (6) whether there is an alternative purpose for it; and (7) whether it is excessive in relation to the alternative purpose assigned.

O'Connor argued that punitive damages are penal under these "*Mendoza-Martinez* factors," and would have remanded the case for further consideration by the lower court for consideration of its proportionality, including use of Punishments Clause proportionality case law. Something else the majority in *Browning-Ferris* left unresolved was the question of whether the Fines Clause applies in civil cases brought by the government, something it would return to four terms later. Justice Blackmun's unanimous ruling in ***AUSTIN v. UNITED STATES***, 509 U.S. 602 (1993) declared that *in rem* civil forfeiture proceedings (where property is confiscated by the government without a criminal conviction) are subject to the limitations of the Eighth Amendment. Petitioner Richard Lyle Austin had been indicted on four counts related to South Dakota's drug laws, pleading guilty to one count of possessing cocaine with intent to distribute and receiving a seven-year prison sentence from the state court. Subsequently, the federal government initiated an *in rem* (against a "thing") action in the U.S. District Court for the District of South Dakota, seeking the forfeiture of Austin's mobile home and auto body shop, which it was alleged he had used to sell cocaine and possess, a .22 caliber revolver, drug paraphernalia, and approximately $4,700 in cash.

The Court first reviewed the text and history of the Eighth Amendment and found that it was not intended to be expressly limited to criminal cases (unlike other constitutional clauses such as those found in the Fifth and Sixth Amendments) and had not been applied in that way historically. Rather, the Justices declared, the crucial question was whether the forfeiture is monetary punishment, engaging the Fines Clause. Because sanctions frequently serve more than one purpose, the Court held, the fact that a forfeiture serves remedial goals will not exclude it from the Clause's purview, as long as there is *at least in part* a punitive justification (citing *Halper*). The Court concluded that forfeiture (generally and *in rem* forfeiture in particular) has long been understood at least in part as punishment, holding that the forfeit imposed against Austin under federal statute was properly considered as punishment and subject to constitutional review, notwithstanding that the legislation also contains a remedial purpose. The Court declined, however, to establish a test for "excessiveness," allowing the lower courts to weigh constitutionality.

"This Court has had little occasion to interpret, and has never actually applied, the Excessive Fines Clause," the majority wrote in ***UNITED STATES v. BAJAKAJIAN***, 524 U.S. 321 (1998). In that ruling, the Supreme Court applied the clause for the first (and, at the time of writing in 2024, only) time to an individual case. Hosep Bajakajian had been apprehended while attempting to leave the United States for Cyprus without reporting the transportation of more than $10,000 in currency, as mandated by federal law. The federal law he was charged with breaching stipulated that a person found guilty of willfully violating this reporting requirement must forfeit to the government "any property . . . involved in such offense." The entire sum of $357,144 , which the respondent failed to declare, was seized—this was upheld on review by the Ninth Circuit, which disregarded the District Court's earlier holding in Bajakajian's favor. That earlier judgment had considered that, (1) as these funds were not linked to any other criminal activity (the purpose behind transporting the money was to repay a lawful debt), and (2) taking into consideration the respondent's failure to report the currency, attributing it to a fear rooted in "cultural differences," the penalty of forfeiture was "extraordinarily harsh" and "grossly disproportionate to the offense in question," reducing the forfeiture to $15,000 plus a $5,000 fine—the maximum permissible under the federal sentencing guidelines. The Ninth Circuit applied a two-part test for satisfying the Excessive Fines Clause, requiring that the forfeited property be (1) an "instrumentality" of the crime and (2) that its value be proportional to the owner's culpability.

At the Supreme Court, Justice Thomas's 5–4 majority in *Bajakajian* ruled in the petitioner's favor, determining that the forfeiture of the entire $357,000 would indeed violate the Excessive Fines Clause. The Court emphasized the principle of proportionality, concurred with the District Court's earlier finding, and established a test that looks solely at whether a forfeiture "is grossly disproportional to the gravity of a defendant's offense," declining to consider effect on a defendant's livelihood. Further, the Court declared that many fines (including customs fines) are "remedial" and, therefore, nonpunitive and not captured by the Excessive Fines Clause. In dissent, Justice Kennedy described the decision as "disturbing," for "the broader upheaval it foreshadows [. . .] portend[ing] serious disruption of a vast range of statutory fines." "In the majority's universe, a fine is not a punishment even if it is much larger than the money owed. This confuses whether a fine is excessive with whether it is a punishment."

Lower-court inconsistency has followed *Bajakajian* within the federal circuits, with the 1st and 2nd Circuits, for example, reading the ruling to open the door to ability-to-pay considerations as part of or in addition to a proportionality enquiry (see *United States v. Viloski*, 814 F.3d 104 (2d Cir. 2016) and *United States v. Levesque*, 546 F.3d 78 (1st Cir. 2008)). Others, the 9th and 11th Circuits, for example, have drawn the precise opposite conclusion, barring (and relying on *Bajakajian* to do so) discussion of a defendant's livelihood in any Fines Clause analysis (see *United States v. Dicter*, 198 F.3d 1284 (11th Cir. 1999) and *United States v. Dubose*, 146 F.3d 1141 (9th Cir. 1998)). The same incongruity has been seen across the nationwide state court level.[2]

Due process claims

As an important aside at this juncture, the Fourteenth Amendment provides its own curtailment of state power in its Due Process Clause, guaranteeing that "nor shall any State deprive any person of life, liberty, or property, without due process of law." Despite uncertainty in the Eighth Amendment space, the Court has consistently held that the Fourteenth prohibits a State from imposing a grossly excessive punishment (such as a disproportionate fine) on a tortfeasor in civil claims. In declaring so in *TXO Production Corp.* v. *Alliance Resources Corp.*, 509 U.S. 443 (1993), the Court nonetheless allowed a $10 million punitive damages payment (despite that amount being 526 times the compensatory damages) for misleading nationwide sales practices, here non-declaration of predelivery damage to cars. Three terms later, the Court heard another automobile challenge, this time in *BMW of North America, Inc. v. Gore*, 517 U.S. 559 (1996). An authorized BMW dealer had sold a car that had been repainted before delivery, unbeknownst to the buyer. Because the $601.37 cost of repainting the car was only about 1.5% of its suggested retail price, BMW did not disclose the damage or repair to the dealer. The jury returned a verdict finding the company liable for compensatory damages of $4,000, assessing $4 million in punitive damages, based on a determination that the nondisclosure policy constituted "gross, oppressive or malicious fraud." The Supreme Court took on the case, holding in a 5–4 decision that the punitive damages were unconstitutionally excessive and violated the Due Process Clause of the Fourteenth Amendment. The Court, in an opinion by Justice John Paul Stevens, provided three "guideposts" for assessing the constitutionality of punitive damages. First, punitive damages should be reasonably proportionate to the degree of reprehensibility of the defendant's conduct. Factors to consider include whether the harm caused was

2 For an excellent analysis of these cases see Harvard Law Review (2019) 'Timbs v. Indiana', *Harvard Law Review*, 133, p. 342.

physical or economic, whether the conduct was intentional, and the level of awareness or disregard for public health and safety. Second, there should be a reasonable relationship between the actual harm suffered by the plaintiff and the punitive damages awarded. Third, punitive damages awarded in similar cases should be considered to ensure that the punishment is not disproportionate. The Supreme Court concluded that the $4 million punitive damages award in the *BMW* case did not meet these criteria and was therefore excessive and unconstitutional under the Due Process Clause.

The decision remains an important precedent in the assessment of punitive damages Fourteenth, providing petitioners with a constitutional line of attack against excessive fines, aside from the Eighth. Subsequent decisions on this precedent by the Supreme Court have further clarified and refined the principles *Gore* set forth. In *State Farm Mutual Automobile Insurance Co. v. Campbell*, 538 U.S. 408 (2003), for example, the Court emphasized key principles for assessing punitive damages. It stressed the importance of considering the reprehensibility of the defendant's conduct, discouraging excessive punitive-to-compensatory damages ratios (suggesting single digits in most cases), and urging consistency by examining sanctions imposed for comparable misconduct. The decision underscored the need for meaningful appellate review to prevent arbitrary and excessive punitive damages awards. Further, in *Exxon Shipping Co. v. Baker*, 554 U.S. 471 (2008), the Justices clarified that maritime law should guide punitive damages in maritime cases, highlighting the importance of a close connection between the defendant's misconduct and the punitive damages award. The decision underscored the necessity for predictability and proportionality in punitive damages, cautioning against unpredictable and excessively massive awards. The Court in *Exxon* recalled the earlier holding in *Browning-Ferris*, stating that it was not at odds with Due Process Clause litigation, emphasizing that "the concerns that animate the Eighth Amendment were about placing limits on the steps a government may take against an individual," noting the similarities of purpose between criminal penalties and punitive damages and distinguishing the two on the basis of their differing levels of state involvement.

Incorporating the Fines Clause

Retaining the status quo further in another Eighth Amendment challenge heard by the Court in *McDonald v. Chicago*, 561 U.S. 742 (2010), the Court declared expressly that the Fines Clause did not apply to the states. As outlined in Chapter 3, Justice Alito's sharply divided 5–4 plurality in *McDonald* had included excessive bail in a footnote, listing it as an incorporated clause (although its status remains less than settled). The judgment was clearer on fines, stating in the subsequent footnote that this clause contained one of "the only rights not fully incorporated." Footnote 13 went on to confirm: "We never have decided whether the [. . .] the Eighth Amendment's prohibition of excessive fines applies to the States through the Due Process Clause," citing *Browning-Ferris Industries*. In 2019, the Court was presented with the chance to extend *McDonald* in this way, which it did through a 9–0 majority authored by leading liberal Justice Ruth Bader Ginsburg. In that case, ***TIMBS v. INDIANA***, 139 S. Ct. 682 (2019), the Supreme Court finally held that the clause was an incorporated protection applicable to the states. Ginsburg's opinion held that the Excessive Fines Clause finds its origins in the Magna Carta, the historic English Bill of Rights, and state constitutions from the colonial era to the present day. As such, it is "fundamental to our scheme of ordered liberty" and "deeply rooted in this Nation's history and tradition." As such, the Fourteenth Amendment's Due Process Clause incorporates the Clause against the states with equal force as against the federal government. Justices Gorsuch and Thomas filed concurring opinions to state that, in their views, the appropriate vehicle for incorporation is the Fourteenth Amendment's Privileges or Immunities Clause, rather than its Due Process Clause.

In 2013, Tyson Timbs was charged with dealing controlled substances (opioids), which he supplied using a $42,000 Land Rover he had purchased with the proceeds of his father's life insurance. A private entity retained by Indiana State filed a civil forfeiture action to seize Timbs's vehicle, worth around four times the $10,000 maximum criminal fine available. The Indiana Court of Appeals applied its own precedent, notwithstanding the lack of full incorporation, protecting Timbs through the Fines Clause, which it held applied to state forfeiture statutes. In applying the clause, the Indiana Court found that the forfeiture was grossly disproportionate to the gravity of the offense. Nonetheless, the Supreme Court of Indiana reversed, noting that the Excessive Fines Clause did not apply against the states. Through Ginsburg's opinion, the U.S. Supreme Court reversed the lower holding, applying the historic incorporation test, which asks whether the relevant Bill of Rights protection is " 'fundamental to our scheme of ordered liberty,' or 'deeply rooted in this Nation's history and tradition' " and finding the argument in favor to be "overwhelming." Justice Ginsburg examined history (as the full text at the end of this chapter shows), concluding that an individual's ability to pay a fine or forfeiture was an essential factor in determining the fine's excessiveness and therefore its constitutionality under the Fines Clause.

Despite achieving long-awaited incorporation, the Fines Clause might not protect individuals as expansively as it might first appear. While its history was acknowledged by the Court, the ruling refrained from setting out a test that would consider a defendant's ability to pay. Instead, it implicitly left that choice to the lower courts. In remaining loyal to a narrow-reading of legal questions, the Court acknowledged—in a sparse opinion—the importance of ability to pay fines, but did not set out (or even recommend) any test that would require assessing such a fine's impact on a defendant's livelihood. Instead, the Court endorsed an open-ended proportionality inquiry. This dissonance between proportionality of the fine and financial ability to pay is most apparent in state-level forfeitures, and so the clause's incorporation may not offer much new protection to defendants in such cases from excessive fines. This was consistent with the lack of doctrinal weight placed on ability to pay in *Austin*, which had neglected to mandate excessive analysis. In a system where federal, state, and local governments depend quite significantly on civil forfeitures for their own revenue, a lack of clear jurisprudence leaves the question to the legislature and its implementation in executive policy. *Timbs* may therefore not deter the mass seizure of lower-value assets, such as petty cash. Such seizures are likely to satisfy the proportionality test even if low-level offenders are unable to pay or are dependent on such cash to survive. Certainly, any speculation that civil asset forfeiture would end as a result of *Timbs* was overstated.

Reference

Harvard Law Review (2019) 'Timbs v. Indiana', *Harvard Law Review*, 133, p. 342.

Cited cases

Austin v. United States, 509 U.S. 602 (1993).
BMW of North America, Inc. v. Gore, 517 U.S. 559 (1996).
Browning-Ferris Industries v. Kelco Disposal, 492 U.S. 257 (1989).
Exxon Shipping Co. v. Baker, 554 U.S. 471 (2008).
McDonald v. Chicago, 561 U.S. 742 (2010).
State Farm Mutual Automobile Insurance Co. v. Campbell, 538 U.S. 408 (2003).
Timbs v. Indiana, 139 S. Ct. 682 (2019).
TXO Production Corp. v. *Alliance Resources Corp*., 509 U. S. 443 (1993).
United States v. Bajakajian, 524 U.S. 321 (1998).
United States v. Dicter, 198 F.3d 1284 (11th Cir. 1999).
United States v. Dubose, 146 F.3d 1141 (9th Cir. 1998).
United States v. Halper, 490 U.S. 435 (1989).
United States v. Levesque, 546 F.3d 78 (1st Cir. 2008).
United States v. Viloski, 814 F.3d 104 (2d Cir. 2016).
Waters-Pierce Oil Co. v. Texas, 212 U.S. 86 (1909).

Cited legislation

Magna Carta, §20, 9 Hen. III, ch. 14, in 1 Eng. Stat. at Large 5 (1225).

BROWNING-FERRIS INDUSTRIES OF VERMONT, INC. v. KELCO DISPOSAL, INC., 492 U.S. 257 (1989)

JUSTICE BLACKMUN delivered the opinion for a unanimous Court with respect to Parts I, III, and IV, and the opinion of the Court with respect to Part II, in which CHIEF JUSTICE REHNQUIST and JUSTICES BRENNAN, WHITE, MARSHALL, SCALIA, and KENNEDY joined.

We face here the questions whether the Excessive Fines Clause of the Eighth Amendment applies to a civil jury award of punitive or exemplary damages, and, if so, whether an award of $6 million was excessive in this particular case. This Court has never held, or even intimated, that the Eighth Amendment serves as a check on the power of a jury to award damages in a civil case. Rather, our concerns in applying the Eighth Amendment have been with criminal process and with direct actions initiated by government to inflict punishment. Awards of punitive damages do not implicate these concerns. We therefore hold, on the basis of the history and purpose of the Eighth Amendment, that its Excessive Fines Clause does not apply to awards of punitive damages in cases between private parties.

I

These weighty questions of constitutional law arise from an unlikely source: the waste-disposal business in Burlington, Vt. Petitioner Browning-Ferris Industries of Vermont, Inc., is a subsidiary of petitioner Browning-Ferris Industries, Inc. (collectively, BFI), which operates a nationwide commercial waste collection and disposal business. In 1973 BFI entered the Burlington area trash collection market, and in 1976 began to offer roll-off collection services. Until 1980, BFI was the sole provider of such services in the Burlington area; that year, respondent Joseph Kelley, who, since 1973, had been BFI's local district manager, went into business for himself, starting respondent Kelco Disposal, Inc. Within a year, Kelco obtained nearly 40% of the Burlington roll-off market, and by 1982, Kelco's market share had risen to 43%. During 1982, BFI reacted by attempting to drive Kelco out of business, first by offering to buy Kelco and then by cutting prices by 40% or more on new business for approximately six months. The orders given to the Burlington BFI office by its regional vice president were clear: "Put [Kelley] out of business. Do whatever it takes. Squish him like a bug."

During the first four months of BFI's predatory campaign, Kelco's revenues dropped 30%. Kelco's attorney wrote to BFI's legal department asserting that BFI's pricing strategy was illegal, and threatened to initiate court proceedings if it continued. BFI did not respond, and continued its price-cutting policy for several more months. BFI's market share remained stable from 1982 to 1984, but by 1985, Kelco had captured 56% of the market. That same year, BFI sold out to a third party and left the Burlington market.

In 1984, Kelco and Kelley brought an action in the United States District Court for the District of Vermont, alleging a violation of § 2 of the Sherman Act for attempts to monopolize the Burlington roll-off market. They also claimed that BFI had interfered with Kelco's contractual relations in violation of Vermont tort law. Kelley's claims were severed from Kelco's, and Kelco's antitrust and tort claims were tried to a jury. After a 6-day trial, BFI was found liable on both counts. A 1-day trial on damages followed, at which Kelco submitted evidence regarding the revenues and profits it lost as a result of BFI's predatory prices. Kelco's attorney urged the jury to return an award of punitive damages, asking the jurors to "deliver a message to Houston [BFI's headquarters]." *Id.* at 53. Kelco also stressed BFI's total revenues of $1.3 billion in the previous year, noting that this figure broke down to $25 million a week. BFI urged that punitive damages were not appropriate, but made no argument as to amount.

The District Court instructed the jury that it could award punitive damages on the state law claims if it found by clear and convincing evidence that BFI's conduct "revealed actual malice, outrageous conduct, or constituted a willful and wanton or reckless disregard of the plaintiff's rights." *Id.* at 81. It also told the jury that, in determining the amount of punitive damages, it could take into account "the character of the defendants, their financial standing, and the nature of their acts." BFI raised no relevant objection to the charge on punitive damages. The jury returned a verdict of $51,146 in compensatory damages on both the federal antitrust and state tort counts, and $6 million in punitive damages.

BFI moved for judgment notwithstanding the verdict, a new trial, or remittitur. The District Court denied these motions and awarded Kelco $153,438 in treble damages and $212,500 in attorney's fees and costs on the antitrust claim, or, in the alternative, $6,066,082.74 in compensatory and punitive damages on the state law claim. BFI appealed. The United States Court of Appeals for the Second Circuit affirmed the judgment both as to liability and as to damages. On the issue of punitive damages, the court noted that the evidence showed that BFI "wilfully and deliberately attempted to drive Kelco out of the market," and found no indication of jury prejudice or bias. Addressing the Eighth Amendment issue, the court noted that, even if the Amendment were applicable "to this nominally civil case," the damages were not "so disproportionate as to be cruel, unusual, or constitutionally excessive," and upheld the award.

II

Given that the Amendment is addressed to bail, fines, and punishments, our cases long have understood it to apply primarily, and perhaps exclusively, to criminal prosecutions and punishments.

To decide the instant case, however, we need not go so far as to hold that the Excessive Fines Clause applies just to criminal cases. Whatever the outer confines of the Clause's reach may be, we now decide only that it does not constrain an award of money damages in a civil suit when the government neither has prosecuted the action nor has any right to receive a share of the damages awarded. To hold otherwise, we believe, would be to ignore the purposes and concerns of the Amendment, as illuminated by its history.

A

The Eighth Amendment received little debate in the First Congress [and] Congress did not discuss what was meant by the term "fines," or whether the prohibition had any application in the civil context. In the absence of direct evidence of Congress' intended meaning, we think it significant that, at the time of the drafting and ratification of the Amendment, the word "fine" was understood to mean a payment to a sovereign as punishment for some offense. Then, as now, fines were assessed in criminal, rather than in private civil, actions.

But there is more than inferential evidence from language to support our conclusion that the Excessive Fines Clause is inapplicable to an award of punitive damages. The undisputed purpose and history of the Amendment generally, and of the Excessive Fines Clause specifically, confirms our reading. The Eighth Amendment clearly was adopted with the particular intent of placing limits on the powers of the new Government.

Simply put, the primary focus of the Eighth Amendment was the potential for governmental abuse of its "prosecutorial" power, not concern with the extent or purposes of civil damages.

This history, when coupled with the fact that the accepted English definition of "fine" in 1689 appears to be identical to that in use in colonial America at the time of our Bill of Rights, seems to us clear support for reading our Excessive Fines Clause as limiting the ability of the sovereign to use its prosecutorial power, including the power to collect fines, for improper ends. Providing even clearer support for this view is the English case law, immediately prior to the enactment of the English Bill of Rights, which stressed the difference between civil damages and criminal fines. In short, nothing in English history suggests that the Excessive Fines Clause of the 1689 Bill of

Rights, the direct ancestor of our Eighth Amendment, was intended to apply to damages awarded in disputes between private parties. Instead, the history of the Eighth Amendment convinces us that the Excessive Fines Clause was intended to limit only those fines directly imposed by, and payable to, the government.

B

Petitioners, however, argue that the Excessive Fines Clause "derives from limitations in English law on monetary penalties exacted in private civil cases to punish and deter misconduct." They recognize that nothing in the history we have recounted thus far espouses that view. To find support, they turn the clock hundreds of years further back to English history prior to Magna Carta, and in particular to the use and abuse of "amercements." According to petitioners, amercements were essentially civil damages, and the limits Magna Carta placed on the use of amercements were the forerunners of the 1689 Bill of Rights' prohibition on excessive fines. In their view, the English Bill of Rights and our Eighth Amendment must be understood as reaching beyond the criminal context, because Magna Carta did. Punitive damages, they suggest, must be within the scope of the Excessive Fines Clause because they are a modern-day analog of 13th-century amercements.

The argument is somewhat intriguing, but we hesitate to place great emphasis on the particulars of 13th-century English practice, particularly when the interpretation we are urged to adopt appears to conflict with the lessons of more recent history. Even so, our understanding of the use of amercements, and the development of actions for damages at common law, convince us that petitioners' view of the relevant history does not support the result they seek.

It is difficult to understand how Magna Carta, or the English Bill of Rights as viewed through the lens of Magna Carta, compels us to read our Eighth Amendment's Excessive Fines Clause as applying to punitive damages when those documents themselves were never so applied.

C

Our conclusion that the Framers of the Eighth Amendment did not expressly intend it to apply to damages awards made by civil juries does not necessarily complete our inquiry. Our Eighth Amendment jurisprudence has not been inflexible.

Furthermore, even if we were prepared to extend the scope of the Excessive Fines Clause beyond the context where the Framers clearly intended it to apply, we would not be persuaded to do so with respect to cases of punitive damages awards in private civil cases, because they are too far afield from the concerns that animate the Eighth Amendment. We think it clear, from both the language of the Excessive Fines Clause and the nature of our constitutional framework, that the Eighth Amendment places limits on the steps a government may take against an individual, whether it be keeping him in prison, imposing excessive monetary sanctions, or using cruel and unusual punishments. The fact that punitive damages are imposed through the aegis of courts, and serve to advance governmental interests, is insufficient to support the step petitioners ask us to take. While we agree with petitioners that punitive damages advance the interests of punishment and deterrence, which are also among the interests advanced by the criminal law, we fail to see how this overlap requires us to apply the Excessive Fines Clause in a case between private parties. Here the government of Vermont has not taken a positive step to punish, as it most obviously does in the criminal context, nor has it used the civil courts to extract large payments or forfeitures for the purpose of raising revenue or disabling some individual. We shall not ignore the language of the Excessive Fines Clause, or its history, or the theory on which it is based, in order to apply it to punitive damages.

III

Petitioners also ask us to review the punitive damages award to determine whether it is excessive under the Due Process Clause of the Fourteenth Amendment. That inquiry must await another day. Because petitioners failed to raise their due process argument before either the District Court or the Court of Appeals, and made no specific mention of it in their petition for certiorari in this Court, we shall not consider its effect on this award.

IV

Petitioners also ask us to hold that this award of punitive damages is excessive as a matter of federal common law. Rather than directing us to a developed body of federal law, however, they merely repeat the standards they urged us to adopt under the Eighth Amendment. It is not our role to review directly the award for excessiveness, or to substitute our judgment for that of the jury.

V

In sum, we conclude that neither federal common law nor the Excessive Fines Clause of the Eighth Amendment provides a basis for disturbing the jury's punitive damages award in this case. Accordingly, the judgment of the Court of Appeals is affirmed.

JUSTICE BRENNAN filed a concurring opinion, joined by JUSTICE MARSHALL.

JUSTICE O'CONNOR filed an opinion concurring in part and dissenting in part, joined by JUSTICE STEVENS

Awards of punitive damages are skyrocketing. As recently as a decade ago, the largest award of punitive damages affirmed by an appellate court in a products liability case was $250,000. Since then, awards more than 30 times as high have been sustained on appeal. The threat of such enormous awards has a detrimental effect on the research and development of new products. Some manufacturers of prescription drugs, for example, have decided that it is better to avoid uncertain liability than to introduce a new pill or vaccine into the market. Similarly, designers of airplanes and motor vehicles have been forced to abandon new projects for fear of lawsuits that can often lead to awards of punitive damages.

The trend toward multimillion dollar awards of punitive damages is exemplified by this case. The Court holds today that the Excessive Fines Clause of the Eighth Amendment places no limits on the amount of punitive damages that can be awarded in a suit between private parties. That result is neither compelled by history nor supported by precedent, and I therefore respectfully dissent from Part II of the Court's opinion.

If a corporation is protected by the Due Process Clause from overbearing and oppressive monetary sanctions, it is also protected from such penalties by the Excessive Fines Clause.

In my view, a chronological account of the Clause and its antecedents demonstrates that the Clause derives from limitations in English law on monetary penalties exacted in civil and criminal cases to punish and deter misconduct. History aside, this Court's cases leave no doubt that punitive damages serve the same purposes—punishment and deterrence—as the criminal law, and that excessive punitive damages present precisely the evil of exorbitant monetary penalties that the Clause was designed to prevent.

In my view, the $6 million award of punitive damages imposed on BFI constitutes a fine subject to the limitations of the Eighth Amendment. In current usage, the word "fine" comprehends a forfeiture or penalty recoverable in a civil action. This plethora of case law on the nature of punitive damages, it seems to me, is sufficient to find the Excessive Fines Clause applicable to the award in this case. There is, however, even more support for the applicability of the Clause. In determining whether a sanction is penal, the Court has generally looked to several factors: (1) whether it involves an affirmative disability; (2) whether it has historically been regarded as punishment; (3) whether it comes into play on a finding of scienter; (4) whether its operation will promote retribution and deterrence; (5) whether the behavior to which it applies is already a crime; (6) whether there is an alternative purpose for it; and (7) whether it is excessive in relation to the alternative purpose assigned. *Kennedy v. Mendoza-Martinez*, 372 U.S. 144, 372 U.S. 168–169 (1963). I agree with those commentators who have found it easy to conclude that punitive damages are penal under the *Mendoza-Martinez* factors.

Determining whether a particular award of punitive damages is excessive is not an easy task. The proportionality framework that the Court has adopted under the Cruel and Unusual Punishments Clause, however, offers some broad guidelines.

The Court of Appeals did not think that the Excessive Fines Clause applied to awards of punitive damages, and therefore did not conduct any sort of proportionality analysis. I would remand the case to the Court of Appeals so that it could, in the first instance, apply the *Solem* framework [. . .] and determine whether the award of over $6 million imposed on BFI violates the Excessive Fines Clause.

AUSTIN v. UNITED STATES, 509 U.S. 602 (1993)

JUSTICE BLACKMUN delivered the unanimous opinion of the Court

In this case, we are asked to decide whether the Excessive Fines Clause of the Eighth Amendment applies to forfeitures of property under 21 U. S. C. §§881(a)(4) and (a)(7). We hold that it does and therefore remand the case for consideration of the question whether the forfeiture at issue here was excessive.

On August 2, 1990, petitioner Richard Lyle Austin was indicted on four counts of violating South Dakota's drug laws. Austin ultimately pleaded guilty to one count of possessing cocaine with intent to distribute and was sentenced by the state court to seven years' imprisonment. On September 7, the United States filed an *in rem* action in the United States District Court for the District of South Dakota seeking forfeiture of Austin's mobile home and auto body shop under 21 U. S. C. §§881(a)(4) and (a)(7).

The United States Court of Appeals for the Eighth Circuit "reluctantly agree[d] with the government" and affirmed.

1 These statutes provide for the forfeiture of:

> "(4) All conveyances, including aircraft, vehicles, or vessels, which are used, or are intended for use, to transport, or in any manner to facilitate the transportation, sale, receipt, possession, or concealment of [controlled substances, their raw materials, and equipment used in their manufacture and distribution]
>
> "(7) All real property, including any right, title, and interest (including any leasehold interest) in the whole of any lot or tract of land and any appurtenances or improvements, which is used, or intended to be used, in any manner or part, to commit, or to facilitate the commission of, a violation of this subchapter punishable by more than one year's imprisonment . . . ."

Each provision has an "innocent owner" exception. See §§881(a)(4)(C) and (a)(7).

II

Austin contends that the Eighth Amendment's Excessive Fines Clause applies to *in rem* civil forfeiture proceedings. We have had occasion to consider this Clause only once before. In *Browning-Ferris*, we held that the Excessive Fines Clause does not limit the award of punitive damages to a private party in a civil suit when the government neither has prosecuted the action nor has any right to receive a share of the damages.

We found it unnecessary to decide in *Browning-Ferris* whether the Excessive Fines Clause applies only to criminal cases. The United States now argues that

> "any claim that the government's conduct in a civil proceeding is limited by the Eighth Amendment generally, or by the Excessive Fines Clause in particular, must fail unless the challenged governmental action, despite its label, would have been recognized as a *criminal* punishment at the time the Eighth Amendment was adopted."

It further suggests that the Eighth Amendment cannot apply to a civil proceeding unless that proceeding is so punitive that it must be considered criminal [. . .] We disagree.

Some provisions of the Bill of Rights are expressly limited to criminal cases. The Fifth Amendment's Self Incrimination Clause, for example, provides: "No person . . . shall be compelled in any criminal case to be a witness against himself." The protections provided by the Sixth Amendment are explicitly confined to "criminal prosecutions." The text of the Eighth Amendment includes no similar limitation. Nor does the history of the Eighth Amendment require such a limitation.

The purpose of the Eighth Amendment, putting the Bail Clause to one side, was to limit the government's power to punish. Thus, the question is not, as the United States would have it, whether forfeiture under §§ 881(a)(4) and (a)(7) is civil or criminal, but rather whether it is punishment.

In considering this question, we are mindful of the fact that sanctions frequently serve more than one purpose. We need not exclude the possibility that a forfeiture serves remedial purposes to conclude that it is subject to the limitations of the Excessive Fines Clause. We, however, must determine that it can only be explained as serving in part to punish. We said in *Halper* that "a civil sanction that cannot fairly be said solely to serve a remedial purpose, but rather can only be explained as also serving either retributive or deterrent purposes, is punishment, as we have come to understand the term." We turn, then, to consider whether, at the time the Eighth Amendment was ratified, forfeiture was understood at least in part as punishment and whether forfeiture under §§ 881(a)(4) and (a)(7) should be so understood today.

Of England's three kinds of forfeiture, only [statutory forfeiture] took hold in the United States. The First Congress passed laws subjecting ships and cargos involved in customs offenses to forfeiture. It does not follow from that fact, however, that the First Congress thought such forfeitures to be beyond the purview of the Eighth Amendment. Indeed, examination of those laws suggests that the First Congress viewed forfeiture as punishment.

Our cases also have recognized that statutory *in rem* forfeiture imposes punishment. In *Peisch* v. *Ware,* 4 Cranch 347 (1808), for example, the Court held that goods removed from the custody of a revenue officer without the payment of duties should not be forfeitable for that reason unless they were removed with the consent of the owner or his agent.

[. . .]

In sum, even though this Court has rejected the "innocence" of the owner as a common-law defense to forfeiture, it consistently has recognized that forfeiture serves, at least in part, to punish the owner. More recently, we have noted that forfeiture serves "punitive and deterrent purposes," and "impos[es] an economic penalty." We conclude, therefore, that forfeiture generally and statutory *in rem* forfeiture in particular historically have been understood, at least in part, as punishment.

We turn next to consider whether forfeitures under 21 U. S. C. §§881(a)(4) and (a)(7) are properly considered punishment today. We find nothing in these provisions or their legislative history to contradict the historical understanding of forfeiture as punishment. Unlike traditional forfeiture statutes, §§881(a)(4) and (a)(7) expressly provide an "innocent owner" defense. See § 881(a)(4)(C) ("[N]o conveyance shall be forfeited under this paragraph to the extent of an interest of an owner, by reason of any act or omission established by that owner to have been committed or omitted without the knowledge, consent, or willful blindness of the owner"); § 881(a)(7) ("[N]o property shall be forfeited under this paragraph, to the extent of an interest of an owner, by reason of any act or omission established by that owner to have been committed or omitted without the knowledge or consent of that owner"). These exemptions serve to focus the provisions on the culpability of the owner in a way that makes them look more like punishment, not less

Furthermore, Congress has chosen to tie forfeiture directly to the commission of drug offenses. Thus, under § 881(a)(4), a conveyance is forfeitable if it is used or intended for use to facilitate the transportation of controlled substances, their raw materials, or the equipment used to manufacture or distribute them. Under § 881(a)(7), real property is forfeitable if it is used or intended for use to facilitate the commission of a drug-related crime punishable by more than one year's imprisonment.

The legislative history of § 881 confirms the punitive nature of these provisions.

Concededly, we have recognized that the forfeiture of contraband itself may be characterized as remedial because it removes dangerous or illegal items from society.

The Government's second argument about the remedial nature of this forfeiture is no more persuasive.

Fundamentally, even assuming that §§881(a)(4) and (a)(7) serve some remedial purpose, the Government's argument must fail. "[A] civil sanction that cannot fairly be said *solely* to serve a remedial purpose, but rather can only be explained as also serving either retributive or deterrent purposes, is punishment, as we have come to understand the term." In light of the historical understanding of forfeiture as punishment, the clear focus of §§ 881(a)(4) and (a)(7) on the culpability of the owner, and the evidence that Congress understood those provisions as serving to deter and to punish, we cannot conclude that forfeiture under §§ 881(a)(4) and (a)(7) serves solely a remedial purpose. We therefore conclude that forfeiture under these provisions constitutes "payment to a sovereign as punishment for some offense," and, as such, is subject to the limitations of the Eighth Amendment's Excessive Fines Clause.

Austin asks that we establish a multifactor test for determining whether a forfeiture is constitutionally "excessive." We decline that invitation.

JUSTICE SCALIA filed an opinion concurring in part and concurring in the judgment

I would have reserved the question without engaging in the misleading discussion of culpability. *Even if* punishment of personal culpability is necessary for a forfeiture to be a fine; and *even if in rem* forfeitures in general do not punish personal culpability; the *in rem* forfeiture in *this* case is a fine. Here, the property must "offend" *and* the owner must not be completely without fault. Nor is there any consideration of compensating for loss, since the value of the property is irrelevant to whether it is forfeited. That is enough to satisfy the *Browning-Ferris* standard, and to make the entire discussion in Part III dictum. Statutory forfeitures under § 881(a) are certainly *payment* (in kind) *to a sovereign* as *punishment* for an *offense*.

Unlike monetary fines, statutory *in rem* forfeitures have traditionally been fixed, not by determining the appropriate value of the penalty in relation to the committed offense, but by determining what property has been "tainted" by unlawful use, to which issue the value of the property is irrelevant. Scales used to measure out unlawful drug sales, for example, are confiscable whether made of the purest gold or the basest metal. But an *in rem* forfeiture goes beyond the traditional limits that the Eighth Amendment permits if it applies to property that cannot properly be regarded as an instrumentality of the offense-the building, for example, in which an isolated drug sale happens to occur. Such a confiscation would be an excessive fine. The question is not *how much* the confiscated property is worth, but *whether* the confiscated property has a close enough relationship to the offense.

JUSTICE KENNEDY filed an opinion concurring in part and concurring in the judgment, joined by CHIEF JUSTICE REHNQUIST and JUSTICE THOMAS

UNITED STATES v. BAJAKAJIAN, 524 U.S. 321 (1998)

JUSTICE THOMAS delivered the opinion of the Court (5–4), joined by JUSTICES STEVENS, SOUTER, GINSBURG, and BREYER

Respondent Hosep Bajakajian attempted to leave the United States without reporting, as required by federal law, that he was transporting more than $10,000 in currency. Federal law also provides that a person convicted of willfully violating this reporting requirement shall forfeit to the Government "any property . . . involved in such offense." 18 U. S. C. § 982(a)(1). The question in this case is whether forfeiture of the entire $357,144 that respondent failed to declare would violate the Excessive Fines Clause of the Eighth Amendment. We hold that it would, because full forfeiture of respondent's currency would be grossly disproportional to the gravity of his offense.

I

[. . .]

Because the Court of Appeals' holding-that the forfeiture ordered by § 982(a)(1) was per se unconstitutional in cases of currency forfeiture-invalidated a portion of an Act of Congress, we granted certiorari.

[. . .] at the time the Constitution was adopted, "the word 'fine' was understood to mean a payment to a sovereign as punishment for some offense." [*Browning-Ferris*]. The Excessive Fines Clause thus "limits the government's power to extract payments, whether in cash or in kind, 'as punishment for some offense.'" [*Austin*].

We have little trouble concluding that the forfeiture of currency ordered by § 982(a)(1) constitutes punishment. The statute directs a court to order forfeiture as an additional sanction when "imposing sentence on a person convicted of" a willful violation of § 5316's reporting requirement. The forfeiture is thus imposed at the culmination of a criminal proceeding and requires conviction of an underlying felony, and it cannot be imposed upon an innocent owner of unreported currency, but only upon a person who has himself been convicted of a § 5316 reporting violation.3 Cf. id., at 619 (holding forfeiture to be a "fine" in part because the forfeiture statute "expressly provide[d] an 'innocent owner' defense" and thus "look[ed] . . . like punishment").

[. . .]

We do not suggest that merely because the forfeiture of respondent's currency in this case would not serve a remedial purpose, other forfeitures may be classified as nonpunitive (and thus not "fines") if they serve some remedial purpose as well as being punishment for an offense. Even if the

Government were correct in claiming that the forfeiture of respondent's currency is remedial in some way, the forfeiture would still be punitive in part. (The Government concedes as much.) This is sufficient to bring the forfeiture within the purview of the Excessive Fines Clause.

III

Because the forfeiture of respondent's currency constitutes punishment and is thus a "fine" within the meaning of the Excessive Fines Clause, we now turn to the question whether it is "excessive."

A

The touchstone of the constitutional inquiry under the Excessive Fines Clause is the principle of proportionality: The amount of the forfeiture must bear some relationship to the gravity of the offense that it is designed to punish. [. . .] If the amount of the forfeiture is grossly disproportional to the gravity of the defendant's offense, it is unconstitutional.

B

Under this standard, the forfeiture of respondent's entire $357,144 would violate the Excessive Fines Clause. Respondent's crime was solely a reporting offense. It was permissible to transport the currency out of the country so long as he reported it. Section 982(a)(1) orders currency to be forfeited for a "willful" violation of the reporting requirement. Thus, the essence of respondent's crime is a willful failure to report the removal of currency from the United States.

[. . .] Comparing the gravity of respondent's crime with the $357,144 forfeiture the Government seeks, we conclude that such a forfeiture would be grossly disproportional to the gravity of his offense.15 It is larger than the $5,000 fine imposed by the District Court by many orders of magnitude, and it bears no articulable correlation to any injury suffered by the Government.

C

Finally, we must reject the contention that the proportionality of full forfeiture is demonstrated by the fact that the First Congress enacted statutes requiring full forfeiture of goods involved in customs offenses or the payment of monetary penalties proportioned to the goods' value. It is argued that the enactment of these statutes at roughly the same time that the Eighth

Amendment was ratified suggests that full forfeiture, in the customs context at least, is a proportional punishment. The early customs statutes, however, do not support such a conclusion because, unlike § 982(a)(1), the type of forfeiture that they imposed was not considered punishment for a criminal offense.

[. . .] the full forfeiture mandated by § 982(a)(1) in this case serves no remedial purpose; it is clearly punishment. The customs statutes enacted by the First Congress, therefore, in no way suggest that § 982(a)(1)'s currency forfeiture is constitutionally proportional.

JUSTICE KENNEDY delivered a dissenting opinion, joined by CHIEF JUSTICE REHNQUIST and JUSTICES O'CONNOR and SCALIA.

TIMBS v. INDIANA, 139 S. CT. 682 (2019)

JUSTICE GINSBURG delivered the opinion of the Court (9–0).

Tyson Timbs pleaded guilty in Indiana state court to dealing in a controlled substance and conspiracy to commit theft. The trial court sentenced him to one year of home detention and five years of probation, which included a court-supervised addiction-treatment program. The sentence also required Timbs to pay fees and costs totaling $1,203. At the time of Timbs's arrest, the police seized his vehicle, a Land Rover SUV Timbs had purchased for about $42,000. Timbs paid for the vehicle with money he received from an insurance policy when his father died.

The State engaged a private law firm to bring a civil suit for forfeiture of Timbs's Land Rover, charging that the vehicle had been used to transport heroin. After Timbs's guilty plea in the criminal case, the trial court held a hearing on the forfeiture demand. Although finding that Timbs's vehicle had been used to facilitate violation of a criminal statute, the court denied the requested forfeiture, observing that Timbs had recently purchased the vehicle for $42,000, more than four times the maximum $10,000 monetary fine assessable against him for his drug conviction. Forfeiture of the Land Rover, the court determined, would be grossly disproportionate to the gravity of Timbs's offense, hence unconstitutional under the Eighth Amendment's Excessive Fines Clause. The Court of Appeals of Indiana affirmed that determination, but the Indiana Supreme Court reversed.

The Indiana Supreme Court did not decide whether the forfeiture would be excessive. Instead, it held that the Excessive Fines Clause constrains only federal action and is inapplicable to state impositions. We granted certiorari.

The question presented: Is the Eighth Amendment's Excessive Fines Clause an "incorporated" protection applicable to the States under the Fourteenth Amendment's Due Process Clause? Like the Eighth Amendment's proscriptions of "cruel and unusual punishment" and "[e]xcessive bail," the protection against excessive fines guards against abuses of government's punitive or criminal-law-enforcement authority. This safeguard, we hold, is "fundamental to our scheme of ordered liberty," with "dee[p] root[s] in [our] history and tradition." The Excessive Fines Clause is therefore incorporated by the Due Process Clause of the Fourteenth Amendment.

Under the Eighth Amendment, "[e]xcessive bail shall not be required, nor excessive fines imposed, nor cruel and unusual punishments inflicted." Taken together, these Clauses place "parallel limitations" on "the power of those entrusted with the criminal-law function of government." Directly at issue here is the phrase "nor excessive fines imposed," which "limits the government's power to extract payments, whether in cash or in kind, 'as punishment for some offense.'" The Fourteenth Amendment, we hold, incorporates this protection.

As relevant here, Magna Carta required that economic sanctions "be proportioned to the wrong" and "not be so large as to deprive [an offender] of his livelihood."

Despite Magna Carta, imposition of excessive fines persisted. The 17th century Stuart kings, in particular, were criticized for using large fines to raise revenue, harass their political foes, and indefinitely detain those un-able to pay. When James II was overthrown in the Glorious Revolution, the attendant English Bill of Rights reaffirmed Magna Carta's guarantee by providing that "excessive Bail ought not to be required, nor excessive Fines imposed; nor cruel and unusual Punishments inflicted."

Across the Atlantic, this familiar language was adopted almost verbatim, first in the Virginia Declaration of Rights, then in the Eighth Amendment, which states: "Excessive bail shall not be required, nor excessive fines imposed, nor cruel and unusual punishments inflicted."

Adoption of the Excessive Fines Clause was in tune not only with English law; the Clause resonated as well with similar colonial-era provisions. See, e.g., Pa. Frame of Govt., Laws Agreed Upon in England, Art. XVIII (1682), in 5 Federal and State Constitutions 3061 (F. Thorpe ed. 1909) ("[A]ll fines shall be moderate, and saving men's contenements, merchandize, or wainage."). In 1787, the constitutions of eight States—accounting for 70% of the U.S. population—forbade excessive fines.

An even broader consensus obtained in 1868 upon ratification of the Fourteenth Amendment. By then, the constitutions of 35 of the 37 States—accounting for over 90% of the U.S. population—expressly prohibited excessive fines.

Notwithstanding the States' apparent agreement that the right guaranteed by the Excessive Fines Clause was fundamental, abuses continued. Following the Civil War, Southern States enacted Black Codes to subjugate newly freed slaves and maintain the prewar racial hierarchy. Among these laws' provisions were draconian fines for violating broad proscriptions on "vagrancy" and other dubious offenses. When newly freed slaves were unable to pay imposed fines, States often demanded involuntary labor instead. Congressional debates over the Civil Rights Act of 1866, the joint resolution that became the Fourteenth Amendment, and similar measures repeatedly mentioned the use of fines to coerce involuntary labor.

Today, acknowledgment of the right's fundamental nature remains widespread. As Indiana itself reports, all 50 States have a constitutional provision prohibiting the imposition of excessive fines either directly or by requiring proportionality. Brief in Opposition 8–9. Indeed, Indiana explains that its own Supreme Court has held that the Indiana Constitution should be interpreted to impose the same restrictions as the Eighth Amendment.

For good reason, the protection against excessive fines has been a constant shield throughout Anglo-American history: Exorbitant tolls undermine other constitutional liberties. Excessive fines can be used, for example, to retaliate against or chill the speech of political enemies, as the Stuarts' critics learned several centuries ago. Even absent a political motive, fines may be employed "in a measure out of accord with the penal goals of retribution and deterrence," for "fines are a source of revenue," while other forms of punishment "cost a State money."

In short, the historical and logical case for concluding that the Fourteenth Amendment incorporates the Excessive Fines Clause is overwhelming. Protection against excessive punitive economic sanctions secured by the Clause is, to repeat, both "fundamental to our scheme of ordered liberty" and "deeply rooted in this Nation's history and tradition."

The State of Indiana does not meaningfully challenge the case for incorporating the Excessive Fines Clause as a general matter. Instead, the State argues that the Clause does not apply to its use of civil *in rem* forfeitures because, the State says, the Clause's specific application to such forfeitures is neither fundamental nor deeply rooted.

In *Austin*, however, this Court held that civil *in rem* forfeitures fall within the Clause's protection when they are at least partially punitive. *Austin* arose in the federal context. But when a Bill of Rights protection is incorporated, the protection applies "identically to both the Federal Government and the States." Accordingly, to prevail, Indiana must persuade us either to overrule our decision in *Austin* or to hold that, in light of *Austin*, the Excessive Fines Clause is not incorporated because the Clause's application to civil *in rem* forfeitures is neither fundamental nor deeply rooted. The first argument is not properly before us, and the second misapprehends the nature of our incorporation inquiry.

In the Indiana Supreme Court, the State argued that forfeiture of Timbs's SUV would not be excessive. It never argued, however, that civil *in rem* forfeitures were categorically beyond the reach of the Excessive Fines Clause. The Indiana Supreme Court, for its part, held that the Clause did not apply to the States at all, and it nowhere addressed the Clause's application to civil *in rem* forfeitures. Accordingly, Timbs sought our review of the question "[w]hether the Eighth Amendment's Excessive Fines Clause is incorporated against the States under the Fourteenth Amendment." In opposing review,

Indiana attempted to reformulate the question to ask "[w]hether the Eighth Amendment's Excessive Fines Clause restricts States' use of civil asset forfeitures." And on the merits, Indiana has argued not only that the Clause is not incorporated, but also that *Austin* was wrongly decided. Respondents' "right, in their brief in opposition, to restate the questions presented," however, "does not give them the power to expand [those] questions." That is particularly the case where, as here, a respondent's reformulation would lead us to address a question neither pressed nor passed upon below. We thus decline the State's invitation to reconsider our unanimous judgment in *Austin* that civil *in rem* forfeitures are fines for purposes of the Eighth Amendment when they are at least partially punitive.

As a fallback, Indiana argues that the Excessive Fines Clause cannot be incorporated if it applies to civil *in rem* forfeitures. We disagree. In considering whether the Fourteenth Amendment incorporates a protection contained in the Bill of Rights, we ask whether the right guaranteed—not each and every particular application of that right—is fundamental or deeply rooted.

Indiana's suggestion to the contrary is inconsistent with the approach we have taken in cases concerning novel applications of rights already deemed incorporated.

[. . .] regardless of whether application of the Excessive Fines Clause to civil *in rem* forfeitures is itself fundamental or deeply rooted, our conclusion that the Clause is incorporated remains unchanged.

For the reasons stated, the judgment of the Indiana Supreme Court is vacated, and the case is remanded for further proceedings not inconsistent with this opinion.

It is so ordered.

JUSTICE GORSUCH filed a concurring opinion. JUSTICE THOMAS filed an opinion concurring in the judgment.

5

THE DEATH PENALTY, FROM *FURMAN* TO *GREGG* AND BEYOND

No book on the Eighth Amendment is complete without close scrutiny of the American institution of the death penalty, and no writing on that subject can avoid the landmark decision in ***FURMAN v. GEORGIA***, 391 U.S. 510 (1972). A brief return to the punishment's American history is pertinent. As already outlined in some depth in Chapter 1, the historical roots of capital punishment within the United States can be traced back to the early colonial period of Virginia, borrowing from English traditions. Captain George Kendall was sentenced to death for espionage and executed in Jamestown in 1608, the first recorded execution in the American colonies. Corporal and capital forms of punishment had been preferred to carceral imprisonment throughout the end of the Middle Ages in England, and this continued in the early American colonies, where the Waltham Black Act 9 Geo. I c. 22 (1723) prevailed. This, or the "Black Code" as it was known, created around 50 capital offenses, mostly property-based. While it is often reported that over 100 offenses were made capital in England during the period of American founding, archival research reveals that the vast majority of death sentences handed down at the time were in practice replaced by transportation to Australian colonies.[1] Of the 51 sentences recorded as imposing death in England during 1789—the year Madison drafted the Bill of Rights—for example, only nine (18%) were carried out. As the Enlightenment reached either side of the Atlantic in the latter half of the 18th century, so did humanitarian reformation. At the same time, the

1 See Eastaugh, C. (2017) *Unconstitutional solitude*. Palgrave Macmillan, Chapter 2.

DOI: 10.4324/9780429398780-6

American colonies adopted and adapted English legal traditions, including the death penalty for a range of offenses. The types of crimes that could warrant capital punishment were diverse, encompassing not only murder but also offenses like witchcraft, arson, burglary, and even certain forms of disrespect or disobedience. The severity of punishments, including the death penalty, was often influenced by the prevailing social, religious, and cultural norms of the time. Public executions were common, serving as both a deterrent and as a form of community spectacle.

Throughout the early history of the United States after independence, the death penalty remained a significant aspect of the legal system—federally and in the states—notwithstanding the Eighth Amendment's proscription of excessive punishments. However, its application and acceptance evolved over time, setting the stage for ongoing debates and reforms in the centuries that followed. Before *Furman* was decided in 1972, state prosecutors generally relied on the death penalty as the ultimate form of punishment without fear of federal court review. Between 1776 and the 1960s, recorded execution numbers ranged from 50 to 200 per year, peaking during World War II. In the ten years from 1966 to 1976, no single sentence of death was carried out in the United States, the longest moratorium period in U.S. history. Even before the Court held the penalty was unconstitutional in 1972, the National Association for the Advancement of Colored People's (NAACP) Legal Defense and Education Fund ("the LDF") had organized an extensive—and highly effective—nationwide campaign to challenge the constitutionality of the death penalty in a massive number of cases spanning dozens of states. The movement essentially blocked the imposition of capital sentences, with *Furman* being the final nail in the coffin, which would commute the sentences of hundreds on death row across the nation.

Before that judgment, though, came an earlier Supreme Court ruling in *Witherspoon v. Illinois*, 391 U.S. 510 (1968), concerning a state scheme where broad discretion had been available to the prosecution when composing juries in capital trials. The Court ruled that a legislative scheme such as that in Illinois, which had permitted juror exclusion on the basis that those individuals had felt unable to impose death due to their principled opposition against capital punishment, was insufficiently impartial by due process standards. While the decision invoked other areas of law besides the Punishments Clause, the majority opinion noted the importance of "the conscience of the community on the ultimate question of life or death," demonstrating a nod toward evolving standards of adjudication and living constitutionalism. The case provided support to the LDF in its struggle against the death penalty and marked the Court's first condemnation of a state's entire capital system, demonstrating a significant step in punishments jurisprudence, but it left unresolved the more fundamental question of the Eighth Amendment's proscription of excessive punishments and whether the death penalty met that bar. *Witherspoon* was handed down in 1968 and set the pace for further abolition of state capital punishments, arriving during a period when around 20 states were seriously considering limiting their death penalty statutes, and seven already had. This arrived at the end of a decade that had seen widespread social justice reform throughout the different branches of federal government, the tail end of the civil rights movement, and significant constitutional protection for the most vulnerable and subjugated members of society. In addition, recorded public support for capital punishment had plummeted to historic lows, and the rate of executions was slowing. This ultimately sparked a *de facto* abolition that would last for ten years, while states fine-tuned their capital statutes and the Court faced various novel challenges to those regimes. Any motion promised by *Witherspoon*'s condemnation of Illinois looked to be short-lived, however, and progress was on the verge of failure just one year later, when Warren stepped down as Chief Justice. Raising the stakes for the LDF's struggle against capital punishment, three significant liberal Justices departed the Court benches. Chief Justice Warren—a leading social justice reformer of the era, responsible for several liberal-leaning revolutions of constitutional law, including desegregation—stepped down to retire, replaced by Warren Burger. Justices Black and Harlan died within three months of one another in 1971, leaving the battle against the death penalty to the lead of Justice Brennan, the liberal champion of the 20th-century Court and one of the most influential American jurists of the era.

Furman reaches the Court

The Justices nominated to replace Black and Harlan were far from moderate. Justice Powell was noted as having criticized Martin Luther King, a sacrilege to civil rights proponents, and Justice Rehnquist was on record defending segregation. It would clearly take more than conventional appeals against the death penalty as an institution to pose serious challenges to its future, and the LDF had the ideal candidate to do so. At oral argument in *Furman*, the LDF's Anthony Amsterdam posed an objective element for his defendant's case, an approach to the Eighth Amendment never before faced by the Court. If a punishment would "be unacceptable to general contemporary conscience and standards of decency," he argued, it would offend the Constitution's proscription of cruel and unusual punishments under the *Weems-Trop* standard. In effect, the decision of which of these standards to follow rested with the Justices' views about the death penalty itself, an issue they had already faced in *Witherspoon*.

Where Amsterdam's argument differed from those the Court had faced previously, however, was with his reference to "objective indications." This required the Justices to interpret value in the Eighth Amendment through objectivity, derived presumably from evidence rather than intuition. Amsterdam's line of attack permitted the nine to consider their judgment of capital punishment without the risk of personal value statements, which might otherwise have been perceived as inapposite and unconstitutionally unsound. Ultimately, Amsterdam won the day, and the Court held in favor of Furman (and a codefendant, Jackson) and in the case of a cross-appeal from a Texan death row inmate, Branch, who had been sentenced in similar circumstances. Abruptly striking down capital statutes in both Georgia and Texas, the Court published a very short *per curiam* decision ruling that the level of discretion those states provided to judges was unacceptable and violated the Punishments Clause. Such schemes, Justice Stewart wrote, lead to the "wanton" and "freakish" imposition of the death penalty.

Many cases are described as "seminal" but few live up to their status as successfully as *Furman*. A truly significant case that changed the face of the death penalty in the United States and set five decades of Eighth Amendment precedent in motion, *Furman* spans 243 pages of the court reports. The nine, extensive, separate opinions amass over 66,000 words—the longest ruling in U.S. Supreme Court history. Clearly, reproducing it in full is not possible here, but salient sections of the concurring opinions are included at the end of the chapter. Chief Justice Burger's 4–5 lead dissent is too an important read, not least, because his words laid the foundations for the Court's reversal of the majority ruling four years later. Despite being notoriously fractured and difficult to decipher, an immediately clear effect of *Furman* was the invalidation of the death penalty. The decision applied to all similar schemes across the United States (which included every death penalty state) and evoked a *de facto* moratorium on capital punishment, reprieving 589 death row inmates (instead of receiving life without parole or whole-life custodial tariffs).

Writing in support of the 5–4 majority, Justice Douglas underscored the discriminatory nature of death sentences, arguing that imposing them based on factors such as race, religion, or social status rendered it unconstitutional as practiced. Justice Brennan claimed that the death penalty, as applied under existing statutes, allowed for arbitrary and capricious decisions by juries, violating the Eighth. He contended that if there was any discernible basis for the selection of individuals sentenced to death, it was the impermissible factor of race. Justice Stewart's concurrence highlighted the arbitrary imposition of death sentences, drawing an analogy to being struck by lightning. He found the death penalty cruel and unusual due to its wanton and unpredictable application, deeming it incompatible with evolving standards of decency. Justice White pointed out the infrequency and inconsistency in applying the death penalty, questioning the meaningful basis for distinguishing cases where it was imposed from those where it was not. He argued that the system lacked rationality and fairness, violating constitutional principles.

In the fifth and final concurrence, leading liberal Justice Thurgood Marshall—the first African American on the Supreme Court—tied the concept of equal protection to the Eighth Amendment, contending that the death penalty's administration, particularly when influenced by race, violated the fundamental theme of equal justice. He emphasized that the constitutionality of a death sentence depended on various factors, including the nature of the offense and the characteristics of the offender. Marshall claimed optimistically that the United States would now become an international beacon of civilization by recording a "magnificent advancement" in achieving "a major milestone in the long road up from barbarism" and joining the "approximately 70 other jurisdictions in the world that celebrate their regard for civilization and humanity by shunning capital punishment." His prediction would be short-lived, however, with two-thirds of the states clamoring to heed the dissent's guidance for new, constitutionally sound legislation. Today, the United States stands alone among fellow Western liberal democracies in imposing the death penalty.

The machinery of death, rebooted

Unsurprisingly, the Court's announcement in *Furman* caused an uproar among retentionist states. In a manifest demonstration of national consensus at the state legislative level, immediately after the decision, 35 individual legislatures across the nation scrambled to rewrite their capital statutes, and quickly enacted fresh legislation to restart executions and clear the five-year backlog since *Witherspoon* (with ten years having passed since the start of the LDF-led moratorium). Legislators looking to retain capital punishment must have known that, although a majority of the Court deemed capital punishment unconstitutional *as applied*, its *per se* constitutionality was a question left unaddressed. Florida was the first state to act, with a new capital scheme following the decision in *Furman* in less than six months. Broadly speaking, legislation could be separated into two groups. The first, in which some states narrowed discretion by providing guidelines for aggravation and mitigation in sentencing, was where Florida rested. Also adopting the Floridian scheme were Georgia and Texas, the states directly involved in the original *Furman* litigation. The second group contained states that attempted to remove the arbitrariness condemned by the Court by requiring mandatory death sentences for capital crimes. North

Carolina and Louisiana took this approach in 1974 and 1975, respectively. Both sets of schemes were to face the Court four years after *Furman*'s lethal prognosis.

Ruling on the constitutionality of this fresh legislation in 1976, ***GREGG v. GEORGIA***, 428 U.S. 325 (1976) emerged as a pivotal case within this post-*Furman* landscape, consolidating three separate appeals challenging the revised death penalty statutes in Georgia, Florida, and Texas (jointly with *Woodson v. North Carolina; Roberts v. Louisiana; Proffitt v. Florida; and Jurek v. Texas*). The legal battleground shifted to the question of whether these new statutes successfully navigated the constitutional pitfalls identified in *Furman*. In the so-called July 2 cases, mandatory sentencing failed constitutional muster. To pass the *Furman* test, the Court held 7–2, states were required to demonstrate that four main elements were protected by their legislation. First, a capital scheme must uphold human dignity. Second, the death penalty must not be inflicted arbitrarily or be seen by society as wrong or excessive. Third, states must not create a substantial risk that the death penalty would be inflicted in an arbitrary and capricious manner, which Louisiana and North Carolina had neglected through their mandatory schemes. Fourth and finally, capital legislation should provide judges and juries with individualized sentencing, taking into account the circumstances of the offense together with the character and propensities of the offender.

The decision marked a delicate equilibrium, allowing states to retain the death penalty while attempting to establish more objective and principled sentencing procedures. The schemes in Georgia, Florida, and Texas—and, by proxy, any other states that had adopted the weighing and balancing approach of aggravation versus mitigation—were upheld. In those states, with Georgia as the principal example on the docket, specific crimes were defined as capital and guilt was determined in the first stage of a bifurcated trial. Next, at sentencing, additional evidence in extenuation, mitigation, and aggravation of punishment was to be provided. Before a sentence of death could be imposed in Georgia, at least one of the ten statutory aggravating circumstances must have been found beyond a reasonable doubt. This scheme passed the four stages of constitutional muster outlined above and satisfied the requisite dignitarian and individualized approach. *Gregg* did not merely conclude a legal case; it reignited the national dialogue on the ethical, moral, and legal considerations surrounding the death penalty. The decision affirmed states authority to continue capital punishment under constitutional guidelines, shaping the trajectory of death penalty jurisprudence in the United States and contributing to the ongoing discourse on the complex issues surrounding the ultimate form of criminal punishment. It demonstrated that the Punishments Clause was applicable not just to the states in abstract but also to the nation's historic death penalty. The ruling might have reinstated this form of punishment, but it ensured that states' liberty to execute their citizens would never again be constitutionally unfettered: a number of new checks and balances would now append to capital sentencing and review. The practical abolition imposed after *Furman* might have fallen, but its legacy continued into a new era of capital punishment jurisprudence and the death penalty would be litigated like never before.

Gregg's legacy

The Court's revised condition of individualized punishment was soon clarified in ***LOCKETT v. OHIO***, 438 U.S. 586 (1978), where the Court examined a capital scheme that provided for only minimal mitigation, such as considerations of the history, character, and condition of the offender. *Lockett* rendered the Eighth Amendment assessment stricter, mandating that sentencing juries must be able to consider *any* aspect of a defendant's character or record and any of the circumstances of the offense. *Eddings v. Oklahoma*, U.S. 104 (1982)—included in Chapter 7—presented the Supreme Court with the opportunity to address whether the Constitution prohibits imposing a death sentence on a juvenile offender. The divided decision concluded that the death penalty was wrongly applied in this instance, emphasizing the trial court's failure to consider mitigating circumstances related to the crime, an obligation established in *Lockett*. Following the *Eddings* verdict, state courts were required to take into account any mitigating factors presented by a juvenile facing the death penalty, with the Court stopping short of resolving the constitutional question of executing a juvenile, leaving it to individual legislatures to resolve (until *Thompson v. Oklahoma*, 487 U.S. 815 (1988)—another case returned to in Chapter 7). *Eddings* effectively expanded the *Gregg-Lockett* standard even further, requiring the inclusion of family history and emotional disturbance in mitigation. In the following term, the Court further clarified that such aggravating factors in capital trials "must genuinely narrow the class of persons eligible for the death penalty" (*Zant v. Stephens* 432 U.S. 862, 877 (1983)), at either trial phase (*Lowenfield v. Phelps* 484 U.S. 231 (1988)).

In essence, Gregg and his progeny achieved a broadening of Eighth Amendment protection. Not only was the evolutive principle of dignity now applicable to the Court's Punishments Clause jurisprudence, including the death penalty, but also the Punishments Clause was interpreted to contain a fundamental proportionality standard, one derived from the early decision in *Weems*. It was in the year following *Gregg*, 1977, when the Court first struck down the death penalty as disproportionate in respect of an entire *category* of offenses as opposed to just the individual application of a punishment. These 1970s judgments founded an important—progressive—generation of punishments jurisprudence, which Chapter 6 turns to. These cases set the scene for the decades that followed, with a slow but persistent return to capital punishment across the nation despite the judicial evolution that would continue to curtail its use to all but the most serious and aggravated capital offenses. Execution totals peaked in the United States at 98 in 1999, with the trend slowing and falling again at a similar rate but in the reverse direction, lower than 30 annually for every year from 2014 to 2023. Indeed, in 2023, only five states executed people and seven imposed new death sentences, the lowest for two decades. Florida (six executions) and Texas (eight) accounted for more than half of the year's total (twenty-four), with Alabama, Missouri, and Oklahoma the remaining three to use the penalty. This steady decline tracks closely nationwide shortages of lethal injection protocols, although, as Chapter 8 shows, key death penalty retentionist states are racing to create novel modes of legal execution, with the U.S. Supreme Court unwilling to rule absolutely against such lethal innovation. (See *Bucklew v. Precythe*, 139 S. Ct. 1112 (2019), where a 5–4 majority rejected a death row inmate's challenge to Missouri's lethal injection protocol and left open the door for alternative methods, including a return to the firing squad and the novel use of nitrogen gas—utilized for the first time in January 2024 in Alabama.)

Reference

Eastaugh, C. (2017) *Unconstitutional solitude*. Palgrave Macmillan.

Cited cases

Bucklew v. Precythe, 139 S.Ct. 1112 (2019).
Eddings v. Oklahoma, 455 U.S. 104 (1982).
Furman v. Georgia, 391 U.S. 510 (1972).
Gregg v. Georgia, 428 U.S. 325 (1976) (jointly with).
Jurek v. Texas, 428 U.S. 262 (1976).
Lockett v. Ohio, 438 U.S. 586 (1978).
Lowenfield v. Phelps, 484 U.S. 231 (1988).
Proffitt v. Florida, 428 U.S. 242 (1976).
Roberts v. Louisiana, 428 U.S. 325 (1976).
Thompson v. Oklahoma, 487 U.S. 815 (1988).
Witherspoon v. Illinois, 391 U.S. 510 (1968).
Woodson v. North Carolina, 428 U.S. 280 (1976).
Zant v. Stephens, 432 U.S. 862 (1983).

Cited legislation

Waltham Black Act, 9 Geo. I c.22 (1723).

FURMAN v. GEORGIA, 408 U.S. 238 (1972)

Per curiam (5–4).

Certiorari was granted limited to the following question: "Does the imposition and carrying out of the death penalty in these cases constitute cruel and unusual punishment in violation of the Eighth and Fourteenth Amendments?"

The Court holds that the imposition and carrying out of the death penalty in these cases constitute cruel and unusual punishment in violation of the Eighth and Fourteenth Amendments. The judgment in each case is therefore reversed insofar as it leaves undisturbed the death sentence imposed, and the cases are remanded for further proceedings.

So ordered.

JUSTICE DOUGLAS, concurring.

It would seem to be incontestable that the death penalty inflicted on one defendant is "unusual" if it discriminates against him by reason of his race, religion, wealth, social position, or class, or if it is imposed under a procedure that gives room for the play of such prejudices. One searches our chronicles in vain for the execution of any member of the affluent strata of this society.

Jackson, a black, convicted of the rape of a white woman, was 21 years old. A court-appointed psychiatrist said that Jackson was of average education and average intelligence, that he was not an imbecile, or schizophrenic, or psychotic, that his traits were the product of environmental influences, and that he was competent to stand trial.

Furman, a black, killed a householder while seeking to enter the home at night. Furman shot the deceased through a closed door. He was 26 years old and had finished the sixth grade in school. Pending trial, he was committed to the Georgia Central State Hospital for a psychiatric examination on his plea of insanity tendered by court-appointed counsel. The superintendent reported that a unanimous staff diagnostic conference had concluded "that this patient should retain his present diagnosis of Mental Deficiency, Mild to Moderate, with Psychotic Episodes associated with Convulsive Disorder." The physicians agreed that "at present the patient is not psychotic, but he is not capable of cooperating with his counsel in the preparation of his defense"; and the staff believed "that he is in need of further psychiatric hospitalization and treatment."

Branch, a black, entered the rural home of a 65-year-old widow, a white, while she slept and raped her, holding his arm against her throat. Thereupon he demanded money, and for 30 minutes or more, the widow searched for money, finding little. As he left, Jackson said if the widow told anyone what happened, he would return and kill her. The record is barren of any medical or psychiatric evidence showing injury to her as a result of Branch's attack. He had previously been convicted of felony theft and found to be a borderline mental deficient and well below the average IQ of Texas prison inmates. He had the equivalent of five and a half years of grade school education. He had a "dull intelligence," and was in the lowest fourth percentile of his class.

We cannot say from facts disclosed in these records that these defendants were sentenced to death because they were black. Yet our task is not restricted to an effort to divine what motives impelled these death penalties. Rather, we deal with a system of law and of justice that leaves to the uncontrolled discretion of judges or juries the determination whether defendants committing these crimes should die or be imprisoned. Under these laws, no standards govern the selection of the penalty. People live or die, dependent on the whim of one man or of 12.

In a Nation committed to equal protection of the laws there is no permissible "caste" aspect of law enforcement. Yet we know that the discretion of judges and juries in imposing the death penalty enables the penalty to be selectively applied, feeding prejudices against the accused if he is poor and despised, and lacking political clout, or if he is a member of a suspect or unpopular minority, and saving those who by social position may be in a more protected position.

A law that stated that anyone making more than $50,000 would be exempt from the death penalty would plainly fall, as would a law that in terms said that blacks, those who never went beyond the fifth grade in school, those who made less than $3,000 a year, or those who were unpopular or unstable should be the only people executed. A law which, in the overall view, reaches that result in practice has no more sanctity than a law which in terms provides the same. Thus, these discretionary statutes are unconstitutional in their operation. They are pregnant with discrimination, and discrimination is an ingredient not compatible with the idea of equal protection of the laws that is implicit in the ban on "cruel and unusual" punishments.

Any law which is nondiscriminatory on its face may be applied in such a way as to violate the Equal Protection Clause of the Fourteenth Amendment. Such conceivably might be the fate of a mandatory death penalty, where equal or lesser sentences were imposed on the elite, a harsher one on the minorities or members of the lower castes. Whether a mandatory death penalty would otherwise be constitutional is a question I do not reach.

JUSTICE BRENNAN, concurring.

The primary principle is that a punishment must not be so severe as to be degrading to the dignity of human beings. Pain, certainly, may be a factor in the judgment. The infliction of an extremely severe punishment will often entail physical suffering.

Death is truly an awesome punishment. The calculated killing of a human being by the State involves, by its very nature, a denial of the executed person's humanity. The contrast with the plight of a person punished by imprisonment is evident. An individual in prison does not lose "the right to have rights." A prisoner retains, for example, the constitutional rights to the free exercise of religion, to be free of cruel and unusual punishments, and to treatment as a "person" for purposes of due process of law and the equal protection of the laws. A prisoner remains a member of the human family. Moreover, he retains the right of access to the courts. His punishment is not irrevocable. Apart from the common charge, grounded upon the recognition of human fallibility, that the punishment of death must inevitably be inflicted upon innocent men, we know that death has been the lot of men whose convictions were unconstitutionally secured in view of later, retroactively applied, holdings of this Court.

In comparison to all other punishments today, then, the deliberate extinguishment of human life by the State is uniquely degrading to human dignity. I would not hesitate to hold, on that ground alone, that death is today a "cruel and unusual" punishment, were it not that death is a punishment of longstanding usage and acceptance in this country. I therefore turn to the second principle—that the State may not arbitrarily inflict an unusually severe punishment.

When the punishment of death is inflicted in a trivial number of the cases in which it is legally available, the conclusion is virtually inescapable that it is being inflicted arbitrarily. Indeed, it smacks of little more than a lottery system. The probability of arbitrariness is sufficiently substantial that it can be relied upon, in combination with the other principles, in reaching a judgment on the constitutionality of this punishment. When there is a strong probability that an unusually severe and degrading punishment is being inflicted arbitrarily, we may well expect that society will disapprove of its infliction.

I turn, therefore, to the third principle. An examination of the history and present operation of the American practice of punishing criminals by death reveals that this punishment has been almost totally rejected by contemporary society. It is this essentially moral conflict that forms the backdrop for the past changes in, and the present operation of, our system of imposing death as a punishment for crime.

Also significant is the drastic decrease in the crimes for which the punishment of death is actually inflicted. In sum, we have made death a rare punishment today. The progressive decline in, and the current rarity of, the infliction of death demonstrate that our society seriously questions the appropriateness of this punishment today.

The final principle to be considered is that an unusually severe and degrading punishment may not be excessive in view of the purposes for which it is inflicted. This principle, too, is related to the others. When there is a strong probability that the State is arbitrarily inflicting an unusually severe punishment that is subject to grave societal doubts, it is likely also that the punishment cannot be shown to be serving any penal purpose that could not be served equally well by some less severe punishment.

In sum, the punishment of death is inconsistent with all four principles: death is an unusually severe and degrading punishment; there is a strong probability that it is inflicted arbitrarily; its rejection by contemporary society is virtually total; and there is no reason to believe that it serves any penal purpose more effectively than the less severe punishment of imprisonment. The function of these principles is to enable a court to determine whether a punishment comports with human dignity. Death, quite simply, does not.

JUSTICE STEWART, concurring.

These death sentences are cruel and unusual in the same way that being struck by lightning is cruel and unusual. For, of all the people convicted of rapes and murders in 1967 and 1968, many just as reprehensible as these, the petitioners are among a capriciously elected random handful upon whom the sentence of death has in fact been imposed.

I simply conclude that the Eighth and Fourteenth Amendments cannot tolerate the infliction of a sentence of death under legal systems that permit this unique penalty to be so wantonly and so freakishly imposed.

JUSTICE WHITE, concurring.

I do not at all intimate that the death penalty is unconstitutional *per se* or that there is no system of capital punishment that would comport with the Eighth Amendment.

The narrower question to which I address myself concerns the constitutionality of capital punishment statutes under which (1) the legislature authorizes the imposition of the death penalty for murder or rape; (2) the legislature does not itself mandate the penalty in any particular class or kind of case (that is, legislative will is not frustrated if the penalty is never imposed), but delegates to judges or juries the decisions as to those cases, if any, in which the penalty will be utilized; and (3) judges and juries have ordered the death penalty with such infrequency that the odds are now very much against imposition and execution of the penalty with respect to any convicted murderer or rapist.

For present purposes, I accept the morality and utility of punishing one person to influence another. I accept also the effectiveness of punishment generally, and need not reject the death penalty as a more effective deterrent than a lesser punishment. But common sense and experience tell us that seldom-enforced laws become ineffective measures for controlling human conduct, and that the death penalty, unless imposed with sufficient frequency, will make little contribution to deterring those crimes for which it may be exacted.

[T]he penalty has not been considered cruel and unusual punishment in the constitutional sense because it was thought justified by the social ends it was deemed to serve. At the moment that it ceases realistically to further these purposes, however, the emerging question is whether its imposition in such circumstances would violate the Eighth Amendment. It is my view that it would, for its imposition would then be the pointless and needless extinction of life with only marginal contributions to any discernible social or public purposes. A penalty with such negligible returns to the State would be patently excessive and cruel and unusual punishment violative of the Eighth Amendment.

I cannot avoid the conclusion that, as the statutes before us are now administered, the penalty is so infrequently imposed that the threat of execution is too attenuated to be of substantial service to criminal justice.

JUSTICE MARSHALL, concurring.

A punishment may be deemed cruel and unusual for any one of four distinct reasons.

First, there are certain punishments that inherently involve so much physical pain and suffering that civilized people cannot tolerate them—e.g., use of the rack, the thumbscrew, or other modes of torture. Regardless of public sentiment with respect to imposition of one of these punishments in a particular case or at any one moment in history, the Constitution prohibits it. These are punishments that have been barred since the adoption of the Bill of Rights.

Second, there are punishments that are unusual, signifying that they were previously unknown as penalties for a given offense.

Third, a penalty may be cruel and unusual because it is excessive and serves no valid legislative purpose. It should also be noted that the "cruel and unusual" language of the Eighth Amendment immediately follows language that prohibits excessive bail and excessive fines. The entire thrust of the Eighth Amendment is, in short, against "that which is excessive."

Fourth, where a punishment is not excessive and serves a valid legislative purpose, it still may be invalid if popular sentiment abhors it. For example, if the evidence clearly demonstrated that capital punishment served valid legislative purposes, such punishment would, nevertheless, be unconstitutional if citizens found it to be morally unacceptable. A general abhorrence on the part of the public would, in effect, equate a modern punishment with those barred since the adoption of the Eighth Amendment.

It is not improper at this point to take judicial notice of the fact that, for more than 200 years, men have labored to demonstrate that capital punishment serves no purpose that life imprisonment could not serve equally well. And they have done so with great success.

There is no rational basis for concluding that capital punishment is not excessive. It therefore violates the Eighth Amendment.

In addition, even if capital punishment is not excessive, it nonetheless violates the Eighth Amendment because it is morally unacceptable to the people of the United States at this time in their history.

Racial or other discriminations should not be surprising. There is also overwhelming evidence that the death penalty is employed against men, and not women. Only 32 women have been executed since 1930, while 3,827 men have met a similar fate. It also is evident that the burden of capital punishment falls upon the poor, the ignorant, and the underprivileged members of society.

Assuming knowledge of all the facts presently available regarding capital punishment, the average citizen would, in my opinion, find it shocking to his conscience and sense of justice. For this reason alone, capital punishment cannot stand.

In striking down capital punishment, this Court does not malign our system of government. On the contrary, it pays homage to it. Only in a free society could right triumph in difficult times, and could civilization record its magnificent advancement. In recognizing the humanity of our fellow beings, we pay ourselves the highest tribute. We achieve "a major milestone in the long road up from barbarism" and join the approximately 70 other jurisdictions in the world which celebrate their regard for civilization and humanity by shunning capital punishment.

CHIEF JUSTICE BURGER, with whom JUSTICES BLACKMUN, POWELL, and REHNQUIST join, dissenting.

Our constitutional inquiry [. . .] must be divorced from personal feelings as to the morality and efficacy of the death penalty, and be confined to the meaning and applicability of the uncertain language of the Eighth Amendment. There is no novelty in being called upon to interpret a constitutional provision that is less than self-defining, but, of all our fundamental guarantees, the ban on "cruel and unusual punishments" is one of the most difficult to translate into judicially manageable terms. The widely divergent views of the Amendment expressed in today's opinions reveal the haze that surrounds this constitutional command. Yet it is essential to our role as a court that we not seize upon the enigmatic character of the guarantee as an invitation to enact our personal predilections into law.

I do not suggest that the presence of the word "unusual" in the Eighth Amendment is merely vestigial, having no relevance to the constitutionality of any punishment that might be devised. But where, as here, we consider a punishment well known to history, and clearly authorized by legislative enactment, it disregards the history of the Eighth Amendment and all the judicial comment that has followed to rely on the term "unusual" as affecting the outcome of these cases. Instead, I view these cases as turning on the single question whether capital punishment is "cruel" in the constitutional sense. The term "unusual" cannot be read as limiting the ban on "cruel" punishments, or as somehow expanding the meaning of the term "cruel." For this reason, I am unpersuaded by the facile argument that, since capital punishment has always been cruel in the everyday sense of the word, and has become unusual due to decreased use, it is, therefore, now "cruel and unusual."

The opening sentence of the Fifth Amendment is a guarantee that the death penalty not be imposed "unless on a presentment or indictment of a Grand Jury." The Double Jeopardy Clause of the Fifth Amendment is a prohibition against being "twice put in jeopardy of life" for the same offense. Similarly, the Due Process Clause commands "due process of law" before an accused can be "deprived of life, liberty, or property." Thus, the explicit language of the Constitution affirmatively acknowledges the legal power to impose capital punishment; it does not expressly or by implication acknowledge the legal power to impose any of the various punishments that have been banned as cruel since 1791. Since the Eighth Amendment was adopted on the same day in 1791 as the Fifth Amendment, it hardly needs more to establish that the death penalty was not "cruel" in the constitutional sense at that time.

In the 181 years since the enactment of the Eighth Amendment, not a single decision of this Court has cast the slightest shadow of a doubt on the constitutionality of capital punishment.

There are no obvious indications that capital punishment offends the conscience of society to such a degree that our traditional deference to the legislative judgment must be abandoned. To [. . .] characterize the rate of imposition as "freakishly rare," as petitioners insist, is unwarranted hyperbole. And regardless of its characterization, the rate, of imposition does not impel the conclusion that capital punishment is now regarded as intolerably cruel or uncivilized.

The rate of imposition of death sentences falls far short of providing the requisite unambiguous evidence that the legislatures of 40 States and the Congress have turned their backs on current or evolving standards of decency in continuing to make the death penalty available. For, if selective imposition evidences a rejection of capital punishment in those cases where it is not imposed, it surely evidences a correlative affirmation of the penalty in those cases where it is imposed. Absent some clear indication that the continued imposition of the death penalty on a selective basis is violative of prevailing standards of civilized conduct, the Eighth Amendment cannot be said to interdict its use.

By pursuing the necessity approach, it becomes even more apparent that it involves matters outside the purview of the Eighth Amendment. Two of the several aims of punishment are generally associated with capital punishment—retribution and deterrence. It is argued that retribution can be discounted because that, after all, is what the Eighth Amendment seeks to eliminate. There is no authority suggesting that the Eighth Amendment was intended to purge the law of its retributive elements, and the Court has consistently assumed that retribution is a legitimate dimension of the punishment of crimes.

As I have earlier stated, the Eighth Amendment forbids the imposition of punishments that are so cruel and inhumane as to violate society's standards of civilized conduct. The Amendment does not prohibit all punishments the States are unable to prove necessary to deter or control crime. The Amendment is not concerned with the process by which a State determines that a particular punishment is to be imposed in a particular case. And the Amendment most assuredly does not speak to the power of legislatures to confer sentencing discretion on juries, rather than to fix all sentences by statute.

To be sure, there is a recitation cast in Eighth Amendment terms: petitioners' sentences are "cruel" because they exceed that which the legislatures have deemed necessary for all cases; petitioners' sentences are "unusual" because they exceed that which is imposed in most cases. This application of the words of the Eighth Amendment suggests that capital punishment can be made to satisfy Eighth Amendment values if its rate of imposition is somehow multiplied; it seemingly follows that the flexible sentencing system created by the legislatures, and carried out by juries and judges, has yielded more mercy than the Eighth Amendment can stand.

Real change could clearly be brought about if legislatures provided mandatory death sentences in such a way as to deny juries the opportunity to bring in a verdict on a lesser charge; under such a system, the death sentence could only be avoided by a verdict of acquittal. If this is the only alternative that the legislatures can safely pursue under today's ruling, I would have preferred that the Court opt for total abolition.

Since there is no majority of the Court on the ultimate issue presented in these cases, the future of capital punishment in this country has been left in an uncertain limbo.

The legislatures are free to eliminate capital punishment for specific crimes or to carve out limited exceptions to a general abolition of the penalty, without adherence to the conceptual strictures of the Eighth Amendment. The legislatures can and should make an assessment of the deterrent influence of capital punishment, both generally and as affecting the commission of specific types of crimes. If legislatures come to doubt the efficacy of capital punishment, they can abolish it, either completely or on a selective basis.

The world-wide trend toward limiting the use of capital punishment, a phenomenon to which we have been urged to give great weight, hardly points the way to a judicial solution in this country under a written Constitution. Rather, the change has generally come about through legislative action, often on a trial basis and with the retention of the penalty for certain limited classes of crimes. Virtually nowhere has change been wrought by so crude a tool as the Eighth Amendment. The complete and unconditional abolition of capital punishment in this country by judicial fiat would have undermined the careful progress of the legislative trend and foreclosed further inquiry on many as yet unanswered questions in this area.

Quite apart from the limitations of the Eighth Amendment itself, the preference for legislative action is justified by the inability of the courts to participate in the debate at the level where the controversy is focused. The case against capital punishment is not the product of legal dialectic, but rests primarily on factual claims, the truth of which cannot be tested by conventional judicial processes. The five opinions in support of the judgments differ in many respects, but they share a willingness to make sweeping factual assertions, unsupported by empirical data, concerning the manner of imposition and effectiveness of capital punishment in this country. Legislatures will have the opportunity to make a more penetrating study of these claims with the familiar and effective tools available to them as they are not to us.

The highest judicial duty is to recognize the limits on judicial power and to permit the democratic processes to deal with matters falling outside of those limits. The "hydraulic pressure[s]" that Holmes spoke of as being generated by cases of great import have propelled the Court to go beyond the limits of judicial power, while fortunately leaving some room for legislative judgment.

JUSTICE BLACKMUN also wrote a dissenting opinion.

JUSTICE POWELL wrote a dissenting opinion, joined by CHIEF JUSTICE BURGER and JUSTICES BLACKMUN and REHNQUIST.

JUSTICE RENQUIST wrote a dissenting opinion, joined by CHIEF JUSTICE BURGER, and JUSTICES BLACKMUN and POWELL.

GREGG v. GEORGIA, 428 U.S. 153 (1976)

Judgment of the Court (7–2), and opinion of JUSTICE STEWART, joined by JUSTICES POWELL and STEVENS

The petitioner, Troy Gregg, was charged with committing armed robbery and murder. In accordance with Georgia procedure in capital cases, the trial was in two stages, a guilt stage and a sentencing stage. The evidence at the guilt trial established that, on November 21, 1973, the petitioner and a traveling companion, Floyd Allen, while hitchhiking north in Florida were picked up by Fred Simmons and Bob Moore. Their car broke down, but they continued north after Simmons purchased another vehicle with some of the cash he was carrying. While still in Florida, they picked up another hitchhiker, Dennis Weaver, who rode with them to Atlanta, where he was let out about 11 p.m. A short time later, the four men interrupted their journey for a rest stop along the highway. The next morning the bodies of Simmons and Moore were discovered in a ditch nearby. The jury found the petitioner guilty of two counts of armed robbery and two counts of murder.

[I]n determining what sentence was appropriate, the jury was free to consider the facts and circumstances, if any, presented by the parties in mitigation or aggravation . . . the judge instructed the jury that it "would not be authorized to consider [imposing] the penalty of death" unless it first found beyond a reasonable doubt one of these aggravating circumstances;

> "One—That the offense of murder was committed while the offender was engaged in the commission of two other capital felonies, to-wit the armed robbery of [Simmons and Moore]."
>
> "Two—That the offender committed the offense of murder for the purpose of receiving money and the automobile described in the indictment."
>
> "Three—The offense of murder was outrageously and wantonly vile, horrible and inhuman, in that they [*sic*] involved the depravity of [the] mind of the defendant."

Finding the first and second of these circumstances, the jury returned verdicts of death on each count.

We address initially the basic contention that the punishment of death for the crime of murder is, under all circumstances, "cruel and unusual" in violation of the Eighth and Fourteenth Amendments of the Constitution. The Court, on a number of occasions, has both assumed and asserted the constitutionality of capital punishment. But until *Furman v. Georgia*, the Court never confronted squarely the fundamental claim that the punishment of death always, regardless of the enormity of the offense or the procedure followed in imposing the sentence, is cruel and unusual punishment in violation of the Constitution. Although this issue was presented and addressed in *Furman*, it was not resolved by the Court.

It is clear from the foregoing precedents that the Eighth Amendment has not been regarded as a static concept. Thus, an assessment of contemporary values concerning the infliction of a challenged sanction is relevant to the application of the Eighth Amendment. As we develop below more fully, this assessment does not call for a subjective judgment. It requires, rather, that we look to objective indicia that reflect the public attitude toward a given sanction.

But our cases also make clear that public perceptions of standards of decency with respect to criminal sanctions are not conclusive. A penalty also must accord with "the dignity of man," which is the "basic concept underlying the Eighth Amendment." *Trop v. Dulles*. This means, at least, that the punishment not be "excessive." When a form of punishment in the abstract (in this case, whether capital punishment may ever be imposed as a sanction for murder), rather than in the particular (the propriety of death as a penalty to be applied to a specific defendant for a specific crime), is under consideration, the inquiry into "excessiveness" has two aspects. First, the punishment must not involve the unnecessary and wanton infliction of pain. Second, the punishment must not be grossly out of proportion to the severity of the crime.

We may not require the legislature to select the least severe penalty possible so long as the penalty selected is not cruelly inhumane or disproportionate to the crime involved. And a heavy burden rests on those who would attack the judgment of the representatives of the people.

This is true in part because the constitutional test is intertwined with an assessment of contemporary standards and the legislative judgment weighs heavily in ascertaining such standards. "[I]n a democratic society, legislatures, not courts, are constituted to respond to the will and consequently the moral values of the people."

A decision that a given punishment is impermissible under the Eighth Amendment cannot be reversed short of a constitutional amendment. The ability of the people to express their preference through the normal democratic processes, as well as through ballot referenda, is shut off. Revisions cannot be made in the light of further experience.

Four years ago, the petitioners in *Furman* and its companion cases predicated their argument primarily upon the asserted proposition that standards of decency had evolved to the point where capital punishment no longer could be tolerated. The petitioners in those cases said, in effect, that the evolutionary process had come to an end, and that standards of decency required that the Eighth Amendment be construed finally as prohibiting capital punishment for any crime, regardless of its depravity and impact on society.

The petitioners in the capital cases before the Court today renew the "standards of decency" argument, but developments during the four years since *Furman* have undercut substantially the assumptions upon which their argument rested. Despite the continuing debate, dating back to the 19th century, over the morality and utility of capital punishment, it is now evident that a large proportion of American society continues to regard it as an appropriate and necessary criminal sanction.

The most marked indication of society's endorsement of the death penalty for murder is the legislative response to *Furman*. The legislatures of at least 35 States have enacted new statutes that provide for the death penalty for at least some crimes that result in the death of another person.

[T]he relative infrequency of jury verdicts imposing the death sentence does not indicate rejection of capital punishment *per se*. Rather, the reluctance of juries in many cases to impose the sentence may well reflect the humane feeling that this most irrevocable of sanctions should be reserved for a small number of extreme cases. Indeed, the actions of juries in many States since *Furman* are fully compatible with the legislative judgments, reflected in the new statutes, as to the continued utility and necessity of capital punishment in appropriate cases.

The death penalty is said to serve two principal social purposes: retribution and deterrence of capital crimes by prospective offenders. Although some of the studies suggest that the death penalty may not function as a significantly greater deterrent than lesser penalties, there is no convincing empirical evidence either supporting or refuting this view. We may nevertheless assume safely that there are murderers, such as those who act in passion, for whom the threat of death has little or no deterrent effect. But for many others, the death penalty undoubtedly is a significant deterrent.

The value of capital punishment as a deterrent of crime is a complex factual issue the resolution of which properly rests with the legislatures, which can evaluate the results of statistical studies in terms of their own local conditions and with a flexibility of approach that is not available to the courts. Indeed, many of the post-*Furman* statutes reflect just such a responsible effort to define those crimes and those criminals for which capital punishment is most probably an effective deterrent.

In sum, we cannot say that the judgment of the Georgia Legislature that capital punishment may be necessary in some cases is clearly wrong.

Considerations of federalism, as well as respect for the ability of a legislature to evaluate, in terms of its particular State, the moral consensus concerning the death penalty and its social utility as a sanction, require us to conclude, in the absence of more convincing evidence, that the infliction of death as a punishment for murder is not without justification, and thus is not unconstitutionally severe.

Finally, we must consider whether the punishment of death is disproportionate in relation to the crime for which it is imposed. There is no question that death, as a punishment, is unique in its severity and irrevocability. But we are concerned here only with the imposition of capital punishment for the crime of murder, and, when a life has been taken deliberately by the offender, we cannot say that the punishment is invariably disproportionate to the crime. It is an extreme sanction, suitable to the most extreme of crimes.

We hold that the death penalty is not a form of punishment that may never be imposed, regardless of the circumstances of the offense, regardless of the character of the offender, and regardless of the procedure followed in reaching the decision to impose it.

We now consider whether Georgia may impose the death penalty on the petitioner in this case. *Furman* mandates that, where discretion is afforded a sentencing body on a matter so grave as the determination of whether a human life should be taken or spared, that discretion must be suitably directed and limited so as to minimize the risk of wholly arbitrary and capricious action.

In summary, the concerns expressed in *Furman* that the penalty of death not be imposed in an arbitrary or capricious manner can be met by a carefully drafted statute that ensures that the sentencing authority is given adequate information and guidance. As a general proposition, these concerns are best met by a system that provides for a bifurcated proceeding at which the sentencing authority is apprised of the information relevant to the imposition of sentence and provided with standards to guide its use of the information.

We now turn to consideration of the constitutionality of Georgia's capital sentencing procedures. In the wake of *Furman*, Georgia amended its capital punishment statute, but chose not to narrow the scope of its murder provisions.

Georgia did act, however, to narrow the class of murderers subject to capital punishment by specifying 10 statutory aggravating circumstances, one of which must be found by the jury to exist beyond a reasonable doubt before a death sentence can ever be imposed. In addition, the jury is authorized to consider any other appropriate aggravating or mitigating circumstances.

In short, Georgia's new sentencing procedures require, as a prerequisite to the imposition of the death penalty, specific jury findings as to the circumstances of the crime or the character of the defendant. Moreover, to guard further against a situation comparable to that presented in *Furman*, the Supreme Court of Georgia compares each death sentence with the sentences imposed on similarly situated defendants to ensure that the sentence of death in a particular case is not disproportionate. On their face, these procedures seem to satisfy the concerns of *Furman*.

The provision for appellate review in the Georgia capital sentencing system serves as a check against the random or arbitrary imposition of the death penalty. In particular, the proportionality review substantially eliminates the possibility that a person will be sentenced to die by the action of an aberrant jury. If a time comes when juries generally do not impose the death sentence in a certain kind of murder case, the appellate review procedures assure that no defendant convicted under such circumstances will suffer a sentence of death.

The new Georgia sentencing procedures, by contrast [to *Furman*], focus the jury's attention on the particularized nature of the crime and the particularized characteristics of the individual defendant. While the jury is permitted to consider any aggravating or mitigating circumstances, it must find and identify at least one statutory aggravating factor before it may impose a penalty of death. In this way, the jury's discretion is channeled. No longer can a jury wantonly and freakishly impose the death sentence; it is always circumscribed by the legislative guidelines. In addition, the review function of the Supreme Court of Georgia affords additional assurance that the concerns that prompted our decision in *Furman* are not present to any significant degree in the Georgia procedure applied here.

For the reasons expressed in this opinion, we hold that the statutory system under which Gregg was sentenced to death does not violate the Constitution. Accordingly, the judgment of the Georgia Supreme Court is affirmed.

It is so ordered.

JUSTICE WHITE, concurred, with whom THE CHIEF JUSTICE and JUSTICE REHNQUIST joined. JUSTICE BLACKMUN also concurred in the judgment.

JUSTICE BRENNAN, dissenting.

This Court inescapably has the duty, as the ultimate arbiter of the meaning of our Constitution, to say whether, when individuals condemned to death stand before our Bar, "moral concepts" require us to hold that the law has progressed to the point where we should declare that the punishment of death, like punishments on the rack, the screw, and the wheel, is no longer morally tolerable in our civilized society. My opinion in *Furman v. Georgia* concluded that our civilization and the law had progressed to this point, and that, therefore, the punishment of death, for whatever crime and under all circumstances, is "cruel and unusual" in violation of the Eighth and Fourteenth Amendments of the Constitution. I shall not again canvass the reasons that led to that conclusion. I emphasize only that foremost among the "moral concepts" recognized in our cases and inherent in the Clause is the primary moral principle that the State, even as it punishes, must treat its citizens in a manner consistent with their intrinsic worth as human beings—a punishment must not be so severe as to be degrading to human dignity. A judicial determination whether the punishment of death comports with human dignity is therefore not only permitted, but compelled, by the Clause.

JUSTICE MARSHALL, dissenting.

Since the decision in *Furman*, the legislatures of 35 States have enacted new statutes authorizing the imposition of the death sentence for certain crimes, and Congress has enacted a law providing the death penalty for air piracy resulting in death. I would be less than candid if I did not acknowledge that these developments have a significant bearing on a realistic assessment of the moral acceptability of the death penalty to the American people. But if the constitutionality of the death penalty turns, as I have urged, on the opinion of an informed citizenry, then even the enactment of new death statutes cannot be viewed as conclusive. In *Furman*, I observed that the American people are largely unaware of the information critical to a judgment on the morality of the death penalty, and concluded that, if they were better informed, they would consider it shocking, unjust, and unacceptable.

Even assuming, however, that the post-*Furman* enactment of statutes authorizing the death penalty renders the prediction of the views of an informed citizenry an uncertain basis for a constitutional decision, the enactment of those statutes has no bearing whatsoever on the conclusion that the death penalty is unconstitutional because it is excessive.

The death penalty, unnecessary to promote the goal of deterrence or to further any legitimate notion of retribution, is an excessive penalty forbidden by the Eighth and Fourteenth Amendments. I respectfully dissent from the Court's judgment upholding the sentences of death imposed upon the petitioners in these cases.

LOCKETT v. OHIO, 438 U.S. 586 (1978)

CHIEF JUSTICE BURGER announced the Court's judgment and delivered an opinion of the Court (7–1) with respect to Parts I and II, in which JUSTICES STEWART, WHITE, BLACKMUN, POWELL, REHNQUIST, and STEVENS joined, and an opinion with respect to Part III, in which JUSTICES STEWART, POWELL, and STEVENS joined.

I

Lockett was charged with aggravated murder with the aggravating specifications (1) that the murder was "committed for the purpose of escaping detection, apprehension, trial, or punishment" for aggravated robbery, and (2) that the murder was "committed while . . . committing, attempting to commit, or fleeing immediately after committing or attempting to commit . . . aggravated robbery."

That offense was punishable by death in Ohio. She was also charged with aggravated robbery. The State's case against her depended largely upon the testimony of a coparticipant, one Al Parker

[. . .]

Lockett's brother and Dew were later convicted of aggravated murder with specifications. Lockett's brother was sentenced to death, but Dew received a lesser penalty because it was determined that his offense was "primarily the product of mental deficiency," one of the three mitigating circumstances specified in the Ohio death penalty statute.

Two weeks before Lockett's separate trial, the prosecutor offered to permit her to plead guilty to voluntary manslaughter and aggravated robbery (offenses which each carried a maximum penalty of 25 years' imprisonment and a maximum fine of $10,000) if she would cooperate with the State, but she rejected the offer. Just prior to her trial, the prosecutor offered to permit her to plead guilty to aggravated murder without specifications, an offense carrying a mandatory life penalty, with the understanding that the aggravated robbery charge and an outstanding forgery charge would be dismissed. Again she rejected the offer.

The court instructed the jury that, before it could find Lockett guilty, it had to find that she purposely had killed the pawnbroker while committing or attempting to commit aggravated robbery. The jury was further charged that one who "purposely aids, helps, associates himself or herself with another for the purpose of committing a crime is regarded as if he or she were the principal offender and is just as guilty as if the person performed every act constituting the offense. . . ."

Regarding the intent requirement, the court instructed: "A person engaged in a common design with others to rob by force and violence an individual or individuals of their property is presumed to acquiesce in whatever may reasonably be necessary to accomplish the object of their enterprise. . . ."

> "If the conspired robbery and the manner of its accomplishment would be reasonably likely to produce death, each plotter is equally guilty with the principal offender as an aider and abettor in the homicide. . . . An intent to kill by an aider and abettor may be found to exist beyond a reasonable doubt under such circumstances."

The jury found Lockett guilty as charged.

Once a verdict of aggravated murder with specifications had been returned, the Ohio death penalty statute required the trial judge to impose a death sentence unless, after "considering the nature and circumstances of the offense" and Lockett's "history, character, and condition," he found by a preponderance of the evidence that (1) the victim had induced or facilitated the offense, (2) it was unlikely that Lockett would have committed the offense but for the fact that she "was under duress, coercion, or strong provocation," or (3) the offense was "primarily the product of [Lockett's] psychosis or mental deficiency."

In accord with the Ohio statute, the trial judge requested a presentence report as well as psychiatric and psychological reports. The reports contained detailed information about Lockett's intelligence, character, and background. The psychiatric and psychological reports described her as a 21-year-old with low-average or average intelligence, and not suffering from a mental deficiency. One of the psychologists reported that "her prognosis for rehabilitation" if returned to society was favorable. The presentence report showed that Lockett had committed no major offenses, although she had a record of several minor ones as a juvenile and two minor offenses as an adult. It also showed that she had once used heroin but was receiving treatment at a drug abuse clinic and seemed to be "on the road to success" as far as her drug problem was concerned. It concluded that Lockett suffered no psychosis and was not mentally deficient.

After considering the reports and hearing argument on the penalty issue, the trial judge concluded that the offense had not been primarily the product of psychosis or mental deficiency. Without specifically addressing the other two statutory mitigating factors, the judge said that he had "no alternative, whether [he] like[d] the law or not," but to impose the death penalty. He then sentenced Lockett to death.

II

A

At the outset, we address Lockett's various challenges to the validity of her conviction. Her first contention is that the prosecutor's repeated references in his closing remarks to the State's evidence as "unrefuted" and "uncontradicted" constituted a comment on her failure to testify and violated her Fifth and Fourteenth Amendment rights. We conclude, however, that the prosecutor's closing comments in this case did not violate constitutional prohibitions.

Lockett's own counsel had clearly focused the jury's attention on her silence, first, by outlining her contemplated defense in his opening statement and, second, by stating to the court and jury near the close of the case, that Lockett would be the "next witness." When viewed against this background, it seems clear that the prosecutor's closing remarks added nothing to the impression that had already been created by Lockett's refusal to testify after the jury had been promised a defense by her lawyer and told that Lockett would take the stand.

B

Lockett also contends that four prospective jurors were excluded from the venire in violation of her Sixth and Fourteenth Amendment rights under the principles established in *Witherspoon*. We do not agree.

C

Lockett's final attack on her conviction, as distinguished from her sentence, merits only brief attention. Specifically, she contends that the Ohio Supreme Court's interpretation of the complicity provision of the statute under which she was convicted, Ohio Rev. Code Ann. § 2923.03(A) (1975), was so unexpected that it deprived her of fair warning of the crime with which she was charged. The opinion of the Ohio Supreme Court belies this claim. It shows clearly that the construction given the statute by the Ohio court was consistent with both prior Ohio law and with the legislative history of the statute. In such circumstances, any claim of inadequate notice under the Due Process Clause of the Fourteenth Amendment must be rejected.

III

Lockett challenges the constitutionality of Ohio's death penalty statute on a number of grounds. We find it necessary to consider only her contention that her death sentence is invalid because the statute under which it was imposed did not permit the sentencing judge to consider, as mitigating factors, her character, prior record, age, lack of specific intent to cause death, and her relatively minor part in the crime. To address her contention from the proper perspective, it is helpful to review the developments in our recent cases where we have applied the Eighth and Fourteenth Amendments to death penalty statutes. We do not write on a "clean slate."

A

[. . .] In the last decade, many of the States have been obliged to revise their death penalty statutes in response to the various opinions supporting the judgments in *Furman* and *Gregg* and its companion cases. The signals from this Court have not, however, always been easy to decipher. The States now deserve the clearest guidance that the Court can provide; we have an obligation to reconcile previously differing views in order to provide that guidance.

B

With that obligation in mind, we turn to Lockett's attack on the Ohio statute. Essentially, she contends that the Eighth and Fourteenth Amendments require that the sentencer be given a full opportunity to consider mitigating circumstances in capital cases, and that the Ohio statute does not comply with that requirement.

We begin by recognizing that the concept of individualized sentencing in criminal cases generally, although not constitutionally required, has long been accepted in this country. Consistent with that concept, sentencing judges traditionally have taken a wide range of factors into account. That States have authority to make aiders and abettors equally responsible, as a matter of law, with principals, or to enact felony murder statutes is beyond constitutional challenge. But the definition of crimes generally has not been thought automatically to dictate what should be the proper penalty. And where sentencing discretion is granted, it generally has been agreed that he sentencing judge's "possession of the fullest information possible concerning the defendant's life and characteristics" is "[h]ighly relevant—*if not essential*—[to the] selection of an appropriate sentence. . . ."

The opinions of this Court going back many years in dealing with sentencing in capital cases have noted the strength of the basis for individualized sentencing.

Although legislatures remain free to decide how much discretion in sentencing should be reposed in the judge or jury in noncapital cases, the plurality opinion in *Woodson*, after reviewing the historical repudiation of mandatory sentencing in capital cases, concluded that "in capital cases the fundamental respect for humanity underlying the Eighth Amendment . . . requires consideration of the character and record of the individual offender and the circumstances of the particular offense as a constitutionally indispensable part of the process of inflicting the penalty of death."

That declaration rested "on the predicate that the penalty of death is qualitatively different" from any other sentence. We are satisfied that this qualitative difference between death and other penalties calls for a greater degree of reliability when the death sentence is imposed. The mandatory death penalty statute in *Woodson* was held invalid because it permitted *no* consideration of "relevant facets of the character and record of the individual offender or the circumstances of the particular offense. The plurality did not attempt to indicate, however, which facets of an offender or his offense it deemed "relevant" in capital sentencing or what degree of consideration of "relevant facets" it would require.

We are now faced with those questions, and we conclude that the Eighth and Fourteenth Amendments require that the sentencer, in all but the rarest kind of capital case, not be precluded from considering, *as a mitigating factor*, any aspect of a defendant's character or record and any of the circumstances of the offense that the defendant proffers as a basis for a sentence less than death.

We recognize that, in noncapital cases, the established practice of individualized sentences rests not on constitutional commands, but on public policy enacted into statutes. The considerations that account for the wide acceptance of individualization of sentences in noncapital cases surely cannot be thought less important in capital cases. Given that the imposition of death by public authority is so profoundly different from all other penalties, we cannot avoid the conclusion that an individualized decision is essential in capital cases. The need for treating each defendant in a capital case with that degree of respect due the uniqueness of the individual is far more important than in noncapital cases. A variety of flexible techniques—probation, parole, work furloughs, to name a few—and various postconviction remedies may be available to modify an initial sentence of confinement in noncapital cases. The nonavailability of corrective or modifying mechanisms with respect to an executed capital sentence underscores the need for individualized consideration as a constitutional requirement in imposing the death sentence.

There is no perfect procedure for deciding in which cases governmental authority should be used to impose death. But a statute that prevents the sentencer in all capital cases from giving independent mitigating weight to aspects of the defendant's character and record and to circumstances of the offense proffered in mitigation creates the risk that the death penalty will be imposed in spite of factors which may call for a less severe penalty. When the choice is between life and death, that risk is unacceptable and incompatible with the commands of the Eighth and Fourteenth Amendments.

C

The Ohio death penalty statute does not permit the type of individualized consideration of mitigating factors we now hold to be required by the Eighth and Fourteenth Amendments in capital cases. Its constitutional infirmities can best be understood by comparing it with the statutes upheld in *Gregg, Proffitt*, and *Jurek*.

None of the statutes we sustained in *Gregg* and the companion cases clearly operated at that time to prevent the sentencer from considering any aspect of the defendant's character and record or any circumstances of his offense as an independently mitigating factor.

In this regard, the statute now before us is significantly different. Once a defendant is found guilty of aggravated murder with at least one of seven specified aggravating circumstances, the death penalty must be imposed unless, considering "the nature and circumstances of the offense and the history, character, and condition of the offender," the sentencing judge determines that at least one of the following mitigating circumstances is established by a preponderance of the evidence:

"(1) The victim of the offense induced or facilitated it."
"(2) It is unlikely that the offense would have been committed, but for the fact that the offender was under duress, coercion, or strong provocation."
"(3) The offense was primarily the product of the offender's psychosis or mental deficiency, though such condition is insufficient to establish the defense of insanity."

The limited range of mitigating circumstances which may be considered by the sentencer under the Ohio statute is incompatible with the Eighth and Fourteenth Amendments. To meet constitutional requirements, a death penalty statute must not preclude consideration of relevant mitigating factors.

Accordingly, the judgment under review is reversed to the extent that it sustains the imposition of the death penalty, and the case is remanded for further proceedings.

JUSTICE BLACKMUN filed an opinion concurring in part and concurring in the judgment, JUSTICE MARSHALL filed an opinion concurring in the judgment, JUSTICE WHITE filed an opinion concurring in part, concurring in the judgment, and dissenting in part, and JUSTICE REHNQUIST filed an opinion concurring in part and dissenting in part, JUSTICE BRENNAN took no part in the consideration or decision of the case.

6

LIMITS ON CAPITAL CATEGORIES

Classes of offense

In the early 1960s, following the incorporation of the Eighth Amendment in *Robinson v. California*, few jurists considered that capital punishment would ever fail constitutional muster. Indeed, it was generally accepted that, with widespread public support, the death penalty was part of the framework of American criminal justice. Furman had reversed that prediction for several years, postponing the penalty and releasing over 600 men from death row (onto whole-life prison sentences), with Gregg's reinstatement ten years later returning the death penalty to the statute books of several dozen states. A judicial review of the nation's ultimate penalty would thereafter turn to the extent of capital punishment's lawfulness in different circumstances rather than the meta question of whether death was constitutionally permissible—something that has been left settled since Gregg's pronouncement, despite the vociferous dissents outlined in the previous pages. Eighth Amendment capital punishment jurisprudence from the 1970s began to refine the imposition of the penalty, divided clearly into two main categories. First, the types of offenses for which capital punishment is permissible, and second, the types of offenders and their relative culpability, and therefore the proportionality and constitutionality of this sentence (primarily in relation to their age and mental capacity).

Non-homicidal rape

Considering the constitutionality of capital punishment for the crime of rape in ***COKER v. GEORGIA***, 433 U.S. 584 (1977), the Court developed a proportionality test comprising an objective determination of the current

DOI: 10.4324/9780429398780-7

national consensus, and a subjective analysis. Under that assessment, the Court condemned death as an unconstitutional punishment for the rape of an adult woman where the victim survived, an offense the majority viewed as falling short of the requisite "severity and irrevocability" for capital punishment to be permitted. Justice White's plurality judgment (6–3 on the categorical constitutional law question) concluded that the sentence of death for this crime is grossly disproportionate and excessive punishment and is therefore forbidden by the Eighth Amendment as cruel and unusual punishment. This was founded on five main grounds.

First, the Court held that the Punishments Clause bars not only those punishments that are barbaric, but also those that are excessive in relation to the crime committed, and a punishment is "excessive" and unconstitutional if it (1) makes no measurable contribution to acceptable goals of punishment, and hence is nothing more than the purposeless and needless imposition of pain and suffering; or (2) is grossly out of proportion to the severity of the crime. Second, death is a disproportionate penalty for rape owing to its status as an outlier, objectively, in contradiction to "present public judgment, as represented by the attitude of state legislatures and sentencing juries," with Georgia the only state to authorize death as a sentence for rape of an adult woman. Moreover, in nine out of ten rape convictions in Georgia since 1973, juries have not imposed the death sentence. Third, the Court noted that "although rape deserves serious punishment," the death penalty is unique in terms of its severity and irrevocability, and it is excessive in comparison to the offense itself, which did not result in the death of the victim: a sort of *lex talionis* eye for an eye argument (which the dissent condemned as being "primitive" in its simplicity). Fourth, the death sentence remains disproportionate, notwithstanding the aggravating circumstances of prior capital felony convictions and the concurrence of the rape with armed robbery. Fifth and finally, in comparison with Georgia's murder statute—which provided that "a deliberate killer cannot be sentenced to death, absent aggravating circumstances"—death as a penalty of rape is further inconsistent, as it would be illogical that any rapist who does not take the life of their victim should be punished more severely than some murderers. Justices Brennan and Marshall repeated their views from both *Furman* and *Gregg* that the death penalty is, in all circumstances, a cruel and unusual punishment.

Justice Powell agreed to rescind the sentence in these circumstances but did not agree with the six-judge majority who struck down Georgia's statute and, with it, abolished capital punishment for the rape of an adult woman. Instead, he argued, a rape committed with excessive brutality where the victim sustained serious or lasting injury could justify a capital sentence. The judgment also left open the question of the rape of a child—something the Court would return to in 2008. Chief Justice Burger, joined by Justice Rehnquist, provided the sole dissenting opinion in *Coker*, condemning the majority for allowing their "personal preferences as to the wisdom of legislative and congressional action," or their "distaste for such action, to guide [their] judicial decision in cases such as these. The temptations to cross that policy line are very great." Echoing Justice Blackmun, dissenting in *Furman*, they concluded: "In fact, as today's decision reveals, they are almost irresistible." The dissenters would instead have left to the States the task of legislating in this area of the law, permitting the Georgia statute, enacted after *Gregg*, "time to take effect, so that data may be evaluated for comparison with the experience of States which have not enacted death penalty statutes."

Felony murder

Half a decade later, the *Coker* position was expanded to incorporate a restriction on capital punishment for felony murderers (accomplices to a distinct criminal offense where a murder took place) in ***ENMUND v. FLORIDA***, 458 U.S. 782 (1982). Forging the objective and subjective elements of the assessment into one, the *Enmund* Court focused on the defendant's "moral responsibility" by examining his intent, to examine whether the correct sentence was one of death. The facts in *Enmund* are relatively straightforward: The defendant acted as a driver for a pair of accomplices who murdered two Floridian pensioners during the course of a robbery. Earl Enmund was subsequently sentenced to death despite lacking homicidal premeditation on his own behalf, a lawful punishment at the state level due to its statutory "felony murder" rule (Fla. Stat. § 921.141(2) (1981)), whereby individuals could be convicted for the same offense as the primary offender—that is, getaway drivers were as culpable as the trigger-pulling shooter or the person wielding the knife that struck the fatal blow.

The U.S. Supreme Court weighed the federal constitutional question regarding this state scheme's propriety, and, in the view of the Justices, an insufficient demonstration of moral responsibility on the part of Enmund, the accomplice, for capital punishment had been presented by the prosecution. Enmund's biological life was spared, his was sentence instead commuted to life without parole. By undertaking a significant review of state legislation to find nationwide "evolving standards" against executing felony murderers—included in full at the end of the chapter—a majority found that only eight U.S. jurisdictions provided for the death penalty where a defendant participated in a robbery in the course of which a murder was committed. In conclusion the Court overturned his death sentence as unconstitutional, being inconsistent with the "evolving standards" test, and noted that robbery itself was not nearly so grievous an affront to humanity that the only adequate response may be the penalty of death. Moreover, the Justices found that neither deterrence of capital crimes nor retribution were sufficient justifications for executing petitioners such as Enmund. Putting him to death to avenge two killings that he did not commit or intend to commit would not, they concluded, measurably contribute to retribution.

Enmund's effect was to categorically prohibit capital punishment for any future "felony murderer" such as accessories or accomplices. A further ruling in *Hitchcock v. Dugger*, 481 U.S. 393 (1987), clarified that, in all capital cases, the sentencer may not refuse to consider or be precluded from considering any relevant mitigating evidence. In 2006, the Court clarified that there is no specific scheme required to uphold this principle (*Kansas v. Marsh*, 548 U.S. 163 (2006) and that factors that are unconstitutionally vague (as prohibited by *Gregg*) are those which have no "common-sense core of meaning [. . .] that criminal juries should be capable of understanding" (*Tuilaepa v. California*, 512 U.S. 967, 973 (1994)). Although *Enmund* symbolized a significant evolution of the Punishments Clause and a consequent restriction of the death penalty, it was not to be for another three decades that the Court would hold that death was unconstitutionally excessive for *all* classes of noncapital crime.

Non-homicidal child rape

In that case, ***KENNEDY v. LOUISIANA***, 544 U.S. 407 (2008), the Court dissolved any residual uncertainty remaining after *Enmund* by creating a *per se* exclusion of capital punishment for all non-homicide offenses. Like many Eighth Amendment cases, the facts in *Kennedy* make for harrowing reading. The offender, Patrick O'Neal Kennedy, was sentenced to death in 2003 after being convicted of raping his eight-year-old stepdaughter in such an aggressive manner that she suffered catastrophic injuries requiring significant invasive emergency surgery. Louisiana's state scheme provided for capital sentencing in cases where the victim of rape was under 12 years old, with Kennedy one of just two (the other was also from Louisiana) on death row for such an offense at the time—the only two such sentences passed in the country since 1964.

Justice Kennedy delivered a 5–4 decision for the Court, holding that the Punishments Clause bars governments from imposing the death penalty for the rape of a child where the crime did not result, and was not intended to result, in the victim's death. In reaching that conclusion and thereby expanding *Coker* explicitly to *all* rapes and *Enmund* to *all* non-homicide offenses, the Justices conducted a significant review of "the evolving standards of decency that mark the progress of a maturing society," citing *Trop*. The Court reviewed contemporaneous state statutes and the number of executions since 1964. Kennedy's majority noted that 37 jurisdictions, including the Federal Government, imposed capital punishment, but only six authorized it for child rape (so in 45, by contrast, offenders could not be executed for child rape of any kind). Extending a turn of logic that had been applied in other cases reviewed shortly, the Court found a "national consensus" against capital punishment for the crime of child rape. Moreover, while several states had permitted capital punishment for adult or child rape for some length of time between *Furman* and *Kennedy*, no individual had been executed for the rape of an adult or child since 1964, and Louisiana swam against a strong national tide.

Next, the Justices dismissed arguments that *Coker*'s ruling in 1977 was ambiguous and that some states had an erroneous understanding of the ruling, with the petitioner arguing that it had been interpreted in too expansive a way, leading some state legislatures to conclude that *Coker* banned the death penalty for child rape when in fact its reasoning did not apply to that specific crime. The Court reviewed this argument carefully and noted that the *Coker* plurality framed the question as regarding "rape of an adult woman" very clearly, using that phrase eight times. There was no strong argument to be maintained, therefore, that state legislatures had been put off passing child rape statutes by mistake, and lower state courts were cited in agreement.[1] Kennedy wrote: "The small number of States that have enacted this penalty, then, is relevant to determining whether there is a consensus against capital punishment for this crime."

Further reviewing national consensus among state legislatures, the Court concluded that six new death penalty statutes being passed in the last 13 years was insufficient demonstration of a "rate of change" in favor of Kennedy's penalty. Unlike in *Atkins v. Virginia*, 536 U.S. 304 (2002), a case returned to shortly in Chapter 7, this rate of legislative change was insufficient to sway the Justices' analysis of national consensus. The evidence, they concluded, closely resembled that in *Enmund*, where the Court found a national consensus against death for felony murder despite eight jurisdictions having authorized it.

1 See, *e.g.*, *State v. Wilson*, 685 So. 2d 1063 (La. 1996), 1066 (upholding the constitutionality of the death penalty for rape of a child and noting that "[t]he plurality [in *Coker*] took great pains in referring only to the rape of adult women throughout their opinion."

Finally, the Court conducted "its independent judgment," expanding the principles set out by *Coker* and *Enmund* to determine that the sentence of death for all noncapital crimes was also objectively excessive. Rejecting any argument that this ruling would effectively block further development of a consensus favoring the death penalty for child rape, the Court concluded that such an imposition was morally and therefore legally barred by the Eighth Amendment. Justice Kennedy wrote:

> Consistent with evolving standards of decency and the teachings of our precedents we conclude that, in determining whether the death penalty is excessive, there is a distinction between intentional first-degree murder on the one hand and nonhomicide crimes against individual persons, even including child rape, on the other. The latter crimes may be devastating in their harm, as here, but in terms of moral depravity and of the injury to the person and to the public, they cannot be compared to murder in their severity and irrevocability.

The significance of the ruling in *Kennedy* is therefore symbolized by its stamp of finality with regard to Eighth Amendment evolution in the realms of restricted categories. Through an expansion of the Punishments Clause, death is now permissible only for the most serious of murders, where aggravating factors have been weighed against mitigating factors. The evolving standards of decency move in one direction under this argument, with state legislatures never able to experiment within their local democracies and apply sentences that have been deemed below the constitutional bar set by the Punishments Clause.

Cited cases

Atkins v. Virginia, 536 U.S. 304 (2002).
Coker v. Georgia, 433 U.S. 584 (1977).
Enmund v. Florida, 458 U.S. 782 (1982).
Hitchcock v. Dugger, 481 U.S. 393 (1987).
Kansas v. Marsh, 548 U.S. 163 (2006).
Kennedy v. Louisiana, 544 U.S. 407 (2008).
State v. Wilson, 685 So. 2d 1063 (La. 1996).
Tuilaepa v. California, 512 U.S. 967 (1994).

COKER v. GEORGIA, 433 U.S. 584 (1977)

JUSTICE WHITE announced the judgment of the Court and filed an opinion in which JUSTICES STEWART, BLACKMUN, and STEVENS, joined.

I

Petitioner Coker was convicted of rape and sentenced to death. Both the conviction and the sentence were affirmed by the Georgia Supreme Court. Coker was granted a writ of certiorari, limited to the single claim, rejected by the Georgia court, that the punishment of death for rape violates the Eighth Amendment, which proscribes "cruel and unusual punishments" and which must be observed by the States as well as the Federal Government.

While serving various sentences for murder, rape, kidnapping, and aggravated assault, petitioner escaped from the Ware Correctional Institution near Waycross, Ga. on September 2, 1974. At approximately 11 o'clock that night, petitioner entered the house of Allen and Elnita Carver through an unlocked kitchen door. Threatening the couple with a "board," he tied up Mr. Carver in the bathroom, obtained a knife from the kitchen, and took Mr. Carver's money and the keys to the family car. Brandishing the knife and saying "you know what's going to happen to you if you try anything, don't you," Coker then raped Mrs. Carver. Soon thereafter, petitioner drove away in the Carver car, taking Mrs. Carver with him. Mr. Carver, freeing himself, notified the police; and not long thereafter petitioner was apprehended. Mrs. Carver was unharmed.

Petitioner was charged with escape, armed robbery, motor vehicle theft, kidnaping, and rape. Counsel was appointed to represent him. Having been found competent to stand trial, he was tried. The jury returned a verdict of guilty, rejecting his general plea of insanity.

The jury's verdict on the rape count was death by electrocution. Both aggravating circumstances on which the court instructed were found to be present by the jury.

II

It is now settled that the death penalty is not invariably cruel and unusual punishment within the meaning of the Eighth Amendment; it is not inherently barbaric or an unacceptable mode of punishment for crime; neither is it always disproportionate to the crime for which it is imposed. It is also established that imposing capital punishment, at least for murder, in accordance with the procedures provided under the Georgia statutes saves the sentence from the infirmities which led the Court to invalidate the prior Georgia capital punishment statute in *Furman*.

In *Gregg*, after giving due regard to such sources, the Court's judgment was that the death penalty for deliberate murder was neither the purposeless imposition of severe punishment nor a punishment grossly disproportionate to the crime. But the Court reserved the question of the constitutionality of the death penalty when imposed for other crimes.

III

That question, with respect to rape of an adult woman, is now before us.

A

As advised by recent cases, we seek guidance in history and from the objective evidence of the country's present judgment concerning the acceptability of death as a penalty for rape of an adult woman. At no time in the last 50 years have a majority of the States authorized death as a punishment for rape. In 1925, 18 States, the District of Columbia, and the Federal Government authorized capital punishment for the rape of an adult female. By 1971, just prior to the decision in *Furman*, that number had declined, but not substantially, to 16 States plus the Federal Government. *Furman* then invalidated most of the capital punishment statutes in this country, including the rape statutes, because, among other reasons, of the manner in which the death penalty was imposed and utilized under those laws.

But if the "most marked indication of society's endorsement of the death penalty for murder is the legislative response to *Furman*," it should also be a telling datum that the public judgment with respect to rape, as reflected in the statutes providing the punishment for that crime, has been dramatically different. In reviving death penalty laws to satisfy Furman's mandate, none of the States that had not previously authorized death for rape chose to include rape among capital felonies. Of the 16 States in which rape had been a capital offense, only three provided the death penalty for rape of an adult woman in their revised statute—Georgia, North Carolina, and Louisiana. In the latter two States, the death penalty was mandatory for those found guilty, and those laws were invalidated by *Woodson* and *Roberts*. When Louisiana and North Carolina, responding to those decisions, again revised their capital punishment laws, they reenacted the death penalty for murder but not for rape; none of the seven other legislatures that to our knowledge have amended or replaced their death penalty statutes since July 2, 1976, including four States (in addition to Louisiana and North Carolina) that had authorized the death sentence for rape prior to 1972 and had reacted to Furman with mandatory statutes, included rape among the crimes for which death was an authorized punishment.

Georgia argues that 11 of the 16 States that authorized death for rape in 1972 attempted to comply with Furman by enacting arguably mandatory death penalty legislation, and that it is very likely that, aside from Louisiana and North Carolina, these States simply chose to eliminate rape as a capital offense rather than to require death for each and every instance of rape. The argument is not without force, but 4 of the 16 States did not take the mandatory course, and also did not continue rape of an adult woman as a capital offense. Further, as we have indicated, the legislatures of 6 of the 11 arguably mandatory States have revised their death penalty laws since *Woodson* and *Roberts* without enacting a new death penalty for rape. And this is to say nothing of 19 other States that enacted nonmandatory, post-Furman statutes and chose not to sentence rapists to death.

It should be noted that Florida, Mississippi, and Tennessee also authorized the death penalty in some rape cases, but only where the victim was a child and the rapist an adult. The Tennessee statute has since been invalidated because the death sentence was mandatory. The upshot is that Georgia is the sole jurisdiction in the United States at the present time that authorizes a sentence of death when the rape victim is an adult woman, and only two other jurisdictions provide capital punishment when the victim is a child.

The current judgment with respect to the death penalty for rape is not wholly unanimous among state legislatures, but it obviously weighs very heavily on the side of rejecting capital punishment as a suitable penalty for raping an adult woman.

B

According to the factual submissions in this Court, out of all rape convictions in Georgia since 1973—and that total number has not been tendered—63 cases had been reviewed by the Georgia Supreme Court as of the time of oral argument; and of these, 6 involved a death sentence, 1 of which was set aside, leaving 5 convicted rapists now under sentence of death in the State of Georgia. Georgia juries have thus sentenced rapists to death six times since 1973. This obviously is not a negligible number; and the State argues that, as a practical matter, juries simply reserve the extreme sanction for extreme cases of rape, and that recent experience surely does not prove that jurors consider the death penalty to be a disproportionate punishment for every conceivable instance of rape, no matter how aggravated. Nevertheless, it is true that, in the vast majority of cases, at least 9 out of 10, juries have not imposed the death sentence.

IV

These recent events evidencing the attitude of state legislatures and sentencing juries do not wholly determine this controversy, for the Constitution contemplates that, in the end, our own judgment will be brought to bear on the question of the acceptability of the death penalty under the Eighth Amendment. Nevertheless, the legislative rejection of capital punishment for rape strongly confirms our own judgment, which is that death is indeed a disproportionate penalty for the crime of raping an adult woman.

We do not discount the seriousness of rape as a crime. It is highly reprehensible, both in a moral sense and in its almost total contempt for the personal integrity and autonomy of the female victim and for the latter's privilege of choosing those with whom intimate relationships are to be established. Short of homicide, it is the "ultimate violation of self." It is also a violent crime because it normally involves force, or the threat of force or intimidation, to overcome the will and the capacity of the victim to resist. Rape is very often accompanied by physical injury to the female and can also inflict mental and psychological damage. Because it undermines the community's sense of security, there is public injury as well.

Rape is without doubt deserving of serious punishment; but in terms of moral depravity and of the injury to the person and to the public, it does not compare with murder, which does involve the unjustified taking of human life. Although it may be accompanied by another crime, rape, by definition, does not include the death of or even the serious injury to another person. The murderer kills; the rapist, if no more than that, does not. Life is over for the victim of the murderer; for the rape victim, life may not be nearly so happy as it was, but it is not over, and normally is not beyond repair.

We note finally that, in Georgia, a person commits murder when he unlawfully and with malice aforethought, either express or implied, causes the death of another human being. He also commits that crime when, in the commission of a felony, he causes the death of another human being, irrespective of malice. But even where the killing is deliberate, it is not punishable by death absent proof of aggravating circumstances. It is difficult to accept the notion, and we do not, that the rapist, with or without aggravating circumstances, should be punished more heavily than the deliberate killer as long as the rapist does not himself take the life of his victim. The judgment of the Georgia Supreme Court upholding the death sentence is reversed, and the case is remanded to that court for further proceedings not inconsistent with this opinion.

JUSTICES BRENNAN, MARSHALL, and POWELL wrote concurring judgments. JUSTICE POWELL dissented in part.

Today, in a case that does not require such an expansive pronouncement, the plurality draws a bright line between murder and all rapes—regardless of the degree of brutality of the rape or the effect upon the victim. I dissent because I am not persuaded that such a bright line is appropriate. The deliberate viciousness of the rapist may be greater than that of the murderer. Rape is never an act committed accidentally. Rarely can it be said to be unpremeditated. There also is wide variation in the effect on the victim. Thus, it may be that the death penalty is not disproportionate punishment for the crime of aggravated rape. Final resolution of the question must await careful inquiry into objective indicators of society's "evolving standards of decency," particularly legislative enactments and the responses of juries in capital cases.

CHIEF JUSTICE BURGER dissented, joined by JUSTICE REHNQUIST.

In a case such as this, confusion often arises as to the Court's proper role in reaching a decision. Our task is not to give effect to our individual views on capital punishment; rather, we must determine what the Constitution permits a State to do under its reserved powers. In striking down the death penalty imposed upon the petitioner in this case, the Court has overstepped the bounds of proper constitutional adjudication by substituting its policy judgment for that of the state legislature. I accept that the Eighth Amendment's concept of disproportionality bars the death penalty for minor crimes. But rape is not a minor crime; hence the Cruel and Unusual Punishments Clause does not give the Members of this Court license to engraft their conceptions of proper public policy onto the considered legislative judgments of the States. Since I cannot agree that Georgia lacked the constitutional power to impose the penalty of death for rape, I dissent from the Court's judgment.

Despite its strong condemnation of rape, the Court reaches the inexplicable conclusion that "the death penalty . . . is an excessive penalty" for the perpetrator of this heinous offense. This, the Court holds, is true even though, in Georgia, the death penalty may be imposed only where the rape is coupled with one or more aggravating circumstances. The process by which this conclusion is reached is as startling as it is disquieting. It represents a clear departure from precedent by making this Court.

However, even were one to give the most charitable acceptance to the plurality's statistical analysis, it still does not, to my mind, support its conclusion. The most that can be claimed is that, for the past year, Georgia has been the only State whose adult rape death penalty statute has not otherwise been invalidated; two other state legislatures had enacted rape death penalty statutes in the last five years, but these were invalidated for reasons unrelated to rape under the Court's decisions last Term. Even if these figures could be read as indicating that no other States view the death penalty as an appropriate punishment for the rape of an adult woman, it would not necessarily follow that Georgia's imposition of such sanction violates the Eighth Amendment.

In order for Georgia's legislative program to develop, it must be given time to take effect, so that data may be evaluated for comparison with the experience of States which have not enacted death penalty statutes. Today, the Court repudiates the State's solemn judgment on how best to deal with the crime of rape before anyone can know whether the death penalty is an effective deterrent for one of the most horrible of all crimes.

Whatever our individual views as to the wisdom of capital punishment, I cannot agree that it is constitutionally impermissible for a state legislature to make the "solemn judgment" to impose such penalty for the crime of rape. Accordingly, I would leave to the States the task of legislating in this area of the law.

ENMUND v. FLORIDA, 458 U.S. 782 (1982)

JUSTICE WHITE delivered the opinion of the Court, joined by JUSTICES BRENNAN, MARSHALL, BLACKMUN, and STEVENS.

On April 1, 1975, at approximately 7:45 a.m., Thomas and Eunice Kersey, aged 86 and 74, were robbed and fatally shot at their farmhouse in central Florida. The evidence showed that Sampson and Jeanette Armstrong had gone to the back door of the Kersey house and asked for water for an overheated car. When Mr. Kersey came out of the house, Sampson Armstrong grabbed him, pointed a gun at him, and told Jeanette Armstrong to take his money. Mr. Kersey cried for help, and his wife came out of the house with a gun and shot Jeanette Armstrong, wounding her. Sampson Armstrong, and perhaps Jeanette Armstrong, then shot and killed both of the Kerseys, dragged them into the kitchen, and took their money and fled.

The jury found both Enmund and Sampson Armstrong guilty of two counts of first-degree murder and one count of robbery. A separate sentencing hearing was held, and the jury recommended the death penalty for both defendants under the Florida procedure whereby the jury advises the trial judge whether to impose the death penalty. The trial judge then sentenced Enmund to death on the two counts of first-degree murder. The trial judge found four statutory aggravating circumstances: the capital felony was committed while Enmund was engaged in or was an accomplice in the commission of an armed robbery; the capital felony was committed for pecuniary gain; it was especially heinous, atrocious, or cruel; and Enmund was previously convicted of a felony involving the use or threat of violence. The court found that "none of the statutory mitigating circumstances applied" to Enmund, and that the aggravating circumstances outweighed the mitigating circumstances. Enmund was therefore sentenced to death on each of the murder counts.

The Florida Supreme Court affirmed Enmund's conviction and sentences.

We granted Enmund's petition for certiorari, presenting the question whether death is a valid penalty under the Eighth and Fourteenth Amendments for one who neither took life, attempted to take life, nor intended to take life.

II

As recounted above, the Florida Supreme Court held that the record supported no more than the inference that Enmund was the person in the car by the side of the road at the time of the killings, waiting to help the robbers escape. This was enough under Florida law to make Enmund a constructive aider and abettor, and hence a principal in first-degree murder upon whom the death penalty could be imposed. It was thus irrelevant to Enmund's challenge to the death sentence that he did not himself kill and was not present at the killings; also beside the point was whether he intended that the Kerseys be killed or anticipated that lethal force would or might be used if necessary to effectuate the robbery or a safe escape. We have concluded that imposition of the death penalty in these circumstances is inconsistent with the Eighth and Fourteenth Amendments.

Thirty-six state and federal jurisdictions presently authorize the death penalty. Of these, only eight jurisdictions authorize imposition of the death penalty solely for participation in a robbery in which another robber takes life. Of the remaining 28 jurisdictions, in 4, felony murder is not a capital crime. Eleven States require some culpable mental state with respect to the homicide as a prerequisite to conviction of a crime for which the death penalty is authorized. Of these 11 States, 8 make knowing, intentional, purposeful, or premeditated killing an element of capital murder. Three other States require proof of a culpable mental state short of intent, such as recklessness or extreme indifference to human life, before the death penalty may be imposed. In these 11 States, therefore, the actors in a felony murder are not subject to the death penalty without proof of their mental state, proof which was not required with respect to Enmund either under the trial court's instructions or under the law announced by the Florida Supreme Court.

Four additional jurisdictions do not permit a defendant such as Enmund to be put to death. Of these, one State flatly prohibits capital punishment in cases where the defendant did not actually commit murder. Two jurisdictions preclude the death penalty in cases, such as this one, where the defendant "was a principal in the offense, which was committed by another, but his participation was relatively minor, although not so minor as to constitute a defense to prosecution." One other State limits the death penalty in felony murders to narrow circumstances not involved here.

Nine of the remaining States deal with the imposition of the death penalty for a vicarious felony murder in their capital sentencing statutes. In each of these States, a defendant may not be executed solely for participating in a felony in which a person was killed if the defendant did not actually cause the victim's death. For a defendant to be executed in these States, typically the statutory aggravating circumstances which are present must outweigh mitigating factors. To be sure, a vicarious felony murderer may be sentenced to death in these jurisdictions absent an intent to kill if sufficient aggravating circumstances are present. However, six of these nine States make it a statutory mitigating circumstance that the defendant was an accomplice in a capital felony committed by another person and his participation was relatively minor. By making minimal participation in a capital felony committed by another person a mitigating circumstance, these sentencing statutes reduce the likelihood that a person will be executed for vicarious felony murder. The remaining three jurisdictions exclude felony murder from their lists of aggravating circumstances that will support a death sentence. In each of these nine States, a nontriggerman guilty of felony murder cannot be sentenced to death for the felony murder absent aggravating circumstances above and beyond the felony murder itself.

Thus, only a small minority of jurisdictions—eight—allow the death penalty to be imposed solely because the defendant somehow participated in a robbery in the course of which a murder was committed. Even if the nine States are included where such a defendant could be executed for an unintended felony murder if sufficient aggravating circumstances are present to outweigh mitigating circumstances—which often include the defendant's minimal participation in the murder—only about a third of American jurisdictions would ever permit a defendant who somehow participated in a robbery where a murder occurred to be sentenced to die. Moreover, of the eight States which have enacted new death penalty statutes since 1978, none authorize capital punishment in such circumstances. While the current legislative judgment with respect to imposition of the death penalty where a defendant did not take life, attempt to take it, or intend to take life is neither "wholly unanimous among state legislatures," nor as compelling as the legislative judgments considered in *Coker*, it nevertheless weighs on the side of rejecting capital punishment for the crime at issue.

Society's rejection of the death penalty for accomplice liability in felony murders is also indicated by the sentencing decisions that juries have made. The evidence is overwhelming that American juries have repudiated imposition of the death penalty for crimes such as petitioner's. First, according to the petitioner, a search of all reported appellate court decisions since 1954 in cases where a defendant was executed for homicide shows that, of the 362 executions, in 339, the person executed personally committed a homicidal assault. In 2 cases, the person executed had another person commit the homicide for him, and, in 16 cases, the facts were not reported in sufficient detail to determine whether the person executed committed the homicide. The survey revealed only 6 cases out of 362 where a nontriggerman felony murderer was executed. All six executions took place in 1955. By contrast, there were 72 executions for rape in this country between 1955 and this Court's decision in *Coker*.

That juries have rejected the death penalty in cases, such as this one, where the defendant did not commit the homicide, was not present when the killing took place, and did not participate in a plot or scheme to murder is also shown by petitioner's survey of the Nation's death-row population. As of October 1, 1981, there were 796 inmates under sentences of death for homicide. Of the 739 for whom sufficient data are available, only 41 did not participate in the fatal assault on the victim. Of the 40 among the 41 for whom sufficient information was available, only 16 were not physically present when the fatal assault was committed. These 16 prisoners included only 3, including petitioner, who were sentenced to die absent a finding that they hired or solicited someone else to kill the victim or participated in a scheme designed to kill the victim. The figures for Florida are similar. Forty-five felony murderers are currently on death row. The Florida Supreme Court either found or affirmed a trial court or jury finding that the defendant intended life to be taken in 36 cases. In eight cases, the courts made no finding with respect to intent, but the defendant was the triggerman in each case. In only one case—Enmund's—there was no finding of an intent to kill and the defendant was not the triggerman.

III

Although the judgments of legislatures, juries, and prosecutors weigh heavily in the balance, it is for us ultimately to judge whether the Eighth Amendment permits imposition of the death penalty on one such as Enmund who aids and abets a felony in the course of which a murder is committed by others but who does not himself kill, attempt to kill, or intend that a killing take place or that lethal force will be employed. We have concluded, along with most legislatures and juries, that it does not.

We have no doubt that robbery is a serious crime deserving serious punishment. It is not, however, a crime "so grievous an affront to humanity that the only adequate response may be the penalty of death."

Here, the robbers did commit murder; but they were subjected to the death penalty only because they killed as well as robbed. The question before us is not the disproportionality of death as a penalty for murder, but rather the validity of capital punishment for Enmund's own conduct. The focus must be on his culpability, not on that of those who committed the robbery and shot the victims, for we insist on "individualized consideration as a constitutional requirement in imposing the death sentence."

Enmund did not kill or intend to kill, and thus his culpability is plainly different from that of the robbers who killed; yet the State treated them alike, and attributed to Enmund the culpability of those who killed the Kerseys. This was impermissible under the Eighth Amendment.

[. . .]

We are quite unconvinced, however, that the threat that the death penalty will be imposed for murder will measurably deter one who does not kill and has no intention or purpose that life will be taken. Instead, it seems likely that "capital punishment can serve as a deterrent only when murder is the result of premeditation and deliberation," for if a person does not intend that life be taken or contemplate that lethal force will be employed by others, the possibility that the death penalty will be imposed for vicarious felony murder will not "enter into the cold calculus that precedes the decision to act."

As for retribution as a justification for executing Enmund, we think this very much depends on the degree of Enmund's culpability—what Enmund's intentions, expectations, and actions were. American criminal law has long considered a defendant's intention—and therefore his moral guilt—to be critical to "the degree of [his] criminal culpability," and the Court has found criminal penalties to be unconstitutionally excessive in the absence of intentional wrongdoing.

For purposes of imposing the death penalty, Enmund's criminal culpability must be limited to his participation in the robbery, and his punishment must be tailored to his personal responsibility and moral guilt. Putting Enmund to death to avenge two killings that he did not commit and had no intention of committing or causing does not measurably contribute to the retributive end of ensuring that the criminal gets his just deserts. This is the judgment of most of the legislatures that have recently addressed the matter, and we have no reason to disagree with that judgment for purposes of construing and applying the Eighth Amendment.

IV

Because the Florida Supreme Court affirmed the death penalty in this case in the absence of proof that Enmund killed or attempted to kill, and regardless of whether Enmund intended or contemplated that life would be taken, we reverse the judgment upholding the death penalty and remand for further proceedings not inconsistent with this opinion.

JUSTICE BRENNAN filed a concurring opinion.

I join the Court's opinion. However, I adhere to my view that the death penalty is in all circumstances cruel and unusual punishment prohibited by the Eighth and Fourteenth Amendments.

JUSTICE O'CONNOR dissented, joined by CHIEF JUSTICE BURGER and JUSTICES POWELL and REHNQUIST.

[. . .] we cannot know the fraction of cases in which juries rejected the death penalty for accomplice felony murder. Moreover, many of these data classify defendants by whether they "personally committed a homicidal assault," and do not show the fraction of capital defendants who were shown to have an intent to kill. While the petitioner relies on the fact that he did not pull the trigger, his principal argument is, and must be, that death is an unconstitutional penalty absent an intent to kill, for otherwise defendants who hire others to kill would escape the death penalty. Thus, the data he presents are not entirely relevant. Even accepting the petitioner's facts as meaningful, they may only reflect that sentencers are especially cautious in imposing the death penalty, and reserve that punishment for those defendants who are sufficiently involved in the homicide, whether or not there was specific intent to kill.

The Court's curious method of counting the States that authorize imposition of the death penalty for felony murder cannot hide the fact that 23 States permit a sentencer to impose the death penalty even though the felony murderer has neither killed nor intended to kill his victim [. . .] in nearly half of the States, and in two-thirds of the States that permit the death penalty for murder, a defendant who neither killed the victim nor specifically intended that the victim die may be sentenced to death for his participation in the robbery-murder.

As I noted earlier, the Eighth Amendment concept of proportionality involves more than merely a measurement of contemporary standards of decency. It requires in addition that the penalty imposed in a capital case be proportional to the harm caused and the defendant's blameworthiness.

Although the Court disingenuously seeks to characterize Enmund as only a "robber," it cannot be disputed that he is responsible, along with Sampson and Jeanette Armstrong, for the murders of the Kerseys. There is no dispute that their lives were unjustifiably taken, and that the petitioner, as one who aided and abetted the armed robbery, is legally liable for their deaths. Quite unlike the defendant in Coker, the petitioner cannot claim that the penalty imposed is "grossly out of proportion" to the harm for which he admittedly is at least partly responsible.

The Court's holding today is especially disturbing because it makes intent a matter of federal constitutional law, requiring this Court both to review highly subjective definitional problems customarily left to state criminal law and to develop an Eighth Amendment meaning of intent.

In sum, the petitioner and the Court have failed to show that contemporary standards, as reflected in both jury determinations and legislative enactments, preclude imposition of the death penalty for accomplice felony murder.

Although I conclude that the death penalty is not disproportionate to the crime of felony murder, I believe that, in light of the State Supreme Court's rejection of critical factual findings, our previous opinions require a remand for a new sentencing hearing.

KENNEDY v. LOUISIANA, 554 U.S. 407 (2008)

JUSTICE KENNEDY delivered the opinion of the Court, joined by JUSTICES STEVENS, SOUTER, GINSBURG, and BREYER.

I

Petitioner's crime was one that cannot be recounted in these pages in a way sufficient to capture in full the hurt and horror inflicted on his victim or to convey the revulsion society, and the jury that represents it, sought to express by sentencing petitioner to death. At 9:18 a.m. on March 2, 1998, petitioner called 911 to report that his stepdaughter, referred to here as L. H., had been raped. He told the 911 operator that L. H. had been in the garage while he readied his son for school. Upon hearing loud screaming, petitioner said, he ran outside and found L. H. in the side yard. Two neighborhood boys, petitioner told the operator, had dragged L. H. from the garage to the yard, pushed her down, and raped her. Petitioner claimed he saw one of the boys riding away on a blue 10-speed bicycle.

L. H. was transported to the Children's Hospital. An expert in pediatric forensic medicine testified that L. H.'s injuries were the most severe he had seen from a sexual assault in his four years of practice. A laceration to the left wall of the vagina had separated her cervix from the back of her vagina, causing her rectum to protrude into the vaginal structure. Her entire perineum was torn from the posterior fourchette to the anus. The injuries required emergency surgery.

The jury having found petitioner guilty of aggravated rape, the penalty phase ensued. The jury unanimously determined that petitioner should be sentenced to death. The Supreme Court of Louisiana affirmed. Because "'children are a class that need special protection,'" the state court reasoned, the rape of a child is unique in terms of the harm it inflicts upon the victim and our society.

II

Evolving standards of decency must embrace and express respect for the dignity of the person, and the punishment of criminals must conform to that rule. As we shall discuss, punishment is justified under one or more of three principal rationales: rehabilitation, deterrence, and retribution.

Based both on consensus and our own independent judgment, our holding is that a death sentence for one who raped but did not kill a child, and who did not intend to assist another in killing the child, is unconstitutional under the Eighth and Fourteenth Amendments.

III

Louisiana reintroduced the death penalty for rape of a child in 1995. Under the current statute, any anal, vaginal, or oral intercourse with a child under the age of 13 constitutes aggravated rape and is punishable by death.

By contrast, 44 States have not made child rape a capital offense. As for federal law, Congress in the Federal Death Penalty Act of 1994 expanded the number of federal crimes for which the death penalty is a permissible sentence, including certain nonhomicide offenses; but it did not do the same for child rape or abuse. Under 18 U. S. C. §2245, an offender is death eligible only when the sexual abuse or exploitation results in the victim's death.

The evidence of a national consensus with respect to the death penalty for child rapists, as with respect to juveniles, mentally retarded offenders, and vicarious felony murderers, shows divided opinion but, on balance, an opinion against it. Thirty-seven jurisdictions—36 States plus the Federal Government—have the death penalty. As mentioned above, only six of those jurisdictions authorize the death penalty for rape of a child. Though our review of national consensus is not confined to tallying the number of States with applicable death penalty legislation, it is of significance that, in 45 jurisdictions, petitioner could not be executed for child rape of any kind. That number surpasses the 30 States in *Atkins* and *Roper* and the 42 States in *Enmund* that prohibited the death penalty under the circumstances those cases considered.

At least one difference between this case and our Eighth Amendment proportionality precedents must be addressed. Respondent and its amici suggest that some States have an "erroneous understanding of this Court's Eighth Amendment jurisprudence." Brief for Missouri Governor Matt Blunt et al. as *Amici Curiae* 10. They submit that the general propositions set out in Coker, contrasting murder and rape, have been interpreted in too expansive a way, leading some state legislatures to conclude that Coker applies to child rape when in fact its reasoning does not, or ought not, apply to that specific crime.

This argument seems logical at first, but in the end it is unsound. [. . .] The position of the state courts, furthermore, to which state legislators look for guidance on these matters, indicates that Coker has not blocked the emergence of legislative consensus. There is no clear indication that state legislatures have misinterpreted Coker to hold that the death penalty for child rape is unconstitutional. The small number of States that have enacted this penalty, then, is relevant to determining whether there is a consensus against capital punishment for this crime.

There are measures of consensus other than legislation. Statistics about the number of executions may inform the consideration whether capital punishment for the crime of child rape is regarded as unacceptable in our society. These statistics confirm our determination from our review of state statutes that there is a social consensus against the death penalty for the crime of child rape.

After reviewing the authorities informed by contemporary norms, including the history of the death penalty for this and other nonhomicide crimes, current state statutes and new enactments, and the number of executions since 1964, we conclude there is a national consensus against capital punishment for the crime of child rape.

IV

As we have said in other Eighth Amendment cases, objective evidence of contemporary values as it relates to punishment for child rape is entitled to great weight, but it does not end our inquiry.

It must be acknowledged that there are moral grounds to question a rule barring capital punishment for a crime against an individual that did not result in death. These facts illustrate the point. Here the victim's fright, the sense of betrayal, and the nature of her injuries caused more prolonged physical and mental suffering than, say, a sudden killing by an unseen assassin. The attack was not just on her but on her childhood.

It does not follow, though, that capital punishment is a proportionate penalty for the crime. The constitutional prohibition against excessive or cruel and unusual punishments mandates that the State's power to punish "be exercised within the limits of civilized standards."

Our concern here is limited to crimes against individual persons. We do not address, for example, crimes defining and punishing treason, espionage, terrorism, and drug kingpin activity, which are offenses against the State. As it relates to crimes against individuals, though, the death penalty should not be expanded to instances where the victim's life was not taken.

Starting with *Gregg*, we have spent more than 32 years articulating limiting factors that channel the jury's discretion to avoid the death penalty's arbitrary imposition in the case of capital murder. Though that practice remains sound, beginning the same process for crimes for which no one has been executed in more than 40 years would require experimentation in an area where a failed experiment would result in the execution of individuals undeserving of the death penalty. Evolving standards of decency are difficult to reconcile with a regime that seeks to expand the death penalty to an area where standards to confine its use are indefinite and obscure.

The judgment of the Supreme Court of Louisiana upholding the capital sentence is reversed. This case is remanded for further proceedings not inconsistent with this opinion.

It is so ordered.

JUSTICE ALITO dissented, joined by CHIEF JUSTICE ROBERTS and JUSTICES SCALIA and THOMAS.

The Court today holds that the Eighth Amendment categorically prohibits the imposition of the death penalty for the crime of raping a child. This is so, according to the Court, no matter how young the child, no matter how many times the child is raped, no matter how many children the perpetrator rapes, no matter how sadistic the crime, no matter how much physical or psychological trauma is inflicted, and no matter how heinous the perpetrator's prior criminal record may be. The Court provides two reasons for this sweeping conclusion: First, the Court claims to have identified "a national consensus" that the death penalty is never acceptable for the rape of a child; second, the Court concludes, based on its "independent judgment," that imposing the death penalty for child rape is inconsistent with "the evolving standards of decency that mark the progress of a maturing society." Because neither of these justifications is sound, I respectfully dissent.

I believe that the "objective indicia" of our society's "evolving standards of decency" can be fairly summarized as follows. Neither Congress nor juries have done anything that can plausibly be interpreted as evidencing the "national consensus" that the Court perceives. State legislatures, for more than 30 years, have operated under the ominous shadow of the *Coker* dicta and thus have not been free to express their own understanding of our society's standards of decency. And in the months following our grant of certiorari in this case, state legislatures have had an additional reason to pause. Yet despite the inhibiting legal atmosphere that has prevailed since 1977, six States have recently enacted new, targeted child-rape laws.

I do not suggest that six new state laws necessarily establish a "national consensus" or even that they are sure evidence of an ineluctable trend. In terms of the Court's metaphor of moral evolution, these enactments might have turned out to be an evolutionary dead end. But they might also have been the beginning of a strong new evolutionary line. We will never know, because the Court today snuffs out the line in its incipient stage.

The Court is willing to block the potential emergence of a national consensus in favor of permitting the death penalty for child rape because, in the end, what matters is the Court's "own judgment" regarding "the acceptability of the death penalty."

In summary, the Court holds that the Eighth Amendment categorically rules out the death penalty in even the most extreme cases of child rape even though: (1) This holding is not supported by the original meaning of the Eighth Amendment; (2) neither Coker nor any other prior precedent commands this result; (3) there are no reliable "objective indicia" of a "national consensus" in support of the Court's position; (4) sustaining the constitutionality of the state law before us would not "extend" or "expand" the death penalty; (5) this Court has previously rejected the proposition that the Eighth Amendment is a one-way ratchet that prohibits legislatures from adopting new capital punishment statutes to meet new problems; (6) the worst child rapists exhibit the epitome of moral depravity; and (7) child rape inflicts grievous injury on victims and on society in general.

7

LIMITS ON CAPITAL OFFENDERS

Alongside the Supreme Court's review of Eighth Amendment limits on the classes of crime punishable by death, the Justices have considered individual culpability, on the basis primarily of mental capacity. Between the 1980s and early 2000s, a series of cases heard by the Court refined the Punishments Clause further in this regard, narrowing the categories of offenders (as well as offenses covered in Chapter 6) for whom the death penalty is constitutional. Age was first declared a valid mitigating factor in capital sentencing in 1978 in *Bell v. Ohio*, 438 U.S. 637 (1978) and *Lockett v. Ohio*, 438 U.S. 586 (1978). In those rulings, the Court reversed two death sentences for aggravated murder committed by juveniles (those aged under 18), holding that the Eighth and Fourteenth Amendments protect the right to enter into mitigation "any aspect of a defendant's character," including age. This would set the foundation for a series of important rulings defining the Punishments Clause as it pertains to those with lower culpability.

Youth in capital sentencing

Further clarifying the *Gregg* requirement of individualized sentencing, the relevance of age to proportionate punishment was later noted in ***EDDINGS v. OKLAHOMA***, 455 U.S. 104 (1982). In that case, Justice Powell declared that age is "more than a chronological fact," striking down a capital sentence imposed on a 16-year-old, because of the trial court's lack of consideration for his individual mitigating circumstances, including his youth and a long history of violence and a personality disorder. "Beginning with *Furman*," Justice Powell's majority ruled, "the Court has attempted to provide

DOI: 10.4324/9780429398780-8

standards for a constitutional death penalty that would serve both goals of measured, consistent application and fairness to the accused," extending *Lockett* to *Eddings*'s case, noting that a state may not, by statute, preclude sentencing judges (or juries) from considering any mitigating factors. Nor, the Court held, may a sentencer refuse to consider such evidence presented to them. This must be weighed, as a matter of constitutional imperative, against aggravating factors before concluding a sentence of death.[1]

THOMPSON v. OKLAHOMA, 487 U.S. 815 (1988) provided the Court with an opportunity to extend *Eddings* to all young offenders. A Justice Stevens-led plurality declared that it would be unconstitutional and "would offend civilized standards of decency" to continue permitting the execution of offenders who were 16 or younger at the time of their offenses. With a weak majority on the constitutional law question of 4–3 (Justice O'Connor agreed with the ruling to set aside the sentence, but not the broad principle, and Justice Kennedy took no part in the case), the Court was sharply divided on two fundamental propositions: (1) There is a certain age, below which a juvenile's crimes can never be constitutionally punished by death, and (2) the Supreme Court precedent requires the Justices to locate this age in light of the "evolving standards of decency that mark the progress of a maturing society." Citing several nationwide displays of legislation considering 15-year-olds as different, the Court held this "consistent with the experience of mankind, as well as the long history of our law, that the normal 15-year-old is not prepared to assume the full responsibilities of an adult."

The main lines of disagreement between the two halves of the bench stemmed from a different evaluation of the "consensus" evidence, included at length at the end of this chapter. In the majority's view, the most relevant states were those 18 that have expressly considered the question of a minimum age for imposition of the death penalty, and have uniformly required that the defendant have attained at least the age of 16 at the time of the capital offense. This, the Court held, supports the conclusion that it would offend civilized standards of decency to execute a person who was less than 16 years old at the time of their offense. Moreover, the behavior

1 Two years of litigation followed. After consideration was given to the circumstances mandated by the Court, Eddings was resentenced to death on remand, which was upheld on appeal. In 1984, seven years after the murder, Oklahoma Court of Criminal Appeals Judge Ed Parks ultimately struck down Eddings's death sentence even before the U.S. Supreme Court would extend such protection categorically in *Thompson*, writing: "It is pertinent to note that Oklahoma has not executed any juveniles for crimes which they have committed. Now is not the time to begin. Life imprisonment, under the circumstances, is punishment enough for this child."

of juries was instructive to this conclusion (as evidenced by statistics demonstrating that, although between 18 and 20 persons under the age of 16 were executed during the first half of the 20th century, no such execution has taken place since 1948). Moreover, emphatically rejected by the dissent, the majority also considered relevant the supporting views expressed by respected professional organizations, by other nations that share the Anglo-American heritage, and by leading members of Western Europe from West Germany to Portugal (as well as by the Soviet Union)—all united in their express rejection of the juvenile death penalty.

The Justices were next presented with an opportunity to clarify their weak majority finding in *Thompson* and redefine the juvenile death penalty one year later, in *Stanford v. Kentucky*, 492 U.S. 361 (1989). In another fractured ruling, Justice Scalia delivered a barely there majority of 5–4 (propped up again by an O'Connor swing vote, this time joining the right side of the Court) and held that the Eighth Amendment's "standards of decency" did not compel application of *Eddings* to 16- and 17-year-olds, permitting consideration of death sentences for juveniles over the age of 15 (thereby refusing to extend *Thompson* protection to *Stanford*'s case). In an important concurrence, Justice O'Connor agreed that no national consensus forbade the imposition of capital punishment on 16- or 17-year-old murderers, but insisted the Court has a constitutional obligation to conduct proportionality analysis and noted that "the day may come" when legislative consensus would bar the juvenile death penalty entirely.

O'Connor's prophecy—though she personally dissented—was realized 15 years later in ***ROPER v. SIMMONS***, 543 U.S. 551 (2005). The Court, more definitively split 5–4, found a "national consensus" against the execution of all juveniles and deemed all statutes that imposed such a penalty *per se* unconstitutional under the Eighth Amendment's Punishments Clause. First finding that the Punishments Clause must be interpreted according to its text, by considering history, tradition, and precedent, Justice Kennedy's ruling turned to legislative consensus and overturned *Thompson* and *Stanford*, in which the Court had found 22 of 37 death penalty States permitting the death penalty for 16-year-old offenders (and 25 of 37 permitting it for 17-year-olds). Referencing *Atkins* (to which this chapter turns shortly), Kennedy concluded that both objective indicia of consensus, as expressed in particular by the enactments of legislatures that have addressed the question, and the Court's own determination in the exercise of its independent judgment, demonstrate that the death penalty is a disproportionate punishment for juveniles. The majority pinned this finding on two headings.

First, a rejection of the juvenile death penalty shown by the majority of States; the infrequency of its use even where it remains on the books; and the consistency in the trend toward abolition of the practice provide sufficient evidence that today society views juveniles, as "categorically less culpable than the average criminal." This review showed 30 states prohibiting the juvenile death penalty, including 12 that have rejected it altogether and 18 that maintain it but, by express provision or judicial interpretation, exclude juveniles from its reach. Moreover, even in the 20 States without a formal prohibition, the execution of juveniles is infrequent.

Second, capital punishment must be limited to those offenders who commit "a narrow category of the most serious crimes" and whose extreme culpability makes them "the most deserving of execution." As Juveniles' susceptibility to immature and irresponsible behavior means "their irresponsible conduct is not as morally reprehensible as that of an adult," their own vulnerability and comparative lack of control over their immediate surroundings mean juveniles have a greater claim than adults to be forgiven for failing to escape negative influences in their whole environment.

In addition, the majority found that an "overwhelming weight of international opinion against the juvenile death penalty," while not controlling, "provides respected and significant confirmation for the Court's determination that the penalty is disproportionate punishment for offenders under 18." Noting that the United States is the only country in the world that continues to give official sanction to the juvenile penalty, the majority found that standing against this tide of "express affirmation of certain fundamental rights by other nations and peoples" was a relevant constitutional consideration in interpreting those same rights into the Eighth Amendment. The Court held that, though international covenants prohibiting the juvenile death penalty were more recent, it was of relevance due to the historic ties with the United States that the United Kingdom abolished the juvenile death penalty long before (an element of the ruling Justice Scalia's dissenting opinion described as "perhaps the most indefensible part").

Scalia's characteristically excoriating dissent described the Court's ruling as "implausible" and the philosophy of the majority as "indulgent," applying the Justices' "current personal views" as reflected by a snapshot of legislative indicia. Scalia's principal objections were (1) that the Constitution's meaning does not evolve with societal change, and (2) that, in this case, the views of "death penalty states" are what is relevant and should be weighed if considering a legislative consensus, not the views of *all* states, including those which do not legislate on the matter at all. Scalia also declared that the Court's proclamation of itself as "sole arbiter of our Nation's moral standards" was wrong, and that "the subjective views of five Members of this Court and like-minded foreigners" were irrelevant in this case and to constitutional interpretation more generally. To continue to evolve the Punishments Clause in this way, he warned, would be "to crown arbitrariness with chaos."

Notwithstanding Scalia's objection to the ruling in applying fidelity to originalist principles, *Roper*'s significant leap in evolutive jurisprudence was extremely important for capital sentencing, aligning the United States with the vast majority of global approaches to the treatment of juveniles in death penalty debates. As a result, the Court's holding limits the death penalty in the United States to those carried out their offenses of murder when aged 18 or above, as bare minimum objective criteria (before further subject criteria—some of which will now be considered).

Intellectually disabled offenders

At the founding of the Union only those who suffered from profound intellectual disabilities, known contemporaneously as "idiots,"[2] were spared from execution under common law. Two centuries later, and during the same period that *Thompson* and *Stanford* were decided, the Court agreed to review two important claims regarding the mental state of capital defendants as a bar to execution. It was long accepted at common law that insanity precluded an offender from death penalty consideration,[3] where culpability for an "insane" defendant's actions (a legal term at the time) was simply not feasible. By "explicitly recogniz[ing] in our law a principle that has long resided there," Justice Thurgood Marshall's 5–4 majority in ***FORD v. WAINWRIGHT***, 477 U.S. 399 (1986) constitutionalized an historic rule designed to protect vulnerable individuals who are incapable of displaying the *mens rea* element of guilt. *Ford* addressed only insanity, not intellectual disability (where guilt was possible). Declaring explicitly for the first time that the Eighth Amendment prohibited the execution of defendants with severe mental disorders, the Court held that: "For centuries, no jurisdiction has countenanced the execution of the insane, yet this Court has never decided whether the Constitution forbids the practice. Today we keep faith with our common law heritage in holding that it does." The majority outlined several procedural protections to achieve this, holding that once a prisoner makes the requisite preliminary showing that his current mental state would bar his execution, the Eighth Amendment entitles him to an adjudication to determine

2 *Penry v. Lynaugh*, 492 U.S. 302 (1989), 333 (defining "idiots" as "persons who had a total lack of reason or understanding, or an inability to distinguish between good and evil"). See also Fitz-Herbert, A. (1794) *Natura Brevium*. 9th edn. p. 233B: "such a person who cannot account or number twenty pence, nor can tell who was his father or mother, nor how old he is, etc., so as it may appear that he hath no understanding of reason what shall be for his profit, or what for his loss."

3 *Nobles v. Georgia*, 168 U.S. 398 (1897); *Phyle v. Duffy*, 334 U.S. 431 (1948).

his condition. This procedure, as set out by the majority, was criticized in concurrence by Justice Powell, who derided it as a "full-scale 'sanity trial.' "[4]

Soon after *Ford* was decided, the Supreme Court bench experienced significant changes. Toward the end of a period when a strong conservative bloc held sway, one that consistently favored states' rights in criminal justice issues,[5] Chief Justice Burger stepped down in 1986, delivering a significant blow to that bloc. President Reagan appointed William Rehnquist to replace him, and Antonin Scalia occupied Rehnquist's vacant Associate seat. Far from the myth of Supreme Court Justices' fidelity to the Constitution above all else, it is commonly accepted that they operate with an underlying positioning on an ideological spectrum, as outlined in Chapter 2. By any measure, Rehnquist and Scalia brought deep conservatism to the bench, by design on Reagan's part: His election emboldened the conservatives in government, extending to the judiciary. The restrictive approach of the later Burger years promised to be strengthened by the new appointments, and that promise was soon fulfilled. It was considered unlikely that the Court would make the unpopular rule in *Ford* even more controversial by expanding it to mental disabilities, and this view was confirmed by the Court in *Penry v. Lynaugh*, 492 U.S. 302 (1989).

Johnny Paul Penry was convicted of the capital rape of a child in 1979 and sentenced to death in Texas despite testimony relating to his "mild to moderate retardation." Organic brain damage had, according to psychiatric reports, led to various IQ test scores of 50–63 points, indicating low functioning and difficulty in reasoning. Nonetheless, the Supreme Court held that the common law protection of insanity did not extend to those deemed competent to stand trial, regardless of the level of their criminal responsibility. A national consensus against a reversal of Penry's sentence—measured by state counting—was considered controlling by the Court, which disregarded an evolutive claim and effectively upheld his execution. In the same year that the Court had refused to protect under-18s

4 Justice Powell, concurring in *Ford*: "The State should provide an impartial officer or board that can receive evidence and argument from the prisoner's counsel, including expert psychiatric evidence that may differ from the State's own psychiatric examination. Beyond these basic requirements, the States should have substantial leeway to determine what process best balances the various interests at stake. As long as basic fairness is observed, I would find due process satisfied, and would apply the presumption of correctness of § 2254(d) on federal habeas corpus."

5 See *Hudson v. Palmer*, 468 U.S. 517 (1984) (no reasonable expectation of privacy in cells); *Block v. Rutherford*, 468 U.S. 576 (1984) (no constitutional right to prison visits); *Whitley v. Albers*, 475 U.S. 312 (1986) ("deliberate indifference" must be shown for a lack of emergency treatment to be unconstitutional).

shortly into the newly inaugurated Rehnquist Court in *Stanford*, it similarly declined Eighth Amendment protection to intellectually disabled offenders (the more modern term).

The *Penry* perspective was to be mirrored throughout the following Presidential election and by the subsequent Republican-led government, where eventual winner Bill Clinton made clear his steadfast support for the death penalty. On the 1992 campaign trail, Clinton returned to his home state of Arkansas to oversee the execution of a man rendered acutely intellectually disabled when he failed to commit suicide following an equally botched robbery. Clinton's backing of congressional policies to secure the most severe sentences, and to cut back on the capital appeals process followed, sustaining a defense against the judiciary's Eighth Amendment evolution over the two decades prior. Congress enacted the Federal Death Penalty Act (18 U.S.C. § 2245) in 1994, expanding the scope of the national government's capital punishment, and in 1995 the Prison Litigation Reform Act (PLRA) (42 U.S.C. § 1997e), which restricted the number of civil law suits a prisoner could bring. This cross-governmental effort to curtail the rights of prisoners led to a sharp decline in the rate of suits brought by prisoners, a trend that continues today.

Nonetheless, the "insanity-protection" rule in *Ford* was to be evolved at an even faster rate than was demonstrated with respect to juveniles in *Roper*, just 13 years after the Court's refused extension in *Penry*. In a dramatic turn of face, the Court in ***ATKINS v. VIRGINIA***, 536 U.S. 304 (2002) was to step off the restrictive approach demonstrated in the 1980s and 1990s. With a composition that the leading liberal Justice Stevens was now able to turn into a majority, the *Atkins* judgment finally prohibited the execution of *any* individuals with intellectual disabilities, after finding a national consensus against such an imposition. Beginning by recalling the *Weems* principles that punishments are unconstitutionally excessive if they are "not graduated and proportioned to the offense," the Court in *Atkins* insisted that objective factors were important in informing such consideration, the "clearest and most reliable of which" is nationwide legislative enactments. Much has changed, Stevens held, since *Penry*'s conclusion 13 years prior that the two state statutes then existing that prohibited such executions, even when added to the 14 States that had rejected capital punishment completely, did not provide sufficient evidence of a consensus. Owing to the uniquely detailed review of "consensus," extensive excerpts from the three major opinions in this case are included at the end of this chapter.

An *amicus curiae* brief filed by the American Psychiatric Association (APA) in *Atkins* noted that an offender who suffered from intellectual disability would typically display diminished capacity to comprehend facts and information; learn from mistakes; engage in logical, consequentialist reasoning; control impulses; communicate; engage in moral reasoning; and to recognize, understand, and demonstrate empathy for the feelings and reactions of others. A number of those mitigating factors had been acknowledged in *Penry* but not constitutionalized as a categorical rule against the imposition of death. Moreover, at oral argument, both the APA's Diagnostic and Statistical Manual of Mental Disorders (DSM) and the American Association on Mental Retardation's (AAMR's) Definition, Classification, and Systems of Supports were cited in support of *Atkins*.[6] Under the similar definitions provided by these organizations, the amici claimed Atkins to be profoundly intellectually disabled. While an individual such as Atkins might be able to commit an act and demonstrate culpability for that act, his defense successfully argued that "as this Court frequently reminds, death is different, a different calculus, a different set of concern. The judgment by the people as expressed in their legislatures has been these are individuals for whom we do not want the death penalty used."

With Atkins's counsel pitching their argument on the Court's precedent and the majoritarian reasoning displayed in *Penry*, the duration of oral argument centered on the "consistency of the direction of change" in state statutes. That is, between 1989 and 2002, the number of states prohibiting the death penalty for intellectually disabled offenders rose from 14 to 30, argued to be a demonstrable "national consensus." The majority, accepting this rate of change argument, noted that even among those 20 states that would have permitted Atkins's sentence of death, "only five have executed offenders possessing a known IQ less than 70 since we decided Penry." This explicit reference to bright-line IQ cutoffs, while well intended by Justice Stevens and his six-Justice majority, would stoke the flames for state legislative disagreement in the years after *Atkins*. Justice Stevens concluded that "today society views mentally retarded offenders as categorically less culpable than the average criminal."

The decision in *Atkins* marked a revival for societally driven evolution of the Eighth Amendment. While the term "professional consensus" would not arrive in the Court's judgments until later, *Atkins* represented a shift toward decent respect for epistemic knowledge in informing Eighth Amendment adjudication. Although most respect was paid to other measures of consensus, it is noteworthy that the Court in *Atkins* admitted that

6 For a more detailed analysis of this case and the contrasting opinions among the relevant epistemic community, see Eastaugh, C. (2017) 'Taking medical judgment seriously: professional consensus as a Trojan Horse for constitutional evolution', *Willamette Law Review*, 53, p. 403.

the views of "several organizations with germane expertise" were complementary to other objective indicia, "reflect[ing] a much broader social and professional consensus." Never before in constitutional law had a psychiatric manual been given such strong credence in decision-making. Indeed, just six months before *Atkins*, the Court emphasized the necessity of separating psychiatry from constitutional rules: "[T]he science of psychiatry [. . .] informs but does not control ultimate legal determinations."[7] Justice Scalia was vehement in dissent, awarding "the Prize for the Court's Most Feeble Effort to fabricate 'national consensus' " to the views "(deservedly relegated to a footnote)" of professional consensus, the "world community," and the results of opinion polls.

Twelve years later, the Court narrowed the discretion under which states can designate an individual convicted in *Hall v. Florida*, 572 U.S. 701 (2014). Through lengthy recitals to detailed amici, again provided by the APA and AAMR (now AAIDD [American Association on Intellectual Development and Disabilities] to reflect the shift in nomenclature), a 5–4 majority eventually discovered an evolving standard of decency in the Eighth Amendment. The Court held in *Hall*'s favor. The Constitution's proscription of cruel and unusual punishment does not permit a bright-line cutoff IQ score as deterministic of his intellectual disability, and therefore Atkins protection against execution. Florida's bright-line rule had led to a neglected consideration of the medical and behavioral history of offenders, which could determine that individuals with IQs above 70 on the standard scale were in fact intellectually disabled. Moreover, the Floridian statute under which Hall had been sentenced to death failed to account for the standard error of measurement. In essence, the Court concluded that "[i]ntellectual disability is a condition, not a number," as warned throughout *Atkins*. Court-watchers could be forgiven for drawing their own bright lines there, concluding that the Court has merely updated the *Atkins* standard with an increased role for expert guidance. Stopping at such a conclusion, however, would be neglectful of the far wider implications of this revolutionary Punishment Clause jurisprudence. The *Hall* Court created a new objective indicia of evolving standards under its own steam: professional consensus. This consensus was borne out of two principal *amici curiae*, each containing empirical, peer-reviewed literature from a variety of scientific journals. Determining that the assessment required a consideration of "psychiatric and professional studies that elaborate on the purpose and meaning of IQ scores," the majority noted that it should be unsurprising "[t]hat this Court, state courts, and state legislatures consult and are

7 *Kansas v. Crane*, 534 U.S. 407, 413 (2002).

informed by the work of medical experts," citing the APA and the AAIDD as the vanguards of this task.

I have argued elsewhere that *Hall* provides a potential "precedential Trojan Horse—one loaded with medical professionals and armed with epistemic knowledge, and one which provides the strongest opportunity for further Eighth Amendment evolution" (Eastaugh, 2017), whereby practices deemed abhorrent by medical professionals and civil liberties organizations across the nation (such as prolonged periods of extreme solitary confinement) could be undermined by professional consensus in evolving standards decision-making. The Court in *Moore v. Texas*, 137 S. Ct. 1039 (2017) undertook such an assessment in determining whether Bobby James Moore (who was due to be executed for the 1980 shooting of a store clerk in Houston) was culpable and whether a framework for intellectual disability assessments developed in 1992 and 2004 (which included, *inter alia*, a "Lennie standard"—by reference to Steinbeck's intellectually disabled character in *Of Mice and Men*) satisfies the *Hall* emphasis on contemporary professional consensus. The Court (led 5–3 by Justice Ginsburg) remanded the decision to consider "prevailing clinical standards."[8] The Court commented further, ruling that although the states have the primary responsibility to develop appropriate ways to enforce the *Ford/Atkins* protections, they must closely take into account the most recent medical guidance and views of professional organizations on intellectual disabilities, further expanding the principle of medical consensus informing constitutional interpretation.[9]

References

Eastaugh, C. (2017) 'Taking medical judgment seriously: professional consensus as a Trojan Horse for constitutional evolution', *Willamette Law Review*, 53, p. 403.

Fitz-Herbert, A. (1794) *Natura Brevium*. 9th edn. London.

8 On a second appeal, *Moore v. Texas II*, 139 S. Ct. 666 (2019), the Court again overturned the subsequent capital resentencing, this time declaring Moore was ineligible for death because of his intellectual disability.

9 The Court has since held, in *Madison v. Alabama*, 139 S. Ct. 718 (2019), that under *Ford*, the Eighth Amendment may permit executing a prisoner even if he cannot remember committing his crime. Such memory loss still may factor into analysis (if that loss combines and interacts with other mental shortfalls to deprive a person of the capacity to comprehend why the State is exacting death as a punishment). Moreover, *Madison* held that the Eighth Amendment may prohibit executing a prisoner even though he suffers from dementia or another disorder rather than psychotic delusions. The important assessment is whether a mental disorder has had a particular effect; it has no interest in establishing any precise cause.

Cited cases

Atkins v. Virginia, 536 U.S. 304 (2002).
Bell v. Ohio, 438 U.S. 637 (1978).
Block v. Rutherford, 468 U.S. 576 (1984).
Eddings v. Oklahoma, 455 U.S. 104 (1982).
Ford v. Wainwright, 477 U.S. 399 (1986).
Hall v. Florida, 572 U.S. 701 (2014).
Hudson v. Palmer, 468 U.S. 517 (1984).
Kansas v. Crane, 534 U.S. 407 (2002).
Lockett v. Ohio, 438 U.S. 586 (1978).
Madison v. Alabama, 139 S. Ct. 718 (2019).
Moore v. Texas, 137 S. Ct. 1039 (2017).
Moore v. Texas II, 139 S. Ct. 666 (2019).
Penry v. Lynaugh, 492 U.S. 302 (1989).
Roper v. Simmons, 543 U.S. 551 (2005).
Stanford v. Kentucky, 492 U.S. 361 (1989).
Thompson v. Oklahoma, 487 U.S. 815 (1988).
Whitley v. Albers, 475 U.S. 312 (1986).

Cited legislation

Federal Death Penalty Act (18 USC § 2245) (1994).
Prison Litigation Reform Act (42 USC § 1997e) (1995).

EDDINGS v. OKLAHOMA, 455 U.S. 104 (1982)

JUSTICE POWELL delivered the opinion of the Court (5–4), in which JUSTICES BRENNAN, MARSHALL, STEVENS, and O'CONNOR joined.

Petitioner Monty Lee Eddings was convicted of first degree murder, and sentenced to death.

On April 4, 1977, Eddings, a 16-year-old youth, and several younger companions ran away from their Missouri homes. They traveled in a car owned by Eddings' brother, and drove without destination or purpose in a southwesterly direction, eventually reaching the Oklahoma Turnpike. Eddings had in the car a shotgun and several rifles he had taken from his father. After he momentarily lost control of the car, he was signalled to pull over by Officer Crabtree of the Oklahoma Highway Patrol. Eddings did so, and when the officer approached the car, Eddings stuck a loaded shotgun out of the window and fired, killing the officer.

Because Eddings was a juvenile, the State moved to have him certified to stand trial as an adult. Finding that there was prosecutive merit to the complaint and that Eddings was not amenable to rehabilitation within the juvenile system, the trial court granted the motion. The ruling was affirmed on appeal. Eddings was then charged with murder in the first degree, and the District Court of Creek County found him guilty upon his plea of *nolo contendere*.

The Oklahoma death penalty statute provides in pertinent part:

> "Upon conviction . . . of guilt of a defendant of murder in the first degree, the court shall conduct a separate sentencing proceeding to determine whether the defendant should be sentenced to death or life imprisonment. . . . In the sentencing proceeding, evidence may be presented as to *any mitigating circumstances* or as to any of the aggravating circumstances enumerated in this act."

Section 701.12 lists seven separate aggravating circumstances; the statute nowhere defines what is meant by "any mitigating circumstances."

At the sentencing hearing, the State alleged three of the aggravating circumstances enumerated in the statute: that the murder was especially heinous, atrocious, or cruel, that the crime was committed for the purpose of avoiding or preventing a lawful arrest, and that there was a probability that the defendant would commit criminal acts of violence that would constitute a continuing threat to society.

In mitigation, Eddings presented substantial evidence at the hearing of his troubled youth. The testimony of his supervising Juvenile Officer indicated that Eddings had been raised without proper guidance. His parents were divorced when he was 5 years old, and until he was 14, Eddings lived with his mother without rules or supervision. There is the suggestion that Eddings' mother was an alcoholic, and possibly a prostitute. By the time Eddings was 14, he no longer could be controlled, and his mother sent him to live with his father. But neither could the father control the boy. Attempts to reason and talk gave way to physical punishment. The Juvenile Officer testified that Eddings was frightened and bitter, that his father overreacted and used excessive physical punishment:

> "Mr. Eddings found the only thing that he thought was effectful with the boy was actual punishment, or physical violence—hitting with a strap or something like this."

Testimony from other witnesses indicated that Eddings was emotionally disturbed in general and at the time of the crime, and that his mental and emotional development were at a level several years below his age. A state psychologist stated that Eddings had a sociopathic or antisocial personality and that approximately 30% of youths suffering from such a disorder grew out of it as they aged. A sociologist specializing in juvenile offenders testified that Eddings was treatable. A psychiatrist testified that Eddings could be rehabilitated by intensive therapy over a 15- to 20-year period.

He testified further that Eddings "did pull the trigger, he did kill someone, but I don't even think he knew that he was doing it." The psychiatrist suggested that, if treated, Eddings would no longer pose a serious threat to society.

At the conclusion of all the evidence, the trial judge weighed the evidence of aggravating and mitigating circumstances. He found that the State had proved each of the three alleged aggravating circumstances beyond a reasonable doubt. Turning to the evidence of mitigating circumstances, the judge found that Eddings' youth was a mitigating factor of great weight:

> "I have given very serious consideration to the youth of the Defendant when this particular crime was committed. Should I fail to do this, I think I would not be carrying out my duty."

But he would not consider in mitigation the circumstances of Eddings' unhappy upbringing and emotional disturbance:

> "[T]he Court cannot be persuaded entirely by the . . . fact that the youth was sixteen years old when this heinous crime was committed. *Nor can*

> *the Court, in following the law, in my opinion, consider the fact of this young man's violent background."*

Finding that the only mitigating circumstance was Eddings' youth, and finding further that this circumstance could not outweigh the aggravating circumstances present, the judge sentenced Eddings to death.

The Court of Criminal Appeals affirmed the sentence of death. It found that each of the aggravating circumstances alleged by the State had been present. It recited the mitigating evidence presented by Eddings in some detail, but, in the end, it agreed with the trial court that only the fact of Eddings' youth was properly considered as a mitigating circumstance:

> "[Eddings] also argues his mental state at the time of the murder. He stresses his family history in saying he was suffering from severe psychological and emotional disorders, and that the killing was, in actuality, an inevitable product of the way he was raised. There is no doubt that the petitioner has a personality disorder. But all the evidence tends to show that he knew the difference between right and wrong at the time he pulled the trigger, and that is the test of criminal responsibility in this State. For the same reason, the petitioner's family history is useful in explaining why he behaved the way he did, but it does not excuse his behavior."

As THE CHIEF JUSTICE explained, the rule in *Lockett* is the product of a considerable history reflecting the law's effort to develop a system of capital punishment at once consistent and principled but also humane and sensible to the uniqueness of the individual. Since the early days of the common law, the legal system has struggled to accommodate these twin objectives. Thus, the common law began by treating all criminal homicides as capital offenses, with a mandatory sentence of death. Later it allowed exceptions, first through an exclusion for those entitled to claim benefit of clergy and then by limiting capital punishment to murders upon "malice prepensed." In this country, we attempted to soften the rigor of the system of mandatory death sentences we inherited from England, first by grading murder into different degrees of which only murder of the first degree was a capital offense and then by committing use of the death penalty to the absolute discretion of the jury.

Beginning with *Furman*, the Court has attempted to provide standards for a constitutional death penalty that would serve both goals of measured, consistent application and fairness to the accused. Thus, in *Gregg v. Georgia*, the principal opinion held that the danger of an arbitrary and capricious death penalty could be met "by a carefully drafted statute that ensures that the sentencing authority is given adequate information and guidance."

Similarly, in *Woodson*, the plurality held that mandatory death sentencing was not a permissible response to the problem of arbitrary jury discretion. As the history of capital punishment had shown, such an approach to the problem of discretion could not succeed while the Eighth Amendment required that the individual be given his due. [. . .] Thus, the rule in *Lockett* followed from the earlier decisions of the Court and from the Court's insistence that capital punishment be imposed fairly, and with reasonable consistency, or not at all.

By holding that the sentencer in capital cases must be permitted to consider any relevant mitigating factor, the rule in *Lockett* recognizes that a consistency produced by ignoring individual differences is a false consistency.

We now apply the rule in *Lockett* to the circumstances of this case. The trial judge stated that "in following the law," he could not "consider the fact of this young man's violent background." There is no dispute that, by "violent background," the trial judge was referring to the mitigating evidence of Eddings' family history. From this statement, it is clear that the trial judge did not evaluate the evidence in mitigation and find it wanting as a matter of fact; rather, he found that, *as a matter of law*, he was unable even to consider the evidence.

The Court of Criminal Appeals took the same approach. It found that the evidence in mitigation was not relevant because it did not tend to provide a legal excuse from criminal responsibility. Thus, the court conceded that Eddings had a "personality disorder," but cast this evidence aside on the basis that "he knew the difference between right and wrong . . . , and that is the test of criminal responsibility." Similarly, the evidence of Eddings' family history was "useful in explaining" his behavior, but it did not "excuse" the behavior. From these statements, it appears that the Court of Criminal Appeals also considered only that evidence to be mitigating which would tend to support a legal excuse from criminal liability.

We find that the limitations placed by these courts upon the mitigating evidence they would consider violated the rule in *Lockett*. Just as the State may not, by statute, preclude the sentencer from considering any mitigating factor, neither may the sentencer refuse to consider, *as a matter of law*, any relevant mitigating evidence. In this instance, it was as if the trial judge had instructed a jury to disregard the mitigating evidence Eddings proffered on his behalf. The sentencer, and the Court of Criminal Appeals on review, may determine the weight to be given relevant mitigating evidence. But they may not give it no weight by excluding such evidence from their consideration.

The trial judge recognized that youth must be considered a relevant mitigating factor. But youth is more than a chronological fact. It is a time and condition of life when a person may be most susceptible to influence and to psychological damage. Our history is replete with laws and judicial recognition that minors, especially in their earlier years, generally are less mature and responsible than adults. Particularly "during the formative years of childhood and adolescence, minors often lack the experience, perspective, and judgment" expected of adults.

Even the normal 16-year-old customarily lacks the maturity of an adult. In this case, Eddings was not a normal 16-year-old; he had been deprived of the care, concern, and paternal attention that children deserve. On the contrary, it is not disputed that he was a juvenile with serious emotional problems, and had been raised in a neglectful, sometimes even violent, family background. In addition, there was testimony that Eddings' mental and emotional development were at a level several years below his chronological age. All of this does not suggest an absence of responsibility for the crime of murder, deliberately committed in this case. Rather, it is to say that, just as the chronological age of a minor is itself a relevant mitigating factor of great weight, so must the background and mental and emotional development of a youthful defendant be duly considered in sentencing.

We are not unaware of the extent to which minors engage increasingly in violent crime. Nor do we suggest an absence of legal responsibility where crime is committed by a minor. We are concerned here only with the manner of the imposition of the ultimate penalty: the death sentence imposed for the crime of murder upon an emotionally disturbed youth with a disturbed child's immaturity.

On remand, the state courts must consider all relevant mitigating evidence and weigh it against the evidence of the aggravating circumstances. We do not weigh the evidence for them. Accordingly, the judgment is reversed to the extent that it sustains the imposition of the death penalty, and the case is remanded for further proceedings not inconsistent with this opinion.

JUSTICE BRENNAN, concurring.

I join the Court's opinion without, however, departing from my view that the death penalty is in all circumstances cruel and unusual punishment prohibited by the Eighth and Fourteenth Amendments.

JUSTICE O'CONNOR also filed a concurring opinion and CHIEF JUSTICE BURGER filed a dissenting opinion, in which JUSTICES WHITE, BLACKMUN, and REHNQUIST joined.

THOMPSON v. OKLAHOMA, 487 U.S. 815 (1988)

JUSTICE STEVENS delivered the opinion of the Court, joined by JUSTICES BRENNAN, MARSHALL, and BLACKMUN. JUSTICE O'CONNOR agreed with the ruling but authored a separate concurrence.

The principal question presented is whether the execution of that sentence would violate the constitutional prohibition against the infliction of "cruel and unusual punishments" because petitioner was only 15 years old at the time of his offense.

I

Because there is no claim that the punishment would be excessive if the crime had been committed by an adult, only a brief statement of facts is necessary. In concert with three older persons, petitioner actively participated in the brutal murder of his former brother-in-law in the early morning hours of January 23, 1983. The evidence disclosed that the victim had been shot twice, and that his throat, chest, and abdomen had been cut. He also had multiple bruises and a broken leg. His body had been chained to a concrete block and thrown into a river, where it remained for almost four weeks. Each of the four participants was tried separately and each was sentenced to death.

II

The authors of the Eighth Amendment drafted a categorical prohibition against the infliction of cruel and unusual punishments, but they made no attempt to define the contours of that category. They delegated that task to future generations of judges, who have been guided by the "evolving standards of decency that mark the progress of a maturing society." In performing that task, the Court has reviewed the work product of state legislatures and sentencing juries, and has carefully considered the reasons why a civilized society may accept or reject the death penalty in certain types of cases. Thus, in confronting the question whether the youth of the defendant—more specifically, the fact that he was less than 16 years old at the time of his offense—is a sufficient reason for denying the State the power to sentence him to death, we first review relevant legislative enactments, then refer to jury determinations, and finally explain why these indicators of contemporary standards of decency confirm our judgment that such a young person is not capable of acting with the degree of culpability that can justify the ultimate penalty.

III

Justice Powell has repeatedly reminded us of the importance of

> "the experience of mankind, as well as the long history of our law, recognizing that there are differences which must be accommodated in determining the rights and duties of children as compared with those of adults. Examples of this distinction abound in our law: in contracts, in torts, in criminal law and procedure, in criminal sanctions and rehabilitation, and in the right to vote and to hold office."

Oklahoma recognizes this basic distinction in a number of its statutes. Thus, a minor is not eligible to vote, to sit on a jury, to marry without parental consent, or to purchase alcohol or cigarettes. Like all other States, Oklahoma has developed a juvenile justice system in which most offenders under the age of 18 are not held criminally responsible. Its statutes do provide, however, that a 16- or 17-year-old charged with murder and other serious felonies shall be considered an adult. Other than the special certification procedure that was used to authorize petitioner's trial in this case "as an adult," apparently there are no Oklahoma statutes, either civil or criminal, that treat a person under 16 years of age as anything but a "child."

The line between childhood and adulthood is drawn in different ways by various States. There is, however, complete or near unanimity among all 50 States and the District of Columbia in treating a person under 16 as a minor for several important purposes. In no State may a 15-year-old vote or serve on a jury. Further, in all but one State, a 15-year-old may not drive without parental consent, and in all but four States, a 15-year-old may not marry without parental consent. Additionally, in those States that have legislated on the subject, no one under age 16 may purchase pornographic materials (50 States), and in most States that have some form of legalized gambling, minors are not permitted to participate without parental consent (42 States). Most relevant, however, is the fact that all States have enacted legislation designating the maximum age for juvenile court jurisdiction at no less than 16. All of this legislation is consistent with the experience of mankind, as well as the long history of our law, that the normal 15-year-old is not prepared to assume the full responsibilities of an adult.

Most state legislatures have not expressly confronted the question of establishing a minimum age for imposition of the death penalty. In 14 States, capital punishment is not authorized at all, and in 19 others, capital punishment is authorized, but no minimum age is expressly stated in the death penalty statute.

If, therefore, we accept the premise that some offenders are simply too young to be put to death, it is reasonable to put this group of statutes to one side because they do not focus on the question of where the chronological age line should be drawn. When we confine our attention to the 18 States that have expressly established a minimum age in their death penalty statutes, we find that all of them require that the defendant have attained at least the age of 16 at the time of the capital offense.

The conclusion that it would offend civilized standards of decency to execute a person who was less than 16 years old at the time of his or her offense is consistent with the views that have been expressed by respected professional organizations, by other nations that share our Anglo-American heritage, and by the leading members of the Western European community.

IV

The second societal factor the Court has examined in determining the acceptability of capital punishment to the American sensibility is the behavior of juries. In fact, the infrequent and haphazard handing out of death sentences by capital juries was a prime factor underlying our judgment in *Furman* [. . .]

While it is not known precisely how many persons have been executed during the 20th century for crimes committed under the age of 16, a scholar has recently compiled a table revealing this number to be between 18 and 20. All of these occurred during the first half of the century, with the last such execution taking place apparently in 1948.

V

"Although the judgments of legislatures, juries, and prosecutors weigh heavily in the balance, it is for us ultimately to judge whether the Eighth Amendment permits imposition of the death penalty" on one such as petitioner who committed a heinous murder when he was only 15 years old. In making that judgment, we first ask whether the juvenile's culpability should be measured by the same standard as that of an adult, and then consider whether the application of the death penalty to this class of offenders "measurably contributes" to the social purposes that are served by the death penalty.

And, even if one posits such a cold-blooded calculation by a 15-year-old, it is fanciful to believe that he would be deterred by the knowledge that a small number of persons his age have been executed during the 20th century. In short, we are not persuaded that the imposition of the death penalty for offenses committed by persons under 16 years of age has made, or can be expected to make, any measurable contribution to the goals that capital punishment is intended to achieve.

JUSTICE SCALIA filed a dissenting opinion, joined by CHIEF JUSTICE REHNQUIST and JUSTICE WHITE.

William Wayne Thompson is not a juvenile caught up in a legislative scheme that unthinkingly lumped him together with adults for purposes of determining that death was an appropriate penalty for him and for his crime. To the contrary, Oklahoma first gave careful consideration to whether, in light of his young age, he should be subjected to the normal criminal system at all. That question having been answered affirmatively, a jury then considered whether, despite his young age, his maturity and moral responsibility were sufficiently developed to justify the sentence of death. In upsetting this particularized judgment on the basis of a constitutional absolute, the plurality pronounces it to be a fundamental principle of our society that no one who is as little as one day short of his 16th birthday can have sufficient maturity and moral responsibility to be subjected to capital punishment for any crime. As a sociological and moral conclusion, that is implausible; and it is doubly implausible as an interpretation of the United States Constitution.

It is thus significant that, only four years ago, in the Comprehensive Crime Control Act of 1984, Pub. L. 98–473, 98 Stat. 2149, Congress expressly addressed the effect of youth upon the imposition of criminal punishment, and changed the law in precisely the opposite direction from that which the plurality's perceived evolution in social attitudes would suggest: it lowered from 16 to 15 the age at which a juvenile's case can, "in the interest of justice," be transferred from juvenile court to Federal District Court, enabling him to be tried and punished as an adult.

Turning to legislation at the state level, one observes the same trend of lowering, rather than raising, the age of juvenile criminal liability. As for the state status quo with respect to the death penalty in particular: the plurality chooses to "confine [its] attention" to the fact that all 18 of the States that establish a minimum age for capital punishment have chosen at least 16. But it is beyond me why an accurate analysis would not include within the computation the larger number of States (19) that have determined that no minimum age for capital punishment is appropriate, leaving that to be governed by their general rules for the age at which juveniles can be criminally responsible. A survey of state laws shows, in other words, that a majority of the States for which the issue exists (the rest do not have capital punishment) are of the view that death is not different insofar as the age of juvenile criminal responsibility is concerned. And the latter age, while presumed to be 16 in all the States, can, in virtually all the States, be less than 16 when individuated consideration of the particular case warrants it. Thus, what Oklahoma has done here is precisely what the majority of capital punishment States would do.

When the Federal Government, and almost 40% of the States, including a majority of the States that include capital punishment as a permissible sanction, allow for the imposition of the death penalty on any juvenile who has been tried as an adult, which category can include juveniles under 16 at the time of the offense, it is obviously impossible for the plurality to rely upon any evolved societal consensus discernible in legislation—or at least discernible in the legislation of this society, which is assuredly all that is relevant.

The evidence that the views of our society, so steadfast and so uniform that they have become part of the agreed-upon laws that we live by, regard that absolute age to be 16 is nonexistent.

JUSTICE KENNEDY took no part in the consideration or decision of the case.

ROPER v. SIMMONS, 543 U.S. 551 (2005)

JUSTICE KENNEDY delivered the opinion of the Court, joined by JUSTICES STEVENS, SOUTER, GINSBURG, and BREYER.

This case requires us to address, for the second time in a decade and a half, whether it is permissible under the Eighth and Fourteenth Amendments to the Constitution of the United States to execute a juvenile offender who was older than 15 but younger than 18 when he committed a capital crime. In *Stanford*, a divided Court rejected the proposition that the Constitution bars capital punishment for juvenile offenders in this age group. We reconsider the question.

I

At the age of 17, when he was still a junior in high school, Christopher Simmons, the respondent here, committed murder. About nine months later, after he had turned 18, he was tried and sentenced to death. There is little doubt that Simmons was the instigator of the crime. Before its commission Simmons said he wanted to murder someone. In chilling, callous terms he talked about his plan, discussing it for the most part with two friends, Charles Benjamin and John Tessmer, then aged 15 and 16 respectively. Simmons proposed to commit burglary and murder by breaking and entering, tying up a victim, and throwing the victim off a bridge. Simmons assured his friends they could "get away with it" because they were minors.

The Missouri Supreme Court agreed. It held that since *Stanford*, "a national consensus has developed against the execution of juvenile offenders, as demonstrated by the fact that eighteen states now bar such executions for juveniles, that twelve other states bar executions altogether, that no state has lowered its age of execution below 18 since Stanford, that five states have legislatively or by case law raised or established the minimum age at 18, and that the imposition of the juvenile death penalty has become truly unusual over the last decade."

On this reasoning it set aside Simmons' death sentence and resentenced him to "life imprisonment without eligibility for probation, parole, or release except by act of the Governor."

We granted certiorari and now affirm.

II

The beginning point is a review of objective indicia of consensus, as expressed in particular by the enactments of legislatures that have addressed the question. This data gives us essential instruction. We then must determine, in the exercise of our own independent judgment, whether the death penalty is a disproportionate punishment for juveniles.

III

A

[I]n this case, 30 States prohibit the juvenile death penalty, comprising 12 that have rejected the death penalty altogether and 18 that maintain it but, by express provision or judicial interpretation, exclude juveniles from its reach [. . .] even in the 20 States without a formal prohibition on executing juveniles, the practice is infrequent.

Since *Stanford*, six States have executed prisoners for crimes committed as juveniles. In the past 10 years, only three have done so: Oklahoma, Texas, and Virginia. In December 2003 the Governor of Kentucky decided to spare the life of Kevin Stanford, and commuted his sentence to one of life imprisonment without parole. By this act the Governor ensured Kentucky would not add itself to the list of States that have executed juveniles within the last 10 years even by the execution of the very defendant whose death sentence the Court had upheld in *Stanford*.

Five States that allowed the juvenile death penalty at the time of Stanford have abandoned it in the intervening 15 years—four through legislative enactments and one through judicial decision [and we] consider the change from *Stanford* to this case to be significant. Since *Stanford*, no State that previously prohibited capital punishment for juveniles has reinstated it. This fact, coupled with the trend toward abolition of the juvenile death penalty, carries special force in light of the general popularity of anticrime legislation, and in light of the particular trend in recent years toward cracking down on juvenile crime in other respects.

When we heard *Stanford*, 12 death penalty States had already prohibited the execution of any juvenile under 18, and 15 had prohibited the execution of any juvenile under 17.

Petitioner cannot show national consensus in favor of capital punishment for juveniles but still resists the conclusion that any consensus exists against it.

B

A majority of States have rejected the imposition of the death penalty on juvenile offenders under 18, and we now hold this is required by the Eighth Amendment.

Three general differences between juveniles under 18 and adults demonstrate that juvenile offenders cannot with reliability be classified among the worst offenders. First, as any parent knows and as the scientific and sociological studies respondent and his amici cite tend to confirm, "[a] lack of maturity and an underdeveloped sense of responsibility are found in youth more often than in adults and are more understandable among the young. These qualities often result in impetuous and ill-considered actions and decisions."

The second area of difference is that juveniles are more vulnerable or susceptible to negative influences and outside pressures, including peer pressure.

The third broad difference is that the character of a juvenile is not as well formed as that of an adult. The personality traits of juveniles are more transitory, less fixed.

In *Thompson*, a plurality of the Court recognized the import of these characteristics with respect to juveniles under 16, and relied on them to hold that the Eighth Amendment prohibited the imposition of the death penalty on juveniles below that age. We conclude the same reasoning applies to all juvenile offenders under 18.

Drawing the line at 18 years of age is subject, of course, to the objections always raised against categorical rules. The qualities that distinguish juveniles from adults do not disappear when an individual turns 18. By the same token, some under 18 have already attained a level of maturity some adults will never reach. For the reasons we have discussed, however, a line must be drawn. The plurality opinion in Thompson drew the line at 16. In the intervening years the Thompson plurality's conclusion that offenders under 16 may not be executed has not been challenged. The logic of Thompson extends to those who are under 18. The age of 18 is the point where society draws the line for many purposes between childhood and adulthood. It is, we conclude, the age at which the line for death eligibility ought to rest.

These considerations mean *Stanford* should be deemed no longer controlling on this issue. To the extent *Stanford* was based on review of the objective indicia of consensus that obtained in 1989, it suffices to note that those indicia have changed. It should be observed, furthermore, that the *Stanford* Court should have considered those States that had abandoned the death penalty altogether as part of the consensus against the juvenile death penalty; a State's decision to bar the death penalty altogether of necessity demonstrates a judgment that the death penalty is inappropriate for all offenders, including juveniles.

In holding that the death penalty cannot be imposed upon juvenile offenders, we take into account the circumstance that some States have relied on

Stanford in seeking the death penalty against juvenile offenders. This consideration, however, does not outweigh our conclusion that *Stanford* should no longer control in those few pending cases or in those yet to arise.

IV

Our determination that the death penalty is disproportionate punishment for offenders under 18 finds confirmation in the stark reality that the United States is the only country in the world that continues to give official sanction to the juvenile death penalty. This reality does not become controlling, for the task of interpreting the Eighth Amendment remains our responsibility.

As respondent and a number of *amici* emphasize, Article 37 of the United Nations Convention on the Rights of the Child, which every country in the world has ratified save for the United States and Somalia, contains an express prohibition on capital punishment for crimes committed by juveniles under 18.

Respondent and his *amici* have submitted, and petitioner does not contest, that only seven countries other than the United States have executed juvenile offenders since 1990: Iran, Pakistan, Saudi Arabia, Yemen, Nigeria, the Democratic Republic of Congo, and China. Since then each of these countries has either abolished capital punishment for juveniles or made public disavowal of the practice. In sum, it is fair to say that the United States now stands alone in a world that has turned its face against the juvenile death penalty.

Though the international covenants prohibiting the juvenile death penalty are of more recent date, it is instructive to note that the United Kingdom abolished the juvenile death penalty before these covenants came into being. The United Kingdom's experience bears particular relevance here in light of the historic ties between our countries and in light of the Eighth Amendment's own origins.

Over time, from one generation to the next, the Constitution has come to earn the high respect and even, as Madison dared to hope, the veneration of the American people. The document sets forth, and rests upon, innovative principles original to the American experience, such as federalism; a proven balance in political mechanisms through separation of powers; specific guarantees for the accused in criminal cases; and broad provisions to secure individual freedom and preserve human dignity. These doctrines and guarantees are central to the American experience and remain essential to our present-day self-definition and national identity. Not the least of the reasons we honor the Constitution, then, is because we know it to be our own. It does not lessen our fidelity to the Constitution or our pride in its origins to acknowledge that the express affirmation of certain fundamental rights by other nations and peoples simply underscores the centrality of those same rights within our own heritage of freedom.

JUSTICE STEVENS filed a concurring opinion, joined by JUSTICE GINSBURG.

JUSTICE O'CONNOR filed a dissenting opinion.

JUSTICE SCALIA filed a dissenting opinion, joined by CHIEF JUSTICE REHNQUIST and JUSTICE THOMAS.

In urging approval of a constitution that gave life-tenured judges the power to nullify laws enacted by the people's representatives, Alexander Hamilton assured the citizens of New York that there was little risk in this, since "[t]he judiciary . . . ha[s] neither FORCE nor WILL but merely judgment." But Hamilton had in mind a traditional judiciary, "bound down by strict rules and precedents which serve to define and point out their duty in every particular case that comes before them." Bound down, indeed. What a mockery today's opinion makes of Hamilton's expectation, announcing the Court's conclusion that the meaning of our Constitution has changed over the past 15 years—not, mind you, that this Court's decision 15 years ago was wrong, but that the Constitution has changed.

The Court thus proclaims itself sole arbiter of our Nation's moral standards—and in the course of discharging that awesome responsibility purports to take guidance from the views of foreign courts and legislatures. Because I do not believe that the meaning of our Eighth Amendment, any more than the meaning of other provisions of our Constitution, should be determined by the subjective views of five Members of this Court and like-minded foreigners, I dissent.

[. . .]

More fundamentally, however, the basic premise of the Court's argument—that American law should conform to the laws of the rest of the world—ought to be rejected out of hand. In fact the Court itself does not believe it. In many significant respects the laws of most other countries differ from our law—including not only such explicit provisions of our Constitution as the right to jury trial and grand jury indictment, but even many interpretations of the Constitution prescribed by this Court itself.

The Court's special reliance on the laws of the United Kingdom is perhaps the most indefensible part of its opinion. It is of course true that we share a common history with the United Kingdom, and that we often consult English sources when asked to discern the meaning of a constitutional text written against the backdrop of 18th-century English law and legal thought. If we applied that approach today, our task would be an easy one.

The Court's parting attempt to downplay the significance of its extensive discussion of foreign law is unconvincing. "Acknowledgment" of foreign approval has no place in the legal opinion of this Court unless it is part of the basis for the Court's judgment—which is surely what it parades as today.

[. . .]

One must admit that the Missouri Supreme Court's action, and this Court's indulgent reaction, are, in a way, understandable. In a system based upon constitutional and statutory text democratically adopted, the concept of "law" ordinarily signifies that particular words have a fixed meaning. Such law does not change, and this Court's pronouncement of it therefore remains authoritative until (confessing our prior error) we overrule. The Court has purported to make of the Eighth Amendment, however, a mirror of the passing and changing sentiment of American society regarding penology. The lower courts can look into that mirror as well as we can; and what we saw 15 years ago bears no necessary relationship to what they see today. Since they are not looking at the same text, but at a different scene, why should our earlier decision control their judgment?

However sound philosophically, this is no way to run a legal system. We must disregard the new reality that, to the extent our Eighth Amendment decisions constitute something more than a show of hands on the current Justices' current personal views about penology, they purport to be nothing more than a snapshot of American public opinion at a particular point in time (with the timeframes now shortened to a mere 15 years). We must treat these decisions just as though they represented real law, real prescriptions democratically adopted by the American people, as conclusively (rather than sequentially) construed by this Court. Allowing lower courts to reinterpret the Eighth Amendment whenever they decide enough time has passed for a new snapshot leaves this Court's decisions without any force—especially since the "evolution" of our Eighth Amendment is no longer determined by objective criteria. To allow lower courts to behave as we do, "updating" the Eighth Amendment as needed, destroys stability and makes our case law an unreliable basis for the designing of laws by citizens and their representatives, and for action by public officials. The result will be to crown arbitrariness with chaos.

FORD v. WAINWRIGHT, 477 U.S. 399 (1986)

JUSTICE MARSHALL announced the judgment of the Court and delivered an opinion of the Court with respect to Parts I and II, in which JUSTICES BRENNAN, BLACKMUN, POWELL, and STEVENS joined, and an opinion with respect to Parts III, IV, and V, in which JUSTICES BRENNAN, BLACKMUN, and STEVENS joined.

For centuries, no jurisdiction has countenanced the execution of the insane, yet this Court has never decided whether the Constitution forbids the practice. Today we keep faith with our common law heritage in holding that it does.

I

Alyin Bernard Ford was convicted of murder in 1974 and sentenced to death. There is no suggestion that he was incompetent at the time of his offense, at trial, or at sentencing.

In early 1982, however, Ford began to manifest gradual changes in behavior. They began as an occasional peculiar idea or confused perception, but became more serious over time. After reading in the newspaper that the Ku Klux Klan had held a rally in nearby Jacksonville, Florida, Ford developed an obsession focused upon the Klan. His letters to various people reveal endless brooding about his "Klan work," and an increasingly pervasive delusion that he had become the target of a complex conspiracy, involving the Klan and assorted others, designed to force him to commit suicide. He believed that the prison guards, part of the conspiracy, had been killing people and putting the bodies in the concrete enclosures used for beds. Later, he began to believe that his women relatives were being tortured and sexually abused somewhere in the prison. This notion developed into a delusion that the people who were tormenting him at the prison had taken members of Ford's family hostage. The hostage delusion took firm hold and expanded, until Ford was reporting that 135 of his friends and family were being held hostage in the prison, and that only he could help them. By "day 287" of the "hostage crisis," the list of hostages had expanded to include "senators, Senator Kennedy, and many other leaders." In a letter to the Attorney General of Florida, written in 1983, Ford appeared to assume authority for ending the "crisis," claiming to have fired a number of prison officials. He began to refer to himself as "Pope John Paul, III," and reported having appointed nine new Justices to the Florida Supreme Court.

Counsel for Ford asked a psychiatrist who had examined Ford earlier, Dr. Jamal Amin, to continue seeing him and to recommend appropriate treatment. On the basis of roughly 14 months of evaluation, taped conversations between Ford and his attorneys, letters written by Ford, interviews with Ford's acquaintances, and various medical records, Dr. Amin concluded in 1983 that Ford suffered from "a severe, uncontrollable, mental disease which closely resembles 'Paranoid Schizophrenia With Suicide Potential' "—a major mental disorder . . . severe enough to substantially affect Mr. Ford's present ability to assist in the defense of his life."

Ford subsequently refused to see Dr. Amin again, believing him to have joined the conspiracy against him, and Ford's counsel sought assistance from Dr. Harold Kaufman, who interviewed Ford in November 1983. Ford told Dr. Kaufman that "I know there is some sort of death penalty, but I'm free to go whenever I want, because it would be illegal and the executioner would be executed." When asked if he would be executed, Ford replied: "I can't be executed because of the landmark case. I won. Ford v. State will prevent executions all over." These statements appeared amidst long streams of seemingly unrelated thoughts in rapid succession. Dr. Kaufman concluded that Ford had no understanding of why he was being executed, made no connection between the homicide of which he had been convicted and the death penalty, and indeed sincerely believed that he would not be executed because he owned the prisons and could control the Governor through mind waves. Dr. Kaufman found that there was "no reasonable possibility that Mr. Ford was dissembling, malingering or otherwise putting on a performance. . . ." The following month, in an interview with his attorneys, Ford regressed further into nearly complete incomprehensibility, speaking only in a code characterized by intermittent use of the word "one," making statements such as "Hands one, face one. Mafia one. God one, father one, Pope one. Pope one. Leader one."

Counsel for Ford invoked the procedures of Florida law governing the determination of competency of a condemned inmate, Fla. Stat. § 922.07 (1985). Following the procedures set forth in the statute, the Governor of Florida appointed a panel of three psychiatrists to evaluate whether, under § 922.07(2), Ford had "the mental capacity to understand the nature of the death penalty and the reasons why it was imposed upon him." At a single meeting, the three psychiatrists together interviewed Ford for approximately 30 minutes. Each doctor then filed a separate two- or three-page report with the Governor, to whom the statute delegates the final decision. One doctor concluded that Ford suffered from "psychosis with paranoia," but had "enough cognitive functioning to understand the nature and the effects of the death penalty, and why it is to be imposed on him." Another found that, although Ford was "psychotic," he did "know fully what can happen to him." The third concluded that Ford had a "severe adaptational disorder," but did "comprehend his total situation including being sentenced to death, and all of the implications of that penalty." He believed that Ford's disorder, "although severe, seem[ed] contrived and recently learned." Thus, the interview produced three different diagnoses, but accord on the question of sanity as defined by state law.

The Governor's decision was announced on April 30, 1984, when, without explanation or statement, he signed a death warrant for Ford's execution. Ford's attorneys unsuccessfully sought a hearing in state court to determine anew Ford's competency to suffer execution. Counsel then filed a petition for habeas corpus in the United States District Court for the Southern District of Florida, seeking an evidentiary hearing on the question of Ford's sanity, proffering the conflicting findings of the Governor-appointed commission and subsequent challenges to their methods by other psychiatrists. The District Court denied the petition without a hearing.

This Court granted Ford's petition for certiorari in order to resolve the important issue whether the Eighth Amendment prohibits the execution of the insane and, if so, whether the District Court should have held a hearing on petitioner's claim.

II

Since this Court last had occasion to consider the infliction of the death penalty upon the insane, our interpretations of the Due Process Clause and the Eighth Amendment have evolved substantially. There is now little room for doubt that the Eighth Amendment's ban on cruel and unusual punishment embraces, at a minimum, those modes or acts of punishment that had been considered cruel and unusual at the time that the Bill of Rights was adopted.

Moreover, the Eighth Amendment's proscriptions are not limited to those practices condemned by the common law in 1789. Not bound by the sparing humanitarian concessions of our forebears, the Amendment also recognizes the "evolving standards of decency that mark the progress of a maturing society." In addition to considering the barbarous methods generally outlawed in the 18th century, therefore, this Court takes into account objective evidence of contemporary values before determining whether a particular punishment comports with the fundamental human dignity that the Amendment protects.

A

We begin, then, with the common law. The bar against executing a prisoner who has lost his sanity bears impressive historical credentials; the practice consistently has been branded "savage and inhuman."

Sir Edward Coke had earlier expressed the same view of the common law of England: "[B]y intendment of Law, the execution of the offender is for example, . . . but so it is not when a mad man is executed, but should be a miserable spectacle, both against Law, and of extream [*sic*] inhumanity and cruelty, and can be no example to others." Further indications suggest that this solid proscription was carried to America, where it was early observed that "the judge is bound" to stay the execution upon insanity of the prisoner.

B

This ancestral legacy has not outlived its time. Today, no State in the Union permits the execution of the insane. It is clear that the ancient and humane limitation upon the State's ability to execute its sentences has as firm a hold upon the jurisprudence of today as it had centuries ago in England. The various reasons put forth in support of the common law restriction have no less logical, moral, and practical force than they did when first voiced. For today, no less than before, we may seriously question the retributive value of executing a person who has no comprehension of why he has been singled out and stripped of his fundamental right to life. Similarly, the natural abhorrence civilized societies feel at killing one who has no capacity to come to grips with his own conscience or deity is still vivid today. And the intuition that such an execution simply offends humanity is evidently shared across this Nation. Faced with such widespread evidence of a restriction upon sovereign power, this Court is compelled to conclude that the Eighth Amendment prohibits a State from carrying out a sentence of death upon a prisoner who is insane. Whether its aim be to protect the condemned from fear and pain without comfort of understanding, or to protect the dignity of society itself from the barbarity of exacting mindless vengeance, the restriction finds enforcement in the Eighth Amendment.

III

The Eighth Amendment prohibits the State from inflicting the penalty of death upon a prisoner who is insane. Petitioner's allegation of insanity in his habeas corpus petition, if proved, therefore, would bar his execution. The question before us is whether the District Court was under an obligation to hold an evidentiary hearing on the question of Ford's sanity. In answering that question, we bear in mind that, while the underlying social values encompassed by the Eighth Amendment are rooted in historical traditions, the manner in which our judicial system protects those values is purely a matter of contemporary law. Once a substantive right or restriction is recognized in the Constitution, therefore, its enforcement is in no way confined to the rudimentary process deemed adequate in ages past.

[. . .]

C

Florida law directs the Governor, when informed that a person under sentence of death may be insane, to stay the execution and appoint a commission of three psychiatrists to examine the prisoner. "The examination of the convicted person shall take place with all three psychiatrists present at the same time." After receiving the report of the commission, the Governor must determine whether "the convicted person has the mental capacity to understand the nature of the death penalty and the reasons why it was imposed on him." If the Governor finds that the prisoner has that capacity, then a death warrant is issued; if not, then the prisoner is committed to a mental health facility. The procedure is conducted wholly within the executive branch, *ex parte*, and provides the exclusive means for determining sanity.

After submission of the reports of the three examining psychiatrists, reaching conflicting diagnoses but agreeing on the ultimate issue of competency, Ford's counsel attempted to submit to the Governor some other written materials, including the reports of the two other psychiatrists who had examined Ford at greater length, one of whom had concluded that the prisoner was not competent to suffer execution. The Governor's office refused to inform counsel whether the submission would be considered. The Governor subsequently issued his decision in the form of a death warrant. That this most cursory form of procedural review fails to achieve even the minimal degree of reliability required for the protection of any constitutional interest, and thus falls short of adequacy under *Townsend*, is self-evident.

IV

The first deficiency in Florida's procedure lies in its failure to include the prisoner in the truth-seeking process. It would be odd were we now to abandon our insistence upon unfettered presentation of relevant information, before the final fact antecedent to execution has been found. Rather, consistent with the heightened concern for fairness and accuracy that has characterized our review of the process requisite to the taking of a human life, we believe that any procedure that precludes the prisoner or his counsel from presenting material relevant to his sanity or bars consideration of that material by the fact finder is necessarily inadequate.

A related flaw in the Florida procedure is the denial of any opportunity to challenge or impeach the state-appointed psychiatrists' opinions. "[C] ross-examination . . . is beyond any doubt the greatest legal engine ever invented for the discovery of truth." The failure of the Florida procedure to afford the prisoner's representative any opportunity to clarify or challenge the state experts' opinions or methods creates a significant possibility that the ultimate decision made in reliance on those experts will be distorted.

Perhaps the most striking defect in the procedures of Fla. Stat. § 922.07, as noted earlier, is the State's placement of the decision wholly within the executive branch. Under this procedure, the person who appoints the experts and ultimately decides whether the State will be able to carry out the sentence that it has long sought is the Governor, whose subordinates have been responsible for initiating every stage of the prosecution of the condemned, from arrest through sentencing. The commander of the State's corps of prosecutors cannot be said to have the neutrality that is necessary for reliability in the fact-finding proceeding.

Having identified various failings of the Florida scheme, we must conclude that the State's procedures for determining sanity are inadequate to preclude federal redetermination of the constitutional issue. We do not here suggest that only a full trial on the issue of sanity will suffice to protect the federal interests; we leave to the State the task of developing appropriate ways to enforce the constitutional restriction upon its execution of sentences.

Yet the lodestar of any effort to devise a procedure must be the overriding dual imperative of providing redress for those with substantial claims and of encouraging accuracy in the fact-finding determination. The stakes are high, and the "evidence" will always be imprecise. It is all the more important that the adversary presentation of relevant information be as unrestricted as possible. Also essential is that the manner of selecting and using the experts responsible for producing that "evidence" be conducive to the formation of neutral, sound, and professional judgments as to the prisoner's ability to comprehend the nature of the penalty. Fidelity to these principles is the solemn obligation of a civilized society.

[. . .]

Today we have explicitly recognized in our law a principle that has long resided there. It is no less abhorrent today than it has been for centuries to exact in penance the life of one whose mental illness prevents him from comprehending the reasons for the penalty or its implications. In light of the clear need for trustworthiness in any factual finding that will prevent or permit the carrying out of an execution, we hold that Fla. Stat. § 922.07 provides inadequate assurances of accuracy. Having been denied a factfinding procedure "adequate to afford a full and fair hearing" on the critical issue, petitioner is entitled to an evidentiary hearing in the District Court, *de novo*, on the question of his competence to be executed.

The judgment of the Court of Appeals is reversed, and the case is remanded for further proceedings consistent with this opinion.

JUSTICE POWELL filed an opinion concurring in part and concurring in the judgment.

While the procedures followed by Florida in this case do not comport with basic fairness, I would not require the kind of full-scale "sanity trial" that JUSTICE MARSHALL appears to find necessary. Due process is a flexible concept, requiring only "such procedural protections as the particular situation demands." In this instance, a number of considerations support the conclusion that the requirements of due process are not as elaborate as JUSTICE MARSHALL suggests.

First, the Eighth Amendment claim at issue can arise only after the prisoner has been validly convicted of a capital crime and sentenced to death. Thus, in this case, the State has a substantial and legitimate interest in taking petitioner's life as punishment for his crime. That interest is not called into question by petitioner's claim. Rather, the only question raised is not whether, but when, his execution may take place. This question is important, but it is not comparable to the antecedent question whether petitioner should be executed at all. It follows that this Court's decisions imposing heightened procedural requirements on capital trials and sentencing proceedings do not apply in this context.

Second, petitioner does not make his claim of insanity against a neutral background. On the contrary, in order to have been convicted and sentenced, petitioner must have been judged competent to stand trial, or his competency must have been sufficiently clear as not to raise a serious question for the trial court. The State therefore may properly presume that petitioner remains sane at the time sentence is to be carried out, and may require a substantial threshold showing of insanity merely to trigger the hearing process.

Finally, the sanity issue in this type of case does not resemble the basic issues at trial or sentencing. Unlike issues of historical fact, the question of petitioner's sanity calls for a basically subjective judgment. And unlike the determination of whether the death penalty is appropriate in a particular case, the competency determination depends substantially on expert analysis in a discipline fraught with "subtleties and nuances." This combination of factors means that ordinary adversarial procedures—complete with live testimony, cross-examination, and oral argument by counsel—are not necessarily the best means of arriving at sound, consistent judgments as to a defendant's sanity.

JUSTICE O'CONNOR filed an opinion concurring in the result in part and dissenting in part, joined by JUSTICE WHITE

I am in full agreement with JUSTICE REHNQUIST's conclusion that the Eighth Amendment does not create a substantive right not to be executed while insane. Accordingly, I do not join the Court's reasoning or opinion. Because, however, the conclusion is for me inescapable that Florida positive law has created a protected liberty interest in avoiding execution while incompetent, and because Florida does not provide even those minimal procedural protections required by due process in this area, I would vacate the judgment and remand to the Court of Appeals with directions that the case be returned to the Florida system so that a hearing can be held in a manner consistent with the requirements of the Due Process Clause. I cannot agree, however, that the federal courts should have any role whatever in the substantive determination of a defendant's competency to be executed.

JUSTICE REHNQUIST dissented, joined by CHIEF JUSTICE BURGER.

The Court today holds that the Eighth Amendment prohibits a State from carrying out a lawfully imposed sentence of death upon a person who is currently insane. This holding is based almost entirely on two unremarkable observations. First, the Court states that it "know[s] of virtually no authority condoning the execution of the insane at English common law." Second, it notes that "[t]oday, no State in the Union permits the execution of the insane." Armed with these facts, and shielded by the claim that it is simply "keep[ing] faith with our common law heritage," the Court proceeds to cast aside settled precedent and to significantly alter both the common law and current practice of not executing the insane. It manages this feat by carefully ignoring the fact that the Florida scheme it finds unconstitutional, in which the Governor is assigned the ultimate responsibility of deciding whether a condemned prisoner is currently insane, is fully consistent with the "common law heritage" and current practice on which the Court purports to rely.

The Court places great weight on the "impressive historical credentials" of the common law bar against executing a prisoner who has lost his sanity. What it fails to mention, however, is the equally important and unchallenged fact that, at common law, it was the executive who passed upon the sanity of the condemned. So when the Court today creates a constitutional right to a determination of sanity outside of the executive branch, it does so not in keeping with, but at the expense of, "our common law heritage."

Since no State sanctions execution of the insane, the real battle being fought in this case is over what procedures must accompany the inquiry into sanity. The Court reaches the result it does by examining the common law, creating a constitutional right that no State seeks to violate, and then concluding that the common law procedures are inadequate to protect the newly created but common-law-based right. I find it unnecessary to "constitutionalize" the already uniform view that the insane should not be executed, and inappropriate to "selectively incorporate" the common law practice. I therefore dissent.

ATKINS v. VIRGINIA, 536 U.S. 304 (2002)

JUSTICE STEVENS delivered the opinion of the Court, joined by JUSTICES O'CONNOR, KENNEDY, SOUTER, GINSBURG, and BREYER.

Those mentally retarded persons who meet the law's requirements for criminal responsibility should be tried and punished when they commit crimes. Because of their disabilities in areas of reasoning, judgment, and control of their impulses, however, they do not act with the level of moral culpability that characterizes the most serious adult criminal conduct. Moreover, their impairments can jeopardize the reliability and fairness of capital proceedings against mentally retarded defendants. Presumably for these reasons, in the 13 years since we decided *Penry*, the American public, legislators, scholars, and judges have deliberated over the question whether the death penalty should ever be imposed on a mentally retarded criminal. The consensus reflected in those deliberations informs our answer to the question presented by this case: whether such executions are "cruel and unusual punishments" prohibited by the Eighth Amendment to the Federal Constitution.

I

Petitioner, Daryl Renard Atkins, was convicted of abduction, armed robbery, and capital murder, and sentenced to death. At approximately midnight on August 16, 1996, Atkins and William Jones, armed with a semiautomatic handgun, abducted Eric Nesbitt, robbed him of the money on his person, drove him to an automated teller machine in his pickup truck where cameras recorded their withdrawal of additional cash, then took him to an isolated location where he was shot eight times and killed.

Jones and Atkins both testified in the guilt phase of Atkins' trial. Each confirmed most of the details in the other's account of the incident, with the important exception that each stated that the other had actually shot and killed Nesbitt. Jones' testimony, which was both more coherent and credible than Atkins', was obviously credited by the jury and was sufficient to establish Atkins' guilt. At the penalty phase of the trial, the State introduced victim impact evidence and proved two aggravating circumstances: future dangerousness and "vileness of the offense." To prove future dangerousness, the State relied on Atkins' prior felony convictions as well as the testimony of four victims of earlier robberies and assaults. To prove the second aggravator, the prosecution relied upon the trial record, including pictures of the deceased's body and the autopsy report.

In the penalty phase, the defense relied on one witness, Dr. Evan Nelson, a forensic psychologist who had evaluated Atkins before trial and concluded that he was "mildly mentally retarded." His conclusion was based on interviews with people who knew Atkins, a review of school and court records, and the administration of a standard intelligence test which indicated that Atkins had a full scale IQ of 59.

The jury sentenced Atkins to death.

The Supreme Court of Virginia affirmed the imposition of the death penalty. Because of the gravity of the concerns expressed by the dissenters, and in light of the dramatic shift in the state legislative landscape that has occurred in the past 13 years, we granted certiorari to revisit the issue that we first addressed in the *Penry* case.

II

A claim that punishment is excessive is judged not by the standards that prevailed in 1685 when Lord Jeffreys presided over the "Bloody Assizes" or when the Bill of Rights was adopted, but rather by those that currently prevail.

Proportionality review under those evolving standards should be informed by " 'objective factors to the maximum possible extent.' " We have pinpointed that the "clearest and most reliable objective evidence of contemporary values is the legislation enacted by the country's legislatures" [so] we shall first review the judgment of legislatures that have addressed the suitability of imposing the death penalty on the mentally retarded and then consider reasons for agreeing or disagreeing with their judgment.

III

The parties have not called our attention to any state legislative consideration of the suitability of imposing the death penalty on mentally retarded offenders prior to 1986. In that year, the public reaction to the execution of a mentally retarded murderer in Georgia apparently led to the enactment of the first state statute prohibiting such executions. In 1988, when Congress enacted legislation reinstating the federal death penalty, it expressly provided that a "sentence of death shall not be carried out upon a person who is mentally retarded." In 1989, Maryland enacted a similar prohibition. It was in that year that we decided *Penry*, and concluded that those two state enactments, "even when added to the 14 States that have rejected capital punishment completely, do not provide sufficient evidence at present of a national consensus."

Much has changed since then. Responding to the national attention received by the Bowden execution and our decision in *Penry*, state legislatures across the country began to address the issue. In 1990, Kentucky and Tennessee enacted statutes similar to those in Georgia and Maryland, as did New Mexico in 1991, and Arkansas, Colorado, Washington, Indiana, and Kansas in 1993 and 1994. In 1995, when New York reinstated its death penalty, it emulated the Federal Government by expressly exempting the mentally retarded. Nebraska followed suit in 1998. There appear to have been no similar enactments during the next two years, but in 2000 and 2001 six more States—South Dakota, Arizona, Connecticut, Florida, Missouri, and North Carolina—joined the procession. The Texas Legislature unanimously adopted a similar bill, and bills have passed at least one house in other States, including Virginia and Nevada.

It is not so much the number of these States that is significant, but the consistency of the direction of change. Given the well-known fact that anticrime legislation is far more popular than legislation providing protections for persons guilty of violent crime, the large number of States prohibiting the execution of mentally retarded persons (and the complete absence of States passing legislation reinstating the power to conduct such executions) provides powerful evidence that today our society views mentally retarded offenders as categorically less culpable than the average criminal. The evidence carries even greater force when it is noted that the legislatures that have addressed the issue have voted overwhelmingly in favor of the prohibition. Moreover, even in those States that allow the execution of mentally retarded offenders, the practice is uncommon. Some States, for example New Hampshire and New Jersey, continue to authorize executions, but none have been carried out in decades. Thus there is little need to pursue legislation barring the execution of the mentally retarded in those States. And it appears that even among those States that regularly execute offenders and that have no prohibition with regard to the mentally retarded, only five have executed offenders possessing a known IQ less than 70 since we decided Penry. The practice, therefore, has become truly unusual, and it is fair to say that a national consensus has developed against it.

To the extent there is serious disagreement about the execution of mentally retarded offenders, it is in determining which offenders are in fact retarded. In this case, for instance, the Commonwealth of Virginia disputes that Atkins suffers from mental retardation. Not all people who claim to be mentally retarded will be so impaired as to fall within the range of mentally retarded offenders about whom there is a national consensus. As was our approach in *Ford* with regard to insanity, "we leave to the State[s] the task of developing appropriate ways to enforce the constitutional restriction upon [their] execution of sentences."

IV

This consensus unquestionably reflects widespread judgment about the relative culpability of mentally retarded offenders, and the relationship between mental retardation and the penological purposes served by the death penalty. Additionally, it suggests that some characteristics of mental retardation undermine the strength of the procedural protections that our capital jurisprudence steadfastly guards.

As discussed above, clinical definitions of mental retardation require not only subaverage intellectual functioning, but also significant limitations in adaptive skills such as communication, self-care, and self-direction that became manifest before age 18. Mentally retarded persons frequently know the difference between right and wrong and are competent to stand trial. Because of their impairments, however, by definition they have diminished capacities to understand and process information, to communicate, to abstract from mistakes and learn from experience, to engage in logical reasoning, to control impulses, and to understand the reactions of others. There is no evidence that they are more likely to engage in criminal conduct than others, but there is abundant evidence that they often act on impulse rather than pursuant to a premeditated plan, and that in group settings they are followers rather than leaders. Their deficiencies do not warrant an exemption from criminal sanctions, but they do diminish their personal culpability.

Our independent evaluation of the issue reveals no reason to disagree with the judgment of "the legislatures that have recently addressed the matter" and concluded that death is not a suitable punishment for a mentally retarded criminal. We are not persuaded that the execution of mentally retarded criminals will measurably advance the deterrent or the retributive purpose of the death penalty. Construing and applying the Eighth Amendment in the light of our "evolving standards of decency," we therefore conclude that such punishment is excessive and that the Constitution "places a substantive restriction on the State's power to take the life" of a mentally retarded offender.

The judgment of the Virginia Supreme Court is reversed, and the case is remanded for further proceedings not inconsistent with this opinion.

CHIEF JUSTICE REHNQUIST filed a dissenting opinion, joined by JUSTICES SCALIA and THOMAS.

The question presented by this case is whether a national consensus deprives Virginia of the constitutional power to impose the death penalty on capital murder defendants like petitioner, i.e., those defendants who indisputably are competent to stand trial, aware of the punishment they are about to suffer and why, and whose mental retardation has been found an insufficiently compelling reason to lessen their individual responsibility for the crime. The Court pronounces the punishment cruel and unusual primarily because 18 States recently have passed laws limiting the death eligibility of certain defendants based on mental retardation alone, despite the fact that the laws of 19 other States besides Virginia continue to leave the question of proper punishment to the individuated consideration of sentencing judges or juries familiar with the particular offender and his or her crime.

I agree with JUSTICE SCALIA['s dissenting opinion], that the Court's assessment of the current legislative judgment regarding the execution of defendants like petitioner more resembles a post hoc rationalization for the majority's subjectively preferred result rather than any objective effort to ascertain the content of an evolving standard of decency. I write separately, however, to call attention to the defects in the Court's decision to place weight on foreign laws, the views of professional and religious organizations, and opinion polls in reaching its conclusion. The Court's suggestion that these sources are relevant to the constitutional question finds little support in our precedents and, in my view, is antithetical to considerations of federalism, which instruct that any "permanent prohibition upon all units of democratic government must [be apparent] in the operative acts (laws and the application of laws) that the people have approved." The Court's uncritical acceptance of the opinion poll data brought to our attention, moreover, warrants additional comment, because we lack sufficient information to conclude that the surveys were conducted in accordance with generally accepted scientific principles or are capable of supporting valid empirical inferences about the issue before us.

In my view, these two sources—the work product of legislatures and sentencing jury determinations—ought to be the sole indicators by which courts ascertain the contemporary American conceptions of decency for purposes of the Eighth Amendment. They are the only objective indicia of contemporary values firmly supported by our precedents. More importantly, however, they can be reconciled with the undeniable precepts that the democratic branches of government and individual sentencing juries are, by design, better suited than courts to evaluating and giving effect to the complex societal and moral considerations that inform the selection of publicly acceptable criminal punishments.

In reaching its conclusion today, the Court does not take notice of the fact that neither petitioner nor his amici have adduced any comprehensive statistics that would conclusively prove (or disprove) whether juries routinely consider death a disproportionate punishment for mentally retarded offenders like petitioner.

I fail to see, however, how the views of other countries regarding the punishment of their citizens provide any support for the Court's ultimate determination. While it is true that some of our prior opinions have looked to "the climate of international opinion" to reinforce a conclusion regarding evolving standards of decency; we have since explicitly rejected the idea that the sentencing practices of other countries could "serve to establish the first Eighth Amendment prerequisite, that [a] practice is accepted among our people."

To further buttress its appraisal of contemporary societal values, the Court marshals public opinion poll results and evidence that several professional organizations and religious groups have adopted official positions opposing the imposition of the death penalty upon mentally retarded offenders. (Citing Brief for American Psychological Association et al. as *Amici Curiae*; Brief for American Association on Mental Retardation et al. as *Amici Curiae*; noting that "representatives of widely diverse religious communities . . . reflecting Christian, Jewish, Muslim, and Buddhist traditions . . . 'share a conviction that the execution of persons with mental retardation cannot be morally justified' "; and stating that "polling data shows a widespread consensus among Americans . . . that executing the mentally retarded is wrong"). In my view, none should be accorded any weight on the Eighth Amendment scale when the elected representatives of a State's populace have not deemed them persuasive enough to prompt legislative action. In *Penry*, we were cited similar data and declined to take them into consideration where the "public sentiment expressed in [them]" had yet to find expression in state law. For the Court to rely on such data today serves only to illustrate its willingness to proscribe by judicial fiat—at the behest of private organizations speaking only for themselves—a punishment about which no across-the-board consensus has developed through the workings of normal democratic processes in the laboratories of the States.

Even if I were to accept the legitimacy of the Court's decision to reach beyond the product of legislatures and practices of sentencing juries to discern a national standard of decency, I would take issue with the blind-faith credence it accords the opinion polls brought to our attention.

JUSTICE SCALIA filed a dissenting opinion, joined by CHIEF JUSTICE REHNQUIST and JUSTICE THOMAS

Today's decision is the pinnacle of our Eighth Amendment death-is-different jurisprudence. Not only does it, like all of that jurisprudence, find no support in the text or history of the Eighth Amendment; it does not even have support in current social attitudes regarding the conditions that render an otherwise just death penalty inappropriate. Seldom has an opinion of this Court rested so obviously upon nothing but the personal views of its Members.

II

The Court makes no pretense that execution of the mildly mentally retarded would have been considered "cruel and unusual" in 1791. Only the severely or profoundly mentally retarded, commonly known as "idiots," enjoyed any special status under the law at that time.

The Court is left to argue, therefore, that execution of the mildly retarded is inconsistent with the "evolving standards of decency that mark the progress of a maturing society." Before today, our opinions consistently emphasized that Eighth Amendment judgments regarding the existence of social "standards" "should be informed by objective factors to the maximum possible extent" and "should not be, or appear to be, merely the subjective views of individual Justices."

The Court pays lip service to these precedents as it miraculously extracts a "national consensus" forbidding execution of the mentally retarded from the fact that 18 States—less than half (47%) of the 38 States that permit capital punishment (for whom the issue exists)—have very recently enacted legislation barring execution of the mentally retarded. Even that 47% figure is a distorted one. If one is to say, as the Court does today, that all executions of the mentally retarded are so morally repugnant as to violate our national "standards of decency," surely the "consensus" it points to must be one that has set its righteous face against all such executions. Not 18 States, but only 7—18% of death penalty jurisdictions—have legislation of that scope. Eleven of those that the Court counts enacted statutes prohibiting execution of mentally retarded defendants convicted after, or convicted of crimes committed after, the effective date of the legislation; those already on death row, or consigned there before the statute's effective date, or even (in those States using the date of the crime as the criterion of retroactivity) tried in the future for murders committed many years ago, could be put to death. That is not a statement of absolute moral repugnance, but one of current preference between two tolerable approaches. Two of these States permit execution of the mentally retarded in other situations as well: Kansas apparently permits execution of all except the severely mentally retarded.

But let us accept, for the sake of argument, the Court's faulty count. That bare number of States alone—18—should be enough to convince any reasonable person that no "national consensus" exists. How is it possible that agreement among 47% of the death penalty jurisdictions amounts to "consensus"? Our prior cases have generally required a much higher degree of agreement before finding a punishment cruel and unusual on "evolving standards" grounds.

Moreover, a major factor that the Court entirely disregards is that the legislation of all 18 States it relies on is still in its infancy. The oldest of the statutes is only 14 years old; five were enacted last year; over half were enacted within the past eight years. Few, if any, of the States have had sufficient experience with these laws to know whether they are sensible in the long term. It is "myopic to base sweeping constitutional principles upon the narrow experience of [a few] years."

The Court attempts to bolster its embarrassingly feeble evidence of "consensus" with the following: "It is not so much the number of these States that is significant, but the consistency of the direction of change." But in what other direction could we possibly see change? Given that 14 years ago all the death penalty statutes included the mentally retarded, any change (except precipitate undoing of what had just been done) was bound to be in the one direction the Court finds significant enough to overcome the lack of real consensus. That is to say, to be accurate the Court's "consistency-of-the-direction-of-change" point should be recast into the following unimpressive observation: "No State has yet undone its exemption of the mentally retarded, one for as long as 14 whole years." In any event, reliance upon "trends," even those of much longer duration than a mere 14 years, is a perilous basis for constitutional adjudication.

But the Prize for the Court's Most Feeble Effort to fabricate "national consensus" must go to its appeal (deservedly relegated to a footnote) to the views of assorted professional and religious organizations, members of the so-called "world community," and respondents to opinion polls.

III

Beyond the empty talk of a "national consensus," the Court gives us a brief glimpse of what really underlies today's decision: pretension to a power confined neither by the moral sentiments originally enshrined in the Eighth

Amendment (its original meaning) nor even by the current moral sentiments of the American people.

[. . .]

The Court throws one last factor into its grab bag of reasons why execution of the retarded is "excessive" in all cases:

Mentally retarded offenders "face a special risk of wrongful execution" because they are less able "to make a persuasive showing of mitigation," "to give meaningful assistance to their counsel," and to be effective witnesses.

"Special risk" is pretty flabby language (even flabbier than "less likely")—and I suppose a similar "special risk" could be said to exist for just plain stupid people, inarticulate people, even ugly people. If this unsupported claim has any substance to it (which I doubt), it might support a due process claim in all criminal prosecutions of the mentally retarded; but it is hard to see how it has anything to do with an Eighth Amendment claim that execution of the mentally retarded is cruel and unusual. We have never before held it to be cruel and unusual punishment to impose a sentence in violation of some other constitutional imperative.

Today's opinion adds one more to the long list of substantive and procedural requirements impeding imposition of the death penalty imposed under this Court's assumed power to invent a death-is-different jurisprudence. None of those requirements existed when the Eighth Amendment was adopted, and some of them were not even supported by current moral consensus.

This newest invention promises to be more effective than any of the others in turning the process of capital trial into a game. One need only read the definitions of mental retardation adopted by the American Association on Mental Retardation and the American Psychiatric Association to realize that the symptoms of this condition can readily be feigned. And whereas the capital defendant who feigns insanity risks commitment to a mental institution until he can be cured (and then tried and executed), the capital defendant who feigns mental retardation risks nothing at all.

8

EXECUTION PROTOCOLS

The U.S. Supreme Court has long recognized that certain methods of execution are categorically off-limits, particularly punishments of pre-Enlightened torture clearly abhorred during the framing of the Constitution. It has held that if a punishment were manifestly cruel and unusual (such as burning at the stake, crucifixion, or breaking on the wheel), it would clearly fall within the Eighth Amendment's ban. The Court has, however, never in its history invalidated a State's chosen procedure for carrying out a sentence of death as the infliction of cruel and unusual punishment (although many states have curtailed certain methods either judicially or by statute). Hanging, for example, is no longer provided for on the statute books of any legislature. Delaware and Washington were the last to repeal it, along with their states' death penalties entirely, in 2016 and 2018, respectively. Lethal injection has been, by some margin, the most prolific method of implementing the death penalty in the United States since 1976, with 1,419 of 1,601 (89%) of executions carried out by that protocol at the time of writing (October 2024). Second is the electric chair, at 163 executions, trailed distantly by lethal gas with 13 and finally, 3 by firing squad (although the last such execution, of Ronnie Gardner in Utah, was carried out in 2010).

Early death penalty methods

Death penalty methods have very seldom been reviewed by the Supreme Court; indeed, it has considered the constitutionality of a specific method of execution on only five occasions: Each of these will be taken in turn. Instead, judicial deference to state legislatures has prevailed in this category,

DOI: 10.4324/9780429398780-9

allowing them to determine the appropriateness of different techniques for implementing capital sentences. One significant early precedent is ***WILKERSON v. UTAH***, 99 U.S. 130 (1878). Wilkerson had been convicted and sentenced to death by firing squad under Utah law, which he appealed as cruel and unusual. The Court noted that "[d]ifficulty would attend the effort to define with exactness the extent of the constitutional provision which provides that cruel and unusual punishments shall not be inflicted," but concluded that it was safe to affirm that torture and punishments that are unnecessarily cruel were in scope. In this instance, the firing squad was not one that failed muster, not least because of its widespread acceptance and practice as a sentence for military crimes sentenced by courts-martial.

Death by hanging was the method of choice of capital sentencers from the foundation of the Union to the early 20th century, when a more publicly appeasing mode was sought. The change was introduced after numerous botched hangings in the late 19th century, giving rise to the observation that it was the public's perception of decency that drove this shift. In 1888, following the recommendation of a commission tasked by the Governor to find the most humane and practical method known to modern science of carrying into effect the sentence of death, New York became the first state to authorize electrocution. By 1915, 11 other states had followed suit, motivated by the well-grounded belief that electrocution is less painful and more humane than hanging. In declining to consider the Eighth Amendment's Punishments Clause relevant, the Court sanctioned this new method's use when handing down ***IN RE KEMMLER***, 136 U.S. 436 (1890). William Kemmler murdered his girlfriend in 1889 and was convicted within weeks, sentenced to death, and destined to become the first person executed by the new electric chair.

The plan to execute Kemmler was embroiled in the *War of the Currents* between Thomas Edison (who had created the Direct Current—DC—method of power transmission) and rival George Westinghouse (who introduced Alternating Current—AC—distribution). As AC had a much higher voltage, it was a Westinghouse generator that would be used to implement this new method, which Edison would portray as the *executioner's current* to undermine its public attraction. Indeed, the *New York Times* proposed *Westinghoused* as the term for this new method (Edison agreed, but *electrocution* was instead adopted) (Moran, 2002, pp. xxi–xxii). Westinghouse supported Kemmler's judicial appeal and attempted to prevent AC from being used to put him to death. While the Supreme Court remained silent on the question of the Eighth Amendment's application in *Kemmler*, it stated that a constitutional test for *cruelty* is a punishment that involves "torture or a lingering death," which was not—it held—provoked by the new electric chair. Death "is not cruel within the meaning of that word as used in the Constitution. It implies there [*sic*] something inhuman and barbarous—something more than the mere extinguishment of life," Chief Justice Fuller's majority ruling concluded. Kemmler was electrocuted soon after, with the national press citing the case ingloriously: The *New York Times* ran with the headline "Far Worse than Hanging: Kemmler's Death Proves an Awful Spectacle" (New York Times, 1890), and the *Washington Post* opting for "'Great God, he is alive!': The first man executed by electric chair died slower than Thomas Edison expected" (Washington Post, 1890).

Half a century later, the Court had the opportunity to review the constitutionality of the electric chair, which had become the most prolific method of execution in the intervening decades. In ***LOUISIANA EX REL. FRANCIS v. RESWEBER***, 329 U.S. 459 (1947), the Court considered the case of Willie Francis, a 16-year-old Black youth who had been sentenced to death for murder. When carrying out his sentence, the state failed to kill him, instead subjecting Francis to a period of violent electrocution while strapped to a chair. The Court considered whether, alongside a double jeopardy question under the Fifth Amendment, subjecting Francis to a second electrocution attempt was cruel and unusual and therefore unconstitutional. Upholding the sentence, the Court held that the case did not call for an examination into any punishments: The psychological strain of preparation for the first electrocution was irrelevant, as his subsequent execution stood on its own as a constitutional punishment. The botched first attempt was, therefore, "an unforeseeable accident" and did not add an element of unlawful cruelty, as any unnecessary pain was inflicted unintentionally. Equipment failure does not bring due process into play, nor does it engage the Eighth's Punishments Clause, which refers to cruelty in method, "not that cruelty which is part of the actual suffering accompanying a lawful sentence of death." Justice Burton's three-judge dissent would have held that the result was relevant, not the intent: "It was the statutory duty of the state officials to make sure that there was no failure," and the high standard of care required to ensure constitutionality had not been discharged in this case. Indeed, the dissent claimed, this was an "unconditional requirement" in the state statute, namely "a single continued application of the current until death results"—something Resweber would receive, in finality, the following year.

The lethal injection

In 1977, legislators in Oklahoma, after consulting with the head of the anesthesiology department at the University of Oklahoma College of Medicine, introduced the first bill proposing lethal injection as the State's method of execution. This swiftly replaced the electric chair as the primary method for executions, a status it retains today in all 27 states with the death penalty, plus the federal government and the military. Primarily carried out by a three-drug cocktail, this "protocol" was first seen to prevent unnecessary pain or suffering by combining the use of the barbiturate sodium thiopental, followed by the muscle relaxant pancuronium bromide, and finally the cardiac-arrest-inducing electrolyte potassium chloride. The Supreme Court reviewed this method for the first time in 2008, the fourth and final instance of it considering the constitutionality of a specific method of execution. In that case, ***BAZE v. REES***, 553 U.S. 35 (2008), the Court held that—insofar as the method did not present a "substantial" or "objectively intolerable" risk of serious harm—it passed constitutional muster under the Eighth Amendment.

The judgment in *Baze* is lengthy, with seven opinions, all failing to carry a majority. Chief Justice Roberts's plurality (joined by Justices Kennedy and Alito in *Baze* and representing a 7–2 holding on the constitutional question) has since been confirmed as controlling.[1] This set a standard that asked whether the method creates an untoward, readily avoidable risk of inflicting severe and unnecessary suffering, considering (1) the degree of risk, (2) the magnitude of pain, and (3) the availability of alternatives. In sum, death itself is not a form of serious and intolerable harm, and lawful capital punishment must have a means of being carried out. The prevailing method of the day, lethal injection, was therefore a legitimate tool to implement a constitutionally proper sentence. In dissent, Justices Ginsburg and Souter would have stuck down Kentucky's statute, arguing that its protocol lacks basic safeguards used by other States to confirm that an inmate is unconscious before injection of the second and third drugs. The *Baze* plurality did not agree with this review, representing a finger on the scale against professional consensus—reviewed in the previous chapter and controlling in "class of offender" cases, particularly regarding intellectual disabilities. Federal courts, Chief Justice Roberts held, should not "embroil [themselves] in ongoing scientific controversies beyond their expertise." The Court was satisfied that the three-drug protocol provided sufficient guarantees, as laid out in detailed legislative schemes, and the issue was seemingly put to sleep. From 2012 to 2015, however, the lethal injection controversy reignited and the post-*Baze* capital picture blurred. Following a nationwide shortage of the three-drug protocol's first two ingredients—sodium thiopental and pancuronium bromide—the states most active in implementing the death penalty altered their lethal drug protocols. Eight states used a single drug for their post-*Baze* executions, with six more announcing similar plans. Moreover, 14 states used pentobarbital in executions, which was heavily criticized as creating an extreme risk of serious harm. This morbid

1 In *Glossip v. Gross*, 576 U.S. 863 (2015).

creativity reached Supreme Court review in 2015, where the Justices heard a challenge to Oklahoma's single-drug protocol.

In that case, ***GLOSSIP v. GROSS***, 576 U.S. 863 (2015), the petitioner alleged that the new scheme would offend the Constitution's proscription of cruel and unusual punishments if they neglected to provide a protocol substantially similar to that considered in *Baze*. While the case had the potential to provide wide-ranging consequences to the abundance of *Baze*-deficient capital statutes across the United States, Justice Alito took the opportunity to block any such argument. In the face of an abundance of scientific professional consensus proffered by *amicus* briefs, Alito condemned their "outlandish rhetoric," dismissing the claim with narrow support from a 5–4 majority. They held that a death row inmate seeking an injunction under the Eighth Amendment against the use of a certain execution method must show that the risk of harm caused by the method is substantial in comparison to a known and available alternative. Moreover, the Court concluded that a requirement of all Eighth Amendment method-of-execution claims was that prisoners must identify a known and available alternative method of execution that entails a lesser risk of pain. Therefore, a method is constitutional as long as the state applying it has used adequate safeguards to minimize risks. This was later clarified in *Bucklew v. Precythe*, 139 S. Ct. 1112 (2019), where a 5–4 majority led by Justice Gorsuch upheld Missouri's use of lethal injection in spite of the death row inmate's assertion—only made after the trial court insisted that the inmate identify an alternative method of execution by which he could be put to death—that execution by nitrogen gas would be less painful. As with other areas of Eighth Amendment law, which are outlined in Chapter 11, what that Amendment prohibits is wanton exposure to "objectively intolerable risk," not merely the possibility of pain.

21st-century innovation

Bucklew has been followed by consistent denials of review by the Court in lethal injection cases,[2] including in permitting the execution by the Federal Government of two inmates in early 2021 who had tested positive for COVID-19 shortly before their sentences were carried out, despite claims that lung damage caused by the virus substantially increased the likelihood

2 For example, *Zagorski v. Parker*, 139 S. Ct. 11 (2018): Justice Sotomayor, dissenting from denial: "Once again, a State hastens to kill a prisoner despite mounting evidence that the sedative to be used, midazolam, will not prevent the prisoner from feeling as if he is "drowning, suffocating, and being burned alive from the inside out" during a process that could last as long as 18 minutes."

of suffering torturous effects if executed with pentobarbital. Further, in 2022, during three consecutive executions by lethal injection in Alabama, prison officials spent multiple hours digging for prisoners' veins in an attempt to set intravenous lines. Two of the men survived and reported experiencing extreme pain, including, in one case, nerve pain equivalent to electrocution. After those executions failed, the State began what it claimed would be a "top-to-bottom" review of its lethal injection process (see *Barber*, 2023).

While very seldom used, a small number of states still provide for the firing squad and the gas chamber as forms of capital punishment. These provisions generally reside in dormant statutes, which have not been invoked for several years: The firing squad has not been used since Utah executed Ronnie Gardner in 2010. Alabama is one of the two remaining states with a live gas chamber statute, carrying out three death-by-nitrogen executions in 2024 (the first since 1999). The recent supply issues and hysteria surrounding the lethal injection have reinvigorated efforts to renew, or in some cases, introduce, historic methods such as the gas chamber (after Oklahoma re-added it to their statute books in 2015). Legislation to introduce nitrogen hypoxia as an execution method is under review in Nebraska and Ohio, though both states have struggled to obtain lethal injection chemicals. It is yet to be seen whether private industrial gas distributors might likewise oppose supplying nitrogen gas for executions, harking back to the AC/DC and *Kemmler* battles surrounding the introduction of the electric chair 135 years ago.

References

Moran, R. (2002) Executioner's current: Thomas Edison, *George Westinghouse, and the invention of the electric chair*. New York: A.A. Knopf.

New York Times (1890) 'The electric chair, "far worse than hanging" ', *New York Times Archive*, 22 March. Available at: https://timesmachine.nytimes.com/timesmachine/1890/08/07/103256332.pdf

Washington Post (1890) '"Great god, he is alive!" The first man executed by electric chair died slower than Thomas Edison expected', *Washington Post Archive*, 22 March. Available at: www.washingtonpost.com/news/retropolis/wp/2017/04/26/thomas-edison-the-electric-chair-and-a-botched-execution-a-death-penalty-primer/

Cited cases

*Barber v. Governor of Ala*bama, 73 F. 4th 1306, 1326–27 (CAll, July 19, 2023).
Baze v. Rees, 553 U.S. 35 (2008).
Bucklew v. Precythe, 139 S. Ct. 1112 (2019).
Glossip v. Gross, 576 U.S. 863 (2015).
In re Kemmler, 136 U.S. 436 (1890).
Louisiana ex rel. Francis v. Resweber, 329 U.S. 459 (1947).
Wilkerson v. Utah, 99 U.S. 130 (1878).
Zagorski v. Parker, 139 S. Ct. 11 (2018).

WILKERSON v. UTAH, 99 U.S. 130 (1878)

JUSTICE CLIFFORD delivered the opinion of the Court.

Sufficient appears to show that the prisoner named in the record was legally charged with the willful, malicious, and premeditated murder of William Baxter with malice aforethought by indictment of the grand jury in due form of law, as fully set forth in the transcript, and that he, upon his arraignment, pleaded that he was not guilty of the alleged offense. Pursuant to the order of the court, a jury for the trial of the prisoner was duly impaneled and sworn, and it appears that the jury, after a full and fair trial, found, by their verdict, that the prisoner was guilty of murder in the first degree.

Provision is also made that every person guilty of murder in the first degree shall suffer death, or, upon the recommendation of the jury, may be imprisoned at hard labor in the penitentiary for life, at the discretion of the court, and that every person guilty of murder in the second degree shall be imprisoned at hard labor in the penitentiary for not less than five nor more than fifteen years.

Duly convicted of murder in the first degree as the prisoner was by the verdict of the jury, it is conceded that the existing law of the territory provides that he "shall suffer death" [. . .]

Construed as that provision must be in connection with the enactment that every person guilty of murder in the first degree shall suffer death, and in view of the fact that the laws of the territory contain no other specific regulation as to the mode of executing such a sentence, the court here is of the opinion that the assignment of error shows no legal ground for reversing the judgment of the court below. Authority to pass such a sentence is certainly not possessed by the circuit courts of the United States, as the act of Congress provides that the manner of inflicting the punishment of death shall be by hanging.

Punishments of the kind are always directed by the circuit courts to be inflicted in that manner, but organized territories are invested with legislative power which extends to all rightful subjects of legislation not inconsistent with the Constitution and laws of the United States. By virtue of that power the legislative branch of the territory may define offenses and prescribe the punishment of the offenders, subject to the prohibition of the Constitution that cruel and unusual punishments shall not be inflicted.

Good reasons exist for supposing that Congress never intended that the provision referred to, that the punishment of death shall be by hanging, should supersede the power of the territories to legislate upon the subject, as the congressional provision is a part of the first crimes act ever passed by the national legislature. Different statutory regulations existed in the territory for nearly a quarter of a century, and the usages of the army to the present day are that sentences of the kind may in certain cases be executed by shooting, and in others by hanging.

Offenses of various kinds are defined in the rules and articles of war where the offender, if duly convicted, may be sentenced to the death penalty. In some of those cases, the provision is that the accused, if convicted, shall suffer death, and in others the punishment to be awarded depends upon the finding of the court-martial; but in none of those cases is the mode of putting to death prescribed in the articles of war or the military regulations.

Repeated instances occur where the death penalty is prescribed in those articles; but the invariable enactment is that the person guilty of the offense shall suffer death, without any specification as to the mode in which the sentence shall be executed, and the regulations of the army are as silent in that respect as the rules and articles of war. Congress having made no regulations in that regard, the custom of war, says a learned writer upon the subject, has, in the absence of statutory law, determined that capital punishment be inflicted by shooting or hanging; and the same author adds to the effect that mutiny, meaning mutiny not resulting in loss of life, desertion, or other military crime, if a capital offense, is commonly punished by shooting; that a spy is always hanged, and that mutiny, if accompanied by loss of life, is punished in the same manner—that is, by hanging.

Military laws, says another learned author, do not say how a criminal offending against such laws shall be put to death, but leave it entirely to the custom of war, and his statement is that shooting or hanging is the method determined by such custom. Like the preceding author, he also proceeds to state that a spy is generally hanged, and that mutiny unaccompanied with loss of life is punished by the same means; and he also concurs with Benet, that desertion, disobedience of orders, or other capital crimes are usually punished by shooting, adding, that the mode in all cases—that is, either shooting or hanging—may be declared in the sentence.

Capital punishment, says the author first named, may be either by shooting or hanging. For mutiny, desertion, or other military crime, it is commonly by shooting; for murder not combined with mutiny, for treason, and piracy accompanied with wounding or attempt to murder, by hanging, as the sentence in England must accord with the law of the country in regard to the punishment of offenders. Exactly the same views are expressed by the other writer, which need not be reproduced.

Cruel and unusual punishments are forbidden by the Constitution, but the authorities referred to are quite sufficient to show that the punishment of shooting as a mode of executing the death penalty for the crime of murder in the first degree is not included in that category within the meaning of the Eighth Amendment. Soldiers convicted of desertion or other capital military offenses are in the great majority of cases sentenced to be shot, and the ceremony for such occasions is given in great fullness by the writers upon the subject of courts-martial.

Where the conviction is in the civil tribunals, the rule of the common law was that the sentence or judgment must be pronounced or rendered by the court in which the prisoner was tried or finally condemned, and the rule was universal that it must be such as is annexed to the crime by law. Of these, says Blackstone, some are capital, which extend to the life of the offender and consist generally in being hanged by the neck till dead.

Difficulty would attend the effort to define with exactness the extent of the constitutional provision which provides that cruel and unusual punishments shall not be inflicted; but it is safe to affirm that punishments of torture, such as those mentioned by the commentator referred to, and all others in the same line of unnecessary cruelty, are forbidden by that amendment to the Constitution.

Concede all that, and still it by no means follows that the sentence of the court in this case falls within that category, or that the supreme court of the territory erred in affirming the judgment of the court of original jurisdiction. Antecedent to the enactment of the code which went into operation March 4, 1876, the statute of the territory passed March 6, 1852, provided that when any person was convicted of any capital offense he shall suffer death by being shot, hanged, or beheaded, as the court may direct, subject to the qualification therein expressed, to the effect that the person condemned might have his option as to the manner of his execution, the meaning of which qualification, as construed, was that the option was limited to the modes prescribed in the statute, and that if it was not exercised, the direction must be given by the court passing the sentence.

Nothing of the kind is contained in the existing code, and the legislature in dropping the provision as to the option failed to enact any specific regulation as to the mode of executing the death penalty. Instead of that, the explicit enactment is that every person guilty of murder in the first degree shall suffer death, or, upon the recommendation of the jury, may be imprisoned at hard labor in the penitentiary for life, at the discretion of the court.

Beyond all question, the first clause of the provision is applicable in this case, as the jury gave no such recommendation as that recited in the second clause, the record showing that their verdict was unconditional and absolute, from which it follows that the sentence that the prisoner shall suffer death is legally correct.

Had the statute prescribed the mode of executing the sentence, it would have been the duty of the court to follow it, unless the punishment to be inflicted was cruel and unusual, within the meaning of the Eighth Amendment to the Constitution, which is not pretended by the counsel of the prisoner. Statutory directions being given that the prisoner when duly convicted shall suffer death, without any statutory regulation specifically pointing out the mode of executing the command of the law, it must be that the duty is devolved upon the court authorized to pass the sentence to determine the mode of execution and to impose the sentence prescribed.

Persons guilty of murder in the first degree "shall suffer death," are the words of the territorial statute, and when that provision is construed in connection with sec. 10 of the code previously referred to, it is clear that it is made obligatory upon the court to prescribe the mode of executing the sentence of death which the code imposes where the conviction is for murder in the first degree, subject, of course, to the constitutional prohibition, that cruel and unusual punishment shall not be inflicted.

IN RE KEMMLER, 136 U.S. 436 (1890)

CHIEF JUSTICE FULLER delivered the opinion of the Court.

[. . .] Copies of the indictment of Kemmler, otherwise called Hort, for the murder of Matilda Zeigler, otherwise called Matilda Hort, the judgment and sentence of the court, and the warrant to the warden to execute the sentence were attached to the petition and return. The conclusion of the warrant, pursuing the sentence, was in these words:

> "Now, therefore, you are hereby ordered, commanded, and required to execute the said sentence upon him, the said William Kemmler, otherwise called John Hort, upon some day within the week commencing on Monday, the 24th day of June, in the year of our Lord one thousand eight hundred and eighty-nine, and within the walls of Auburn State Prison, or within the yard or inclosure adjoining thereto, by then and there causing to pass through the body of him the said William Kemmler, otherwise called John Hort, a current of electricity of sufficient intensity to cause death, and that the application of such current of electricity be continued until he, the said William Kemmler, otherwise called John Hort, be dead."

Upon the return of the writ before the county judge, counsel for the petitioner offered to prove that the infliction of death by the application of electricity as directed

> "is a cruel and unusual punishment, within the meaning of the Constitution, and that it cannot therefore be lawfully inflicted, and to establish the facts upon which the court can pass as to the character of the penalty. The Attorney General objected to the taking of testimony as to the constitutionality of this law on the ground that the court has no authority to take such proof. The objection was thereupon overruled, and the Attorney General excepted."

A voluminous mass of evidence was then taken as to the effect of electricity as an agent of death, and upon that evidence it was argued that the punishment in that form was cruel and unusual, within the inhibition of the Constitutions of the United States and of the State of New York, and that therefore the act in question was unconstitutional.

The county judge observed that the

> "Constitution of the United States and that of the State of New York, in language almost identical, provide against cruel and inhuman punishment, but it may be remarked in passing that with the former we have no present concern, as the prohibition therein contained has no reference to punishments inflicted in state courts for crimes against the State, but is addressed solely to the national government, and operates as a restriction on its power."

He held that the presumption of constitutionality had not been overcome by the prisoner, because he had not

> "made it appear, by proofs or otherwise, beyond doubt, that the statute of 1888 in regard to the infliction of the death penalty provides a cruel and unusual, and therefore unconstitutional, punishment, and that a force of electricity sufficient to kill any human subject with celerity and certainty, when scientifically applied, cannot be generated."

He therefore made an order dismissing the writ of habeas corpus, and remanding the relator to the custody of the respondent. From this order, an appeal was taken to the Supreme Court, which affirmed the judgment of the county judge. The Supreme Court was of opinion that it was not competent to support the contention of the relator by proofs aliunde the statute; that there was nothing in the constitution of the government or in the nature of things giving any color to the proposition that, upon a mere question of fact involved in legislation, the judgment of a court is superior to that of the legislature itself, nor was there any authority for the proposition that, in respect to such questions, relating either to the manner or the matter of legislation, the decision of the legislature could be reviewed by the court; and that the presumption that the legislature had ascertained the facts necessary to determine that death by the mode prescribed was not a cruel punishment was conclusive upon the court. And Dwight, J., delivering the opinion, also said:

> "We have read with much interest the evidence returned to the county judge, and we agree with him that the burden of the proof is not successfully borne by the relator. On the contrary, we think that the evidence is clearly in favor of the conclusion that it is within easy reach of electrical science at this day to so generate and apply to the person of the convict a current of electricity of such known and sufficient force as certainly to produce instantaneous, and therefore painless, death."

From this judgment of the Supreme Court an appeal was prosecuted to the Court of Appeals, and the order appealed from was affirmed. It is said in the opinion by O'Brien, J.:

> "The only question involved in this appeal is whether this enactment is in conflict with the provision of the state Constitution which forbids the infliction of cruel and unusual punishment. . . . If it cannot be made to appear that a law is in conflict with the Constitution, by argument deduced from the language of the law itself, or from matters of which a court can take judicial notice, then the act must stand. The testimony of expert or other witnesses is not admissible to show that, in carrying out a law enacted by the legislature, some provision of the Constitution may possibly be violated."

The determination of the legislature that the use of electricity as an agency for producing death constituted a more humane method of executing the judgment of the court in capital cases was held conclusive. The opinion concludes as follows:

> "We have examined this testimony, and can find but little in it to warrant the belief that this new mode of execution is cruel, within the meaning of the Constitution, though it is certainly unusual. On the contrary, we agree with the court below that it removes every reasonable doubt that the application of electricity to the vital parts of the human body, under such conditions and in the manner contemplated by the statute, must result in instantaneous, and consequently in painless, death."

At the same term of the Court of Appeals, the appeal of the relator from the judgment on the indictment against him was heard, and that judgment affirmed. Among other points made upon that appeal was this: that the sentence imposed was illegal and unconstitutional, as being a cruel and unusual punishment; but the court decided, as in the case of the appeal from the order under consideration here, that the position was untenable, and that the act was not unconstitutional because of the new mode adopted to bring about death.

We find, then, the law held constitutional by the court of Oyer and Terminer in rendering the original judgment; by the Supreme Court and the Court of Appeals in affirming it; by the county judge in the proceedings upon the writ of habeas corpus; by the Supreme Court in affirming the order of the county judge; and by the Court of Appeals in affirming that judgment of the Supreme Court. It appears that the first step which led to the enactment of the law was a statement contained in the annual message of the Governor of the State of New York, transmitted to the legislature January 6, 1885, as follows:

> "The present mode of executing criminals by hanging has come down to us from the dark ages, and it may well be questioned whether the science of the present day cannot provide a means for taking the life of such as are condemned to die in a less barbarous manner. I commend this suggestion to the consideration of the legislature."

The legislature accordingly appointed a commission to investigate and report "the most humane and practical method known to modern science of carrying into effect the sentence of death in capital cases." This commission reported in favor of execution by electricity, and accompanied their report by a bill which was enacted and became chapter 489 of the Laws of 1888. Laws of New York, 1888, 778. Among other changes, section 505 of the Code of Criminal Procedure of New York was amended so as to read as follows:

> "§ 505. The punishment of death must, in every case, be inflicted by causing to pass through the body of the convict a current of electricity of sufficient intensity to cause death, and the application of such current must be continued until such convict is dead."

Punishments are cruel when they involve torture or a lingering death; but the punishment of death is not cruel within the meaning of that word as used in the Constitution. It implies there something inhuman and barbarous—something more than the mere extinguishment of life. The courts of New York held that the mode adopted in this instance might be said to be unusual because it was new, but that it could not be assumed to be cruel in the light of that common knowledge which has stamped certain punishments as such; that it was for the legislature to say in what manner sentence of death should be executed; that this act was passed in the effort to devise a more humane method of reaching the result; that the courts were bound to presume that the legislature was possessed of the facts upon which it took action; and that, by evidence taken aliunde the statute, that presumption could not be overthrown. They went further, and expressed the opinion that, upon the evidence, the legislature had attained by the act the object had in view in its passage. The decision of the state courts sustaining the validity of the act under the state Constitution is not reexaminable here, nor was that decision against any title, right, privilege, or immunity specially set up or claimed by the petitioner under the Constitution of the United States.

Treating it as involving an adjudication that the statute was not repugnant to the federal Constitution, that conclusion was so plainly right that we should not be justified in allowing the writ upon the ground that error might have supervene therein. The Fourteenth Amendment did not radically change the whole theory of the relations of the state and federal governments to each other, and of both governments to the people. The same person may be at the same time a citizen of the United States and a citizen of a State. Protection to life, liberty, and property rests primarily with the States, and the amendment furnishes an additional guaranty against any encroachment by the States upon those fundamental rights which belong to citizenship, and which the state governments were created to secure. The privileges and immunities of citizens of the United States, as distinguished from the privileges and immunities of citizens of the States, are indeed protected by it; but those are privileges and immunities arising out of the nature and essential character of the national government, and granted or secured by the Constitution of the United States.

[. . .]

In order to reverse the judgment of the highest court of the State of New York, we should be compelled to hold that it had committed an error so gross as to amount in law to a denial by the State of due process of law to one accused of crime, or of some right secured to him by the Constitution of the United States. We have no hesitation in saying that this we cannot do upon the record before us. The application for a writ of error is denied.

LOUISIANA EX REL. FRANCIS v. RESWEBER, 329 U.S. 459 (1947)

JUSTICE REED announced the judgment of the Court, joined by CHIEF JUSTICE VINSON and JUSTICES BLACK and JACKSON. JUSTICE FRANKFURTER filed a concurring opinion.

This writ of certiorari brings before this Court a unique situation. The petitioner, Willie Francis, is a colored citizen of Louisiana. He was duly convicted of murder, and, in September 1945, sentenced to be electrocuted for the crime. Upon a proper death warrant, Francis was prepared for execution and on May 3, 1946, pursuant to the warrant, was placed in the official electric chair of the State of Louisiana in the presence of the authorized witnesses. The executioner threw the switch, but, presumably because of some mechanical difficulty, death did not result. He was thereupon removed from the chair and returned to prison, where he now is. A new death warrant was issued by the Governor of Louisiana, fixing the execution for May 9, 1946.

Applications to the Supreme Court of the state were filed for writs of certiorari, mandamus, prohibition and habeas corpus, directed to the appropriate officials in the state. Execution of the sentence was stayed. By the applications, petitioner claimed the protection of the due process clause of the Fourteenth Amendment on the ground that an execution under the circumstances detailed would deny due process to him because of the double jeopardy provision of the Fifth Amendment and the cruel and unusual punishment provision of the Eighth Amendment. These federal constitutional protections, petitioner claimed, would be denied because he had once gone through the difficult preparation for execution, and had once received through his body a current of electricity intended to cause death. The Supreme Court of Louisiana denied the applications on the ground of a lack of any basis for judicial relief. That is, the state court concluded there was no violation of state or national law alleged in the various applications. It spoke of the fact that no "current of sufficient intensity to cause death" passed through petitioner's body. It referred specifically to the fact that the applications of petitioner invoked the provisions of the Louisiana Constitution against cruel and inhuman punishments and putting one in jeopardy of life or liberty twice for the same offense. We granted certiorari on a petition setting forth the aforementioned contentions to consider the alleged violations of rights under the Federal Constitution in the unusual circumstances of this case.

To determine whether or not the execution of the petitioner may fairly take place after the experience through which he passed, we shall examine the circumstances under the assumption, but without so deciding, that violation of the principles of the Fifth and Eighth Amendments as to double jeopardy and cruel and unusual punishment would be violative of the due process clause of the Fourteenth Amendment. As nothing has been brought to our attention to suggest the contrary, we must and do assume that the state officials carried out their duties under the death warrant in a careful and humane manner. Accidents happen for which no man is to blame. We turn to the question as to whether the proposed enforcement of the criminal law of the state is offensive to any constitutional requirements to which reference has been made.

[. . .]

We find nothing in what took place here which amounts to cruel and unusual punishment in the constitutional sense. The case before us does not call for an examination into any punishments except that of death. The traditional humanity of modern Anglo-American law forbids the infliction of unnecessary pain in the execution of the death sentence. Prohibition against the wanton infliction of pain has come into our law from the Bill of Rights of 1688. The identical words appear in our Eighth Amendment. The Fourteenth would prohibit by its due process clause execution by a state in a cruel manner.

Petitioner's suggestion is that, because he once underwent the psychological strain of preparation for electrocution, now to require him to undergo this preparation again subjects him to a lingering or cruel and unusual punishment. Even the fact that petitioner has already been subjected to a current of electricity does not make his subsequent execution any more cruel in the constitutional sense than any other execution. The cruelty against which the Constitution protects a convicted man is cruelty inherent in the method of punishment, not the necessary suffering involved in any method employed to extinguish life humanely. The fact that an unforeseeable accident prevented the prompt consummation of the sentence cannot, it seems to us, add an element of cruelty to a subsequent execution. There is no purpose to inflict unnecessary pain, nor any unnecessary pain involved in the proposed execution. The situation of the unfortunate victim of this accident is just as though he had suffered the identical amount of mental anguish and physical pain in any other occurrence, such as, for example, a fire in the cell block. We cannot agree that the hardship imposed upon the petitioner rises to that level of hardship denounced as denial of due process because of cruelty.

JUSTICE BURTON filed a dissenting opinion, joined by JUSTICES DOUGLAS, MURPHY, and RUTLEDGE.

[T]he State's brief says:

> "Through a latent electrical defect, the attempt to electrocute Francis failed, the State contending no current whatsoever reached Francis' body,

> the relator contending a current of electricity did pass through his body; but, in any event, Willie Francis was not put to death."

On May 8, the death warrant was canceled, and the relator's execution has been stayed pending completion of these proceedings. The Governor proposes to issue another death warrant for the relator's electrocution, and the relator now asks this Court to prevent it for the reason that, under the present unique circumstances, his electrocution will be so cruel and unusual as to violate the due process clause of the Fourteenth Amendment to the Constitution of the United States.

That Amendment provides: "nor shall any State deprive any person of life, liberty or property, without due process of law; . . ." When this was adopted in 1868, there long had been imbedded deeply in the standards of this nation a revulsion against subjecting guilty persons to torture culminating in death. Pre-constitutional American history reeked with cruel punishment to such an extent that, in 1791, the Eighth Amendment to the Constitution of the United States expressly imposed upon federal agencies a mandate that "Excessive bail shall not be required, nor excessive fines imposed, nor cruel and unusual punishments inflicted." Louisiana and many other states have adopted like constitutional provisions.

The capital case before us presents an instance of the violation of constitutional due process that is more clear than would be presented by many lesser punishments prohibited by the Eighth Amendment or its state counterparts. Taking human life by unnecessarily cruel means shocks the most fundamental instincts of civilized man. It should not be possible under the constitutional procedure of a self-governing people. Abhorrence of the cruelty of ancient forms of capital punishment has increased steadily until, today, some states have prohibited capital punishment altogether. It is unthinkable that any state legislature in modern times would enact a statute expressly authorizing capital punishment by repeated applications of an electric current separated by intervals of days or hours until finally death shall result. The Legislature of Louisiana did not do so. The Supreme Court of Louisiana did not say that it did. The Supreme Court of Louisiana said merely that the pending petitions for relief in this case presented an executive, rather than a judicial, question and, by that mistake of law, it precluded itself from discussing the constitutional issue before us.

In determining whether the proposed procedure is unconstitutional, we must measure it against a lawful electrocution. The contrast is that between instantaneous death and death by installments—caused by electric shocks administered after one or more intervening periods of complete consciousness of the victim. Electrocution, when instantaneous, *can* be inflicted by a state in conformity with due process of law. The Supreme Court of Louisiana has held that electrocution, in the manner prescribed in its statute, is more humane than hanging.

The all-important consideration is that the execution shall be so instantaneous and substantially painless that the punishment shall be reduced, as nearly as possible, to no more than that of death itself. Electrocution has been approved only in a form that eliminates suffering.

The Louisiana statute makes this clear. It provides that:

> "Every sentence of death imposed in this State shall be by electrocution; that is, causing to pass through the body of the person convicted a current of electricity of sufficient intensity to cause death, and the application and continuance of such current through the body of the person convicted until such person is dead. . . ."

It does not provide for electrocution by interrupted or repeated applications of electric current at intervals of several days or even minutes. It does not provide for the application of electric current of an intensity less than that sufficient to cause death. It prescribes expressly and solely for the application of a current of sufficient intensity to cause death and for the continuance of that application until death results. Prescribing capital punishment, it should be construed strictly. There can be no implied provision for a second, third or multiple application of the current. There is no statutory or judicial precedent upholding a delayed process of electrocution.

These considerations were emphasized in *In re Kemmler*, when an early New York statute authorizing electrocution was attacked as violative of the due process clause of the Fourteenth Amendment because prescribing a cruel and unusual punishment. In upholding that statute, this Court stressed the fact that the electric current was to cause instantaneous death. Like the Louisiana statute before us, that statute called expressly for the continued application of a sufficient electric current to cause death. It was the resulting "instantaneous" and "painless" death that was referred to as "humane."

If the state officials deliberately and intentionally had placed the relator in the electric chair five times and, each time, had applied electric current to his body in a manner not sufficient, until the final time, to kill him, such a form of torture would rival that of burning at the stake. Although the failure of the first attempt, in the present case, was unintended, the reapplication of the electric current will be intentional. How many deliberate and intentional reapplications of electric current does it take to produce a cruel, unusual and unconstitutional punishment? While five applications would be more cruel and unusual than one, the uniqueness of the present case demonstrates that, today, two separated applications are sufficiently "cruel and unusual" to be prohibited. If five attempts would be "cruel and unusual," it would be difficult to draw the line between two, three, four and five. It is not difficult, however, as we here contend, to draw the line between the one continuous application prescribed by statute and any other application of the current.

Lack of intent that the first application be less than fatal is not material. The intent of the executioner cannot lessen the torture or excuse the result. It was the statutory duty of the state officials to make sure that there was no failure. The procedure in this case contrasts with common knowledge of precautions generally taken elsewhere to insure against failure of electrocutions. The high standard of care generally taken evidences the significance properly attached to the unconditional requirement of a single continued application of the current until death results. In our view of this case, we are giving careful recognition to the law of Louisiana. Neither the Legislature nor the Supreme Court of Louisiana has expressed approval of electrocution other than by one continuous application of a lethal current.

Executive clemency provides a common means of avoiding unconstitutional or otherwise questionable executions. When, however, the unconstitutionality of proposed executive procedure is brought before this Court, as in this case, we should apply the constitutional protection. In this case, final recourse is had to the high trusteeship vested in this Court by the people of the United States over the constitutional process by which their own lives may be taken.

In determining whether a case of cruel and unusual punishment constitutes a violation of due process of law, each case must turn upon its particular facts. The record in this case is not limited to an instance where a prisoner was placed in the electric chair and released before being subjected to the electric current. It presents more than a case of mental anguish, however severe such a case might be. The petition to the Supreme Court of Louisiana expressly states that a current of electricity was caused to pass through the body of the relator. This allegation was denied in the answer, and no evidence was presented by either side.

[. . .]

For the reasons stated, we are unable to concur in the judgment of this Court which affirms the judgment below.

BAZE v. REES, 553 U.S. 35 (2008)

CHIEF JUSTICE ROBERTS announced the judgment of the Court and delivered an opinion, joined by JUSTICES KENNEDY and ALITO.

Like 35 other States and the Federal Government, Kentucky has chosen to impose capital punishment for certain crimes. As is true with respect to each of these States and the Federal Government, Kentucky has altered its method of execution over time to more humane means of carrying out the sentence. That progress has led to the use of lethal injection by every jurisdiction that imposes the death penalty.

Petitioners in this case—each convicted of double homicide—acknowledge that the lethal injection procedure, if applied as intended, will result in a humane death. They nevertheless contend that the lethal injection protocol is unconstitutional under the Eighth Amendment's ban on "cruel and unusual punishments," because of the risk that the protocol's terms might not be properly followed, resulting in significant pain. They propose an alternative protocol, one that they concede has not been adopted by any State and has never been tried.

The trial court held extensive hearings and entered detailed Findings of Fact and Conclusions of Law. It recognized that "[t]here are no methods of legal execution that are satisfactory to those who oppose the death penalty on moral, religious, or societal grounds," but concluded that Kentucky's procedure "complies with the constitutional requirements against cruel and unusual punishment." App. 769. The State Supreme Court affirmed. We too agree that petitioners have not carried their burden of showing that the risk of pain from maladministration of a concededly humane lethal injection protocol, and the failure to adopt untried and untested alternatives, constitute cruel and unusual punishment. The judgment below is affirmed.

I

[. . .]

Kentucky replaced electrocution with lethal injection in 1998. The Kentucky statute does not specify the drugs or categories of drugs to be used during an execution, instead mandating that "every death sentence shall be executed by continuous intravenous injection of a substance or combination of substances sufficient to cause death." Prisoners sentenced before 1998 have the option of electing either electrocution or lethal injection, but lethal injection is the default if—as is the case with petitioners—the prisoner refuses to make a choice at least 20 days before the scheduled execution. If a court invalidates Kentucky's lethal injection method, Kentucky law provides that the method of execution will revert to electrocution.

Currently, Kentucky uses a certified phlebotomist and an emergency medical technician (EMT) to perform the venipunctures necessary for the catheters. They have up to one hour to establish both primary and secondary peripheral intravenous sites in the arm, hand, leg, or foot of the inmate. Other personnel are responsible for mixing the solutions containing the three drugs and loading them into syringes.

Kentucky's execution facilities consist of the execution chamber, a control room separated by a one-way window, and a witness room. The warden and deputy warden remain in the execution chamber with the prisoner, who is strapped to a gurney. The execution team administers the drugs remotely from the control room through five feet of IV tubing. If, as determined by the warden and deputy warden through visual inspection, the prisoner is not unconscious within 60 seconds following the delivery of the sodium thiopental to the primary IV site, a new 3-gram dose of thiopental is administered to the secondary site before injecting the pancuronium and potassium chloride. In addition to assuring that the first dose of thiopental is successfully administered, the warden and deputy warden also watch for any problems with the IV catheters and tubing.

A physician is present to assist in any effort to revive the prisoner in the event of a last-minute stay of execution. By statute, however, the physician is prohibited from participating in the "conduct of an execution," except to certify the cause of death. An electrocardiogram (EKG) verifies the death of the prisoner. Only one Kentucky prisoner, Eddie Lee Harper, has been executed since the Commonwealth adopted lethal injection. There were no reported problems at Harper's execution.

Petitioners Ralph Baze and Thomas C. Bowling were each convicted of two counts of capital murder and sentenced to death.

After exhausting their state and federal collateral remedies, Baze and Bowling sued three state officials in the Franklin Circuit Court for the Commonwealth of Kentucky, seeking to have Kentucky's lethal injection protocol declared unconstitutional. After a 7-day bench trial during which the trial court received the testimony of approximately 20 witnesses, including numerous experts, the court upheld the protocol, finding there to be minimal risk of various claims of improper administration of the protocol. On appeal, the Kentucky Supreme Court stated that a method of execution violates the Eighth Amendment when it "creates a substantial risk of wanton and unnecessary infliction of pain, torture or lingering death." Applying that standard, the court affirmed.

We granted certiorari to determine whether Kentucky's lethal injection protocol satisfies the Eighth Amendment. We hold that it does.

II

Some risk of pain is inherent in any method of execution—no matter how humane—if only from the prospect of error in following the required procedure. It is clear, then, that the Constitution does not demand the avoidance of all risk of pain in carrying out executions.

Petitioners do not claim that it does. Rather, they contend that the Eighth Amendment prohibits procedures that create an "unnecessary risk" of pain. Petitioners envision that the quantum of risk necessary to make out an Eighth Amendment claim will vary according to the severity of the pain and the availability of alternatives, but that the risk must be "significant" to trigger Eighth Amendment scrutiny.

A

This Court has never invalidated a State's chosen procedure for carrying out a sentence of death as the infliction of cruel and unusual punishment.

B

Petitioners do not claim that lethal injection or the proper administration of the particular protocol adopted by Kentucky by themselves constitute the cruel or wanton infliction of pain. Quite the contrary, they concede that "if performed properly," an execution carried out under Kentucky's procedures would be "humane and constitutional."

Instead, petitioners claim that there is a significant risk that the procedures will *not* be properly followed—in particular, that the sodium thiopental will not be properly administered to achieve its intended effect—resulting in severe pain when the other chemicals are administered. Our cases recognize that subjecting individuals to a risk of future harm—not simply actually inflicting pain—can qualify as cruel and unusual punishment. To establish that such exposure violates the Eighth Amendment, however, the conditions presenting the risk must be "*sure or very likely* to cause serious illness and needless suffering," and give rise to "sufficiently *imminent* dangers."

Simply because an execution method may result in pain, either by accident or as an inescapable consequence of death, does not establish the sort of "objectively intolerable risk of harm" that qualifies as cruel and unusual.

C

Much of petitioners' case rests on the contention that they have identified a significant risk of harm that can be eliminated by adopting alternative procedures, such as a one-drug protocol that dispenses with the use of pancuronium and potassium chloride, and additional monitoring by trained personnel to ensure that the first dose of sodium thiopental has been adequately delivered. Given what our cases have said about the nature of the risk of harm that is actionable under the Eighth Amendment, a condemned prisoner cannot successfully challenge a State's method of execution merely by showing a slightly or marginally safer alternative.

Permitting an Eighth Amendment violation to be established on such a showing would threaten to transform courts into boards of inquiry charged with determining "best practices" for executions, with each ruling supplanted by another round of litigation touting a new and improved methodology. Such an approach finds no support in our cases, would embroil the courts in ongoing scientific controversies beyond their expertise, and would substantially intrude on the role of state legislatures in implementing their execution procedures—a role that by all accounts the States have fulfilled with an earnest desire to provide for a progressively more humane manner of death.

Instead, the proffered alternatives must effectively address a "substantial risk of serious harm." To qualify, the alternative procedure must be feasible, readily implemented, and in fact significantly reduce a substantial risk of severe pain. If a State refuses to adopt such an alternative in the face of these documented advantages, without a legitimate penological justification for adhering to its current method of execution, then a State's refusal to change its method can be viewed as "cruel and unusual" under the Eighth Amendment.

III

In applying these standards to the facts of this case, we note at the outset that it is difficult to regard a practice as "objectively intolerable" when it is in fact widely tolerated. Thirty-six States that sanction capital punishment have adopted lethal injection as the preferred method of execution. The Federal Government uses lethal injection as well. This broad consensus goes not just to the method of execution, but also to the specific three-drug combination used by Kentucky. Thirty States, as well as the Federal Government, use a series of sodium thiopental, pancuronium bromide, and potassium chloride, in varying amounts. No State uses or has ever used the alternative one-drug protocol belatedly urged by petitioners. This consensus is probative but not conclusive with respect to that aspect of the alternatives proposed by petitioners.

A

Petitioners contend that there is a risk of improper administration of thiopental because the doses are difficult to mix into solution form and load into syringes; because the protocol fails to establish a rate of injection, which could lead to a failure of the IV; because it is possible that the IV catheters will infiltrate into surrounding tissue, causing an inadequate dose to be delivered to the vein; because of inadequate facilities and training; and because Kentucky has no reliable means of monitoring the anesthetic depth of the prisoner after the sodium thiopental has been administered.

As for the risk that the sodium thiopental would be improperly prepared, petitioners contend that Kentucky employs untrained personnel who are unqualified to calculate and mix an adequate dose, especially in light of the omission of volume and concentration amounts from the written protocol. The state trial court, however, specifically found that "[i]f the manufacturers' instructions for reconstitution of Sodium Thiopental are followed, . . . there would be minimal risk of improper mixing, despite converse testimony that a layperson would have difficulty performing this task."

Likewise, the asserted problems related to the IV lines do not establish a sufficiently substantial risk of harm to meet the requirements of the Eighth Amendment. Kentucky has put in place several important safeguards to ensure that an adequate dose of sodium thiopental is delivered to the condemned prisoner. The most significant of these is the written protocol's requirement that members of the IV team must have at least one year of professional experience as a certified medical assistant, phlebotomist, EMT, paramedic, or military corpsman. Kentucky currently uses a phlebotomist and an EMT, personnel who have daily experience establishing IV catheters for inmates in Kentucky's prison population. Moreover, these IV team members, along with the rest of the execution team, participate in at least 10 practice sessions per year. These sessions, required by the written protocol, encompass a complete walk-through of the execution procedures, including the siting of IV catheters into volunteers. In addition, the protocol calls for the IV team to establish both primary and backup lines and to prepare two sets of the lethal injection drugs before the execution commences. These redundant measures ensure that if an insufficient dose of sodium thiopental is initially administered through the primary line, an additional dose can be given through the backup line before the last two drugs are injected.

The IV team has one hour to establish both the primary and backup IVs, a length of time the trial court found to be "not excessive but rather necessary," contrary to petitioners' claim that using an IV inserted after any "more than ten or fifteen minutes of unsuccessful attempts is dangerous because the IV is almost certain to be unreliable." And, in any event, merely because the protocol gives the IV team one hour to establish intravenous access does not mean that team members are required to spend the entire hour in a futile attempt to do so. The qualifications of the IV team also substantially reduce the risk of IV infiltration.

In addition, the presence of the warden and deputy warden in the execution chamber with the prisoner allows them to watch for signs of IV problems, including infiltration. Three of the Commonwealth's medical experts testified that identifying signs of infiltration would be "very obvious," even to the average person, because of the swelling that would result. Kentucky's protocol specifically requires the warden to redirect the flow of chemicals to the backup IV site if the prisoner does not lose consciousness within 60 seconds. In light of these safeguards, we cannot say that the risks identified by petitioners are so substantial or imminent as to amount to an Eighth Amendment violation.

B

Nor does Kentucky's failure to adopt petitioners' proposed alternatives demonstrate that the Commonwealth's execution procedure is cruel and unusual.

First, petitioners contend that Kentucky could switch from a three-drug protocol to a one-drug protocol by using a single dose of sodium thiopental or other barbiturate. That alternative was not proposed to the state courts below. As a result, we are left without any findings on the effectiveness of petitioners' barbiturate-only protocol, despite scattered references in the trial testimony to the sole use of sodium thiopental or pentobarbital as a preferred method of execution.

In any event, the Commonwealth's continued use of the three-drug protocol cannot be viewed as posing an "objectively intolerable risk" when no other State has adopted the one-drug method and petitioners proffered no study showing that it is an equally effective manner of imposing a death sentence.

Petitioners also contend that Kentucky should omit the second drug, pancuronium bromide, because it serves no therapeutic purpose while suppressing muscle movements that could reveal an inadequate administration of the first drug. The state trial court, however, specifically found that pancuronium serves two purposes. First, it prevents involuntary physical movements during unconsciousness that may accompany the injection of potassium chloride. The Commonwealth has an interest in preserving the dignity of the procedure, especially where convulsions or seizures could be misperceived as signs of consciousness or distress. Second, pancuronium stops respiration, hastening death. Kentucky's decision to include the drug does not offend the Eighth Amendment.

Petitioners' barbiturate-only protocol, they contend, is not untested; it is used routinely by veterinarians in putting animals to sleep. Moreover, 23 States, including Kentucky, bar veterinarians from using a neuromuscular paralytic agent like pancuronium bromide, either expressly or, like Kentucky, by specifically directing the use of a drug like sodium pentobarbital.

[. . .]

The dissent would continue the stay of these executions (and presumably the many others held in abeyance pending decision in this case) and send the case back to the lower courts to determine whether such added measures redress an "untoward" risk of pain. But an inmate cannot succeed on an Eighth Amendment claim simply by showing one more step the State could take as a failsafe for other, independently adequate measures. This approach would serve no meaningful purpose and would frustrate the State's legitimate interest in carrying out a sentence of death in a timely manner.

Justice Stevens suggests that our opinion leaves the disposition of other cases uncertain, but the standard we set forth here resolves more challenges than he acknowledges. A stay of execution may not be granted on grounds such as those asserted here unless the condemned prisoner establishes that the State's lethal injection protocol creates a demonstrated risk of severe pain. He must show that the risk is substantial when compared to the known and available alternatives. A State with a lethal injection protocol substantially similar to the protocol we uphold today would not create a risk that meets this standard.

Reasonable people of good faith disagree on the morality and efficacy of capital punishment, and for many who oppose it, no method of execution would ever be acceptable. But as Justice Frankfurter stressed in *Resweber*, "[o]ne must be on guard against finding in personal disapproval a reflection of more or less prevailing condemnation." This Court has ruled that capital punishment is not prohibited under our Constitution, and that the States may enact laws specifying that sanction. "[T]he power of a State to pass laws means little if the State cannot enforce them." State efforts to implement capital punishment must certainly comply with the Eighth Amendment, but what that Amendment prohibits is wanton exposure to "objectively intolerable risk," not simply the possibility of pain.

Kentucky has adopted a method of execution believed to be the most humane available, one it shares with 35 other States. Petitioners agree that, if administered as intended, that procedure will result in a painless death. The risks of maladministration they have suggested—such as improper mixing of chemicals and improper setting of IVs by trained and experienced personnel—cannot remotely be characterized as "objectively intolerable." Kentucky's decision to adhere to its protocol despite these asserted risks, while adopting safeguards to protect against them, cannot be viewed as probative of the wanton infliction of pain under the Eighth Amendment. Finally, the alternative that petitioners belatedly propose has problems of its own, and has never been tried by a single State.

Throughout our history, whenever a method of execution has been challenged in this Court as cruel and unusual, the Court has rejected the challenge. Our society has nonetheless steadily moved to more humane methods of carrying out capital punishment. The firing squad, hanging, the electric chair, and the gas chamber have each in turn given way to more humane methods, culminating in today's consensus on lethal injection. The broad framework of the Eighth Amendment has accommodated this progress toward more humane methods of execution, and our approval of a particular method in the past has not precluded legislatures from taking the steps they deem appropriate, in light of new developments, to ensure humane capital punishment. There is no reason to suppose that today's decision will be any different.

JUSTICE ALITO filed a concurring opinion.

Prominent among the practical constraints that must be taken into account in considering the feasibility and availability of any suggested modification of a lethal injection protocol are the ethical restrictions applicable to medical professionals. The first step in the lethal injection protocols currently in use is the anesthetization of the prisoner. If this step is carried out properly, it is agreed, the prisoner will not experience pain during the remainder of the procedure. Every day, general anesthetics are administered to surgical patients in this country, and if the medical professionals who participate in these surgeries also participated in the anesthetization of prisoners facing execution by lethal injection, the risk of pain would be minimized. But the ethics rules of medical professionals—for reasons that I certainly do not question here—prohibit their participation in executions.

Misinterpretation of the standard set out in the plurality opinion or adoption of the standard favored by the dissent and Justice Breyer would create a grave danger of extended delay. The dissenters and Justice Breyer would hold that the protocol used in carrying out an execution by lethal injection violates the Eighth Amendment if it creates an "*untoward*, readily avoidable risk of inflicting severe and unnecessary pain." Determining whether a risk is "untoward," we are told, requires a weighing of three factors—the severity of the pain that may occur, the likelihood of this pain, and the availability of alternative methods. We are further informed that "[t]he three factors are interrelated; a strong showing on one reduces the importance of others."

An "untoward" risk is presumably a risk that is "unfortunate" or "marked by or causing trouble or unhappiness." This vague and malleable standard would open the gates for a flood of litigation that would go a long way toward bringing about the end of the death penalty as a practical matter. While I certainly do not suggest that this is the intent of the Justices who favor this test, the likely consequences are predictable.

JUSTICE STEVENS filed a concurring opinion.

When we granted certiorari in this case, I assumed that our decision would bring the debate about lethal injection as a method of execution to a close. It now seems clear that it will not. The question whether a similar three-drug protocol may be used in other States remains open, and may well be answered differently in a future case on the basis of a more complete record. Instead of ending the controversy, I am now convinced that this case will generate debate not only about the constitutionality of the three-drug protocol, and specifically about the justification for the use of the paralytic agent, pancuronium bromide, but also about the justification for the death penalty itself.

Because it masks any outward sign of distress, pancuronium bromide creates a risk that the inmate will suffer excruciating pain before death occurs. There is a general understanding among veterinarians that the risk of pain is sufficiently serious that the use of the drug should be proscribed when an animal's life is being terminated. As a result of this understanding among knowledgeable professionals, several States—including Kentucky—have enacted legislation prohibiting use of the drug in animal euthanasia.

II

The thoughtful opinions written by the Chief Justice and by Justice Ginsburg have persuaded me that current decisions by state legislatures, by the Congress of the United States, and by this Court to retain the death penalty as a part of our law are the product of habit and inattention rather than an acceptable deliberative process that weighs the costs and risks of administering that penalty against its identifiable benefits, and rest in part on a faulty assumption about the retributive force of the death penalty.

The conclusion that I have reached with regard to the constitutionality of the death penalty itself makes my decision in this case particularly difficult. It does not, however, justify a refusal to respect precedents that remain a part of our law. This Court has held that the death penalty is constitutional, and has established a framework for evaluating the constitutionality of particular methods of execution. Under those precedents, whether as interpreted by the Chief Justice or Justice Ginsburg, I am persuaded that the evidence adduced by petitioners fails to prove that Kentucky's lethal injection protocol violates the Eighth Amendment. Accordingly, I join the Court's judgment.

JUSTICE THOMAS filed a concurring opinion, joined by JUSTICE SCALIA

Although I agree that petitioners have failed to establish that Kentucky's lethal injection protocol violates the Eighth Amendment, I write separately because I cannot subscribe to the plurality opinion's formulation of the governing standard. As I understand it, that opinion would hold that a method of execution violates the Eighth Amendment if it poses a substantial risk of severe pain that could be significantly reduced by adopting readily available alternative procedures. This standard—along with petitioners' proposed "unnecessary risk" standard and the dissent's "untoward risk" standard—finds no support in the original understanding of the Cruel and Unusual Punishments Clause or in our previous method-of-execution cases; casts constitutional doubt on long-accepted methods of execution; and injects the Court into matters it has no institutional capacity to resolve. Because, in my view, a method of execution violates the Eighth Amendment only if it is deliberately designed to inflict pain, I concur only in the judgment.

JUSTICE SCALIA filed a concurring opinion, joined by JUSTICE THOMAS.

I write separately to provide what I think is needed response to Justice Stevens' separate opinion.

Purer expression cannot be found of the principle of rule by judicial fiat. In the face of Justice Stevens' experience, the experience of all others is, it appears, of little consequence. The experience of the state legislatures and the Congress—who retain the death penalty as a form of punishment—is dismissed as "the product of habit and inattention rather than an acceptable deliberative process." The experience of social scientists whose studies indicate that the death penalty deters crime is relegated to a footnote. The experience of fellow citizens who support the death penalty is described, with only the most thinly veiled condemnation, as stemming from a "thirst for vengeance." It is Justice Stevens' experience that reigns over all.

I take no position on the desirability of the death penalty, except to say that its value is eminently debatable and the subject of deeply, indeed passionately, held views—which means, to me, that it is preeminently not a matter to be resolved here. And especially not when it is explicitly permitted by the Constitution.

JUSTICE BREYER filed a concurring opinion.

Assuming the lawfulness of the death penalty itself, petitioners argue that Kentucky's method of execution, lethal injection, nonetheless constitutes a constitutionally forbidden, "cruel and usual punishmen[t]. In respect to *how* a court should review such a claim, I agree with Justice Ginsburg. She highlights the relevant question, whether the method creates an untoward, readily avoidable risk of inflicting severe and unnecessary suffering. I agree that the relevant factors—the "degree of risk," the "magnitude of pain," and the "availability of alternatives"—are interrelated and each must be considered.

[. . .]

The upshot is that I cannot find, either in the record or in the readily available literature that I have seen, sufficient grounds to believe that Kentucky's method of lethal injection creates a significant risk of unnecessary suffering.

JUSTICE GINSBURG filed a dissenting opinion, joined by JUSTICE SOUTER.

It is undisputed that the second and third drugs used in Kentucky's three-drug lethal injection protocol, pancuronium bromide and potassium chloride, would cause a conscious inmate to suffer excruciating pain. Pancuronium bromide paralyzes the lung muscles and results in slow asphyxiation. Potassium chloride causes burning and intense pain as it circulates throughout the body. Use of pancuronium bromide and potassium chloride on a conscious inmate, the plurality recognizes, would be "constitutionally unacceptable."

The constitutionality of Kentucky's protocol therefore turns on whether inmates are adequately anesthetized by the first drug in the protocol, sodium thiopental. Kentucky's system is constitutional, the plurality states, because "petitioners have not shown that the risk of an inadequate dose of the first drug is substantial." I would not dispose of the case so swiftly given the character of the risk at stake. Kentucky's protocol lacks basic safeguards used by other States to confirm that an inmate is unconscious before injection of the second and third drugs. I would vacate and remand with instructions to consider whether Kentucky's omission of those safeguards poses an untoward, readily avoidable risk of inflicting severe and unnecessary pain.

II

A consciousness check supplementing the warden's visual observation before injection of the second drug is easily implemented and can reduce a risk of dreadful pain. Pancuronium bromide is a powerful paralytic that prevents all voluntary muscle movement. Once it is injected, further monitoring of the inmate's consciousness becomes impractical without sophisticated equipment and training. Even if the inmate were conscious and in excruciating pain, there would be no visible indication.

Recognizing the importance of a window between the first and second drugs, other States have adopted safeguards not contained in Kentucky's protocol.

In Missouri, "medical personnel must examine the prisoner physically to confirm that he is unconscious using standard clinical techniques and must inspect the catheter site again."

In California, a member of the IV team brushes the inmate's eyelashes, speaks to him, and shakes him at the halfway point and, again, at the completion of the sodium thiopental injection.

In Alabama, a member of the execution team "begin[s] by saying the condemned inmate's name. If there is no response, the team member will gently stroke the condemned inmate's eyelashes. If there is no response, the team member will then pinch the condemned inmate's arm."

In Indiana, officials inspect the injection site after administration of sodium thiopental, say the inmate's name, touch him, and use ammonia tablets to test his response to a noxious nasal stimulus.

These checks provide a degree of assurance—missing from Kentucky's protocol—that the first drug has been properly administered. They are simple and essentially costless to employ, yet work to lower the risk that the inmate will be subjected to the agony of conscious suffocation caused by pancuronium bromide and the searing pain caused by potassium chloride. The record contains no explanation why Kentucky does not take any of these elementary measures.

[. . .] I would therefore remand with instructions to consider whether the failure to include readily available safeguards to confirm that the inmate is unconscious after injection of sodium thiopental, in combination with the other elements of Kentucky's protocol, creates an untoward, readily avoidable risk of inflicting severe and unnecessary pain.

GLOSSIP v. GROSS, 576 U.S. 863 (2015)

JUSTICE ALITO delivered the opinion of the Court, joined by CHIEF JUSTICE ROBERTS and JUSTICES SCALIA, KENNEDY, and THOMAS.

Our decisions in this area have been animated in part by the recognition that because it is settled that capital punishment is constitutional, "[i]t necessarily follows that there must be a [constitutional] means of carrying it out." And because some risk of pain is inherent in any method of execution, we have held that the Constitution does not require the avoidance of all risk of pain. After all, while most humans wish to die a painless death, many do not have that good fortune. Holding that the Eighth Amendment demands the elimination of essentially all risk of pain would effectively outlaw the death penalty altogether.

Baze cleared any legal obstacle to use of the most common three-drug protocol that had enabled States to carry out the death penalty in a quick and painless fashion. But a practical obstacle soon emerged, as anti-death-penalty advocates pressured pharmaceutical companies to refuse to supply the drugs used to carry out death sentences. The sole American manufacturer of sodium thiopental, the first drug used in the standard three-drug protocol, was persuaded to cease production of the drug.

After other efforts to procure sodium thiopental proved unsuccessful, States sought an alternative, and they eventually replaced sodium thiopental with pentobarbital, another barbiturate. In December 2010, Oklahoma became the first State to execute an inmate using pentobarbital. That execution occurred without incident, and States gradually shifted to pentobarbital as their supplies of sodium thiopentalran out. It is reported that pentobarbital was used in all of the 43 executions carried out in 2012.

Before long, however, pentobarbital also became unavailable. Anti-death-penalty advocates lobbied the Danish manufacturer of the drug to stop selling it for use in executions. That manufacturer opposed the death penalty and took steps to block the shipment of pentobarbital for use in executions in the United States. Oklahoma eventually became unable to acquire the drug through any means. The District Court below found that both sodium thiopental and pentobarbital are now unavailable to Oklahoma.

Unable to acquire either sodium thiopental or pentobarbital, some States have turned to midazolam, a sedative in the benzodiazepine family of drugs. In October 2013, Florida became the first State to substitute midazolam for pentobarbital as part of a three-drug lethal injection protocol. In 2014, Oklahoma also substituted midazolam for pentobarbital as part of its three-drug protocol. Oklahoma has already used this three-drug protocol twice: to execute Clayton Lockett in April 2014 and Charles Warner in January 2015. (Warner was one of the four inmates who moved for a preliminary injunction in this case.)

II

A

In June 2014, after Oklahoma switched from pentobarbital to midazolam and executed Lockett, 21 Oklahoma death row inmates filed an action under 42 U. S. C. §1983 challenging the State's new lethal injection protocol. The complaint alleged that Oklahoma's use of midazolam violates the Eighth Amendment's prohibition of cruel and unusual punishment.

In November 2014, four of those plaintiffs—Richard Glossip, Benjamin Cole, John Grant, and Warner—filed a motion for a preliminary injunction. All four men had been convicted of murder and sentenced to death by Oklahoma juries.

The Oklahoma Court of Criminal Appeals affirmed the murder conviction and death sentence of each offender. Each of the men then unsuccessfully sought both state postconviction and federal habeas corpus relief. Having exhausted the avenues for challenging their convictions and sentences, they moved for a preliminary injunction against Oklahoma's lethal injection protocol.

The controlling opinion summarized the requirements of an Eighth Amendment method-of-execution claim as follows: "A stay of execution may not be granted on grounds such as those asserted here unless the condemned prisoner establishes that the State's lethal injection protocol creates a demonstrated risk of severe pain. [And] [h]e must show that the risk is substantial when compared to the known and available alternatives." The preliminary injunction posture of the present case thus requires petitioners to establish a likelihood that they can establish both that Oklahoma's lethal injection protocol creates a demonstrated risk of severe pain and that the risk is substantial when compared to the known and available alternatives.

IV

Our first ground for affirmance is based on petitioners' failure to satisfy their burden of establishing that any risk of harm was substantial when compared to a known and available alternative method of execution. In their amended complaint, petitioners proffered that the State could use sodium thiopental as part of a single-drug protocol. They have since suggested that it might also be constitutional for Oklahoma to use pentobarbital. But the District Court found that both sodium thiopental and pentobarbital are now unavailable to Oklahoma's Department of Corrections. The Court of Appeals affirmed that finding, and it is not clearly erroneous. On the contrary, the record shows that Oklahoma has been unable to procure those drugs despite a good-faith effort to do so.

Petitioners do not seriously contest this factual finding, and they have not identified any available drug or drugs that could be used in place of those that Oklahoma is now unable to obtain. Nor have they shown a risk of pain so great that other acceptable, available methods must be used. Instead, they argue that they need not identify a known and available method of execution that presents less risk. But this argument is inconsistent with the controlling opinion in *Baze*, which imposed a requirement that the Court now follows.

V

We also affirm for a second reason: The District Court did not commit clear error when it found that midazolam is highly likely to render a person unable to feel pain during an execution.

[. . .] numerous courts have concluded that the use of midazolam as the first drug in a three-drug protocol is likely to render an inmate insensate to pain that might result from administration of the paralytic agent and potassium chloride.

Although we must invalidate a lethal injection protocol if it violates the Eighth Amendment, federal courts should not "embroil [themselves] in ongoing scientific controversies beyond their expertise." Accordingly, an inmate challenging a protocol bears the burden to show, based on evidence presented to the court, that there is a substantial risk of severe pain.

Oklahoma has also adopted important safeguards to ensure that midazolam is properly administered. The District Court emphasized three requirements in particular: The execution team must secure both a primary and backup IV access site, it must confirm the viability of the IV sites, and it must continuously monitor the offender's level of consciousness. The District Court did not commit clear error in concluding that these safeguards help to minimize any risk that might occur in the event that midazolam does not operate as intended. Indeed, we concluded in *Baze* that many of the safeguards that Oklahoma employs—including the establishment of a primary and backup IV and the presence of personnel to monitor an inmate—help in significantly reducing the risk that an execution protocol will violate the Eighth Amendment. And many other safeguards that Oklahoma has adopted mirror those that the dissent in *Baze* complained were absent from Kentucky's protocol in that case. For example, the dissent argued that because a consciousness check before injection of the second drug "can reduce a risk of dreadful pain," Kentucky's failure to include that step in its procedure was unconstitutional. The dissent also complained that Kentucky did not monitor the effectiveness of the first drug or pause between injection of the first and second drugs. Oklahoma has accommodated each of those concerns.

[. . .] petitioners argue that difficulties with Oklahoma's execution of Lockett and Arizona's July 2014 execution of Joseph Wood establish that midazolam is sure or very likely to cause serious pain. We are not persuaded. Aside from the Lockett execution, 12 other executions have been conducted using the three-drug protocol at issue here, and those appear to have been conducted without any significant problems.

Finally, we find it appropriate to respond to the principal dissent's groundless suggestion that our decision is tantamount to allowing prisoners to be "drawn and quartered, slowly tortured to death, or actually burned at the stake." That is simply not true, and the principal dissent's resort to this outlandish rhetoric reveals the weakness of its legal arguments.

JUSTICE SCALIA filed a concurring opinion, joined by JUSTICE THOMAS.

I join the opinion of the Court, and write to respond to Justice Breyer's plea for judicial abolition of the death penalty.

Welcome to Groundhog Day. The scene is familiar: Petitioners, sentenced to die for the crimes they committed (including, in the case of one petitioner since put to death, raping and murdering an 11-month-old baby), come before this Court asking us to nullify their sentences as "cruel and unusual" under the Eighth Amendment. They rely on this provision because it is the only provision they can rely on. They were charged by a sovereign State with murder. They were afforded counsel and tried before a jury of their peers—tried twice, once to determine whether they were guilty and once to determine whether death was the appropriate sentence. They were duly convicted and sentenced. They were granted the right to appeal and to seek postconviction relief, first in state and then in federal court. And now, acknowledging that their convictions are unassailable, they ask us for clemency, as though clemency were ours to give.

The response is also familiar: A vocal minority of the Court, waving over their heads a ream of the most recent abolitionist studies (a superabundant genre) as though they have discovered the lost folios of Shakespeare, insist that now, at long last, the death penalty must be abolished for good. Mind you, not once in the history of the American Republic has this Court ever suggested the death penalty is categorically impermissible. The reason is obvious: It is impossible to hold unconstitutional that which the Constitution explicitly contemplates. The Fifth Amendment provides that "[n]o person shall be held to answer for a capital . . . crime, unless on a presentment or indictment of a Grand Jury," and that no person shall be "deprived of life . . . without due process of law." Nevertheless, today Justice Breyer takes on the role of the abolitionists in this long-running drama, arguing that the text of the Constitution and two centuries of history must yield to his "20 years of experience on this Court," and inviting full briefing on the continued permissibility of capital punishment.

Even accepting Justice Breyer's rewriting of the Eighth Amendment, his argument is full of internal contradictions and (it must be said) gobbledy-gook. He says that the death penalty is cruel because it is unreliable; but it is convictions, not punishments, that are unreliable. Moreover, the "pressure on police, prosecutors, and jurors to secure a conviction," which he claims increases the risk of wrongful convictions in capital cases, flows from the nature of the crime, not the punishment that follows its commission. Justice Breyer acknowledges as much: "[T]he crimes at issue in capital cases are typically horrendous murders, and thus accompanied by intense community pressure." That same pressure would exist, and the same risk of wrongful convictions, if horrendous death-penalty cases were converted into equally horrendous life-without-parole cases. The reality is that any innocent defendant is infinitely better off appealing a death sentence than a sentence of life imprisonment.

Of course, this delay is a problem of the Court's own making. As Justice Breyer concedes, for more than 160 years, capital sentences were carried out in an average of two years or less. But by 2014, he tells us, it took an average of 18 years to carry out a death sentence. What happened in the intervening years? Nothing other than the proliferation of labyrinthine restrictions on capital punishment, promulgated by this Court under an interpretation of the Eighth Amendment that empowered it to divine "the evolving standards of decency that mark the progress of a maturing society,"—a task for which we are eminently ill suited. Indeed, for the past two decades, Justice Breyer has been the Drum Major in this parade. His invocation of the resultant delay as grounds for abolishing the death penalty calls to mind the man sentenced to death for killing his parents, who pleads for mercy on the ground that he is an orphan. Amplifying the surrealism of his argument, Justice Breyer uses the fact that many States have abandoned capital punishment—have abandoned it precisely because of the costs those suspect decisions have imposed—to conclude that it is now "unusual." (A caution to the reader: Do not use the creative arithmetic that Justice Breyer employs in counting the number of States that use the death penalty when you prepare your next tax return; outside the world of our Eighth Amendment abolitionist-inspired jurisprudence, it will be regarded as more misrepresentation than math.)

Capital punishment presents moral questions that philosophers, theologians, and statesmen have grappled with for millennia. The Framers of our Constitution disagreed bitterly on the matter. For that reason, they handled it the same way they handled many other controversial issues: they left it to the People to decide. By arrogating to himself the power to overturn that decision, Justice Breyer does not just reject the death penalty, he rejects the Enlightenment.

JUSTICE THOMAS filed a concurring opinion, joined by JUSTICE SCALIA.

Whatever one's views on the permissibility or wisdom of the death penalty, I doubt anyone would disagree that each of these crimes was egregious enough to merit the severest condemnation that society has to offer. The only constitutional problem with the fact that these criminals were spared that condemnation, while others were not, is that their amnesty came in the form of unfounded claims. Arbitrariness has nothing to do with it. To the extent that we are ill at ease with these disparate outcomes, it seems to me that the best solution is for the Court to stop making up Eighth Amendment claims in its ceaseless quest to end the death penalty through undemocratic means.

JUSTICE SOTOMAYOR filed a dissenting opinion, joined by JUSTICES GINSBURG, BREYER, and KAGAN.

Petitioners, three inmates on Oklahoma's death row, challenge the constitutionality of the State's lethal injection protocol. The State plans to execute petitioners using three drugs: midazolam, rocuronium bromide, and potassium chloride. The latter two drugs are intended to paralyze the inmate and stop his heart. But they do so in a torturous manner, causing burning, searing pain. It is thus critical that the first drug, midazolam, do what it is supposed to do, which is to render and keep the inmate unconscious. Petitioners claim that midazolam cannot be expected to perform that function, and they have presented ample evidence showing that the State's planned use of this drug poses substantial, constitutionally intolerable risks.

Nevertheless, the Court today turns aside petitioners' plea that they at least be allowed a stay of execution while they seek to prove midazolam's inadequacy. The Court achieves this result in two ways: first, by deferring to the District Court's decision to credit the scientifically unsupported and implausible testimony of a single expert witness; and second, by faulting petitioners for failing to satisfy the wholly novel requirement of proving the availability of an alternative means for their own executions. On both counts the Court errs. As a result, it leaves petitioners exposed to what may well be the chemical equivalent of being burned at the stake.

[. . .]

The Court not only disregards this record evidence of midazolam's inadequacy, but also fails to fully appreciate the procedural posture in which this case arises. Petitioners have not been accorded a full hearing on the merits of their claim. They were granted only an abbreviated evidentiary proceeding that began less than three months after the State issued its amended execution protocol; they did not even have the opportunity to present rebuttal evidence after Dr. Evans testified. They sought a preliminary injunction, and thus were not required to prove their claim, but only to show that they were likely to succeed on the merits.

Perhaps the State could prevail after a full hearing, though this would require more than Dr. Evans' unsupported testimony. At the preliminary injunction stage, however, petitioners presented compelling evidence suggesting that midazolam will not work as the State intends. The State, by contrast, offered absolutely no contrary evidence worth crediting. Petitioners are thus at the very least *likely* to prove that, due to midazolam's inherent deficiencies, there is a constitutionally intolerable risk that they will be awake, yet unable to move, while chemicals known to cause "excruciating pain" course through their veins.

The Court's determination that the use of midazolam poses no objectively intolerable risk of severe pain is factually wrong. The Court's conclusion that petitioners' challenge also fails because they identified no available alternative means by which the State may kill them is legally indefensible.

[. . .]

In reengineering *Baze* to support its newfound rule, the Court appears to rely on a flawed syllogism. If the death penalty is constitutional, the Court reasons, then there must be a means of accomplishing it, and thus some available method of execution must be constitutional. But even accepting that the death penalty is, in the abstract, consistent with evolving standards of decency, but the Court's conclusion does not follow. The constitutionality of the death penalty may inform our conception of the degree of pain that would render a particular method of imposing it unconstitutional.

If all available means of conducting an execution constitute cruel and unusual punishment, then conducting the execution will constitute cruel and usual punishment. Nothing compels a State to perform an execution. It does not get a constitutional free pass simply because it desires to deliver the ultimate penalty; its ends do not justify any and all means. If a State wishes to carry out an execution, it must do so subject to the constraints that our Constitution imposes on it, including the obligation to ensure that its chosen method is not cruel and unusual. Certainly the condemned has no duty to devise or pick a constitutional instrument of his or her own death.

For these reasons, the Court's available-alternative requirement leads to patently absurd consequences. Petitioners contend that Oklahoma's current protocol is a barbarous method of punishment—the chemical equivalent of being burned alive. But under the Court's new rule, it would not matter whether the State intended to use midazolam, or instead to have petitioners drawn and quartered, slowly tortured to death, or actually burned at the stake: because petitioners failed to prove the availability of sodium thiopental or pentobarbital, the State could execute them using whatever means it designated. The Eighth Amendment cannot possibly countenance such a result.

"By protecting even those convicted of heinous crimes, the Eighth Amendment reaffirms the duty of the government to respect the dignity of all persons." Today, however, the Court absolves the State of Oklahoma of this duty. It does so by misconstruing and ignoring the record evidence regarding the constitutional insufficiency of midazolam as a sedative in a three-drug lethal injection cocktail, and by imposing a wholly unprecedented obligation on the condemned inmate to identify an available means for his or her own execution. The contortions necessary to save this particular lethal injection protocol are not worth the price. I dissent.

JUSTICE BREYER filed a dissenting opinion, joined by JUSTICE GINSBURG.

For the reasons stated in Justice Sotomayor's opinion, I dissent from the Court's holding. But rather than try to patch up the death penalty's legal wounds one at a time, I would ask for full briefing on a more basic question: whether the death penalty violates the Constitution.

9

EQUAL APPLICATION AND RACIAL BIAS

A sector of death penalty jurisprudence that has yet to experience the same application of the Eighth Amendment is the issue of racial bias in capital sentencing. It was written in 1981 that "[i]f a black man kill a white man, that be first degree murder; if a white man kill a white man, that be second degree murder; if a black man kill a black man, that be manslaughter; but if a white man kill a black man, that be excusable homicide" (Zeisel, 1981, p. 467). The meteoric rise of African American overrepresentation in prison continued well into this century, termed *The New Jim Crow* by Michelle Alexander, who condemns the current American criminal justice framework for instituting a new caste system (Alexander, 2010). Decades of "tough on crime" policies—and strict sentencing guidelines targeted at mandatory minimums for offenses associated with crack cocaine, for example—have led to disproportionate enforcement of drug laws against Black Americans. This has, in turn, produced gratuitously racially disproportionate incarceration rates. In California, for example, around 6% of the adult population is Black, compared to almost one-third of the prison population. When combined with overcrowding in the same prisons, the effect of every element of the justice system, from arrest, charge, conviction, sentence, to treatment in prison, is compounded. These themes and their impact on Eighth Amendment adjudication are covered in more detail in Chapters 10 and 11, when examining the constitutionality of noncapital sentences and confinement conditions in turn. The vast majority of race-based equal application challenges in constitutional law are not brought under this Amendment, and so this chapter is limited to one key case, although its infamy in the annals of punishments jurisprudence warrants inclusion.

DOI: 10.4324/9780429398780-10

Statistically, race plays a huge role in the probability of a sentence of death in the United States—this was one of many issues at play in *Furman v. Georgia*, outlined at length in Chapter 5. In that famously fractured 5–4 ruling, two of the concurrences, by Justices Brennan and Marshall, would have found that the death penalty was unconstitutional in all circumstances and emphasized the "arbitrariness" and "untrammeled discretion" of juries, amounting to an "open invitation" to engage in racial discrimination. A third justice, Justice Douglas, decried how unfettered discretion led to racist results. Justices Stewart and White avoided referring in particular to race but condemned the arbitrary application no less. Justice Stewart's opinion is best summed up by his oft-quoted line: "These death sentences are cruel and unusual in the same way that being struck by lightning is cruel and unusual." As *Furman* was confined to history by the *Gregg-Lockett-Eddings* requirements for individualized sentencing, the liberal-leaning Justices repeatedly argued that the these requirements could successfully curb racist death sentences. This was the subject of a major Supreme Court ruling handed down in ***McCLESKEY v. KEMP***, 481 U.S. 279 (1987).

McCleskey was a Black man who, ten years prior, had killed a white police officer during the course of a robbery. He claimed that the Georgia statute under which his penalty of death had been imposed was administered in a racially discriminatory manner, in violation of both the Eighth and Fourteenth Amendments. In support of the claim, the petitioner proffered a statistical study (the "Baldus study") demonstrating a disparity in the imposition of the death sentence in Georgia based on the murder victim's race and, to a lesser extent, the defendant's race (Baldus, Pulaski and Woodworth, 1983).

That study, based on 2,000 Georgian murder cases from the 1970s, indicated that Black defendants who killed white victims have the greatest likelihood of receiving the death penalty (4.3 times more likely than the counterfactual). In addition, the study showed that Black defendants were 1.1 times more likely to receive a death sentence than non-Black defendants. Rejecting his constitutional claims, the Court found 5–4 against McCleskey's arguments and found the statistics insufficient to demonstrate the irrationality, arbitrariness, and capriciousness required to succeed under Eighth Amendment analysis. Justice Powell's majority held that the opportunities for discretionary leniency under state law did not render the capital sentences imposed arbitrary and capricious. Because the petitioner's sentence was imposed under a sentencing regime focused on "the particularized nature of the crime and the particularized characteristics of the individual defendant," it was not "wantonly and freakishly" as proscribed by the Punishments Clause (the *Gregg* criteria). Controversially to the commentariat, the Court held further that even though the study might demonstrate likely racial prejudice, this did not constitute the constitutional measure of an unacceptable risk of racial prejudice.

The Court accepted that "the criminal justice system was probably inherently racist," but denied Eighth Amendment protection until *deliberate* government bias could be proven—a similar standard of proof to the *Baze* principles of harm outlined in the previous chapter. While Powell's majority acknowledged that "the power to be lenient [also] is the power to discriminate," he contended that, on the whole, the benefits of expansive juror discretion outweighed the costs. Praising the jury as "a criminal defendant's fundamental 'protection of life and liberty against race or color prejudice,'" Powell cited broad juror discretion as a gift to defendants because jury decisions to acquit or to bestow mercy are not reviewable. "As we have stated specifically in the context of capital punishment," he wrote, "the Constitution does not place totally unrealistic conditions on its use." The implications of Powell's words were that the individualized sentencing requirement permitted jurors to rely on racial considerations to spare white defendants and defendants convicted of murdering Black victims, for instance, and that a few "undeserving" individuals were receiving mercy.

In an impassioned dissent, Justice Brennan argued against the constitutionality of the Georgia capital sentencing scheme, emphasizing the necessity of individualized sentencing. "[I]t has been scarcely a generation since this Court's first decision striking down racial segregation, and barely two decades since the legislative prohibition of racial discrimination in major domains of national life," he wrote, arguing that the United States had not yet escaped the strong grip of centuries of this historical legacy. While "honorable steps" were taken, Warren McCleskey's evidence was ignored at their peril: "[W]e remain imprisoned by the past as long as we deny its influence in the present." Brennan asserted that considering the race of a defendant or victim when deciding on the death penalty is fundamentally incompatible with the principle of evaluating each person as unique. He criticized racially influenced decisions for relying on a generalized assessment of human worth based on color, which disregards the individual qualities of the people involved. He warned that judicial discretion should serve as a tool, not a goal, to ensure that the requirement for individualized sentencing acts as a safeguard against racially biased outcomes. Furthermore, he stated that "[discretion] is bestowed in order to permit the sentencer to 'trea[t] each defendant in a capital case with that degree of respect due the uniqueness of the individual.'"

Brennan's dissent highlighted the stark reality of the unadjusted data, revealing that the capital sentencing rate for cases involving white victims was nearly 11 times higher than for cases with Black victims. Additionally,

Black defendants with white victims faced death sentences almost 22 times more frequently than Black defendants with Black victims and over seven times more often than white defendants with Black victims. The Baldus study provided further evidence, showing that prosecutors sought the death penalty in 70% of cases involving Black defendants with white victims, but only in 15% of cases with Black defendants and Black victims, and 19% for white defendants with Black victims. Brennan criticized the majority's slippery slope analysis, which had warned that a ruling in favor of McCleskey could undermine the entire legal system by prompting similar claims regarding other penalties, thereby challenging the foundational principles of criminal justice. Brennan decried this as a "fear of too much justice." He contended that any reasonable analysis of the Baldus study would find the risk of racial influence in McCleskey's sentence intolerable by any standard:

> It is tempting to pretend that minorities on death row share a fate in no way connected to our own, that our treatment of them sounds no echoes beyond the chambers in which they die. Such an illusion is ultimately corrosive, for the reverberations of injustice are not so easily confined. "The destinies of the two races in this country are indissolubly linked together" and the way in which we choose those who will die reveals the depth of moral commitment among the living.
>
> The Court's decision today will not change what attorneys in Georgia tell other Warren McCleskeys about their chances of execution. Nothing will soften the harsh message they must convey, nor alter the prospect that race undoubtedly will continue to be a topic of discussion. McCleskey's evidence will not have obtained judicial acceptance, but that will not affect what is said on death row. However many criticisms of today's decision may be rendered, these painful conversations will serve as the most eloquent dissents of all.

Just 15 years after it suspended the death penalty nationally because it was incurably infected with racial bias, the Court in *McCleskey* faced unequivocal evidence that efforts to eliminate arbitrariness and racial bias in the death penalty had failed, but the Justices nonetheless declined to strike down the Georgia statute. Anthony Amsterdam, who had successfully argued *Furman* for the NAACP Legal Defense and Educational Fund, described *McCleskey* as "the *Dred Scott* decision of our time," by reference to the decision 130 years earlier upholding slavery.[1] The case had wide-ranging

1 *Dred Scott v. Sandford*, 60 U.S. 393 (1856).

impacts and has been described as a missed opportunity for the majority of Justices, with three of them (Stevens, Powell, and Blackmun) later becoming ardent opponents of capital punishments and have since been on record as having regretted their decisions in that judgment. Those regrets were fruitless. On September 25, 1991, the same year retired Justice Powell expressed regret over his McCleskey vote and advocated for the abolition of capital punishment, Warren McCleskey was executed by electrocution.

The Supreme Court grew even more conservative after Powell departed, and though lower courts might have shown willing to condemn the decision,[2] the nation's highest tribunal has yet to resolve the issue of race in capital sentencing. Race is reported to have been the elephant in the room during *Furman*: Justice Brennan—while vehemently against the death penalty and in favor of the LDF's arguments—allegedly regularly persuaded his colleagues to remove references to race, and Chief Justice Warren agreed.[3] A grant of *certiorari* in June 2015 appeared to offer a route to further scrutiny. That challenge, *Foster v. Chatman*, 136 S. Ct. 1737 (2016), asked whether the Georgia Supreme Court failed to recognize racial discrimination in a capital appeal. Specifically, when it had become apparent that prosecutors wrongly offered "race-neutral" justifications for what could in fact be deemed willful and unconstitutional discrimination. The Court decided in favor of the defendant, 7–1, concluding that the Supreme Court of Georgia's decision that Foster failed to show purposeful discrimination was clearly erroneous. The racial references plainly belied the State's claim that it exercised its strikes in a "color-blind" manner. That decision, however, was so tightly focused on the immediate case that far-reaching consequences seem unlikely: No reference was made to the Eighth Amendment and *McCleskey* remains controlling.

More recent research expanding on the Baldus study has demonstrated that the impact of race on death penalty outcomes is even greater than previously known, with a 2020 report finding that defendants convicted of murder in cases with white victims were 17 times more likely to be executed than those convicted of killing a Black person (Phillips and Marceau, 2020). More than three-quarters of those executed in the United States since *McCleskey* were condemned to death for killing white people, even though the number of Black homicide victims over the same period has exceeded that of white homicide victims by at least 13,000 people.

2 Justice Borden wrote for a unanimous Appellate Court in *Abdullah v. Commissioner of Correction* 1 A. 3d. 1102 (Conn. App. Ct. 2010) indicating *McCleskey* as an outlier but deferring due to its federal precedence.

3 See Mandery, E. (2014) *A Wild Justice*. New York: W.W. Norton, pp.181–182 and generally, on *Furman* and relevant 1970s jurisprudence.

Recent research building on the Baldus study has revealed that the racial impact on death penalty outcomes is even more significant than previously understood.

References

Alexander, M. (2010) *The new Jim Crow*. New York: The New Press.
Baldus, D.C., Pulaski, C. and Woodworth, G. (1983) 'Comparative review of death sentences: an empirical study of the Georgia experience', *Journal of Criminal Law and Criminology*, 74, p. 661.
Mandery, E. (2014) *A Wild Justice*. New York: W.W. Norton.
Phillips, S. and Marceau, J. (2020) 'Whom the state kills', *Harvard Civil Rights-Civil Liberties Law Review*, 55(2), pp. 585–656.
Zeisel, H. (1981) 'Race bias in the administration of the death penalty—the Florida experience', *Harvard Law Review*, 95, p. 456.

Cited cases

Abdullah v. Commissioner of Correction, 1 A. 3d. 1102 (Conn. App. Ct.) (2010).
Dred Scott v. Sandford, 60 U.S. 393 (1856).
Eddings v. Oklahoma, 455 U.S. 104 (1982).
Foster v. Chatman, 136 S. Ct. 1737 (2016).
Furman v. Georgia, 408 U.S. 238 (1972).
Gregg v. Georgia, 428 U.S. 153 (1976).
Lockett v. Ohio, 438 U.S. 586 (1978).
McCleskey v. Kemp, 481 U.S. 279 (1987).

McCLESKEY v. KEMP, 481 U.S. 279 (1987)

JUSTICE POWELL delivered the opinion of the Court, joined by CHIEF JUSTICE REHNQUIST and JUSTICES WHITE, O'CONNOR, and SCALIA.

This case presents the question whether a complex statistical study that indicates a risk that racial considerations enter into capital sentencing determinations proves that petitioner McCleskey's capital sentence is unconstitutional under the Eighth or Fourteenth Amendment.

McCleskey next filed a petition for a writ of habeas corpus in the Federal District Court for the Northern District of Georgia. His petition raised 18 claims, one of which was that the Georgia capital sentencing process is administered in a racially discriminatory manner in violation of the Eighth and Fourteenth Amendments to the United States Constitution. In support of his claim, McCleskey proffered a statistical study performed by Professors David C. Baldus, Charles Pulaski, and George Woodworth, and (the Baldus study) that purports to show a disparity in the imposition of the death sentence in Georgia based on the race of the murder victim and, to a lesser extent, the race of the defendant. The Baldus study is actually two sophisticated statistical studies that examine over 2,000 murder cases that occurred in Georgia during the 1970's. The raw numbers collected by Professor Baldus indicate that defendants charged with killing white persons received the death penalty in 11% of the cases, but defendants charged with killing blacks received the death penalty in only 1% of the cases. The raw numbers also indicate a reverse racial disparity according to the race of the defendant: 4% of the black defendants received the death penalty, as opposed to 7% of the white defendants.

Baldus also divided the cases according to the combination of the race of the defendant and the race of the victim. He found that the death penalty was assessed in 22% of the cases involving black defendants and white victims; 8% of the cases involving white defendants and white victims; 1% of the cases involving black defendants and black victims; and 3% of the cases involving white defendants and black victims. Similarly, Baldus found that prosecutors sought the death penalty in 70% of the cases involving black defendants and white victims; 32% of the cases involving white defendants and white victims; 15% of the cases involving black defendants and black victims; and 19% of the cases involving white defendants and black victims.

Baldus subjected his data to an extensive analysis, taking account of 230 variables that could have explained the disparities on nonracial grounds. One of his models concludes that, even after taking account of

39 nonracial variables, defendants charged with killing white victims were 4.3 times as likely to receive a death sentence as defendants charged with killing blacks. According to this model, black defendants were 1.1 times as likely to receive a death sentence as other defendants. Thus, the Baldus study indicates that black defendants, such as McCleskey, who kill white victims have the greatest likelihood of receiving the death penalty.

III

McCleskey also argues that the Baldus study demonstrates that the Georgia capital sentencing system violates the Eighth Amendment.

In the cases decided after *Gregg*, the Court has imposed a number of requirements on the capital sentencing process to ensure that capital sentencing decisions rest on the individualized inquiry contemplated in Gregg. [. . .] In sum, our decisions since Furman have identified a constitutionally permissible range of discretion in imposing the death penalty. First, there is a required threshold below which the death penalty cannot be imposed. In this context, the State must establish rational criteria that narrow the decisionmaker's judgment as to whether the circumstances of a particular defendant's case meet the threshold. Moreover, a societal consensus that the death penalty is disproportionate to a particular offense prevents a State from imposing the death penalty for that offense. Second, States cannot limit the sentencer's consideration of any relevant circumstance that could cause it to decline to impose the penalty. In this respect, the State cannot channel the sentencer's discretion, but must allow it to consider any relevant information offered by the defendant.

IV

A

In light of our precedents under the Eighth Amendment, McCleskey cannot argue successfully that his sentence is "disproportionate to the crime in the traditional sense."

On the one hand, he cannot base a constitutional claim on an argument that his case differs from other cases in which defendants did receive the death penalty. On automatic appeal, the Georgia Supreme Court found that McCleskey's death sentence was not disproportionate to other death sentences imposed in the State. The court supported this conclusion with an appendix containing citations to 13 cases involving generally similar murders. Moreover, where the statutory procedures adequately channel the sentencer's discretion, such proportionality review is not constitutionally required.

On the other hand, absent a showing that the Georgia capital punishment system operates in an arbitrary and capricious manner, McCleskey cannot prove a constitutional violation by demonstrating that other defendants who may be similarly situated did not receive the death penalty.

Because McCleskey's sentence was imposed under Georgia sentencing procedures that focus discretion "on the particularized nature of the crime and the particularized characteristics of the individual defendant," we lawfully may presume that McCleskey's death sentence was not "wantonly and freakishly" imposed, and thus that the sentence is not disproportionate within any recognized meaning under the Eighth Amendment.

B

Although our decision in *Gregg* as to the facial validity of the Georgia capital punishment statute appears to foreclose McCleskey's disproportionality argument, he further contends that the Georgia capital punishment system is arbitrary and capricious in application, and therefore his sentence is excessive, because racial considerations may influence capital sentencing decisions in Georgia. We now address this claim.

To evaluate McCleskey's challenge, we must examine exactly what the Baldus study may show. Even Professor Baldus does not contend that his statistics prove that race enters into any capital sentencing decisions or that race was a factor in McCleskey's particular case. Statistics at most may show only a likelihood that a particular factor entered into some decisions. There is, of course, some risk of racial prejudice influencing a jury's decision in a criminal case. There are similar risks that other kinds of prejudice will influence other criminal trials. McCleskey asks us to accept the likelihood allegedly shown by the Baldus study as the constitutional measure of an unacceptable risk of racial prejudice influencing capital sentencing decisions. This we decline to do.

Individual jurors bring to their deliberations "qualities of human nature and varieties of human experience, the range of which is unknown and perhaps unknowable." The capital sentencing decision requires the individual jurors to focus their collective judgment on the unique characteristics of a particular criminal defendant. It is not surprising that such collective judgments often are difficult to explain. But the inherent lack of predictability of jury decisions does not justify their condemnation. On the contrary, it is the jury's function to make the difficult and uniquely human judgments that defy codification and that "buil[d] discretion, equity, and flexibility into a legal system."

McCleskey's argument that the Constitution condemns the discretion allowed decisionmakers in the Georgia capital sentencing system is antithetical to the fundamental role of discretion in our criminal justice system. Discretion in the criminal justice system offers substantial benefits to the criminal defendant. Not only can a jury decline to impose the death sentence, it can decline to convict or choose to convict of a lesser offense. Whereas decisions against a defendant's interest may be reversed by the trial judge or on appeal, these discretionary exercises of leniency are final and unreviewable. Similarly, the capacity of prosecutorial discretion to provide individualized justice is "firmly entrenched in American law."

C

At most, the Baldus study indicates a discrepancy that appears to correlate with race. Apparent disparities in sentencing are an inevitable part of our criminal justice system. The discrepancy indicated by the Baldus study is "a far cry from the major systemic defects identified in *Furman*." As this Court has recognized, any mode for determining guilt or punishment "has its weaknesses and the potential for misuse." Where the discretion that is fundamental to our criminal process is involved, we decline to assume that what is unexplained is invidious. In light of the safeguards designed to minimize racial bias in the process, the fundamental value of jury trial in our criminal justice system, and the benefits that discretion provides to criminal defendants, we hold that the Baldus study does not demonstrate a constitutionally significant risk of racial bias affecting the Georgia capital sentencing process.

V

Two additional concerns inform our decision in this case. First, McCleskey's claim, taken to its logical conclusion, throws into serious question the principles that underlie our entire criminal justice system. The Eighth Amendment is not limited in application to capital punishment, but applies to all penalties. Thus, if we accepted McCleskey's claim that racial bias has impermissibly tainted the capital sentencing decision, we could soon be faced with similar claims as to other types of penalty. Moreover, the claim that his sentence rests on the irrelevant factor of race easily could be extended to apply to claims based on unexplained discrepancies that correlate to membership in other minority groups, and even to gender. Similarly, since McCleskey's claim relates to the race of his victim, other claims could apply with equally logical force to statistical disparities that correlate with the race or sex of other actors in the criminal justice system, such as defense attorneys, or judges. Also, there is no logical reason that such a claim need be limited to racial or sexual bias. If arbitrary and capricious punishment is the touchstone under the Eighth Amendment, such a claim could—at least in theory—be based upon any arbitrary variable, such as the defendant's facial characteristics, or the physical attractiveness of the defendant or the victim, that some statistical study indicates may be influential in jury decisionmaking. As these examples illustrate, there is no limiting principle to the type of challenge brought by McCleskey. The Constitution does not require that a State eliminate any demonstrable disparity that correlates with a potentially irrelevant factor in order to operate a criminal justice system that includes capital punishment. As we have stated specifically in the context of capital punishment, the Constitution does not "plac[e] totally unrealistic conditions on its use."

Capital punishment is now the law in more than two-thirds of our States. It is the ultimate duty of courts to determine on a case-by-case basis whether these laws are applied consistently with the Constitution. Despite McCleskey's wide-ranging arguments that basically challenge the validity of capital punishment in our multiracial society, the only question before us is whether in his case, the law of Georgia was properly applied. We agree with the District Court and the Court of Appeals for the Eleventh Circuit that this was carefully and correctly done in this case.

JUSTICE BRENNAN filed a dissenting opinion, joined by JUSTICE MARSHALL and (in all but Part I), by JUSTICES BLACKMUN and STEVENS.

I

Adhering to my view that the death penalty is in all circumstances cruel and unusual punishment forbidden by the Eighth and Fourteenth Amendments, I would vacate the decision below insofar as it left undisturbed the death sentence imposed in this case.

I write separately to emphasize how conclusively McCleskey has also demonstrated precisely the type of risk of irrationality in sentencing that we have consistently condemned in our Eighth Amendment jurisprudence.

II

At some point in this case, Warren McCleskey doubtless asked his lawyer whether a jury was likely to sentence him to die. A candid reply to this question would have been disturbing. First, counsel would have to tell McCleskey that few of the details of the crime or of McCleskey's past criminal conduct were more important than the fact that his victim was white. Furthermore, counsel would feel bound to tell McCleskey that defendants charged with killing white victims in Georgia are 4.3 times as likely to be sentenced to death as defendants charged with killing blacks. In addition, frankness would compel the disclosure that it was more likely than not that the race of McCleskey's victim would determine whether he received a death sentence: 6 of every 11 defendants convicted of killing a white person would not have received the death penalty if their victims had been black, while, among defendants with aggravating and mitigating factors comparable to McCleskey's, 20 of every 34 would not have been sentenced to die if their victims had been black. Finally, the assessment would not be complete without the information that cases involving black defendants and white victims are more likely to result in a death sentence than cases featuring any other racial combination of defendant and victim. The story could be told in a variety of ways, but McCleskey could not fail to grasp its essential narrative line: there was a significant chance that race would play a prominent role in determining if he lived or died.

The Court today holds that Warren McCleskey's sentence was constitutionally imposed. It finds no fault in a system in which lawyers must tell their clients that race casts a large shadow on the capital sentencing process. The Court arrives at this conclusion by stating that the Baldus study cannot "prove that race enters into any capital sentencing decisions or that race was a factor in McCleskey's particular case." Since, according to Professor Baldus, we cannot say "to a moral certainty" that race influenced a decision, we can identify only "a likelihood that a particular factor entered into some decisions," and "a discrepancy that appears to correlate with race." This "likelihood" and "discrepancy," holds the Court, is insufficient to establish a constitutional violation. The Court reaches this conclusion by placing four factors on the scales opposite McCleskey's evidence: the desire to encourage sentencing discretion, the existence of "statutory safeguards" in the Georgia scheme, the fear of encouraging widespread challenges to other sentencing decisions, and the limits of the judicial role. The Court's evaluation of the significance of petitioner's evidence is fundamentally at odds with our consistent concern for rationality in capital sentencing, and the considerations that the majority invokes to discount that evidence cannot justify ignoring its force.

III

A

It is important to emphasize at the outset that the Court's observation that McCleskey cannot prove the influence of race on any particular sentencing decision is irrelevant in evaluating his Eighth Amendment claim.

Defendants challenging their death sentences thus never have had to prove that impermissible considerations have actually infected sentencing decisions. We have required instead that they establish that the system under which they were sentenced posed a significant risk of such an occurrence. McCleskey's claim does differ, however, in one respect from these earlier cases: it is the first to base a challenge not on speculation about how a system might operate, but on empirical documentation of how it does operate.

The Court assumes the statistical validity of the Baldus study, and acknowledges that McCleskey has demonstrated a risk that racial prejudice plays a role in capital sentencing in Georgia, Nonetheless, it finds the probability of prejudice insufficient to create constitutional concern. Close analysis of the Baldus study, however, in light of both statistical principles and human experience, reveals that the risk that race influenced McCleskey's sentence is intolerable by any imaginable standard.

B

The Baldus study indicates that, after taking into account some 230 nonracial factors that might legitimately influence a sentencer, the jury more likely than not would have spared McCleskey's life had his victim been black. The study distinguishes between those cases in which (1) the jury exercises virtually no discretion because the strength or weakness of aggravating factors usually suggests that only one outcome is appropriate; and (2) cases reflecting an "intermediate" level of aggravation, in which the jury has considerable discretion in choosing a sentence. McCleskey's case falls into the intermediate range. In such cases, death is imposed in 34% of white-victim crimes and 14% of black-victim crimes, a difference of 139% in the rate of imposition of the death penalty. In other words, just under 59%—almost 6 in 10—defendants comparable to McCleskey would not have received the death penalty if their victims had been black.

Furthermore, even examination of the sentencing system as a whole, factoring in those cases in which the jury exercises little discretion, indicates the influence of race on capital sentencing. For the Georgia system as a whole, race accounts for a six percentage point difference in the rate at which capital punishment is imposed. Since death is imposed in 11% of all white-victim cases, the rate in comparably aggravated black-victim cases is 5%. The rate of capital sentencing in a white-victim case is thus 120% greater than the rate in a black-victim case. Put another way, over half—55%—of defendants in white-victim crimes in Georgia would not have been sentenced to die if their victims had been black. Of the more than 200 variables potentially relevant to a sentencing decision, race of the victim is a powerful explanation for variation in death sentence rates—as powerful as nonracial aggravating factors such as a prior murder conviction or acting as the principal planner of the homicide.

Data unadjusted for the mitigating or aggravating effect of other factors show an even more pronounced disparity by race. The capital sentencing rate for all white-victim cases was almost 11 times greater than the rate for black-victim cases. Furthermore, blacks who kill whites are sentenced to death at nearly 22 times the rate of blacks who kill blacks, and more than 7 times the rate of whites who kill blacks. In addition, prosecutors seek the death penalty for 70% of black defendants with white victims, but for only 15% of black defendants with black victims, and only 19% of white defendants with black victims. Since our decision upholding the Georgia capital sentencing system in *Gregg*, the State has executed seven persons. All of the seven were convicted of killing whites, and six of the seven executed were black. Such execution figures are especially striking in light of the fact that, during the period encompassed by the Baldus study, only 9.2% of Georgia homicides involved black defendants and white victims, while 60.7% involved black victims.

McCleskey's statistics have particular force because most of them are the product of sophisticated multiple-regression analysis. Such analysis is designed precisely to identify patterns in the aggregate, even though we may not be able to reconstitute with certainty any individual decision that goes to make up that pattern. Multiple-regression analysis is particularly well suited to identify the influence of impermissible considerations in sentencing, since it is able to control for permissible factors that may explain an apparent arbitrary pattern.

The statistical evidence in this case thus relentlessly documents the risk that McCleskey's sentence was influenced by racial considerations. This evidence shows that there is a better than even chance in Georgia that race will influence the decision to impose the death penalty: a majority of defendants in white-victim crimes would not have been sentenced to die if their victims had been black. In determining whether this risk is acceptable, our judgment must be shaped by the awareness that "[t]he risk of racial prejudice infecting a capital sentencing proceeding is especially serious in light of the complete finality of the death sentence," and that "[i]t is of vital importance to the defendant and to the community that any decision to impose the death sentence be, and appear to be, based on reason rather than caprice or emotion." In determining the guilt of a defendant, a State must prove its case beyond a reasonable doubt. That is, we refuse to convict if the chance of error is simply less likely than not. Surely, we should not be willing to take a person's life if the chance that his death sentence was irrationally imposed is more likely than not. In light of the gravity of the interest at stake, petitioner's statistics on their face are a powerful demonstration of the type of risk that our Eighth Amendment jurisprudence has consistently condemned.

[. . .]

The majority thus misreads our Eighth Amendment jurisprudence in concluding that McCleskey has not demonstrated a degree of risk sufficient to raise constitutional concern. The determination of the significance of his evidence is at its core an exercise in human moral judgment, not a mechanical statistical analysis. It must first and foremost be informed by awareness of the fact that death is irrevocable, and that as a result "the qualitative difference of death from all other punishments requires a greater degree of scrutiny of the capital sentencing determination." For this reason, we have demanded a uniquely high degree of rationality in imposing the death penalty. A capital sentencing system in which race more likely than not plays a role does not meet this standard. It is true that every nuance of decision cannot be statistically captured, nor can any individual judgment be plumbed with absolute certainty. Yet the fact that we must always act without the illumination of complete knowledge cannot induce paralysis when we confront what is literally an issue of life and death. Sentencing data, history, and experience all counsel that Georgia has provided insufficient assurance of the heightened rationality we have required in order to take a human life.

V

At the time our Constitution was framed 200 years ago this year, blacks "had for more than a century before been regarded as beings of an inferior order, and altogether unfit to associate with the white race, either in social or political relations; and so far inferior, that they had no rights which the white man was bound to respect." Only 130 years ago, this Court relied on these observations to deny American citizenship to blacks. A mere three generations ago, this Court sanctioned racial segregation, stating that "[i]f one race be inferior to the other socially, the Constitution of the United States cannot put them upon the same plane."

In more recent times, we have sought to free ourselves from the burden of this history. Yet it has been scarcely a generation since this Court's first decision striking down racial segregation, and barely two decades since the legislative prohibition of racial discrimination in major domains of national life. These have been honorable steps, but we cannot pretend that in three decades we have completely escaped the grip of a historical legacy spanning centuries. Warren McCleskey's evidence confronts us with the subtle and persistent influence of the past. His message is a disturbing one to a society that has formally repudiated racism, and a frustrating one to a Nation accustomed to regarding its destiny as the product of its own will. Nonetheless, we ignore him at our peril, for we remain imprisoned by the past as long as we deny its influence in the present.

It is tempting to pretend that minorities on death row share a fate in no way connected to our own, that our treatment of them sounds no echoes beyond the chambers in which they die. Such an illusion is ultimately corrosive, for the reverberations of injustice are not so easily confined. "The destinies of the two races in this country are indissolubly linked together," and the way in which we choose those who will die reveals the depth of moral commitment among the living.

The Court's decision today will not change what attorneys in Georgia tell other Warren McCleskeys about their chances of execution. Nothing will soften the harsh message they must convey, nor alter the prospect that race undoubtedly will continue to be a topic of discussion. McCleskey's evidence will not have obtained judicial acceptance, but that will not affect what is said on death row. However many criticisms of today's decision may be rendered, these painful conversations will serve as the most eloquent dissents of all.

JUSTICE BLACKMUN filed a dissenting opinion, joined by JUSTICES MARSHALL and STEVENS and (in all but Part IV-B), by JUSTICE BRENNAN.

The Court today sanctions the execution of a man despite his presentation of evidence that establishes a constitutionally intolerable level of racially based discrimination leading to the imposition of his death sentence. I am disappointed with the Court's action not only because of its denial of constitutional guarantees to petitioner McCleskey individually, but also because of its departure from what seems to me to be well-developed constitutional jurisprudence.

[. . .] McCleskey's case raises concerns that are central not only to the principles underlying the Eighth Amendment, but also to the principles underlying the Fourteenth Amendment. Analysis of his case in terms of the Fourteenth Amendment is consistent with this Court's recognition that racial discrimination is fundamentally at odds with our constitutional guarantee of equal protection. The protections afforded by the Fourteenth Amendment are not left at the courtroom door.

The Court's assertion that the fact of McCleskey's conviction undermines his constitutional claim is inconsistent with a long and unbroken line of this Court's case law. The Court on numerous occasions during the past century has recognized that an otherwise legitimate basis for a conviction does not outweigh an equal protection violation. In cases where racial discrimination in the administration of the criminal justice system is established, it has held that setting aside the conviction is the appropriate remedy.

The Court's reliance on legitimate interests underlying the Georgia Legislature's enactment of its capital punishment statute is likewise inappropriate.

When questioned directly as to how the office decided whether to seek the death penalty, Slaton listed several factors he thought relevant to that decision, including the strength of the evidence, the atrociousness of the crime, and the likelihood that a jury would impose the death sentence. He explained that the attorneys did not seek the death penalty in every case in which statutory aggravating factors existed.

In addition to this showing that the challenged system was susceptible to abuse, McCleskey presented evidence of the history of prior discrimination in the Georgia system.

[. . .]

I disagree with the Court's assertion that there are fewer variables relevant to the decisions of jury commissioners or prosecutors in their selection of jurors, or to the decisions of employers in their selection, promotion, or discharge of employees. Such decisions involve a multitude of factors, some rational, some irrational. Second, I disagree with the comment that the venire-selection and employment decisions are "made by fewer entities." Certainly in the employment context, personnel decisions are often the product of several levels of decisionmaking within the business or government structure. The Court's statement that the decision to impose death is made by the petit jury also disregards the fact that the prosecutor screens the cases throughout the pretrial proceedings and decides to seek the death penalty and to pursue a capital case to the penalty phase where a death sentence can be imposed. McCleskey's claim in this regard lends itself to analysis under the framework we apply in assessing challenges to other prosecutorial actions.

IV

A

One of the final concerns discussed by the Court may be the most disturbing aspect of its opinion. Granting relief to McCleskey in this case, it is said, could lead to further constitutional challenges. That, of course, is no reason to deny McCleskey his rights under the Equal Protection Clause. If a grant of relief to him were to lead to a closer examination of the effects of racial considerations throughout the criminal justice system, the system, and hence society, might benefit. Where no such factors come into play, the integrity of the system is enhanced. Where such considerations are shown to be significant, efforts can be made to eradicate their impermissible influence and to ensure an evenhanded application of criminal sanctions.

B

Like Justice STEVENS, I do not believe acceptance of McCleskey's claim would eliminate capital punishment in Georgia. Justice STEVENS points out that the evidence presented in this case indicates that in extremely aggravated murders the risk of discriminatory enforcement of the death penalty is minimized. I agree that narrowing the class of death-eligible defendants is not too high a price to pay for a death penalty system that does not discriminate on the basis of race. Moreover, the establishment of guidelines for Assistant District Attorneys as to the appropriate basis for exercising their discretion at the various steps in the prosecution of a case would provide at least a measure of consistency. The Court's emphasis on the procedural safeguards in the system ignores the fact that there are none whatsoever during the crucial process leading up to trial. As Justice WHITE stated for the plurality in *Turner v. Murray*, I find "the risk that racial prejudice may have infected petitioner's capital sentencing unacceptable in light of the ease with which that risk could have been minimized." I dissent.

JUSTICE STEVENS filed a dissenting opinion, joined by JUSTICE BLACKMUN.

In this case it is claimed—and the claim is supported by elaborate studies which the Court properly assumes to be valid that the jury's sentencing process was likely distorted by racial prejudice. The studies demonstrate a strong probability that McCleskey's sentencing jury, which expressed "the community's outrage—its sense that an individual has lost his moral entitlement to live," was influenced by the fact that McCleskey is black and his victim was white, and that this same outrage would not have been generated if he had killed a member of his own race. This sort of disparity is constitutionally intolerable. It flagrantly violates the Court's prior "insistence that capital punishment be imposed fairly, and with reasonable consistency, or not at all."

The Court's decision appears to be based on a fear that the acceptance of McCleskey's claim would sound the death knell for capital punishment in Georgia. If society were indeed forced to choose between a racially discriminatory death penalty (one that provides heightened protection against murder "for whites only") and no death penalty at all, the choice mandated by the Constitution would be plain. But the Court's fear is unfounded. One of the lessons of the Baldus study is that there exist certain categories of extremely serious crimes for which prosecutors consistently seek, and juries consistently impose, the death penalty without regard to the race of the victim or the race of the offender. If Georgia were to narrow the class of death-eligible defendants to those categories, the danger of arbitrary and discriminatory imposition of the death penalty would be significantly decreased, if not eradicated. As Justice BRENNAN has demonstrated in his dissenting opinion, such a restructuring of the sentencing scheme is surely not too high a price to pay.

Like Justice BRENNAN, I would therefore reverse the judgment of the Court of Appeals. I believe, however, that further proceedings are necessary in order to determine whether McCleskey's death sentence should be set aside. First, the Court of Appeals must decide whether the Baldus study is valid. I am persuaded that it is, but orderly procedure requires that the Court of Appeals address this issue before we actually decide the question. Second, it is necessary for the District Court to determine whether the particular facts of McCleskey's crime and his background place this case within the range of cases that present an unacceptable risk that race played a decisive role in McCleskey's sentencing.

Accordingly, I respectfully dissent.

10

NONCAPITAL PROSCRIPTIONS

Having spent five chapters documenting the Supreme Court's treatment of Punishments Clause adjudication, the following and final two substantive chapters turn to noncapital punishment. That is, custodial sentences and the treatment and conditions associated with such imprisonment. This chapter delves into landmark cases that have shaped the interpretation of the Eighth Amendment. From the principle of proportionality in sentencing to the abolition of life without parole for juveniles, these cases illustrate the Court's application of the evolving standards of decency principle to a far wider set of issues in the criminal justice system.

Life imprisonment and proportionality

Following a decade of litigation in the death penalty sphere, the Court first turned to the question of noncapital sentences in *Rummel v. Estelle*, 445 U.S. 263 (1980). In that case, the Justices confirmed that a life sentence under a "three-strikes" law did not constitute cruel and unusual punishment, even for nonviolent felonies. This case affirmed that states have broad discretion in sentencing habitual offenders, emphasizing the state's interest in deterring recidivism. The defendant had, on two previous occasions, been convicted in Texas state courts and sentenced to prison for felonies (fraudulent use of a credit card to obtain $80 worth of goods or services, and passing a forged check in the amount of $28). As a "third strike" he was convicted of a further felony, obtaining $120 by false pretenses, and received a mandatory life sentence pursuant to Texas' recidivist "three strikes and you're out" statute.

DOI: 10.4324/9780429398780-11

Justice Rehnquist's 5–4 majority noted that Texas's interest was not simply that of making criminal the unlawful acquisition of another person's property, but it was designed to deal in a harsher manner with those who, by repeated criminal acts, "have shown that they are incapable of conforming to the norms of society as established by its criminal law." The Texas statute was upheld as a "societal decision" about the treatment of reoffenders. While the third "strike" was in relation to a meager $120 fraud offense, the majority concluded that the state was entitled to make its own judgment as to the dividing line between felony theft and petty larceny and therefore impose strict sentences in whichever way it saw fit—in this case, three relatively minor financial crimes were compounded and assessed to meet that threshold. In an impassioned dissent in *Rummel*, Justice Powell wrote that the Punishments Clause extended not only to barbarous methods but also to those punishments that are grossly disproportionate, including that in this case, in his view. Reviewing the history of the Eighth, Powell concluded that the principle of disproportionality plays just as important a role in the review of sentences imposing noncapital punishments, citing deep roots first found in English constitutional law, including Magna Carta of 1215, which ensured that "[a] free man shall not be [fined] for a trivial offence, except in accordance with the degree of the offence; and for a serious offence he shall be [fined] according to its gravity."

That minority was reversed and secured a majority three years later in ***SOLEM v. HELM***, 463 U.S. 277 (1983), introducing for the first time a clear principle of proportionality to the Eighth Amendment, agnostic of the type of sentence, although dissenters over the following decades would continue to maintain that there was no such principle intended by this clause. In *Solem*, South Dakota, the defendant was convicted of "uttering a *no account* check for $100 ." Ordinarily, the maximum punishment would have been five years' imprisonment and a $5,000 fine, but he was sentenced to life imprisonment without the possibility of parole because of his six prior felony convictions (all of which were nonviolent). This time writing for the majority (again 5–4, but with Justice Blackmun providing the swing in moving to the liberal side on this occasion), Justice Powell delivered a landmark ruling, holding that the Eighth Amendment's proscription of cruel and unusual punishments prohibits not only barbaric punishments but also sentences that are disproportionate to the crime committed, on extremely similar lines to the dissent in *Rummel*, again citing Magna Carta and centuries of application by English courts. Moreover, the Court held that this constitutional principle of proportionality had been recognized explicitly in several cases since *Weems* and that no penalty is *per se* constitutional.

Second, *Solem* established a three-part objective test based on previous case law to determine if a punishment is cruel and unusual, considering: "(i) the gravity of the offense and the harshness of the penalty; (ii) the sentences imposed on other criminals in the same jurisdiction; and (iii) the sentences imposed for commission of the same crime in other jurisdictions." The majority concluded that courts are competent to judge the gravity of an offense, at least on a relative scale, noting other accepted principles that courts may apply in measuring the harm caused or threatened to the victim or society. Finally, the majority accepted that their list was by no means exhaustive, noting that the "absolute magnitude" of the crime may be relevant, as will the individual culpability of the particular offender (an important point that will be returned to later and has influenced much of the capital sentencing adjudication outlined in previous chapter).

Revisiting proportionality

In three further cases that followed the *Rummel-Solem* debate over the following two decades, the Court revisited proportionality and declined to increase the Eighth Amendment's reach on each occasion. First in ***HARMELIN v. MICHIGAN***, 501 U.S. 957 (1991), a 5–4 plurality opinion complicated the proportionality principle established in *Solem*, upholding a mandatory life sentence without parole for a nonviolent drug offense. While not explicitly overruling *Solem*, the decision signaled a shift in the Court's approach, suggesting that grossly disproportionate sentences might not be subject to strict proportionality review under the Eighth Amendment. Harmelin was convicted of possessing more than 1.5 pounds of cocaine and received a mandatory sentence of life imprisonment without the possibility of parole under Michigan law. This raised questions about the severity of the punishment for a nonviolent drug offense. Justice Scalia's plurality opinion held that this sentence was not unconstitutional merely because it was mandatory in nature and allowed the sentencer no opportunity to consider "mitigating factors." Severe, mandatory penalties may be cruel, the plurality held, but they are not unusual in the constitutional sense, having been employed in various forms throughout the Nation's history. Justice Scalia (joined by Chief Justice Rehnquist) would have concluded that the Eighth Amendment contains no proportionality guarantee at all, undertaking an extensive review of the original meaning of the Eighth to demonstrate their argument. Justice White's dissent conceded that the Punishments Clause did not refer to proportionality in so many words, but noted that it does forbid "excessive" fines, a restraint that suggests that a determination of excessiveness should be based, at least in part, on whether the fine imposed is disproportionate to the crime committed.

While concurring with the conclusion of the judgment, Justice Kennedy expressed reservations about the lack of proportionality analysis in *Harmelin. Stare decisis*, he concluded, counseled adherence to a narrow proportionality principle that had existed in Eighth Amendment jurisprudence for 80 years, but joined the plurality in upholding the constitutionality of the particular sentence (which was the same as in *Solem*) for not being grossly disproportionate in this instance. In asserting the constitutionality of this mandatory sentence, "I offer no judgment on its wisdom," Kennedy summarized, noting that such punishments can be criticized for depriving judges of the power to exercise individual discretion, but that such sentencing schemes are for legislatures to resolve and not courts. Kennedy's conclusion (joined by Justices O'Connor and Souter) noted that Harmelin's "suggestion that the crime was nonviolent and victimless is false to the point of absurdity," citing the grave threat that illegal drugs, and particularly cocaine, pose to society in terms of violence, crime, and social displacement. This concurrence sets the stage for future cases where the Court might revisit the issue of proportionality in noncapital sentences. Unlike death penalty cases, where the Court has developed clear proportionality standards, *Harmelin* left the door open for states to impose severe noncapital sentences for nonviolent crimes without violating the Constitution. The decision contributed to the broader legal landscape surrounding mandatory minimum sentences and "three-strikes" laws, allowing states to enact stringent sentencing measures for certain offenses. Over a decade later, the Court took the opportunity to review another three-strikes law and clarify how limited the *Solem* precedent should be applied in two cases handed down on the same day in 2003.

First, in ***EWING v. CALIFORNIA***, 538 U.S. 11 (2003), the Supreme Court upheld a 25-year-to-life sentence for an offender who committed a minor theft, concluding that California's recidivist statute was proportionate. The decision—another fractured 5–4 majority with a plurality ruling authored by Justice O'Connor—reinforced the state's authority to impose harsh penalties on habitual offenders, highlighting the balance between public safety and individual rights. While on parole, Ewing had been convicted of felony grand theft for stealing three golf clubs worth $399 apiece. Ewing had been convicted previously of four serious or violent felonies, so the theft offense triggered the state's "three-strikes" law. In sentencing him to 25 years to life, the court refused to exercise its discretion to reduce the conviction to a misdemeanor under a state law that permits certain offenses, known as "wobblers," to be classified as either misdemeanors or felonies, or to dismiss the allegations of some or all of his prior relevant convictions. Justice O'Connor's three-Justice plurality (5–4 on the constitutional question) applied *Harmelin* and concluded that Ewing's sentence was not grossly disproportionate and therefore did not violate the Eighth Amendment's prohibition on cruel and unusual punishments. In a separate concurrence, Justice Scalia agreed that petitioner's sentence does not violate the Eighth Amendment's prohibition against cruel and unusual punishments, but on the ground that that prohibition was aimed at excluding only certain *modes* of punishment, arguing that the case demonstrated why a proportionality principle cannot be intelligently applied and why *Solem* should, in his view, be overruled (which it was not, expressly, in either *Harmelin* or *Ewing*).

Second, the Court considered the parallel case of ***LOCKYER v. ANDRADE***, 538 U.S. 63 (2003), in which two consecutive 25-year-to-life sentences had been imposed on a repeat offender convicted of petty theft under the same California three-strikes law. The Court also upheld this penalty, emphasizing deference to state legislative judgments in determining such schemes. In a lead judgment also authored by Justice O'Connor (this time joined for a clear 5–4 majority), the Court held that the only "clearly established" law emerging from the Court's jurisprudence in this area (through *Rummel, Solem*, and *Harmelin*) is that a gross disproportionality principle applies to such sentences, but that the principle's precise contours are unclear, applicable only in the "exceedingly rare" and "extreme" case, citing Justice Kennedy's concurrence in *Harmelin* as controlling on the matter. The dissenters concluded that "if Andrade's sentence is not grossly disproportionate, the principle has no meaning."

Juveniles and noncapital proportionality

In the 28 years since *Solem*, the "exceedingly rare" principle espoused in *Harmelin* remained controlling, with the Court rejecting all three such challenges it agreed to hear. In 2010, a newly composed bench would return to *Solem*'s case-by-case proportionality standard for noncapital sentences, considering life-without-parole sentences imposed on juvenile non-homicide offenders. As Chapter 7 demonstrated, age was first declared a valid mitigating factor in capital sentencing in 1978 in *Bell* and *Lockett*, where two death sentences for aggravated murder committed by juveniles (those aged under 18) were reversed. These cases, built on by *Eddings* and its precedents, laid the foundation for a series of important rulings defining the Punishments Clause as it pertains to those with lower culpability. In declaring that age is "more than a chronological fact" in *Eddings*, Justice Powell struck down a capital sentence imposed on a 16-year-old—a principle that was later expanded to all under-18 offenders—but failed to increase its reach beyond the death penalty context.

GRAHAM v. FLORIDA, 560 U.S. 48 (2010), presented a fourth opportunity to review a sentence under the *Solem* proportionality principle, this time of a 16-year-old who had committed armed burglary, after which he violated the terms of his probation by committing additional offenses. Graham was sentenced to life in prison for the original burglary due to the reoffending (and, because Florida had abolished its parole system, this left him with no possibility of release except executive clemency). In a 5–4 majority, the Court reasserted the principle that youth matters in sentencing. Reviewing the case under *Weems* principles of proportionality and extending the capital sentencing jurisprudence to non-homicide offenses such as Graham's, the Justices applied "objective indicia of society's standards, as expressed in legislative enactments and state practice" and "the standards elaborated by controlling precedents and by the Court's own understanding and interpretation of the Eighth Amendment's text, history, meaning, and purpose." By combining these precedents with the categorical approach in *Atkins-Roper-Kennedy* (principles of subjective offender assessments), a majority was convinced that the sentencing practice at issue was *per se* unconstitutional, not just in *Graham*'s case.

First, six jurisdictions did not permit life without parole for juvenile offenders under any circumstances, and seven allowed it only for homicide offenses. In 37 states, the District of Columbia, and the Federal Government, juvenile offenders could receive life without parole for non-homicide offenses under certain conditions. Florida argued that these figures indicated no national consensus against this sentencing practice. However, an analysis of actual sentencing practices revealed a different picture: [O]nly 129 juveniles nationwide were serving life without parole for non-homicide crimes. Notably, 77 of these were in Florida, and the remaining 52 were spread across just 10 states and the federal system, showing that only 12 jurisdictions actively imposed this sentence. In contrast, 26 states and the District of Columbia did not impose it, despite statutory allowances. These statistics indicated how infrequently such sentences were actually imposed, even where they were legally permissible.

Second, the Court found that life without parole for juvenile non-homicide offenders was unjustifiable under penological theory, given the limited culpability of such offenders and the severity of the sentence. *Roper*'s conclusion that juveniles were less culpable and thus less deserving of the harshest punishments remained valid: Juveniles who did not kill or intend to kill were less deserving of extreme punishments than murderers and serious non-homicide crimes (such as in *Graham*'s case), while harmful, did not match the moral depravity or irreversible harm of murder. Since society marked 18 as the boundary between childhood and adulthood, the majority ruled that offenders below this age should not have been sentenced to life without parole for non-homicide crimes. Third, a categorical rule was necessary due to the inadequacies of other approaches in addressing constitutional concerns, and fourth, further support for the Court's conclusion came from the global rejection of this sentencing practice—references to international consensus that sparked fury among the dissenters. The United States stood alone in imposing life without parole for juvenile non-homicide offenders, contributing to the conclusion that the Eighth Amendment's evolving standards of decent compelled a higher bar. Justice Thomas condemned the ruling for eviscerating the distinction of capital punishment: " 'Death is different' no longer," he declared, noting that the Court now claims that " 'less culpable' persons are categorically exempt from the '*second* most severe penalty.' " and that, by way of slippery-slope argument, "[n]o reliable limiting principle remains to prevent the Court from immunizing any class of offenders from the law's third, fourth, fifth, or fiftieth most severe penalties as well."

Two years later, the Court permitted life-without-parole sentences for defendants who committed *homicide* when they were under 18, but only so long as the sentence is not mandatory—that is, only so long as the sentencer has discretion to "consider the mitigating qualities of youth" and impose a lesser punishment. In so doing, the Court declared unconstitutional any scheme of mandatory life without parole for non-homicide juvenile offenders. In that case, ***MILLER v. ALABAMA***, 567 U.S. 460 (2012), the Justices considered the joint cases of 14-year-olds, Miller and Jackson, who had been convicted of murder and sentenced to mandatory terms of life imprisonment without the possibility of parole. In Justice Kagan's 5–4 majority opinion, the Court applied the two lines of precedent concerning proportionate punishment in *Graham* (first, the categorical bans on sentencing practices where there is a mismatch between the offender's culpability and the severity of the penalty, and second, where sentencing authorities must consider the defendant's characteristics and offense details before imposing the death penalty). Kagan noted that both *Roper* and *Graham* establish that juveniles are constitutionally different from adults for sentencing purposes due to their lack of maturity, underdeveloped sense of responsibility, and vulnerability to negative influences. These differences diminish the justifications for imposing the harshest sentences on juveniles, even for serious crimes, her majority concluded, and extended *Graham*'s reasoning applies to any life-without-parole sentence for juveniles.

In sum, mandatory penalty schemes that prevent consideration of a juvenile's youth and circumstances violate the foundational principle that juveniles should not be sentenced as if they were adults. Although they did not foreclose a sentencer's ability to make the judgment of whether a juvenile deserves a life without parole in homicide cases, they did clarify a constitutional requirement for them to "take into account how children are different, and how those differences counsel against irrevocably sentencing them to a lifetime in prison." Justice Alito's dissent (joined by Justice Scalia) continued to expose growing concerns from the Court's conservative half (in 2024, a strong majority view), writing in opposition to the evolving standards test: "Unless our cases change course, we will continue to march toward some vision of evolutionary culmination that the Court has not yet disclosed. The Constitution does not authorize us to take the country on this journey."

The *Miller* rule was later extended by *Montgomery v. Louisiana*, 136 S. Ct. 718 (2016), with Chief Justice Roberts joining to bolster a 6–3 majority on that occasion. The Court held that the mandatory scheme ruled unconstitutional in *Miller* must be applied retroactively, allowing those previously sentenced to mandatory life without parole as juveniles to seek resentencing or parole (such as Henry Montgomery himself, whose offense had been carried out 50 years prior, when he was 17). This case underscored the commitment to fair sentencing practices and the ongoing evolution of the Eighth Amendment's application, and was limited in *Jones v. Mississippi*, 141 S. Ct. 1307 (2021), where the appellant contended that a sentencer must make a separate factual finding that a murderer under 18 is permanently incorrigible before sentencing the offender to life without parole. A six-Justice majority opinion authored by Justice Kavanaugh found that, in cases of defendants who committed a homicide when they were under 18 years old, *Miller* and *Montgomery* do not require the sentencer to make a separate factual finding of "permanent incorrigibility" before sentencing the defendant to life without parole. In such a case, a discretionary sentencing system is both constitutionally necessary and constitutionally sufficient. The dissenters, led by Justice Sotomayor, wrote that the majority opinion was "an abrupt break from precedent" and indicated that a state should, in most cases, "consider whether a juvenile offender has demonstrated maturity and rehabilitation sufficient to merit a chance at life beyond the prison in which he has grown up"—something denied by the ruling in *Jones*, although leaving unaffected the categorical bars from *Graham* (against mandatory juvenile life-without-parole schemes) *and Miller* (against all life-without-parole sentences imposed on juveniles who did not commit homicide offenses).

Cited cases

Atkins v. Virginia, 536 U.S. 304 (2002).
Bell v. Ohio, 438 U.S. 637 (1978).
Eddings v. Oklahoma, 455 U.S. 104 (1982).
Ewing v. California, 538 U.S. 11 (2003).
Graham v. Florida, 560 U.S. 48 (2010).

Harmelin v. Michigan, 501 U.S. 957 (1991).
Jones v. Mississippi, 141 S. Ct. 1307 (2021).
Kennedy v. Louisiana, 554 U.S. 407 (2008).
Lockyer v. Andrade, 538 U.S. 63 (2003).
Lockett v. Ohio, 438 U.S. 586 (1978).
Miller v. Alabama, 567 U.S. 460 (2012).
Montgomery v. Louisiana, 136 S. Ct. 718 (2016).
Roper v. Simmons, 543 U.S. 551 (2005).
Rummel v. Estelle, 445 U.S. 263 (1980).
Solem v. Helm, 463 U.S. 277 (1983).
Weems v. United States, 217 U.S. 349 (1910).

***SOLEM v. HELM*, 463 U.S. 277 (1983)**

JUSTICE POWELL delivered the opinion of the Court, joined by JUSTICES BRENNAN, MARSHALL, BLACKMUN, and STEVENS.

I

The issue presented is whether the Eighth Amendment proscribes a life sentence without possibility of parole for a seventh nonviolent felony.

By 1975, the State of South Dakota had convicted respondent Jerry Helm of six nonviolent felonies. In 1964, 1966, and 1969, Helm was convicted of third-degree burglary. In 1972, he was convicted of obtaining money under false pretenses. In 1973, he was convicted of grand larceny. And in 1975, he was convicted of third-offense driving while intoxicated. The record contains no details about the circumstances of any of these offenses, except that they were all nonviolent, none was a crime against a person, and alcohol was a contributing factor in each case.

In 1979, Helm was charged with uttering a "no account" check for $100. The only details we have of the crime are those given by Helm to the state trial court: " 'I was working in Sioux Falls, and got my check that day, was drinking, and I ended up here in Rapid City with more money than I had when I started. I knew I'd done something, I didn't know exactly what. If I would have known this, I would have picked the check up. I was drinking, and didn't remember, stopped several places.' "

After offering this explanation, Helm pleaded guilty. Ordinarily, the maximum punishment for uttering a "no account" check would have been five years' imprisonment in the state penitentiary and a $5,000 fine. As a result of his criminal record, however, Helm was subject to South Dakota's recidivist statute:

> "When a defendant has been convicted of at least three prior convictions [*sic*] in addition to the principal felony, the sentence for the principal felony shall be enhanced to the sentence for a Class 1 felony." The maximum penalty for a "Class 1 felony" was life imprisonment in the state penitentiary and a $25,000 fine. Moreover, South Dakota law explicitly provides that parole is unavailable: "A person sentenced to life imprisonment is not eligible for parole by the board of pardons and paroles."

Immediately after accepting Helm's guilty plea, the South Dakota Circuit Court sentenced Helm to life imprisonment.

II

The Eighth Amendment declares: "Excessive bail shall not be required, nor excessive fines imposed, nor cruel and unusual punishments inflicted." The final clause prohibits not only barbaric punishments, but also sentences that are disproportionate to the crime committed.

The principle that a punishment should be proportionate to the crime is deeply rooted and frequently repeated in common law jurisprudence. In 1215, three chapters of Magna Carta were devoted to the rule that "amercements" may not be excessive. And the principle was repeated and extended in the First Statute of Westminster, 3 Edw. I, ch. 6 (1275). These were not hollow guarantees, for the royal courts relied on them to invalidate disproportionate punishments. When prison sentences became the normal criminal sanctions, the common law recognized that these, too, must be proportional.

The English Bill of Rights repeated the principle of proportionality in language that was later adopted in the Eighth Amendment: "excessive Baile ought not to be required nor excessive Fines imposed nor cruell and unusuall Punishments inflicted." Although the precise scope of this provision is uncertain, it at least incorporated "the longstanding principle of English law that the punishment . . . should not be, by reason of its excessive length or severity, greatly disproportionate to the offense charged."

Thus our Bill of Rights was designed in part to ensure that these rights were preserved. Although the Framers may have intended the Eighth Amendment to go beyond the scope of its English counterpart, their use of the language of the English Bill of Rights is convincing proof that they intended to provide at least the same protection—including the right to be free from excessive punishments.

The constitutional principle of proportionality has been recognized explicitly in this Court for almost a century. In the leading case of *Weems v. United States* [t]he Court endorsed the principle of proportionality as a constitutional standard. The Court next applied the principle to invalidate a criminal sentence in *Robinson v. California*. Most recently, the Court has applied the principle of proportionality to hold capital punishment excessive in certain circumstances. *Enmund v. Florida*.

There is no basis for the State's assertion that the general principle of proportionality does not apply to felony prison sentences. The constitutional language itself suggests no exception for imprisonment. We have recognized that the Eighth Amendment imposes "parallel limitations" on bail, fines, and other punishments.

When we have applied the proportionality principle in capital cases, we have drawn no distinction with cases of imprisonment.

III

When sentences are reviewed under the Eighth Amendment, courts should be guided by objective factors that our cases have recognized. First, we look to the gravity of the offense and the harshness of the penalty. In *Enmund*, for example, the Court examined the circumstances of the defendant's crime in great detail.

Second, it may be helpful to compare the sentences imposed on other criminals in the same jurisdiction. If more serious crimes are subject to the same penalty, or to less serious penalties, that is some indication that the punishment at issue may be excessive. Thus, in *Enmund*, the Court noted that all of the other felony murderers on death row in Florida were more culpable than the petitioner there. The *Weems* Court identified an impressive list of more serious crimes that were subject to less serious penalties.

Third, courts may find it useful to compare the sentences imposed for commission of the same crime in other jurisdictions. In *Enmund*, the Court conducted an extensive review of capital punishment statutes and determined that "only about a third of American jurisdictions would ever permit a defendant [such as Enmund] to be sentenced to die."

In sum, a court's proportionality analysis under the Eighth Amendment should be guided by objective criteria, including (i) the gravity of the offense and the harshness of the penalty; (ii) the sentences imposed on other criminals in the same jurisdiction; and (iii) the sentences imposed for commission of the same crime in other jurisdictions.

B

Application of these factors assumes that courts are competent to judge the gravity of an offense, at least on a relative scale. In a broad sense, this assumption is justified, and courts traditionally have made these judgments—just as legislatures must make them in the first instance.

There are other accepted principles that courts may apply in measuring the harm caused or threatened to the victim or society. The absolute magnitude of the crime may be relevant.

Turning to the culpability of the offender, there are again clear distinctions that courts may recognize and apply.

This list is by no means exhaustive. It simply illustrates that there are generally accepted criteria for comparing the severity of different crimes on a broad scale, despite the difficulties courts face in attempting to draw distinctions between similar crimes.

C

Application of the factors that we identify also assumes that courts are able to compare different sentences. This assumption, too, is justified. The easiest comparison, of course, is between capital punishment and noncapital punishments, for the death penalty is different from other punishments in kind rather than degree. For sentences of imprisonment, the problem is not so much one of ordering, but one of line-drawing. It is clear that a 25-year sentence generally is more severe than a 15-year sentence, but in most cases it would be difficult to decide that the former violates the Eighth Amendment while the latter does not. Decisions of this kind, although troubling, are not unique to this area. The courts are constantly called upon to draw similar lines in a variety of contexts.

IV

It remains to apply the analytical framework established by our prior decisions to the case before us. We first consider the relevant criteria, viewing Helm's sentence as life imprisonment without possibility of parole. We then consider the State's argument that the possibility of commutation is sufficient to save an otherwise unconstitutional sentence.

[. . .]

Applying objective criteria, we find that Helm has received the penultimate sentence for relatively minor criminal conduct. He has been treated more harshly than other criminals in the State who have committed more serious crimes. He has been treated more harshly than he would have been in any other jurisdiction, with the possible exception of a single State. We conclude that his sentence is significantly disproportionate to his crime, and is therefore prohibited by the Eighth Amendment.

CHIEF JUSTICE BURGER filed a dissenting opinion, joined by JUSTICES WHITE, REHNQUIST, and O'CONNOR.

It is indeed a curious business for this Court to so far intrude into the administration of criminal justice to say that a state legislature is barred by the Constitution from identifying its habitual criminals and removing them from the streets. Surely seven felony convictions warrant the conclusion that respondent is incorrigible. It is even more curious that the Court should brush aside controlling precedents that are barely in the bound volumes of the United States Reports. The Court would do well to heed Justice Black's comments about judges overruling the considered actions of legislatures under the guise of constitutional interpretation:

> "Such unbounded authority in any group of politically appointed or elected judges would unquestionably be sufficient to classify our Nation as a government of men, not the government of laws of which we boast. With a 'shock the conscience' test of constitutionality, citizens must guess what is the law, guess what a majority of nine judges will believe fair and reasonable. Such a test willfully throws away the certainty and security that lies in a written constitution, one that does not alter with a judge's health, belief, or his politics."

HARMELIN v. MICHIGAN, 501 U.S. 957 (1991)

JUSTICE SCALIA announced the judgment of the Court and delivered the opinion of the Court with respect to Part IV, joined by CHIEF JUSTICE REHNQUIST, JUSTICES O'CONNOR, KENNEDY, and SOUTER.

Parts I, II, and III were joined only by CHIEF JUSTICE REHNQUIST.

I

Petitioner was convicted of possessing 672 grams of cocaine and sentenced to a mandatory term of life in prison without possibility of parole.

Petitioner claims that his sentence is unconstitutionally "cruel and unusual" for two reasons: first, because it is "significantly disproportionate" to the crime he committed; second, because the sentencing judge was statutorily required to impose it, without taking into account the particularized circumstances of the crime and of the criminal.

[O]ur 5-to-4 decision eight years ago in *Solem* was scarcely the expression of clear and well accepted constitutional law. We have long recognized, of course, that the doctrine of *stare decisis* is less rigid in its application to constitutional precedents, and we think that to be especially true of a constitutional precedent that is both recent and in apparent tension with other decisions. Accordingly, we have addressed anew, and in greater detail, the question whether the Eighth Amendment contains a proportionality guarantee—with particular attention to the background of the Eighth Amendment (which *Solem* discussed in only two pages) and to the understanding of the Eighth Amendment before the end of the 19th century (which *Solem* discussed not at all). We conclude from this examination that *Solem* was simply wrong; the Eighth Amendment contains no proportionality guarantee.

[. . .]

Perhaps the Americans of 1791 understood the Declaration's language precisely as the Englishmen of 1689 did—though, as we shall discuss later, that seems unlikely. Or perhaps the colonists meant to incorporate the content of that antecedent by reference, *whatever* the content might have been. *Solem* suggested something like this, arguing that, since Americans claimed "all the rights of English subjects," "their use of the language of the English Bill of Rights is convincing proof that they intended to provide at least the same protection." Thus, not only is the original meaning of the 1689 Declaration of Rights relevant, but also the circumstances of its enactment, insofar as they display the particular "rights of English subjects" it was designed to vindicate.

As *Solem* observed, the principle of proportionality was familiar to English law at the time the Declaration of Rights was drafted. Most historians agree that the "cruell and unusuall Punishments" provision of the English Declaration of Rights was prompted by the abuses attributed to the infamous Lord Chief Justice Jeffreys of the King's Bench during the Stuart reign of James II. They do not agree, however, on which abuses.

But the vicious punishments for treason decreed in the Bloody Assizes (drawing and quartering, burning of women felons, beheading, disembowling [*sic*], etc.) were common in that period—indeed, they were specifically authorized by law, and remained so for many years afterwards.

In sum, we think it most unlikely that the English Cruell and Unusuall Punishments Clause was meant to forbid "disproportionate" punishments. There is even less likelihood that proportionality of punishment was one of the traditional "rights and privileges of Englishmen" apart from the Declaration of Rights, which happened to be included in the Eighth Amendment. Indeed, even those scholars who believe the principle to have been included within the Declaration of Rights do not contend that such a prohibition was reflected in English practice—nor could they.

Unless one accepts the notion of a blind incorporation, however, the ultimate question is not what "cruell and unusuall punishments" meant in the Declaration of Rights, but what its meaning was to the Americans who adopted the Eighth Amendment. Even if one assumes that the Founders knew the precise meaning of that English antecedent, a direct transplant of the English meaning to the soil of American constitutionalism would, in any case, have been impossible. There were no common law punishments in the federal system, so that the provision must have been meant as a check not upon judges, but upon the Legislature.

Wrenched out of its common law context, and applied to the actions of a legislature, the word "unusual" could hardly mean "contrary to law." But it continued to mean (as it continues to mean today) "such as [does not] occu[r] in ordinary practice."

The language bears the construction, however—and here we come to the point crucial to resolution of the present case—that "cruelty and unusualness" are to be determined not solely with reference to the punishment at issue ("Is life imprisonment a cruel and unusual punishment?"), but with reference to the crime for which it is imposed, as well ("Is life imprisonment cruel and unusual punishment for possession of unlawful drugs?"). The latter interpretation would make the provision a form of proportionality guarantee. The arguments against it, however, seem to us conclusive.

First of all, to use the phrase "cruel and unusual punishment" to describe a requirement of proportionality would have been an exceedingly vague and oblique way of saying what Americans were well accustomed to saying more directly. The notion of "proportionality" was not a novelty (though then, as now, there was little agreement over what it entailed). In 1778, for example, the Virginia Legislature narrowly rejected a comprehensive "Bill for Proportioning Punishments" introduced by Thomas Jefferson. Proportionality provisions had been included in several state constitutions. There is little doubt that those who framed, proposed, and ratified the Bill of Rights were aware of such provisions, yet chose not to replicate them. Both the New Hampshire Constitution, adopted 8 years before ratification of the Eighth Amendment, and the Ohio Constitution, adopted 12 years after, contain, in separate provisions, a prohibition of "cruel and unusual punishments" ("cruel or unusual," in New Hampshire's case) *and* a requirement that "all penalties ought to be proportioned to the nature of the offence."

Secondly, it would seem quite peculiar to refer to cruelty and unusualness *for the offense in question*, in a provision having application only to a new government that had never before defined offenses, and that would be defining new and peculiarly national ones. Finally, and most conclusively, [. . .] the fact that what was "cruel and unusual" under the Eighth Amendment was to be determined without reference to the particular offense is confirmed by all available evidence of contemporary understanding.

The actions of the First Congress, which are, of course, persuasive evidence of what the Constitution means, belie any doctrine of proportionality.

II

We think it enough that those who framed and approved the Federal Constitution chose, for whatever reason, not to include within it the guarantee against disproportionate sentences that some State Constitutions contained. It is worth noting, however, that there was good reason for that choice—a reason that reinforces the necessity of overruling *Solem*. While there are relatively clear historical guidelines and accepted practices that enable judges to determine which modes of punishment are "cruel and unusual," proportionality does not lend itself to such analysis. Neither Congress nor any state legislature has ever set out with the objective of crafting a penalty that is "disproportionate"; yet, as some of the examples mentioned above indicate, many enacted dispositions seem to be so—because they were made for other times or other places, with different social attitudes, different criminal epidemics, different public fears, and different prevailing theories of penology.

This is not to say that there are no absolutes; one can imagine extreme examples that no rational person, in no time or place, could accept. But, for the same reason, these examples are easy to decide, they are certain never to occur. The real function of a constitutional proportionality principle, if it exists, is to enable judges to evaluate a penalty that *some* assemblage of men and women *has* considered proportionate—and to say that it is not. For that real-world enterprise, the standards seem so inadequate that the proportionality principle becomes an invitation to imposition of subjective values.

This becomes clear, we think, from a consideration of the three factors that *Solem* found relevant to the proportionality determination: (1) the inherent gravity of the offense, (2) the sentences imposed for similarly grave offenses in the same jurisdiction, and (3) sentences imposed for the same crime in other jurisdictions.

The Eighth Amendment is not a ratchet, whereby a temporary consensus on leniency for a particular crime fixes a permanent constitutional maximum, disabling the States from giving effect to altered beliefs and responding to changed social conditions.

III

Our 20th-century jurisprudence has not remained entirely in accord with the proposition that there is no proportionality requirement in the Eighth Amendment, but neither has it departed to the extent that *Solem* suggests.

IV [the only element of the per curiam ***which carried a 5–4 majority]***

Petitioner claims that his sentence violates the Eighth Amendment for a reason in addition to its alleged disproportionality. He argues that it is "cruel and unusual" to impose a mandatory sentence of such severity, without any consideration of so-called mitigating factors such as, in his case, the fact that he had no prior felony convictions. He apparently contends that the Eighth Amendment requires Michigan to create a sentencing scheme whereby life in prison without possibility of parole is simply the most severe of a range of available penalties that the sentencer may impose after hearing evidence in mitigation and aggravation.

As our earlier discussion should make clear, this claim has no support in the text and history of the Eighth Amendment. Severe, mandatory penalties may be cruel, but they are not unusual in the constitutional sense, having been employed in various forms throughout our Nation's history. As noted earlier, mandatory death sentences abounded in our first Penal Code. They were also common in the several States—both at the time of the founding and throughout the 19th century. There can be no serious contention, then, that a sentence which is not otherwise cruel and unusual becomes so simply because it is "mandatory."

Petitioner's "required mitigation" claim, like his proportionality claim, does find support in our death penalty jurisprudence. We have held that a capital sentence is cruel and unusual under the Eighth Amendment if it is imposed without an individualized determination that that punishment is "appropriate"—whether or not the sentence is "grossly disproportionate." Petitioner asks us to extend this so-called "individualized capital sentencing doctrine," to an "individualized mandatory life in prison without parole sentencing doctrine." We refuse to do so.

It is true that petitioner's sentence is unique in that it is the second most severe known to the law; but life imprisonment with possibility of parole is also unique in that it is the third most severe. And if petitioner's sentence forecloses some "flexible techniques" for later reducing his sentence, it does not foreclose all of them, since there remain the possibilities of retroactive legislative reduction and executive clemency. In some cases, moreover, there will be negligible difference between life without parole and other sentences of imprisonment—for example, a life sentence with eligibility for parole after 20 years, or even a lengthy term sentence without eligibility for parole, given to a 65-year-old man. But even where the difference is the greatest, it cannot be compared with death. We have drawn the line of required individualized sentencing at capital cases, and see no basis for extending it further.

JUSTICE KENNEDY filed an opinion concurring in part and concurring in the judgment, joined by JUSTICES O'CONNOR and SOUTER.

I concur in Part IV of the Court's opinion and in the judgment. I write this separate opinion because my approach to the Eighth Amendment proportionality analysis differs from JUSTICE SCALIA's.

Though our decisions recognize a proportionality principle, its precise contours are unclear. This is so, in part, because we have applied the rule in few cases, and even then to sentences of different types. Our most recent pronouncement on the subject in *Solem*, furthermore, appeared to apply a different analysis than *Rummel* and *Davis*. *Solem* twice stated, however, that its decision was consistent with *Rummel*, and thus did not overrule it.

The first of these principles is that the fixing of prison terms for specific crimes involves a substantive penological judgment that, as a general matter, is "properly within the province of legislatures, not courts."

The second principle is that the Eighth Amendment does not mandate adoption of any one penological theory.

Third, marked divergences both in underlying theories of sentencing and in the length of prescribed prison terms are the inevitable, often beneficial, result of the federal structure.

All of these principles—the primacy of the legislature, the variety of legitimate penological schemes, the nature of our federal system, and the requirement that proportionality review be guided by objective factors—inform the final one: the Eighth Amendment does not require strict proportionality between crime and sentence. Rather, it forbids only extreme sentences that are "grossly disproportionate" to the crime.

II

The Michigan scheme does possess mechanisms for consideration of individual circumstances. Prosecutorial discretion before sentence and executive or legislative clemency afterwards provide means for the State to avert or correct unjust sentences. Here the prosecutor may have chosen to seek the maximum penalty because petitioner possessed 672.5 grams of undiluted cocaine and several other trappings of a drug trafficker, including marijuana cigarettes, four brass cocaine straws, a cocaine spoon, 12 Percodan tablets, 25 tablets of Phendimetrazine Tartrate, a Motorola beeper, plastic bags containing cocaine, a coded address book, and $3,500 in cash.

A penalty as severe and unforgiving as the one imposed here would make this a most difficult and troubling case for any judicial officer. Reasonable minds may differ about the efficacy of Michigan's sentencing scheme, and it is far from certain that Michigan's bold experiment will succeed. The accounts of pickpockets at Tyburn hangings are a reminder of the limits of the law's deterrent force, but we cannot say the law before us has no chance of success, and is, on that account, so disproportionate as to be cruel and unusual punishment. The dangers flowing from drug offenses and the circumstances of the crime committed here demonstrate that the Michigan penalty scheme does not surpass constitutional bounds. Michigan may use its criminal law to address the issue of drug possession in wholesale amounts in the manner that it has in this sentencing scheme.

For the foregoing reasons, I conclude that petitioner's sentence of life imprisonment without parole for his crime of possession of more than 650 grams of cocaine does not violate the Eighth Amendment.

JUSTICE WHITE, with whom JUSTICE BLACKMUN and JUSTICE STEVENS join, dissenting.

The language of the Amendment does not refer to proportionality in so many words, but it does forbid "excessive" fines, a restraint that suggests that a determination of excessiveness should be based, at least in part, on whether the fine imposed is disproportionate to the crime committed. Nor would it be unreasonable to conclude that it would be both cruel and unusual to punish overtime parking by life imprisonment, or, more generally, to impose any punishment that is grossly disproportionate to the offense for which the defendant has been convicted.

[. . .]

Application of *Solem's* proportionality analysis leaves no doubt that the Michigan statute at issue fails constitutional muster. The statutorily mandated penalty of life without possibility of parole for possession of narcotics is unconstitutionally disproportionate in that it violates the Eighth Amendment's prohibition against cruel and unusual punishment. Consequently, I would reverse the decision of the Michigan Court of Appeals.

JUSTICE WHITE filed a dissenting opinion, joined by JUSTICES BLACKMUN and STEVENS.

JUSTICE MARSHALL filed a dissenting opinion.

JUSTICE STEVENS filed a dissenting opinion, joined by JUSTICE BLACKMUN.

EWING v. CALIFORNIA, 538 U.S. 11 (2003)

JUSTICE O'CONNOR announced the judgment of the Court and delivered an opinion, joined by CHIEF JUSTICE REHNQUIST and JUSTICE KENNEDY.

In this case, we decide whether the Eighth Amendment prohibits the State of California from sentencing a repeat felon to a prison term of 25 years to life under the State's "Three Strikes and You're Out" law.

[. . .]

Three years after *Rummel*, in *Solem*, we held that the Eighth Amendment prohibited "a life sentence without possibility of parole for a seventh nonviolent felony." We specifically stated that the Eighth Amendment's ban on cruel and unusual punishments "prohibits . . . sentences that are disproportionate to the crime committed," and that the "constitutional principle of proportionality has been recognized explicitly in this Court for almost a century."

Eight years after *Solem*, we grappled with the proportionality issue again in *Harmelin*. *Harmelin* was not a recidivism case, but rather involved a first-time offender convicted of possessing 672 grams of cocaine. He was sentenced to life in prison without possibility of parole. A majority of the Court rejected Harmelin's claim that his sentence was so grossly disproportionate that it violated the Eighth Amendment. The Court, however, could not agree on why his proportionality argument failed.

The proportionality principles in our cases distilled in JUSTICE KENNEDY'S concurrence guide our application of the Eighth Amendment in the new context that we are called upon to consider.

[. . .]

We hold that Ewing's sentence of 25 years to life in prison, imposed for the offense of felony grand theft under the three strikes law, is not grossly disproportionate and therefore does not violate the Eighth Amendment's prohibition on cruel and unusual punishments.

JUSTICE SCALIA filed an opinion concurring in the judgment.

JUSTICE THOMAS filed an opinion concurring in the judgment.

JUSTICE STEVENS filed a dissenting opinion, joined by JUSTICES SOUTER, GINSBURG, and BREYER.

JUSTICE BREYER filed a dissenting opinion, joined by JUSTICES STEVENS, SOUTER, and GINSBURG.

LOCKYER v. ANDRADE, 538 U.S. 63 (2003)

JUSTICE O'CONNOR delivered the opinion of the Court, joined by CHIEF JUSTICE REHNQUIST and JUSTICES SCALIA, KENNEDY, and THOMAS.

This case raises the issue whether the United States Court of Appeals for the Ninth Circuit erred in ruling that the California Court of Appeal's decision affirming Leandro Andrade's two consecutive terms of 25 years to life in prison for a "third strike" conviction is contrary to, or an unreasonable application of, clearly established federal law.

On November 4, 1995, Leandro Andrade stole five videotapes worth $84.70 from a Kmart store in Ontario, California. Security personnel detained Andrade as he was leaving the store. On November 18, 1995, Andrade entered a different Kmart store in Montclair, California, and placed four videotapes worth $68.84 in the rear waistband of his pants. Again, security guards apprehended Andrade as he was exiting the premises. Police subsequently arrested Andrade for these crimes.

These two incidents were not Andrade's first or only encounters with law enforcement. According to the state probation officer's presentence report, Andrade has been in and out of state and federal prison since 1982. In January 1982, he was convicted of a misdemeanor theft offense and was sentenced to 6 days in jail with 12 months' probation. Andrade was arrested again in November 1982 for multiple counts of first-degree residential burglary. He pleaded guilty to at least three of those counts, and in April of the following year he was sentenced to 120 months in prison. In 1988, Andrade was convicted in federal court of "[t]ransportation of [m]arijuana," and was sentenced to eight years in federal prison. In 1990, he was convicted in state court for a misdemeanor petty theft offense and was ordered to serve 180 days in jail. In September 1990, Andrade was convicted again in federal court for the same felony of "[t]ransportation of [m]arijuana," and was sentenced to 2,191 days in federal prison. And in 1991, Andrade was arrested for a state parole violation-escape from federal prison. He was paroled from the state penitentiary system in 1993.

Because of his 1990 misdemeanor conviction, the State charged Andrade in this case with two counts of petty theft with a prior conviction, in violation of Cal. Penal Code Ann. § 666 (West Supp. 2002). Under California law, petty theft with a prior conviction is a so-called "wobbler" offense because it is punishable either as a misdemeanor or as a felony. The decision to prosecute petty theft with a prior conviction as a misdemeanor or as a felony is in the discretion of the prosecutor. The trial court also has discretion to reduce the charge to a misdemeanor at the time of sentencing.

Under California's three-strikes law, any felony can constitute the third strike, and thus can subject a defendant to a term of 25 years to life in prison. In this case, the prosecutor decided to charge the two counts of theft as felonies rather than misdemeanors. The trial court denied Andrade's motion to reduce the offenses to misdemeanors, both before the jury verdict and again in state habeas proceedings.

A jury found Andrade guilty of two counts of petty theft with a prior conviction. According to California law, a jury must also find that a defendant has been convicted of at least two serious or violent felonies that serve as qualifying offenses under the three-strikes regime. In this case, the jury made a special finding that Andrade was convicted of three counts of first-degree residential burglary. A conviction for first-degree residential burglary qualifies as a serious or violent felony for the purposes of the three strikes law. As a consequence, each of Andrade's convictions for theft triggered a separate application of the three strikes law. Pursuant to California law, the judge sentenced Andrade to two consecutive terms of 25 years to life in prison.

[. . .]

Andrade's argument in this Court is that two consecutive terms of 25 years to life for stealing approximately $150 in videotapes is grossly disproportionate in violation of the Eighth Amendment. Andrade similarly maintains that the state court decision affirming his sentence is "contrary to, or involved an unreasonable application of, clearly established Federal law, as determined by the Supreme Court of the United States."

Through this thicket of Eighth Amendment jurisprudence, one governing legal principle emerges as "clearly established": A gross disproportionality principle is applicable to sentences for terms of years.

Our cases exhibit a lack of clarity regarding what factors may indicate gross disproportionality. [. . .] the "precise contours" of the proportionality principle "are unclear." Thus, in this case, the only relevant clearly established law amenable to the "contrary to" or "unreasonable application of" framework is the gross disproportionality principle, the precise contours of which are unclear, applicable only in the "exceedingly rare" and "extreme" case.

The gross disproportionality principle reserves a constitutional violation for only the extraordinary case.

JUSTICE SOUTER, with whom JUSTICES STEVENS, GINSBURG, and BREYER join, dissenting.

This is the rare sentence of demonstrable gross disproportionality, as the California Legislature may well have recognized when it specifically provided that a prosecutor may move to dismiss or strike a prior felony conviction "in the furtherance of justice." In this case, the statutory safeguard failed, and the state court was left to ensure that the Eighth Amendment prohibition on grossly disproportionate sentences was met. If Andrade's sentence is not grossly disproportionate, the principle has no meaning. The California court's holding was an unreasonable application of clearly established precedent.

JUSTICE SOUTER filed a dissenting opinion, joined by JUSTICES STEVENS, GINSBURG, and BREYER.

GRAHAM v. FLORIDA, 560 U.S. 48 (2010)

JUSTICE KENNEDY delivered the opinion of the Court, joined by JUSTICES STEVENS, GINSBURG, BREYER, and SOTOMAYOR.

The issue before the Court is whether the Constitution permits a juvenile offender to be sentenced to life in prison without parole for a nonhomicide crime. The sentence was imposed by the State of Florida. Petitioner challenges the sentence under the Eighth Amendment's Cruel and Unusual Punishments Clause.

I

Petitioner is Terrance Jamar Graham. He was born on January 6, 1987. Graham's parents were addicted to crack cocaine, and their drug use persisted in his early years. Graham was diagnosed with attention deficit hyperactivity disorder in elementary school. He began drinking alcohol and using tobacco at age 9 and smoked marijuana at age 13.

In July 2003, when Graham was age 16, he and three other school-age youths attempted to rob a barbeque restaurant in Jacksonville, Florida. One youth, who worked at the restaurant, left the back door unlocked just before closing time. Graham and another youth, wearing masks, entered through the unlocked door. Graham's masked accomplice twice struck the restaurant manager in the back of the head with a metal bar. When the manager started yelling at the assailant and Graham, the two youths ran out and escaped in a car driven by the third accomplice. The restaurant manager required stitches for his head injury. No money was taken.

Graham was arrested for the robbery attempt. Under Florida law, it is within a prosecutor's discretion whether to charge 16- and 17-year-olds as adults or juveniles for most felony crimes. Graham's prosecutor elected to charge Graham as an adult. The charges against Graham were armed burglary with assault or battery, a first-degree felony carrying a maximum penalty of life imprisonment without the possibility of parole; and attempted armed-robbery, a second-degree felony carrying a maximum penalty of 15 years' imprisonment.

On December 18, 2003, Graham pleaded guilty to both charges under a plea agreement. Graham wrote a letter to the trial court. After reciting "this is my first and last time getting in trouble," he continued "I've decided to turn my life around."

The trial court accepted the plea agreement. The court withheld adjudication of guilt as to both charges and sentenced Graham to concurrent 3-year terms of probation. Graham was required to spend the first 12 months of his probation in the county jail, but he received credit for the time he had served awaiting trial, and was released on June 25, 2004.

Less than 6 months later, on the night of December 2, 2004, Graham again was arrested. The State's case was as follows: Earlier that evening, Graham participated in a home invasion robbery. His two accomplices were Meigo Bailey and Kirkland Lawrence, both 20-year-old men. According to the State, at 7 p.m. that night, Graham, Bailey, and Lawrence knocked on the door of the home where Carlos Rodriguez lived. Graham, followed by Bailey and Lawrence, forcibly entered the home and held a pistol to Rodriguez's chest. For the next 30 minutes, the three held Rodriguez and another man, a friend of Rodriguez, at gunpoint while they ransacked the home searching for money. Before leaving, Graham and his accomplices barricaded Rodriguez and his friend inside a closet.

The State further alleged that Graham, Bailey, and Lawrence, later the same evening, attempted a second robbery, during which Bailey was shot. Graham, who had borrowed his father's car, drove Bailey and Lawrence to the hospital and left them there. As Graham drove away, a police sergeant signaled him to stop. Graham continued at a high speed but crashed into a telephone pole. He tried to flee on foot but was apprehended. Three handguns were found in his car.

When detectives interviewed Graham, he denied involvement in the crimes. He said he encountered Bailey and Lawrence only after Bailey had been shot. One of the detectives told Graham that the victims of the home invasion had identified him. He asked Graham, "Aside from the two robberies tonight how many more were you involved in?" Graham responded, "Two to three before tonight." The night that Graham allegedly committed the robbery, he was 34 days short of his 18th birthday.

On December 13, 2004, Graham's probation officer filed with the trial court an affidavit asserting that Graham had violated the conditions of his probation by possessing a firearm, committing crimes, and associating with persons engaged in criminal activity. The trial court held hearings on Graham's violations about a year later, in December 2005 and January 2006. The judge who presided was not the same judge who had accepted Graham's guilty plea to the earlier offenses.

Graham maintained that he had no involvement in the home invasion robbery; but, even after the court underscored that the admission could expose him to a life sentence on the earlier charges, he admitted violating probation conditions by fleeing. The State presented evidence related to the home invasion, including testimony from the victims. The trial court noted that Graham, in admitting his attempt to avoid arrest, had acknowledged violating his probation. The court further found that Graham had violated his probation by committing a home invasion robbery, by possessing a firearm, and by associating with persons engaged in criminal activity.

The trial court held a sentencing hearing. Under Florida law the minimum sentence Graham could receive absent a downward departure by the judge was 5 years' imprisonment. The maximum was life imprisonment. Graham's attorney requested the minimum nondeparture sentence of 5 years. A presentence report prepared by the Florida Department of Corrections recommended that Graham receive an even lower sentence—at most 4 years' imprisonment. The State recommended that Graham receive 30 years on the armed burglary count and 15 years on the attempted armed robbery count.

After hearing Graham's testimony, the trial court explained the sentence it was about to pronounce:

> "Mr. Graham, as I look back on your case, yours is really candidly a sad situation. You had, as far as I can tell, you have quite a family structure. You had a lot of people who wanted to try and help you get your life turned around including the court system, and you had a judge who took the step to try and give you direction through his probation order to give you a chance to get back onto track. And at the time you seemed through your letters that that is exactly what you wanted to do. And I don't know why it is that you threw your life away. I don't know why.
>
> "But you did, and that is what is so sad about this today is that you have actually been given a chance to get through this, the original charge, which were very serious charges to begin with. . . . The attempted robbery with a weapon was a very serious charge. . . .
>
> [. . .]
>
> "I have reviewed the statute. I don't see where any further juvenile sanctions would be appropriate. I don't see where any youthful offender sanctions would be appropriate. Given your escalating pattern of criminal conduct, it is apparent to the Court that you have decided that this is the way you are going to live your life and that the only thing I can do now is to try and protect the community from your actions."

The trial court found Graham guilty of the earlier armed burglary and attempted armed robbery charges. It sentenced him to the maximum sentence authorized by law on each charge: life imprisonment for the armed burglary and 15 years for the attempted armed robbery. Because Florida has abolished its parole system, a life sentence gives a defendant no possibility of release unless he is granted executive clemency.

II

The controlling opinion in *Harmelin* explained its approach for determining whether a sentence for a term of years is grossly disproportionate for a particular defendant's crime.

The second classification of cases has used categorical rules to define Eighth Amendment standards. The previous cases in this classification involved the death penalty. The classification in turn consists of two subsets, one considering the nature of the offense, the other considering the characteristics of the offender. With respect to the nature of the offense, the Court has concluded that capital punishment is impermissible for nonhomicide crimes against individuals.

In the cases adopting categorical rules the Court has taken the following approach. The Court first considers "objective indicia of society's standards, as expressed in legislative enactments and state practice" to determine whether there is a national consensus against the sentencing practice at issue. Next, guided by "the standards elaborated by controlling precedents and by the Court's own understanding and interpretation of the Eighth Amendment's text, history, meaning, and purpose," the Court must determine in the exercise of its own independent judgment whether the punishment in question violates the Constitution.

The present case involves an issue the Court has not considered previously: a categorical challenge to a term-of-years sentence. The approach in cases such as *Harmelin* and *Ewing* is suited for considering a gross proportionality challenge to a particular defendant's sentence, but here a sentencing practice itself is in question. This case implicates a particular type of sentence as it applies to an entire class of offenders who have committed a range of crimes. As a result, a threshold comparison between the severity of the penalty and the gravity of the crime does not advance the analysis. Here, in addressing the question presented, the appropriate analysis is the one used in cases that involved the categorical approach, specifically *Atkins*, *Roper*, and *Kennedy*.

III

A

The analysis begins with objective indicia of national consensus. Six jurisdictions do not allow life without parole sentences for any juvenile offenders. Seven jurisdictions permit life without parole for juvenile offenders, but only for homicide crimes. Thirty-seven States as well as the District of Columbia permit sentences of life without parole for a juvenile nonhomicide offender in some circumstances. Federal law also allows for the possibility of life without parole for offenders as young as 13. Relying on this metric, the State and its *amici* argue that there is no national consensus against the sentencing practice at issue.

This argument is incomplete and unavailing. Actual sentencing practices are an important part of the Court's inquiry into consensus. Here, an examination of actual sentencing practices in jurisdictions where the sentence in question is permitted by statute discloses a consensus against its use. Although these statutory schemes contain no explicit prohibition on sentences of life without parole for juvenile nonhomicide offenders, those sentences are most infrequent. According to a recent study, nationwide there are only 109 juvenile offenders serving sentences of life without parole for nonhomicide offenses.

The State contends that this study's tally is inaccurate because it does not count juvenile offenders who were convicted of both a homicide and a nonhomicide offense, even when the offender received a life-without-parole sentence for the nonhomicide. This distinction is unpersuasive. Juvenile offenders who committed both homicide and nonhomicide crimes present a different situation for a sentencing judge than juvenile offenders who committed no homicide. It is difficult to say that a defendant who receives a life sentence on a nonhomicide offense but who was at the same time convicted of homicide is not in some sense being punished in part for the homicide when the judge makes the sentencing determination. The instant case concerns only those juvenile offenders sentenced to life without parole solely for a nonhomicide offense.

The numbers cited above reflect all current convicts in a jurisdiction's penal system, regardless of when they were convicted. It becomes all the more clear how rare these sentences are, even within the jurisdictions that do sometimes impose them, when one considers that a juvenile sentenced to life without parole is likely to live in prison for decades. Thus, these statistics likely reflect nearly all juvenile nonhomicide offenders who have received a life-without-parole sentence stretching back many years. It is not certain that this opinion has identified every juvenile nonhomicide offender nationwide serving a life-without-parole sentence, for the statistics are not precise. The available data, nonetheless, are sufficient to demonstrate how rarely these sentences are imposed even if there are isolated cases that have not been included in the presentations of the parties or the analysis of the Court.

It must be acknowledged that in terms of absolute numbers juvenile life-without-parole sentences for nonhomicides are more common than the sentencing practices at issue in some of this Court's other Eighth Amendment cases.

The evidence of consensus is not undermined by the fact that many jurisdictions do not prohibit life without parole for juvenile nonhomicide offenders. The Court confronted a similar situation in *Thompson*, where a plurality concluded that the death penalty for offenders younger than 16 was unconstitutional. A number of States then allowed the juvenile death penalty if one considered the statutory scheme. As is the case here, those States authorized the transfer of some juvenile offenders to adult court; and at that point there was no statutory differentiation between adults and juveniles with respect to authorized penalties.

The same reasoning obtains here. Many States have chosen to move away from juvenile court systems and to allow juveniles to be transferred to, or charged directly in, adult court under certain circumstances. Once in adult court, a juvenile offender may receive the same sentence as would be given to an adult offender, including a life-without-parole sentence. But the fact that transfer and direct charging laws make life without parole possible for some juvenile nonhomicide offenders does not justify a judgment that many States intended to subject such offenders to life-without-parole sentences.

For example, under Florida law a child of any age can be prosecuted as an adult for certain crimes and can be sentenced to life without parole. The State acknowledged at oral argument that even a 5-year-old, theoretically, could receive such a sentence under the letter of the law. All would concede this to be unrealistic, but the example underscores that the statutory eligibility of a juvenile offender for life without parole does not indicate that the penalty has been endorsed through deliberate, express, and full legislative consideration. Similarly, the many States that allow life without parole for juvenile nonhomicide offenders but do not impose the punishment should not be treated as if they have expressed the view that the sentence is appropriate. The sentencing practice now under consideration is exceedingly rare. And "it is fair to say that a national consensus has developed against it."

B

Community consensus, while "entitled to great weight," is not itself determinative of whether a punishment is cruel and unusual.

No recent data provide reason to reconsider the Court's observations in *Roper* about the nature of juveniles. As petitioner's *amici* point out, developments in psychology and brain science continue to show fundamental differences between juvenile and adult minds. For example, parts of the brain involved in behavior control continue to mature through late adolescence. It remains true that "[f]rom a moral standpoint it would be misguided to equate the failings of a minor with those of an adult, for a greater possibility exists that a minor's character deficiencies will be reformed." These matters relate to the status of the offenders in question; and it is relevant to consider next the nature of the offenses to which this harsh penalty might apply.

The Court has recognized that defendants who do not kill, intend to kill, or foresee that life will be taken are categorically less deserving of the most serious forms of punishment than are murderers.

It follows that, when compared to an adult murderer, a juvenile offender who did not kill or intend to kill has a twice diminished moral culpability. The age of the offender and the nature of the crime each bear on the analysis.

As for the punishment, life without parole is "the second most severe penalty permitted by law."

Life without parole is an especially harsh punishment for a juvenile. Under this sentence a juvenile offender will on average serve more years and a greater percentage of his life in prison than an adult offender. A 16-year-old and a 75-year-old each sentenced to life without parole receive the same punishment in name only.

Retribution is a legitimate reason to punish, but it cannot support the sentence at issue here. Society is entitled to impose severe sanctions on a juvenile nonhomicide offender to express its condemnation of the crime and to seek restoration of the moral imbalance caused by the offense. But "[t]he heart of the retribution rationale is that a criminal sentence must be directly related to the personal culpability of the criminal offender."

Deterrence does not suffice to justify the sentence either. *Roper* noted that "the same characteristics that render juveniles less culpable than adults suggest . . . that juveniles will be less susceptible to deterrence." Because juveniles' "lack of maturity and underdeveloped sense of responsibility . . . often result in impetuous and ill-considered actions and decisions," they are less likely to take a possible punishment into consideration when making decisions. This is particularly so when that punishment is rarely imposed.

Incapacitation, a third legitimate reason for imprisonment, does not justify the life-without-parole sentence in question here. Recidivism is a serious risk to public safety, and so incapacitation is an important goal. But while incapacitation may be a legitimate penological goal sufficient to justify life without parole in other contexts, it is inadequate to justify that punishment for juveniles who did not commit homicide. To justify life without parole on the assumption that the juvenile offender forever will be a danger to society requires the sentencer to make a judgment that the juvenile is incorrigible. The characteristics of juveniles make that judgment questionable. "It is difficult even for expert psychologists to differentiate between the juvenile offender whose crime reflects unfortunate yet transient immaturity, and the rare juvenile offender whose crime reflects irreparable corruption." As one court concluded in a challenge to a life-without-parole sentence for a 14-year-old, "incorrigibility is inconsistent with youth."

Finally there is rehabilitation, a penological goal that forms the basis of parole systems. The concept of rehabilitation is imprecise; and its utility and proper implementation are the subject of a substantial, dynamic field of inquiry and dialogue. It is for legislatures to determine what rehabilitative techniques are appropriate and effective.

A sentence of life imprisonment without parole, however, cannot be justified by the goal of rehabilitation. The penalty forswears altogether the rehabilitative ideal.

C

Terrance Graham's sentence guarantees he will die in prison without any meaningful opportunity to obtain release, no matter what he might do to demonstrate that the bad acts he committed as a teenager are not representative of his true character, even if he spends the next half century attempting to atone for his crimes and learn from his mistakes. The State has denied him any chance to later demonstrate that he is fit to rejoin society based solely on a nonhomicide crime that he committed while he was a child in the eyes of the law. This the Eighth Amendment does not permit.

D

There is support for our conclusion in the fact that, in continuing to impose life-without-parole sentences on juveniles who did not commit homicide, the United States adheres to a sentencing practice rejected the world over. This observation does not control our decision. The judgments of other nations and the international community are not dispositive as to the meaning of the Eighth Amendment. But " '[t]he climate of international opinion concerning the acceptability of a particular punishment' " is also " 'not irrelevant.' "

Today we continue that longstanding practice in noting the global consensus against the sentencing practice in question. A recent study concluded that only 11 nations authorize life without parole for juvenile offenders under any circumstances; and only 2 of them, the United States and Israel, ever impose the punishment in practice.

Thus, as petitioner contends and respondent does not contest, the United States is the only Nation that imposes life-without-parole sentences on juvenile nonhomicide offenders. We also note, as petitioner and his *amici* emphasize, that Article 37(a) of the United Nations Convention on the Rights of the Child, ratified by every nation except the United States and Somalia, prohibits the imposition of "life imprisonment without possibility of release . . . for offences committed by persons below eighteen years of age." As we concluded in *Roper* with respect to the juvenile death penalty, "the United States now stands alone in a world that has turned its face against" life without parole for juvenile nonhomicide offenders.

[. . .]

The Constitution prohibits the imposition of a life-without-parole sentence on a juvenile offender who did not commit homicide. A State need not guarantee the offender eventual release, but if it imposes a sentence of life it must provide him or her with some realistic opportunity to obtain release before the end of that term. The judgment of the First District Court of Appeal of Florida affirming Graham's conviction is reversed, and the case is remanded for further proceedings not inconsistent with this opinion.

JUSTICE STEVENS filed a concurring opinion, joined by JUSTICES GINSBURG and SOTOMAYOR.

While Justice Thomas would apparently not rule out a death sentence for a $50 theft by a 7-year-old, the Court wisely rejects his static approach to the law. Standards of decency have evolved since 1980. They will never stop doing so.

CHIEF JUSTICE ROBERTS filed a concurring opinion.

JUSTICE THOMAS filed a dissenting opinion, joined by JUSTICE SCALIA, and joined by JUSTICE ALITO as to Parts I and III.

Until today, the Court has based its categorical proportionality rulings on the notion that the Constitution gives special protection to capital defendants because the death penalty is a uniquely severe punishment that must be reserved for only those who are "most deserving of execution."

Today's decision eviscerates that distinction. "Death is different" no longer. The Court now claims not only the power categorically to reserve the "most severe punishment" for those the Court thinks are "'the most deserving of execution,'" *but also* to declare that "less culpable" persons are categorically exempt from the "*second* most severe penalty." No reliable limiting principle remains to prevent the Court from immunizing any class of offenders from the law's third, fourth, fifth, or fiftieth most severe penalties as well.

The Court's departure from the "death is different" distinction is especially mystifying when one considers how long it has resisted crossing that divide.

Indeed, for a time the Court declined to apply proportionality principles to noncapital sentences at all, emphasizing that "a sentence of death differs in kind from any sentence of imprisonment, *no matter how long*." Based on that rationale, the Court found that the excessiveness of one prison term as compared to another was "properly within the province of legislatures, not courts," precisely because it involved an "*invariably . . . subjective determination*, there being no clear way to make 'any constitutional distinction between one term of years and a shorter or longer term of years.' "

They have been rare indeed. In the 28 years since *Solem*, the Court has considered just three such challenges and has rejected them all, largely on the theory that criticisms of the "wisdom, cost-efficiency, and effectiveness" of term-of-years prison sentences are "appropriately directed at the legislature[s]," not the courts.

Remarkably, the Court today does more than return to *Solem*'s case-by-case proportionality standard for noncapital sentences; it hurtles past it to impose a *categorical* proportionality rule banning life-without-parole sentences not just in this case, but in *every* case involving a juvenile nonhomicide offender, no matter what the circumstances. Neither the Eighth Amendment nor the Court's precedents justify this decision.

[. . .]

The ultimate question in this case is not whether a life-without-parole sentence 'fits' the crime at issue here or the crimes of juvenile nonhomicide offenders more generally, but to whom the Constitution assigns that decision. The Florida Legislature has concluded that such sentences should be available for persons under 18 who commit certain crimes, and the trial judge in this case decided to impose that legislatively authorized sentence here. Because a life-without-parole prison sentence is not a "cruel and unusual" method of punishment under any standard, the Eighth Amendment gives this Court no authority to reject those judgments.

It would be unjustifiable for the Court to declare otherwise even if it could claim that a bare majority of state laws supported its independent moral view. The fact that the Court categorically prohibits life-without-parole sentences for juvenile nonhomicide offenders in the face of an overwhelming legislative majority *in favor* of leaving that sentencing option available under certain cases simply illustrates how far beyond any cognizable constitutional principle the Court has reached to ensure that its own sense of morality and retributive justice pre-empts that of the people and their representatives.

I agree with Justice Stevens that "[w]e learn, sometimes, from our mistakes." Perhaps one day the Court will learn from this one.

JUSTICE ALITO filed a dissenting opinion.

MILLER v. ALABAMA, 567 U.S. 460 (2012)

JUSTICE Kagan delivered the opinion of the Court, joined by JUSTICES KENNEDY, GINSBURG, BREYER, and SOTOMAYOR.

The two 14-year-old offenders in these cases were convicted of murder and sentenced to life imprisonment without the possibility of parole. In neither case did the sentencing authority have any discretion to impose a different punishment. State law mandated that each juvenile die in prison even if a judge or jury would have thought that his youth and its attendant characteristics, along with the nature of his crime, made a lesser sentence (for example, life *with* the possibility of parole) more appropriate. Such a scheme prevents those meting out punishment from considering a juvenile's "lessened culpability" and greater "capacity for change," and runs afoul of our cases' requirement of individualized sentencing for defendants facing the most serious penalties. We therefore hold that mandatory life without parole for those under the age of 18 at the time of their crimes violates the Eighth Amendment's prohibition on "cruel and unusual punishments."

I

A

In November 1999, petitioner Kuntrell Jackson, then 14 years old, and two other boys decided to rob a video store. En route to the store, Jackson learned that one of the boys, Derrick Shields, was carrying a sawed-off shotgun in his coat sleeve. Jackson decided to stay outside when the two other boys entered the store. Inside, Shields pointed the gun at the store clerk, Laurie Troup, and demanded that she "give up the money." Troup refused. A few moments later, Jackson went into the store to find Shields continuing to demand money. When Troup threatened to call the police, Shields shot and killed her. The three boys fled empty-handed.

Arkansas law gives prosecutors discretion to charge 14-year-olds as adults when they are alleged to have committed certain serious offenses. The prosecutor here exercised that authority by charging Jackson with capital felony murder and aggravated robbery. A jury later convicted Jackson of both crimes. Noting that "in view of [the] verdict, there's only one possible punishment," the judge sentenced Jackson to life without parole.

[. . .] Jackson filed a state petition for habeas corpus. He argued, based on *Roper*'s reasoning, that a mandatory sentence of life without parole for a 14-year-old also violates the Eighth Amendment. The circuit court rejected that argument and granted the State's motion to dismiss. While that ruling was on appeal, this Court held in *Graham* v. *Florida* that life without parole violates the Eighth Amendment when imposed on juvenile nonhomicide offenders. After the parties filed briefs addressing that decision, the Arkansas Supreme Court affirmed the dismissal of Jackson's petition.

B

Like Jackson, petitioner Evan Miller was 14 years old at the time of his crime. Miller had by then been in and out of foster care because his mother suffered from alcoholism and drug addiction and his stepfather abused him. Miller, too, regularly used drugs and alcohol; and he had attempted suicide four times, the first when he was six years old.

One night in 2003, Miller was at home with a friend, Colby Smith, when a neighbor, Cole Cannon, came to make a drug deal with Miller's mother. The two boys followed Cannon back to his trailer, where all three smoked marijuana and played drinking games. When Cannon passed out, Miller stole his wallet, splitting about $300 with Smith. Miller then tried to put the wallet back in Cannon's pocket, but Cannon awoke and grabbed Miller by the throat. Smith hit Cannon with a nearby baseball bat, and once released, Miller grabbed the bat and repeatedly struck Cannon with it. Miller placed a sheet over Cannon's head, told him " 'I am God, I've come to take your life,' " and delivered one more blow. The boys then retreated to Miller's trailer, but soon decided to return to Cannon's to cover up evidence of their crime. Once there, they lit two fires. Cannon eventually died from his injuries and smoke inhalation.

Alabama law required that Miller initially be charged as a juvenile, but allowed the District Attorney to seek removal of the case to adult court. [. . .] The State accordingly charged Miller as an adult with murder in the course of arson. That crime (like capital murder in Arkansas) carries a mandatory minimum punishment of life without parole.

II

The cases before us implicate two strands of precedent reflecting our concern with proportionate punishment. The first has adopted categorical bans on sentencing practices based on mismatches between the culpability of a class of offenders and the severity of a penalty.

To start with the first set of cases: *Roper* and *Graham* establish that children are constitutionally different from adults for purposes of sentencing.

Roper and *Graham* emphasized that the distinctive attributes of youth diminish the penological justifications for imposing the harshest sentences on juvenile offenders, even when they commit terrible crimes. Because " '[t] he heart of the retribution rationale' " relates to an offender's blameworthiness, " 'the case for retribution is not as strong with a minor as with an adult.' "

Graham concluded from this analysis that life-without-parole sentences, like capital punishment, may violate the Eighth Amendment when imposed on children. To be sure, *Graham*'s flat ban on life without parole applied only to nonhomicide crimes, and the Court took care to distinguish those offenses from murder, based on both moral culpability and consequential harm. But none of what it said about children—about their distinctive (and transitory) mental traits and environmental vulnerabilities—is crime-specific. Those features are evident in the same way, and to the same degree, when (as in both cases here) a botched robbery turns into a killing. So *Graham*'s reasoning implicates any life-without-parole sentence imposed on a juvenile, even as its categorical bar relates only to nonhomicide offenses.

Most fundamentally, *Graham* insists that youth matters in determining the appropriateness of a lifetime of incarceration without the possibility of parole. In the circumstances there, juvenile status precluded a life-without-parole sentence, even though an adult could receive it for a similar crime. And in other contexts as well, the characteristics of youth, and the way they weaken rationales for punishment, can render a life-without-parole sentence disproportionate.

But the mandatory penalty schemes at issue here prevent the sentencer from taking account of these central considerations. By removing youth from the balance—by subjecting a juvenile to the same life-without-parole sentence applicable to an adult—these laws prohibit a sentencing authority from assessing whether the law's harshest term of imprisonment proportionately punishes a juvenile offender. That contravenes *Graham*'s (and also *Roper*'s) foundational principle: that imposition of a State's most severe penalties on juvenile offenders cannot proceed as though they were not children.

And *Graham* makes plain these mandatory schemes' defects in another way: by likening life-without-parole sentences imposed on juveniles to the death penalty itself. Life-without-parole terms, the Court wrote, "share some characteristics with death sentences that are shared by no other sentences." Imprisoning an offender until he dies alters the remainder of his life "by a forfeiture that is irrevocable." And this lengthiest possible incarceration is an "especially harsh punishment for a juvenile," because he will almost inevitably serve "more years and a greater percentage of his life in prison than an adult offender." The penalty when imposed on a teenager, as compared with an older person, is therefore "the same . . . in name only." All of that suggested a distinctive set of legal rules: In part because we viewed this ultimate penalty for juveniles as akin to the death penalty, we treated it similarly to that most severe punishment. We imposed a categorical ban on the sentence's use, in a way unprecedented for a term of imprisonment. And the bar we adopted mirrored a proscription first established in the death penalty context—that the punishment cannot be imposed for any nonhomicide crimes against individuals.

Of special pertinence here, we insisted in these rulings that a sentencer have the ability to consider the "mitigating qualities of youth." Everything we said in *Roper* and *Graham* about that stage of life also appears in these decisions. As we observed, "youth is more than a chronological fact."

In light of *Graham*'s reasoning, these decisions too show the flaws of imposing mandatory life-without-parole sentences on juvenile homicide offenders. Such mandatory penalties, by their nature, preclude a sentencer from taking account of an offender's age and the wealth of characteristics and circumstances attendant to it. Under these schemes, every juvenile will receive the same sentence as every other—the 17-year-old and the 14-year-old, the shooter and the accomplice, the child from a stable household and the child from a chaotic and abusive one. And still worse, each juvenile (including these two 14-year-olds) will receive the same sentence as the vast majority of adults committing similar homicide offenses—but really, as *Graham* noted, a *greater* sentence than those adults will serve. In meting out the death penalty, the elision of all these differences would be strictly forbidden. And once again, *Graham* indicates that a similar rule should apply when a juvenile confronts a sentence of life (and death) in prison.

So *Graham* and *Roper* and our individualized sentencing cases alike teach that in imposing a State's harshest penalties, a sentencer misses too much if he treats every child as an adult. To recap: Mandatory life without parole for a juvenile precludes consideration of his chronological age and its hallmark features—among them, immaturity, impetuosity, and failure to appreciate risks and consequences. It prevents taking into account the family and home environment that surrounds him—and from which he cannot usually extricate himself—no matter how brutal or dysfunctional. It neglects the circumstances of the homicide offense, including the extent of his participation in the conduct and the way familial and peer pressures may have affected him. Indeed, it ignores that he might have been charged and convicted of a lesser offense if not for incompetencies associated with youth—for example, his inability to deal with police officers or prosecutors (including on a plea agreement) or his incapacity to assist his own attorneys. And finally, this mandatory punishment disregards the possibility of rehabilitation even when the circumstances most suggest it.

Both cases before us illustrate the problem. Take Jackson's first. As noted earlier, Jackson did not fire the bullet that killed Laurie Troup; nor did the State argue that he intended her death. Jackson's conviction was instead based on an aiding-and-abetting theory. [. . .] At the least, a sentencer should look at such facts before depriving a 14-year-old of any prospect of release from prison.

That is true also in *Miller*'s case. No one can doubt that he and Smith committed a vicious murder. But they did it when high on drugs and alcohol consumed with the adult victim. And if ever a pathological background might have contributed to a 14-year-old's commission of a crime, it is here. Miller's stepfather physically abused him; his alcoholic and drug-addicted mother neglected him; he had been in and out of foster care as a result; and he had tried to kill himself four times, the first when he should have been in kindergarten. Nonetheless, Miller's past criminal history was limited—two instances of truancy and one of "second-degree criminal mischief." That Miller deserved severe punishment for killing Cole Cannon is beyond question. But once again, a sentencer needed to examine all these circumstances before concluding that life without any possibility of parole was the appropriate penalty.

We therefore hold that the Eighth Amendment forbids a sentencing scheme that mandates life in prison without possibility of parole for juvenile offenders. By making youth (and all that accompanies it) irrelevant to imposition of that harshest prison sentence, such a scheme poses too great a risk of disproportionate punishment. Because that holding is sufficient to decide these cases, we do not consider Jackson's and Miller's alternative argument that the Eighth Amendment requires a categorical bar on life without parole for juveniles, or at least for those 14 and younger. But given all we have said in *Roper*, *Graham*, and this decision about children's diminished culpability and heightened capacity for change, we think appropriate occasions for sentencing juveniles to this harshest possible penalty will be uncommon. That is especially so because of the great difficulty we noted in *Roper* and *Graham* of distinguishing at this early age between "the juvenile offender whose crime reflects unfortunate yet transient immaturity, and the rare juvenile offender whose crime reflects irreparable corruption." Although we do not foreclose a sentencer's ability to make that judgment in homicide cases, we require it to take into account how children are different, and how those differences counsel against irrevocably sentencing them to a lifetime in prison.

[. . .]

Graham and *Thompson* provide special guidance, because they considered the same kind of statutes we do and explained why simply counting them would present a distorted view. Most jurisdictions authorized the death penalty or life without parole for juveniles only through the combination of two independent statutory provisions. One allowed the transfer of certain juvenile offenders to adult court, while another (often in a far-removed part of the code) set out the penalties for any and all individuals tried there. We reasoned that in those circumstances, it was impossible to say whether a legislature had endorsed a given penalty for children (or would do so if presented with the choice). In *Thompson*, we found that the statutes "t[old] us that the States consider 15-year-olds to be old enough to be tried in criminal court for serious crimes (or too old to be dealt with effectively in juvenile court), but t[old] us nothing about the judgment these States have made regarding the appropriate punishment for such youthful offenders."

And *Graham* echoed that reasoning: Although the confluence of state laws "ma[de] life without parole possible for some juvenile nonhomicide offenders," it did not "justify a judgment" that many States actually "intended to subject such offenders" to those sentences.

All that is just as true here. Almost all jurisdictions allow some juveniles to be tried in adult court for some kinds of homicide. But most States do not have separate penalty provisions for those juvenile offenders. Of the 29 jurisdictions mandating life without parole for children, more than half do so by virtue of generally applicable penalty provisions, imposing the sentence without regard to age. And indeed, some of those States set no minimum age for who may be transferred to adult court in the first instance, thus applying life-without-parole mandates to children of any age—be it 17 or 14 or 10 or 6. As in *Graham*, we think that "underscores that the statutory eligibility of a juvenile offender for life without parole does not indicate that the penalty has been endorsed through deliberate, express, and full legislative consideration." That Alabama and Arkansas can count to 29 by including these possibly (or probably) inadvertent legislative outcomes does not preclude our determination that mandatory life without parole for juveniles violates the Eighth Amendment.

B

Nor does the presence of discretion in some jurisdictions' transfer statutes aid the States here. Alabama and Arkansas initially ignore that many States use mandatory transfer systems: A juvenile of a certain age who has committed a specified offense will be tried in adult court, regardless of any individualized circumstances. Of the 29 relevant jurisdictions, about half place at least some juvenile homicide offenders in adult court automatically, with no apparent opportunity to seek transfer to juvenile court. Moreover, several States at times lodge this decision exclusively in the hands of prosecutors, again with no statutory mechanism for judicial reevaluation. And those "prosecutorial discretion laws are usually silent regarding standards, protocols, or appropriate considerations for decisionmaking."

Even when States give transfer-stage discretion to judges, it has limited utility. First, the decisionmaker typically will have only partial information at this early, pretrial stage about either the child or the circumstances of his offense. *Miller*'s case provides an example. As noted earlier, the juvenile court denied Miller's request for his own mental-health expert at the transfer hearing, and the appeals court affirmed on the ground that Miller was not then entitled to the protections and services he would receive at trial. But by then, of course, the expert's testimony could not change the sentence; whatever she said in mitigation, the mandatory life-without-parole prison term would kick in. The key moment for the exercise of discretion is the transfer—and as *Miller*'s case shows, the judge often does not know then what she will learn, about the offender or the offense, over the course of the proceedings.

Second and still more important, the question at transfer hearings may differ dramatically from the issue at a post-trial sentencing. Because many juvenile systems require that the offender be released at a particular age or after a certain number of years, transfer decisions often present a choice between extremes: light punishment as a child or standard sentencing as an adult (here, life without parole). In many States, for example, a child convicted in juvenile court must be released from custody by the age of 21. Discretionary sentencing in adult court would provide different options: There, a judge or jury could choose, rather than a life-without-parole sentence, a lifetime prison term *with* the possibility of parole or a lengthy term of years. It is easy to imagine a judge deciding that a minor deserves a (much) harsher sentence than he would receive in juvenile court, while still not thinking life-without-parole appropriate. For that reason, the discretion available to a judge at the transfer stage cannot substitute for discretion at post-trial sentencing in adult court—and so cannot satisfy the Eighth Amendment.

IV

Graham, *Roper*, and our individualized sentencing decisions make clear that a judge or jury must have the opportunity to consider mitigating circumstances before imposing the harshest possible penalty for juveniles. By requiring that all children convicted of homicide receive lifetime incarceration without possibility of parole, regardless of their age and age-related characteristics and the nature of their crimes, the mandatory sentencing schemes before us violate this principle of proportionality, and so the Eighth Amendment's ban on cruel and unusual punishment. We accordingly reverse the judgments of the Arkansas Supreme Court and Alabama Court of Criminal Appeals and remand the cases for further proceedings not inconsistent with this opinion.

JUSTICE BREYER filed a concurring opinion, joined by JUSTICE SOTOMAYOR.

CHIEF JUSTICE ROBERTS filed a dissenting opinion, joined by JUSTICES SCALIA, THOMAS, and ALITO.

[. . .] Mercy toward the guilty can be a form of decency, and a maturing society may abandon harsh punishments that it comes to view as unnecessary or unjust. But decency is not the same as leniency. A decent society protects the innocent from violence. A mature society may determine that this requires removing those guilty of the most heinous murders from its midst, both as protection for its other members and as a concrete expression of its standards of decency. As judges we have no basis for deciding that progress toward greater decency can move only in the direction of easing sanctions on the guilty.

It is a great tragedy when a juvenile commits murder—most of all for the innocent victims. But also for the murderer, whose life has gone so wrong so early. And for society as well, which has lost one or more of its members to deliberate violence, and must harshly punish another. In recent years, our society has moved toward requiring that the murderer, his age notwithstanding, be imprisoned for the remainder of his life. Members of this Court may disagree with that choice. Perhaps science and policy suggest society should show greater mercy to young killers, giving them a greater chance to reform themselves at the risk that they will kill again. But that is not our decision to make. Neither the text of the Constitution nor our precedent prohibits legislatures from requiring that juvenile murderers be sentenced to life without parole. I respectfully dissent.

JUSTICE THOMAS filed a dissenting opinion joined by JUSTICE SCALIA.

JUSTICE ALITO filed a dissenting opinion, joined by JUSTICE SCALIA.

What today's decision shows is that our Eighth Amendment cases are no longer tied to any objective indicia of society's standards. Our Eighth Amendment case law is now entirely inward looking. After entirely disregarding objective indicia of our society's standards in *Graham*, the Court now extrapolates from *Graham*. Future cases may extrapolate from today's holding, and this process may continue until the majority brings sentencing practices into line with whatever the majority views as truly evolved standards of decency.

The Eighth Amendment imposes certain limits on the sentences that may be imposed in criminal cases, but for the most part it leaves questions of sentencing policy to be determined by Congress and the state legislatures—and with good reason. Determining the length of imprisonment that is appropriate for a particular offense and a particular offender inevitably involves a balancing of interests. If imprisonment does nothing else, it removes the criminal from the general population and prevents him from committing additional crimes in the outside world. When a legislature prescribes that a category of killers must be sentenced to life imprisonment, the legislature, which presumably reflects the views of the electorate, is taking the position that the risk that these offenders will kill again outweighs any countervailing consideration, including reduced culpability due to immaturity or the possibility of rehabilitation. When the majority of this Court countermands that democratic decision, what the majority is saying is that members of society must be exposed to the risk that these convicted murderers, if released from custody, will murder again.

Unless our cases change course, we will continue to march toward some vision of evolutionary culmination that the Court has not yet disclosed. The Constitution does not authorize us to take the country on this journey.

11

CONFINEMENT CONDITIONS AND INMATE RIGHTS

As has been shown throughout earlier chapters, the mid-1970s marked the dawn of a new generation for the Eighth Amendment. Around the same time that two-thirds of the states were reenacting capital codes to reinstate the death penalty in *Gregg*, the Court opened the gates to prisoner litigation. In that case, *Wolff v. McDonnell*, 418 U.S. 539 (1974), the Justices examined prison disciplinary hearings in light of the due process clause of the Fourteenth Amendment and determined what rights must be afforded to state prison inmates facing internal disciplinary proceedings. Attempting to establish a definitive set of guidelines and to settle the disparate results reached by the lower federal courts, the Supreme Court called for a balancing of the state's interest in orderly disciplinary hearings with that of the inmate in obtaining a just resolution of the proceedings. Following the ruling, the iron curtain that had previously isolated prisoners from constitutional claims was lifted, and such litigation thrived. In the Eighth Amendment sphere, though, silence surrounded the constitutionality of confinement conditions themselves. Due process in sentencing was the most frequent channel for prisoners' civil rights suits and, as such, that was the matter to which the Supreme Court paid most attention.

Extending punishments adjudication to prison health and safety

At the same time that the Burger Court was reacting to an overabundance of prison litigation in procedural and substantive due process, noncapital Eighth Amendment challenges were amplified. Amid battles for the

DOI: 10.4324/9780429398780-12

death penalty's reinstatement, ***ESTELLE v. GAMBLE***, 429 U.S. 97 (1976), reached the Supreme Court. Faced with a challenge to treatment during confinement, the next line of the Eighth Amendment attack was drawn. The central legal issue in *Estelle* was whether the failure to provide adequate medical care to an inmate constituted cruel and unusual punishment in violation of the Eighth. In that case, prisoner Gamble had been injured during manual labor, with weeks of persistent pain following the incident. Texas prison authorities moved him to "administrative segregation," a form of solitary confinement, for several more weeks, during which his condition worsened. Gamble alleged that his subsequent official treatment was constitutionally insufficient. Considering the role of prison authorities with regard to treating the medical needs of inmates, the Justices held that serious neglect may actually produce physical "torture or a lingering death," as prohibited by the Eighth under *Kemmler*. Creating a subjective, intent-based standard, the *Estelle* majority held that "deliberate indifference to serious medical needs of prisoners" constitutes the "unnecessary and wanton infliction of pain" prohibited by the Punishments Clause.

Regardless of how evidenced, an 8–1 majority held that "deliberate indifference to a prisoner's serious illness or injury states a cause of action under § 1983," with reference to 42 U.S. Code § 1983 (civil action for deprivation of rights). The Court concluded that, however, not every claim by a prisoner that he has not received adequate medical treatment states a violation of the Eighth. An accident, for example—as much as it might produce added anguish—is not on that basis sufficient for a successful Punishments Clause claim, as the infliction of pain in such circumstances would be neither wanton nor unnecessary. Similarly to *Resweber*, where the Court upheld a second-time execution attempt after the first failed, in the medical context, an inadvertent failure to provide adequate medical care cannot be said to constitute such infliction: "Thus, a complaint that a physician has been negligent in diagnosing or treating a medical condition does not state a valid claim of medical mistreatment under the Eighth Amendment. Medical malpractice does not become a constitutional violation merely because the victim is a prisoner. In order to state a cognizable claim, a prisoner must allege acts or omissions sufficiently harmful to evidence deliberate indifference to serious medical needs."

While on the merits question Gamble's claim was unsuccessful, the Court's *Estelle* judgment was significant in that it established the "deliberate indifference" test and emphasized that prison officials must take care, under the Constitution, to ensure the health and safety of inmates. It marked an expansion of the scope of the Eighth Amendment, moving beyond considerations of physical punishment to include the provision of essential services and recognizing that inadequate medical care could be a form of punishment in and of itself. This opened the way for conditions of confinement case law, which is outlined throughout this chapter and continues today, establishing precedent for § 1983 claims and allowing prisoners to bring lawsuits against state officials for violating their constitutional rights, including the right to be free from cruel and unusual punishment. In ***HUTTO v. FINNEY***, 437 U.S. 678 (1978), the petitioner succeeded where Gamble had failed, representing the first successful lawsuit filed by an inmate against a correctional institution.

Conditions in the Arkansas prison system were ruled to constitute cruel and unusual punishment in violation of the Eighth and Fourteenth Amendments, upholding a District Court order placing a maximum limit of 30 days on confinement in punitive isolation. In *Hutto*, the routine conditions that an Arkansas convict had to endure were characterized as "a dark and evil world completely alien to the free world," with harsh "punitive isolation" imposed on the average inmate. Around 4, sometimes as many as 11, prisoners were crowded into windowless 8 by 10 feet cells containing no furniture other than a toilet that could only be flushed from outside the cell. Prisoners in such isolation received fewer than 1,000 calories each day, with "meals" comprising "grue," a substance created by mashing meat, potatoes, vegetables, and eggs into a paste before baking the mixture and apportioning it into squares. While such treatment might be to tolerate for a few days, the Court ruled, a filthy, overcrowded cell and a diet of "grue" might well be assessed as intolerably cruel when imposed for weeks or months—as it was in this case.

With a strong conservative bloc, the Justices consistently favored states' rights over those of prisoners during the final six years of Burger's chiefdom. First, in *Bell v. Wolfish*, 441 U.S. 520 (1979), the Court held that it had its first opportunity to review double-celling, a practice common in federal and state prisons. The Court declined to condemn these conditions, describing them as innocuous and reasonable. "Prison administrators," a majority held, "should be accorded wide-ranging deference in the adoption and execution of policies and practices that in their judgment are needed to preserve internal order and discipline and to maintain institutional security." The Justices clarified the position even more strongly in *Rhodes v. Chapman*, 452 U.S. 337 (1981). While *Wolff* might have spoken of a lifted iron curtain between prisoners and constitutional rights, *Rhodes* declared that "the Constitution does not mandate comfortable prisons, and prisons . . . cannot be free of discomfort." This line of ruling has been characterized as the "hands-off doctrine" and was later bolstered in *Hudson v. Palmer*, 468 U.S. 517 (1984) (finding no reasonable expectation of privacy in cells) and *Block v. Rutherford*, 468 U.S. 576 (1984) (finding no constitutional right to prison visits). The final nail in the coffin for 1980s Eighth

Amendment adjudication in prison conditions cases came in the form of a 5–4 ruling in ***WHITLEY v. ALBERS***, 475 U.S. 312 (1986).

During the course of a riot at Oregon State Penitentiary, a prison officer was taken hostage in a cell, after which the prison's security manager attempted to quell subsequent disorder with officers firing shots, one of which hit the respondent in the knee, giving rise to a constitutional claim for the pain inflicted on him in the course of his confinement. The *Whitley* Court held that the shooting did not violate the petitioner's Eighth Amendment right to be free from cruel and unusual punishments: It is "obduracy and wantonness, not inadvertence or error in good faith," the Court held, that characterize the conduct restricted by the Punishments Clause. Such infliction of pain in the course of a security measure, therefore, does not amount to cruel and unusual punishment, even if, with hindsight, it appears gratuitous or unnecessary. Although the specific circumstances (as Justice Marshall pointed out in his dissent) went beyond the shooting—with the petitioner "losing a great deal of blood" and having "the barrel of a gun or gas pistol" put in his face, he "left lying and bleeding profusely for approximately 10 or 15 more minutes"—these circumstances were incidental. They were not material to the constitutional question, which is whether force was "applied in a good faith effort to maintain or restore discipline," rather than "maliciously and sadistically" with the intention of causing harm, which these acts were not. Prison officials cannot, the Court concluded, "realistically be expected to consider every contingency or minimize every risk," setting a high bar for successful appeals in future similar circumstances and deferring to prison security in decision-making during instances of disorder.

In *DeShaney v. Winnebago County Department of Social Services*, 489 U.S. 189 (1989), the Court made clear the "corresponding duty to assume some responsibility for his safety and general well being" by a state that takes a person into custody. "The rationale for this principle is simple enough," the Justices concluded: "[W]hen the State by the affirmative exercise of its power so restrains an individual's liberty that it renders him unable to care for himself, and at the same time fails to provide for his basic human needs—*e.g.*, food, clothing, shelter, medical care, and reasonable safety—it transgresses the substantive limits on state action set by the Eighth Amendment."

Confinement conditions at the turn of the century: caveating the limitations

A further set of relevant cases, beginning with ***WILSON v. SEITER***, 501 U.S. 294 (1991), reviewed *Estelle*'s "deliberate indifference" test. Wilson was an Ohio prison inmate and alleged that certain conditions of his confinement constituted constitutionally violative punishment. Culpability was the key theme of Justice Scalia's slim majority ruling, where Wilson's suggested distinction between "short-term" or "one-time" prison conditions (in which a state of mind requirement would apply) and "continuing" or "systemic" conditions (where an official state of mind would be irrelevant) was rejected. Under *Estelle* and *Whitley*, the "wantonness" of conduct depends not on its effect on the prisoner but on the constraints facing the official. *Estelle*'s "deliberate indifference" test applied, therefore, to confinement conditions claims. Justice White concurred in *Wilson* but warned that the majority's "intent requirement" was a departure from precedent, which would be impossible to apply in many cases, as inhumane prison conditions often are the result of cumulative actions and inactions, sometimes over a long period: circumstances in which the majority offers no real guidance.

In the following term, the Court admitted, in ***HUDSON v. MCMILLIAN***, 503 U.S. 1 (1992), that excessive force could constitute cruel and unusual punishment but, again, only if inflicted intentionally. Hudson had suffered bruising, loosened teeth, and a cracked dental plate resulting from a beating by prison guards, *which was unconstitutional under the Eighth Amendment*, even though the injury suffered was not "serious." What was most important in this case was again the subjective intent of the officials: Here it was unnecessary, violative of the Punishments Clause and not applied in a good-faith effort to maintain or restore discipline. This holding extended *Whitley's* application of the "unnecessary and wanton infliction of pain" standard to all allegations of force, whether the prison disturbance is a riot or a lesser disruption. In the excessive force context, the Court held, evolving standards of decency are violated when prison officials maliciously and sadistically use force to cause harm, whether or not significant injury is evident. In a concurring opinion, Justice Blackmun summarized the majority's conclusion and commended it for "appropriately put[ting] to rest a seriously misguided view that pain inflicted by an excessive use of force is actionable under the Eighth Amendment only when coupled with 'significant injury,' *e.g.*, injury that requires medical attention or leaves permanent marks," listing the sorts of treatment now clearly outlawed by the ruling in *Hudson* ("lashing prisoners with leather straps, whipping them with rubber hoses, beating them with naked fists, shocking them with electric currents, asphyxiating them short of death, intentionally exposing them to undue heat or cold, or forcibly injecting them with psychosis-inducing drugs [all of which are] hardly unknown within this Nation's prisons"). A further term later, the Court would review the involuntary exposure of an inmate to environmental tobacco smoke ("ETS") from other inmates' cigarettes, which he claimed posed an unreasonable risk to his health. In that case, ***HELLING v. McKINNEY***, 509 U.S. 25 (1993), a 7–2 majority upheld the claim and deemed such treatment deliberately indifferent to McKinney's health, with ETS levels that posed an unreasonable risk to him in the future: further clarifying *Estelle*'s application to another set of circumstances (although Justice Scalia's dissent rejected the very notion of Eighth Amendment engagement, arguing that such environmental concerns are not themselves *punishments* and therefore unprotected by the clause of the same description).

In 1994, another confinement conditions challenge was placed on the Court's docket, directly challenging the "hands-off" declaration from *Rhodes*. Despite an opportunity to do so, the Justices continued to ignore the growing problems of contemporary imprisonment in that case, ***FARMER v. BRENNAN***, 511 U.S. 825 (1994). Farmer was a "preoperative transsexual who projects feminine characteristics" and had been incarcerated with males in the federal prison system, sometimes in the general prison population but more often in segregation. He claimed to have been beaten and raped by another inmate after being transferred to a higher-security facility (typically with more troublesome prisoners) and placed in its general population. Farmer claimed that these actions had constituted "deliberate indifference" to his safety in violation of the Eighth Amendment because they knew that the penitentiary had a violent environment and a history of inmate assaults and that he would therefore be particularly vulnerable to sexual attack. The Supreme Court held that a prison official may be held liable for acting with such deliberate indifference only if he knows that inmates face "a substantial risk of serious harm" and "disregards that risk by failing to take reasonable measures to abate it": In this case, such deprivation was not "sufficiently serious." Such indifference is more than mere negligence, and a subjective recklessness test was applied, inspired by that used in criminal law. This gave little slack to prisoners seeking to challenge the serious harm they suffered, solidifying a continuing trend from 1976 to 1995, namely that inmates, while engaging in litigation at a rate never seen before, were not finding success with Eighth Amendment challenges against their confinement conditions. Congress next enacted the PRLA in 1995 to restrict the number of civil (§ 1983) lawsuits a prisoner could bring, and to limit the power of Federal judges on the circuit. This cross-governmental effort to curtail the rights of prisoners was successful, with a sharp decline in the rate of suits brought by prisoners from 1995 onward. The *Estelle-Farmer* standard continues in 2025 to represent the most recent precedent by which to deal explicitly with confinement conditions challenges under the Punishments Clause.

In a further and final decision on confinement conditions adjudication, the Court reviewed the treatment of an Alabaman prisoner, handcuffed to a hitching post in hot, exposed weather and humiliated by guards. A reasonable officer, as the Court held in ***HOPE v. PELZER***, 536 U.S. 730 (2002), would have known that this conduct was unlawful. It was obviously cruel, inherent in practicing such treatment, and this should have provided the prison authorities with sufficient notice that an Eighth Amendment claim was sustainable against them. The Eighth Amendment violation was described by the majority as "obvious on the facts alleged," outlined as follows: Hope (the petitioner) "was twice handcuffed to a hitching post for disruptive conduct. . . . He was handcuffed above shoulder height, and when he tried moving his arms to improve circulation, the handcuffs cut into his wrists, causing pain and discomfort . . . he was ordered to take off his shirt, thus exposing himself to the sun, and spent seven hours on the hitching post. While there, he was given one or two water breaks but no bathroom breaks, and a guard taunted him about his thirst." This treatment, Justice Stevens's 6–3 majority concluded, was despite a clear lack of emergency, no compelling case of necessity, and therefore the guards knowingly subjected Hope to a substantial risk of physical harm. The subsequent unnecessary pain created a risk of particular discomfort and humiliation. Such inflictions were "unnecessary and wanton," constituting cruel and unusual punishment forbidden by the Amendment, particularly as they were "totally without penological justification" (with reference to *Rhodes*).

Mass incarceration on trial

Until 2011, the Supreme Court had not extended *Estelle*'s "deliberate indifference" standard to psychiatric care, despite a burgeoning field of academic literature calling for the introduction of limits to the severity of modern imprisonment. Although the Court has never upheld a challenge to solitary confinement in and of itself, it did once accept that such hardship could become so extreme that it constitutes psychological torture. In the same term that the Court held that electrocution was inoffensive to the Eighth Amendment in *Kemmler*, the majority in *In Re Medley*, 134 U.S. 160 (1890) described solitary as creating "one of the most horrible feelings to which [an inmate] can be subjected." The only Roberts Court decision to cite *Rhodes*, the case that announced prisons as vestibules of permissible and expected discomfort, came in a challenge to the Californian prison system. That case, ***BROWN v. PLATA***, 563 U.S. 493 (2011), arose from a decision handed down by a special, PLRA-created, three-judge federal court that had reviewed the system in 2009. In the earlier decision—the first ever litigation against mass incarceration—the lower federal court heard how California held approximately 156,000 inmates in a network of prisons designed for 85,000, or 83% overcapacity.[1] The system was found unfit for purpose, as it had subjected a mass of prisoners to undue hardship in conditions such as triple-bunked beds, contained in wards, which more closely resembled refugee camps than modern prisons. As a result of these findings, the three judges recommended diversion from prisons, insisting that lesser culpability offenses should not be matched with custodial sentences, and ordering a 46,000-prisoner reduction in California's inmate population within two years. After that time had passed, *Plata* was decided by the Supreme Court.

A 5–4 majority acknowledged that prisoners "retain the essence of human dignity inherent in all persons," holding the entire state prison system in violation of the Eighth Amendment for lacking adequate safeguards for physical and mental safety. In sum, the Justices upheld the three-judge court's mandated population limit as necessary to remedy the violation of prisoners' constitutional rights and concluded that it was authorized by the PLRA. Moreover, if a prison deprives prisoners of basic sustenance, including adequate medical care, the courts have a responsibility to remedy the resulting Eighth Amendment violation. It was permissible for the three-judge court to conclude that overcrowding was the "primary," but not the only, cause of the violations and that reducing crowding would not entirely cure the violations. As noted previously, until *Plata* the Court had never equated mental health with physical needs. Justice Kennedy's majority expanded the approach significantly, paying particular attention to the evolving standards element of the assessment. To "subject sick and mentally ill prisoners in California to 'substantial risk of serious harm' cause[s] the delivery of care in the prisons to fall below the evolving standards of decency that mark the progress of a maturing society," he concluded.

The *Plata* majority "broke with the posture of extreme deference toward imprisonment choices" (Simon, 2014, p. 152), although the "potential sea change" it could have unleashed—according to Jonathan Simon, who has examined the judgment in some detail—has not been seen. This resurrection of federal judicial scrutiny of prisons from the Supreme Court's 20-year deep freeze opened the prospect of a legal dismantling of mass incarceration, but the results were implemented at the legislative state-level rather than in further Eighth Amendment case law. The most marked immediate effects of *Plata* were in California itself, with reforms in its sentencing and parole policies (for instance, reclassifying certain drug and property offenses from felonies to misdemeanors in 2014, reducing the prison

1 *Coleman v. Schwarzenegger*; *Plata v. Schwarzenegger* (Nos Civ S-90–0520; C01–1351) (ED CA; ND CA 2009) (three-judge court).

population). The state met initial court-imposed benchmarks and made several changes to its sentencing policy. Instead of releasing state prison inmates, though, California transferred them to county jails. State officials deemed it inefficient to reduce the state prison population by 46,000 inmates while county jails had 10,000 empty beds. Consequently, the legislation restructured California's penal system. Nearly 500 felonies were redefined, so offenders could serve time in county jails, and nonserious, nonviolent, and nonsexual offenders were mandated to serve time in such facilities. From 2010 to 2012, California's prison population decreased by 18%, while its jail population grew by 12%. The state-run probation system saw a 46% drop, whereas the county-run parole population increased by 34%. This realignment led to the largest reduction in California's prison population since the 1969–1976 period.

Mass incarceration did dwindle nationally, with a reduction in the overall American prison population in 2012 for the first time since the 1960s, a reducing trend that continued for a decade before a 2% uptick in 2022 (Carson, 2023). *Plata* might have temporarily reinforced the role of judicial oversight in ensuring that state prison systems comply with constitutional standards, but the ruling has not been referenced in any substantively meaningful way by the Supreme Court in the 14 years since, and the current composition of the bench makes it unlikely this will change anytime soon.

Unconstitutional solitude?

I have written elsewhere about solitary confinement, in which around 100,000 prisoners are held in the United States (Eastaugh, 2017). Extending *Rhodes* to solitary (as a totality of conditions that might amount to inhuman treatment) is a subject not addressed substantively by the Supreme Court. In *Davis v. Ayala*, 576 U.S. 257 (2015), a case primarily concerning the Fourteenth, Justice Kennedy concurred to question the propriety of Ayala's placement in solitary, observing that Ayala had spent more than a quarter of a century in such solitude, in "a windowless cell no larger than a typical parking spot for 23 hours a day; and in the one hour when he leaves it, he likely is allowed little or no opportunity for conversation or interaction with anyone." Kennedy concluded that the "human toll wrought by extended terms of isolation long has been understood, and questioned, by writers and commentators," and that he would review it on the same lines as the Court has examined the death penalty. Justice Breyer added his voice to this chorus of discontent, this time concerning prolonged detention in solitary confinement on death row. Dissenting in *Smith v. Ryan*, 137 S. Ct. 1283 (2017) (*cert. denied*), Breyer asked: "What legitimate purpose does it serve to hold any human being in solitary confinement for 40 years awaiting execution?" Adding to another dissent from denial in 2021 his belief that "excessive delay both undermines the death penalty's penological rationale and is in and of itself especially cruel because it subjects death row inmates to decades of especially severe, dehumanizing conditions of confinement."[2] Justice Kennedy retired in 2018 and Breyer in 2022, after which the Court does not appear to provide any prospect of such review in the near future.

Moreover, UN bodies and regional institutions such as the European Court of Human Rights and the Inter-American Court of Human Rights (IACtHR) have applied similar principles to those established in the cases outlined in this chapter to curtail solitary. The IACtHR has deemed "prolonged isolation and deprivation of communication"[3] in breach of its Convention and has ruled that solitary cells must be used "only during the time necessary and in strict compliance with the criteria of reasonability, necessity and legality."[4] Despite reliance on international comparators in other areas of Eighth Amendment law, the Court has yet to accept review of a challenge against solitary itself, although a number of federal circuits have extended Fourteenth Amendment due process review to solitary.[5]

References

Carson, E.A. (2023) *Prisoners in 2022—statistical tables*. U.S. Department of Justice Office of Justice. November, NCJ 307149. Available at: https://bjs.ojp.gov/document/p22st.pdf

Eastaugh, C. (2017) *Unconstitutional solitude*. Palgrave Macmillan.

Simon, J. (2014) *Mass incarceration on trial: a remarkable court decision and the future of prisons in America*. New York: The New Press.

Cited cases

Bell v. Wolfish, 441 U.S. 520 (1979).

Buniton v. Lumpkin, 142 S. Ct. 3 (2021) (cert. denied, Justice Breyer dissenting).

Coleman v. Schwarzenegger; *Plata v. Schwarzenegger*, Nos Civ S-90–0520; C01–1351, ED CA; ND CA (2009).

Davis v. Ayala, 576 U.S. 257 (2015).

DeShaney v. Winnebago County Dept. of Social Services, 489 U.S. 189 (1989).

2 *Buniton v. Lumpkin*, 142 S. Ct. 3 (2021) (*cert. denied*) (Justice Breyer, dissenting). See also *Lackey v. Texas*, 514 U.S. 1045 (1995) (*cert. denied*); *Knight v. Florida*, 528 U.S. 990 (1999) (*cert. denied*); *Smith v. Arizona*, 128 S. Ct. 466 (2007) (*cert. denied*).

3 *Velasquez Rodriguez v. Honduras*, IACtHR Series C No. 4 [516] (1988).

4 *Montero Aranguren et al. v. Venezuela*, IACtHR Series C No. 150 [117] (2006).

5 See *Wilkinson v. Austin*, 545 U.S. 209 (2005), applied to solitary in: *Williams v. Secretary Pennsylvania DoC*; *Walker v. Farnan* (Nos 14–1469; 15–1390) (3rd Cir. 2017); *Incumaa v. Stirling*, 791 F.3d. 517 (4th Cir. 2015); *Harden-Bey v. Rutter* 524 F.3d. 789 (6th Cir. 2008).

Estelle v. Gamble, 429 U.S. 97 (1976).
Farmer v. Brennan, 511 U.S. 825 (1994).
Harden-Bey v. Rutter, 524 F. 3d. 789 (6th Cir. 2008).
Helling v. McKinney, 509 U.S. 25 (1993).
Hope v. Pelzer, 536 U.S. 730 (2002).
Hudson v. McMillian, 503 U.S. 1 (1992).
Hutto v. Finney, 437 U.S. 678 (1978).
In Re Medley, 134 U.S. 160 (1890).
Incumaa v. Stirling, 791 F. 3d. 517 (4th Cir. 2015).
Knight v. Florida, 528 U.S. 990 (1999) (cert. denied).
Lackey v. Texas, 514 U.S. 1045 (1995) (cert. denied).
Montero Aranguren et al. v. Venezuela, IACtHR Series C No 150 (2006).
Rhodes v. Chapman, 452 U.S. 337 (1981).
Smith v. Arizona, 128 S. Ct. 466 (2007) (cert. denied).
Smith v. Ryan, 137 S. Ct. 1283 (2017) (cert. denied).
Velasquez Rodriguez v. Honduras, IACtHR Series C No 4 (1988).
Whitley v. Albers, 475 U.S. 312 (1986).
Wilkinson v. Austin, 545 U.S. 209 (2005).
Williams v. Secretary Pennsylvania DoC; *Walker v. Farnan*, Nos 14–1469; 15–1390, 3rd Cir (2017).
Wilson v. Seiter, 501 U.S. 294 (1991).
Wolff v. McDonnell, 418 U.S. 539 (1974).

Cited legislation

42 U.S.C. § 1983 (2018).
Prison Litigation Reform Act of 1995, 42 U.S.C. § 1997e (1995).

ESTELLE v. GAMBLE, 429 U.S. 97 (1976)

JUSTICE MARSHALL delivered the opinion of the Court, joined by CHIEF JUSTICE BURGER and JUSTICES BRENNAN, STEWART, WHITE, POWELL, and REHNQUIST. JUSTICE BLACKMUN concurred in the judgment.

Respondent J. W. Gamble, an inmate of the Texas Department of Corrections, was injured on November 9, 1973, while performing a prison work assignment. On February 11, 1974, he instituted this civil rights action under 42 U.S.C. § 1983, complaining of the treatment he received after the injury.

According to the complaint, Gamble was injured on November 9, 1973, when a bale of cotton fell on him while he was unloading a truck. He continued to work, but, after four hours, he became stiff and was granted a pass to the unit hospital. At the hospital, a medical assistant, "Captain" Blunt, checked him for a hernia and sent him back to his cell. Within two hours, the pain became so intense that Gamble returned to the hospital, where he was given pain pills by an inmate nurse and then was examined by a doctor. The following day, Gamble saw a Dr. Astone, who diagnosed the injury as a lower back strain, prescribed Zactirin (a pain reliever) and Robaxin (a muscle relaxant), and placed respondent on "cell pass, cell feed" status for two days, allowing him to remain in his cell at all times except for showers. On November 12, Gamble again saw Dr. Astone, who continued the medication and cell pass, cell feed for another seven days. He also ordered that respondent be moved from an upper to a lower bunk for one week, but the prison authorities did not comply with that directive. The following week, Gamble returned to Dr. Astone. The doctor continued the muscle relaxant but prescribed a new pain reliever, Febridyne, and placed respondent on cell-pass for seven days, permitting him to remain in his cell except for meals and showers. On November 26, respondent again saw Dr. Astone, who put respondent back on the original pain reliever for five days and continued the cell-pass for another week.

On December 3, despite Gamble's statement that his back hurt as much as it had the first day, Dr. Astone took him off cell-pass, thereby certifying him to be capable of light work. At the same time, Dr. Astone prescribed Febridyne for seven days. Gamble then went to a Major Muddox and told him that he was in too much pain to work. Muddox had respondent moved to "administrative segregation." On December 5, Gamble was taken before the prison disciplinary committee, apparently because of his refusal to work. When the committee heard his complaint of back pain and high blood pressure, it directed that he be seen by another doctor.

On December 6, respondent saw petitioner Gray, who performed a urinalysis, blood test, and blood pressure measurement. Dr. Gray prescribed the drug Ser-Ap-Es for the high blood pressure and more Febridyne for the back pain. The following week respondent again saw Dr. Gray, who continued the Ser-Ap-Es for an additional 30 days. The prescription was not filled for four days, however, because the staff lost it. Respondent went to the unit hospital twice more in December; both times he was seen by Captain Blunt, who prescribed Tiognolos (described as a muscle relaxant). For all of December, respondent remained in administrative segregation.

In early January, Gamble was told on two occasions that he would be sent to the "farm" if he did not return to work. He refused, nonetheless, claiming to be in too much pain. On January 7, 1974, he requested to go on sick call for his back pain and migraine headaches. After an initial refusal, he saw Captain Blunt, who prescribed sodium salicylate (a pain reliever) for several days and Ser-Ap-Es for 30 days. Respondent returned to Captain Blunt on January 17 and January 25, and received renewals of the pain reliever prescription both times. Throughout the month, respondent was kept in administrative segregation.

On January 31, Gamble was brought before the prison disciplinary committee for his refusal to work in early January. He told the committee that he could not work because of his severe back pain and his high blood pressure. Captain Blunt testified that Gamble was in "first class" medical condition. The committee, with no further medical examination or testimony, placed respondent in solitary confinement.

Four days later, on February 4, at 8 am., respondent asked to see a doctor for chest pains and "blank outs." It was not until 7:30 that night that a medical assistant examined him and ordered him hospitalized. The following day, a Dr. Heaton performed an electrocardiogram; one day later, respondent was placed on Quinidine for treatment of irregular cardiac rhythm and moved to administrative segregation. On February 7, respondent again experienced pain in his chest, left arm, and back and asked to see a doctor. The guards refused. He asked again the next day. The guards again refused. Finally, on February 9, he was allowed to see Dr. Heaton, who ordered the Quinidine continued for three more days. On February 11, he swore out his complaint.

II

The gravamen of respondent's § 1983 complaint is that petitioners have subjected him to cruel and unusual punishment in violation of the Eighth Amendment, made applicable to the States by the Fourteenth.

[The] elementary principles establish the government's obligation to provide medical care for those whom it is punishing by incarceration. An inmate must rely on prison authorities to treat his medical needs; if the authorities fail to do so, those needs will not be met. In the worst cases, such a failure may actually produce physical "torture or a lingering death," the evils of most immediate concern to the drafters of the Amendment. In less serious cases, denial of medical care may result in pain and suffering which no one suggests would serve any penological purpose. The infliction of such unnecessary suffering is inconsistent with contemporary standards of decency as manifested in modern legislation codifying the common law view that "it is but just that the public be required to care for the prisoner, who cannot, by reason of the deprivation of his liberty, care for himself."

We therefore conclude that deliberate indifference to serious medical needs of prisoners constitutes the "unnecessary and wanton infliction of pain," proscribed by the Eighth Amendment. This is true whether the indifference is manifested by prison doctors in their response to the prisoner's needs or by prison guards in intentionally denying or delaying access to medical care or intentionally interfering with the treatment once prescribed. Regardless of how evidenced, deliberate indifference to a prisoner's serious illness or injury states a cause of action under § 1983.

This conclusion does not mean, however, that every claim by a prisoner that he has not received adequate medical treatment states a violation of the Eighth Amendment. An accident, although it may produce added anguish, is not on that basis alone to be characterized as wanton infliction of unnecessary pain.

Similarly [to *Resweber*], in the medical context, an inadvertent failure to provide adequate medical care cannot be said to constitute "an unnecessary and wanton infliction of pain" or to be "repugnant to the conscience of mankind." Thus, a complaint that a physician has been negligent in diagnosing or treating a medical condition does not state a valid claim of medical mistreatment under the Eighth Amendment. Medical malpractice does not become a constitutional violation merely because the victim is a prisoner. In order to state a cognizable claim, a prisoner must allege acts or omissions sufficiently harmful to evidence deliberate indifference to serious medical needs. It is only such indifference that can offend "evolving standards of decency" in violation of the Eighth Amendment.

III

[. . .] however, Gamble's claims against Dr. Gray, both in his capacity as treating physician and as medical director of the Corrections Department, are not cognizable under § 1983. Gamble was seen by medical personnel on 17 occasions spanning a three-month period: by Dr. Astone five times; by Dr. Gray twice; by Dr. Heaton three times; by an unidentified doctor and inmate nurse on the day of the injury; and by medical assistant Blunt six times. They treated his back injury, high blood pressure, and heart problems. Gamble has disclaimed any objection to the treatment provided for his high blood pressure and his heart problem; his complaint is "based solely on the lack of diagnosis and inadequate treatment of his back injury." The doctors diagnosed his injury as a lower back strain and treated it with bed rest, muscle relaxants, and pain relievers. Respondent contends that more should have been done by way of diagnosis and treatment, and suggests a number of options that were not pursued.

The Court of Appeals agreed, stating:

> "Certainly an X-ray of [Gamble's] lower back might have been in order and other tests conducted that would have led to appropriate diagnosis and treatment for the daily pain and suffering he was experiencing."

But the question whether an X-ray—or additional diagnostic techniques or forms of treatment—is indicated is a classic example of a matter for medical judgment. A medical decision not to order an X-ray, or like measures, does not represent cruel and unusual punishment. At most, it is medical malpractice, and, as such, the proper forum is the state court under the Texas Tort Claims Act. The Court of Appeals was in error in holding that the alleged insufficiency of the medical treatment required reversal and remand. That portion of the judgment of the District Court should have been affirmed.

The Court of Appeals focused primarily on the alleged actions of the doctors, and did not separately consider whether the allegations against the Director of the Department of Corrections, Estelle, and the warden of the prison, Husbands, stated a cause of action. Although we reverse the judgment as to the medical director, we remand the case to the Court of Appeals to allow it an opportunity to consider, in conformity with this opinion, whether a cause of action has been stated against the other prison officials.

It is so ordered.

JUSTICE STEVENS filed a dissenting opinion.

Most of what is said in the Court's opinion is entirely consistent with the way the lower federal courts have been processing claims that the medical treatment of prison inmates is so inadequate as to constitute the cruel and unusual punishment prohibited by the Eighth Amendment. I have no serious disagreement with the way this area of the law has developed thus far, or with the probable impact of this opinion. Nevertheless, there are three reasons why I am unable to join it. First, insofar as the opinion orders the dismissal of the complaint against the chief medical officer of the prison, it is not faithful to the rule normally applied in construing the allegations in a pleading prepared by an uncounseled inmate. Second, it does not adequately explain why the Court granted certiorari in this case. Third, it describes the State's duty to provide adequate medical care to prisoners in ambiguous terms which incorrectly relate to the subjective motivation of persons accused of violating the Eighth Amendment, rather than to the standard of care required by the Constitution.

[. . .]

III

By its reference to the accidental character of the first unsuccessful attempt to electrocute the prisoner in *Louisiana ex rel. Francs v. Resweber* and by its repeated references to "deliberate indifference" and the "intentional" denial of adequate medical care, I believe the Court improperly attaches significance to the subjective motivation of the defendant as a criterion for determining whether cruel and unusual punishment has been inflicted. Subjective motivation may well determine what, if any, remedy is appropriate against a particular defendant. However, whether the constitutional standard has been violated should turn on the character of the punishment, rather than the motivation of the individual who inflicted it. Whether the conditions in Andersonville were the product of design, negligence, or mere poverty, they were cruel and inhuman.

In sum, I remain convinced that the petition for certiorari should have been denied. It having been granted, I would affirm the judgment of the Court of Appeals.

HUTTO v. FINNEY, 437 U.S. 678 (1978)

JUSTICE STEVENS delivered the opinion of the Court, joined by JUSTICES BRENNAN, STEWART, MARSHALL, and BLACKMUN, with WHITE, J., joining in Part I, and CHIEF JUSTICE BURGER and JUSTICE POWELL joining in Parts I and II-A.

After finding that conditions in the Arkansas penal system constituted cruel and unusual punishment, the District Court entered a series of detailed remedial orders. On appeal to the United States Court of Appeals for the Eighth Circuit, petitioners challenged two aspects of that relief: (1) an order placing a maximum limit of 30 days on confinement in punitive isolation; and (2) an award of attorney's fees to be paid out of Department of Correction funds.

[. . .]

The routine conditions that the ordinary Arkansas convict had to endure were characterized by the District Court as "a dark and evil world completely alien to the free world." That characterization was amply supported by the evidence.

The punishments for misconduct not serious enough to result in punitive isolation were cruel, unusual, and unpredictable. It is the discipline known as "punitive isolation" that is most relevant for present purposes.

Confinement in punitive isolation was for an indeterminate period of time. An average of 4, and sometimes as many as 10 or 11, prisoners were crowded into windowless 8′ × 10′ cells containing no furniture other than a source of water and a toilet that could only be flushed from outside the cell. At night, the prisoners were given mattresses to spread on the floor. Although some prisoners suffered from infectious diseases such as hepatitis and venereal disease, mattresses were removed and jumbled together each morning, then returned to the cells at random in the evening. Prisoners in isolation received fewer than 1,000 calories a day; their meals consisted primarily of 4-inch squares of "grue," a substance created by mashing meat, potatoes, oleo, syrup, vegetables, eggs, and seasoning into a paste and baking the mixture in a pan.

After finding the conditions of confinement unconstitutional, the District Court did not immediately impose a detailed remedy of its own. Instead, it directed the Department of Correction to "make a substantial start" on improving conditions and to file reports on its progress. When the Department's progress proved unsatisfactory, a second hearing was held. The District Court found some improvements, but concluded that prison conditions remained unconstitutional. Again the court offered prison administrators an opportunity to devise a plan of their own for remedying the constitutional violations, but this time the court issued guidelines, identifying four areas of change that would cure the worst evils: improving conditions in the isolation cells, increasing inmate safety, eliminating the barracks sleeping arrangements, and putting an end to the trusty system. The Department was ordered to move as rapidly as funds became available.

I

Confinement in a prison or in an isolation cell is a form of punishment subject to scrutiny under Eighth Amendment standards. Petitioners do not challenge this proposition; nor do they disagree with the District Court's original conclusion that conditions in Arkansas' prisons, including its punitive isolation cells, constituted cruel and unusual punishment. Rather, petitioners single out that portion of the District Court's most recent order that forbids the Department to sentence inmates to more than 30 days in punitive isolation. Petitioners assume that the District Court held that indeterminate sentences to punitive isolation always constitute cruel and unusual punishment. This assumption misreads the District Court's holding.

Read in its entirety, the District Court's opinion makes it abundantly clear that the length of isolation sentences was not considered in a vacuum. In the court's words, punitive isolation "is not necessarily unconstitutional, but it may be, depending on the duration of the confinement and the conditions thereof." It is perfectly obvious that every decision to remove a particular inmate from the general prison population for an indeterminate period could not be characterized as cruel and unusual. If new conditions of confinement are not materially different from those affecting other prisoners, a transfer for the duration of a prisoner's sentence might be completely unobjectionable, and well within the authority of the prison administrator. It is equally plain, however, that the length of confinement cannot be ignored in deciding whether the confinement meets constitutional standards. A filthy, overcrowded cell and a diet of "grue" might be tolerable for a few days and intolerably cruel for weeks or months.

The question before the trial court was whether past constitutional violations had been remedied. The court was entitled to consider the severity of those violations in assessing the constitutionality of conditions in the isolation cells. The court took note of the inmates' diet, the continued overcrowding, the rampant violence, the vandalized cells, and the "lack of professionalism and good judgment on the part of maximum security personnel." The length of time each inmate spent in isolation was simply one consideration among many. We find no error in the court's conclusion that, taken as a whole, conditions in the isolation cells continued to violate the prohibition against cruel and unusual punishment.

In fashioning a remedy, the District Court had ample authority to go beyond earlier orders and to address each element contributing to the violation. The District Court had given the Department repeated opportunities to remedy the cruel and unusual conditions in the isolation cells. If petitioners had fully complied with the court's earlier orders, the present time limit might well have been unnecessary. But taking the long and unhappy history of the litigation into account, the court was justified in entering a comprehensive order to insure against the risk of inadequate compliance.

The order is supported by the interdependence of the conditions producing the violation. The vandalized cells and the atmosphere of violence were attributable, in part, to overcrowding and to deep-seated enmities growing out of months of constant daily friction. The 30-day limit will help to correct these conditions. Moreover, the limit presents little danger of interference with prison administration, for the Commissioner of Correction himself stated that prisoners should not ordinarily be held in punitive isolation for more than 14 days. Finally, the exercise of discretion in this case is entitled to special deference because of the trial judge's years of experience with the problem at hand and his recognition of the limits on a federal court's authority in a case of this kind. Like the Court of Appeals, we find no error in the inclusion of a 30-day limitation on sentences to punitive isolation as a part of the District Court's comprehensive remedy.

JUSTICE BRENNAN filed a concurring opinion.

JUSTICE POWELL filed an opinion concurring in part and dissenting in part, joined by CHIEF JUSTICE BURGER, and joined in the dissenting portion by JUSTICES WHITE and REHNQUIST.

JUSTICE REHNQUIST filed a dissenting opinion, joined in Part II by JUSTICE WHITE.

WHITLEY v. ALBERS, 475 U.S. 312 (1986)

JUSTICE O'CONNOR delivered the opinion of the Court, joined by CHIEF JUSTICE BURGER, and JUSTICES WHITE, POWELL, and REHNQUIST.

This case requires us to decide what standard governs a prison inmate's claim that prison officials subjected him to cruel and unusual punishment by shooting him during the course of their attempt to quell a prison riot.

At the time he was injured, respondent Gerald Albers was confined in cellblock "A" of the Oregon State Penitentiary. Cellblock "A" consists of two tiers of barred cells housing some 200 inmates. The two tiers are connected by a stairway that offers the only practical way to move from one tier to another.

At about 8:30 on the evening of June 27, 1980, several inmates were found intoxicated at the prison annex. Prison guards attempted to move the intoxicated prisoners, some of whom resisted, to the penitentiary's isolation and segregation facility. This incident could be seen from the cell windows in cellblock "A," and some of the onlookers became agitated because they thought that the guards were using unnecessary force. Acting on instructions from their superiors, Officers Kemper and Fitts, who were on duty in cellblock "A," ordered the prisoners to return to their cells. The order was not obeyed. Several inmates confronted the two officers, who were standing in the open area of the lower tier. One inmate, Richard Klenk, jumped from the second tier and assaulted Officer Kemper. Kemper escaped, but Officer Fitts was taken hostage. Klenk and other inmates then began breaking furniture and milling about.

Upon being informed of the disturbance, petitioner Harol Whitley, the prison security manager, entered cellblock "A" and spoke with Klenk. Captain Whitley agreed to permit four residents of cellblock "A" to view the inmates who had been taken to segregation earlier. These emissaries reported back that the prisoners in segregation were intoxicated but unharmed. Nonetheless, the disturbance in cellblock "A" continued.

Whitley returned to the cellblock and confirmed that Fitts was not harmed. Shortly thereafter, Fitts was moved from an office on the lower tier to cell 201 on the upper tier, and Klenk demanded that media representatives be brought into the cellblock. In the course of the negotiations, Klenk, who was armed with a homemade knife, informed Whitley that one inmate had already been killed, and other deaths would follow. In fact, an inmate had been beaten but not killed by other prisoners.

Captain Whitley left the cellblock to organize an assault squad. When Whitley returned to cellblock "A," he was taken to see Fitts in cell 201. Several inmates assured Whitley that they would protect Fitts from harm, but Klenk threatened to kill the hostage if an attempt was made to lead an assault. Klenk and at least some other inmates were aware that guards had assembled outside the cellblock and that shotguns had been issued. Meanwhile, respondent had left his cell on the upper tier to see if elderly prisoners housed on the lower tier could be moved out of harm's way in the event that tear gas was used. Respondent testified that he asked Whitley for the key to the row of cells housing the elderly prisoners, and Whitley indicated that he would return with the key. Whitley denied that he spoke to respondent at any time during the disturbance.

Whitley next consulted with his superiors, petitioners Cupp, the prison Superintendent, and Kenney, the Assistant Superintendent. They agreed that forceful intervention was necessary to protect the life of the hostage and the safety of the inmates who were not rioting, and ruled out tear gas as an unworkable alternative. Cupp ordered Whitley to take a squad armed with shotguns into cellblock "A."

Whitley gave the final orders to the assault team, which was assembled in the area outside cellblock "A." Petitioner Kennicott and two other officers armed with shotguns were to follow Whitley, who was unarmed, over the barricade the inmates had constructed at the cellblock entrance. A second group of officers, without firearms, would be behind them. Whitley ordered Kennicott to fire a warning shot as he crossed the barricade. He also ordered Kennicott to shoot low at any prisoners climbing the stairs toward cell 201, since they could pose a threat to the safety of the hostage or to Whitley himself, who would be climbing the stairs in an attempt to free the hostage in cell 201.

At about 10:30 p.m., Whitley reappeared just outside the barricade. By this time, about a half hour had elapsed since the earlier breaking of furniture, and the noise level in the cellblock had noticeably diminished. Respondent, who was standing at the bottom of the stairway, asked about the key. Whitley replied "No," clambered over the barricade, yelled "shoot the bastards," and ran toward the stairs after Klenk, who had been standing in the open areaway along with a number of other inmates. Kennicott fired a warning shot into the wall opposite the cellblock entrance as he followed Whitley over the barricade. He then fired a second shot that struck a post near the stairway. Meanwhile, Whitley chased Klenk up the stairs, and shortly thereafter respondent started up the stairs. Kennicott fired a third shot that struck respondent in the left knee. Another inmate was shot on the stairs, and several others on the lower tier were wounded by gunshot. The inmates in cell 201 prevented Klenk from entering, and Whitley subdued Klenk at the cell door, freeing the hostage.

As a result of the incident, respondent sustained severe damage to his left leg and mental and emotional distress. He subsequently commenced this action pursuant to 42 U.S.C. § 1983, alleging that petitioners deprived him of his rights under the Eighth and Fourteenth Amendments and raising pendent state law claims for assault and battery and negligence. Many of the facts were stipulated, but both sides also presented testimony from witnesses to the disturbance and the rescue attempt, as well as from expert witnesses with backgrounds in prison discipline and security. At the conclusion of trial, the District Judge directed a verdict for petitioners.

II

"After incarceration, only the '*unnecessary and wanton infliction of pain*' " . . . *constitutes cruel and unusual punishment forbidden by the Eighth Amendment.*"

Ingraham v. Wright (quoting *Estelle v. Gamble*). To be cruel and unusual punishment, conduct that does not purport to be punishment at all must involve more than ordinary lack of due care for the prisoner's interests or safety. It is obduracy and wantonness, not inadvertence or error in good faith, that characterize the conduct prohibited by the Cruel and Unusual Punishments Clause, whether that conduct occurs in connection with establishing conditions of confinement, supplying medical needs, or restoring official control over a tumultuous cellblock. The infliction of pain in the course of a prison security measure, therefore, does not amount to cruel and unusual punishment simply because it may appear in retrospect that the degree of force authorized or applied for security purposes was unreasonable, and hence unnecessary in the strict sense.

The general requirement that an Eighth Amendment claimant allege and prove the unnecessary and wanton infliction of pain should also be applied with due regard for differences in the kind of conduct against which an Eighth Amendment objection is lodged. The deliberate indifference standard articulated in *Estelle* was appropriate in the context presented in that case because the State's responsibility to attend to the medical needs of prisoners does not ordinarily clash with other equally important governmental responsibilities. Consequently, "deliberate indifference to a prisoner's serious illness or injury," can typically be established or disproved without the necessity of balancing competing institutional concerns for the safety of prison staff or other inmates. But, in making and carrying out decisions involving the use of force to restore order in the face of a prison disturbance, prison officials undoubtedly must take into account the very real threats the unrest presents to inmates and prison officials alike, in addition to the possible harms to inmates against whom force might be used. As we said in *Hudson v. Palmer*, prison administrators are charged with the responsibility of ensuring the safety of the prison staff, administrative personnel, and visitors, as well as the "obligation to take reasonable measures to guarantee the safety of the inmates themselves." In this setting, a deliberate indifference standard does not adequately capture the importance of such competing obligations, or convey the appropriate hesitancy to critique in hindsight decisions necessarily made in haste, under pressure, and frequently without the luxury of a second chance.

Where a prison security measure is undertaken to resolve a disturbance, such as occurred in this case, that indisputably poses significant risks to the safety of inmates and prison staff, we think the question whether the measure taken inflicted unnecessary and wanton pain and suffering ultimately turns on "whether force was applied in a good faith effort to maintain or restore discipline or maliciously and sadistically for the very purpose of causing harm."

When the "ever-present potential for violent confrontation and conflagration" ripens into actual unrest and conflict, the admonition that "a prison's internal security is peculiarly a matter normally left to the discretion of prison administrators" carries special weight.

"Prison administrators . . . should be accorded wide-ranging deference in the adoption and execution of policies and practices that in their judgment are needed to preserve internal order and discipline and to maintain institutional security." [*Bell v. Wolfish*]

That deference extends to a prison security measure taken in response to an actual confrontation with riotous inmates, just as it does to prophylactic or preventive measures intended to reduce the incidence of these or any other breaches of prison discipline. It does not insulate from review actions taken in bad faith and for no legitimate purpose, but it requires that neither judge nor jury freely substitute their judgment for that of officials who have made a considered choice. Accordingly, in ruling on a motion for a directed verdict in a case such as this, courts must determine whether the evidence goes beyond a mere dispute over the reasonableness of a particular use of force or the existence of arguably superior alternatives. Unless it appears that the evidence, viewed in the light most favorable to the plaintiff, will support a reliable inference of wantonness in the infliction of pain under the standard we have described, the case should not go to the jury.

III

To begin with, although the evidence could be taken to show that the general disturbance had quieted down, a guard was still held hostage, Klenk was armed and threatening, several other inmates were armed with homemade clubs, numerous inmates remained outside their cells, and the cellblock remained in the control of the inmates. The situation remained dangerous and volatile. As respondent concedes, at the time he was shot, "an officer's safety was in question and . . . an inmate was armed and dangerous." Prison officials had no way of knowing what direction matters would take if they continued to negotiate or did nothing, but they had ample reason to believe that these options presented unacceptable risks.

Respondent's expert testimony is likewise unavailing. One of respondent's experts opined that petitioners gave inadequate consideration to less forceful means of intervention, and that the use of deadly force under the circumstances was not necessary to "prevent imminent danger" to the hostage guard or other inmates. Respondent's second expert testified that prison officials were "possibly a little hasty in using the firepower" on the inmates. At most, this evidence, which was controverted by petitioners' experts, establishes that prison officials arguably erred in judgment when they decided on a plan that employed potentially deadly force. It falls far short of a showing that there was no plausible basis for the officials' belief that this degree of force was necessary. Indeed, any such conclusion would run counter to common sense, in light of the risks to the life of the hostage and the safety of inmates that demonstrably persisted notwithstanding repeated attempts to defuse the situation. An expert's after-the-fact opinion that danger was not "imminent" in no way establishes that there was no danger, or that a conclusion by the officers that it was imminent would have been wholly unreasonable.

Once the basic design of the plan was in place, moreover, it is apparent why any inmate running up the stairs after Captain Whitley, or interfering with his progress towards the hostage, could reasonably be thought to present a threat to the success of the rescue attempt and to Whitley—particularly after a warning shot was fired. A sizable group of inmates, in defiance of the cell-in order and in apparent support of Klenk, continued to stand in the open area on the lower tier.

[. . .]

As petitioners' own experts conceded, a verbal warning would have been desirable, in addition to a warning shot, if circumstances permitted it to be given without undue risk. While a jury might conclude that this omission was unreasonable, we think that an inference of wantonness could not properly be drawn. First, some warning was given in the form of the first shot fired by Officer Kennicott. Second, the prison officials could have believed in good faith that such a warning might endanger the success of the security measure because of the risk that it would have allowed one or more inmates to climb the stairs before they could be stopped. The failure to provide for verbal warnings is thus not so insupportable as to be wanton. Accordingly, a jury could not properly find that this omission, coupled with the order to shoot, offended the Eighth Amendment.

To be sure, the plan was not adapted to take into account the appearance of respondent on the scene, and, on the facts as we must take them, Whitley was aware that respondent was present on the first tier for benign reasons. Conceivably, Whitley could have added a proviso exempting respondent from his order to shoot any prisoner climbing the stairs. But such an oversight simply does not rise to the level of an Eighth Amendment violation. Officials cannot realistically be expected to consider every contingency or minimize every risk, and it was far from inevitable that respondent would react as he did. Whitley was about to risk his life in an effort to rescue the hostage, and he was understandably focusing on the orders essential to the success of the plan. His failure to make special provision for respondent may have been unfortunate, but is hardly behavior from which a wanton willingness to inflict unjustified suffering on respondent can be inferred.

Once it is established that the order to shoot low at anyone climbing the stairs after a warning shot was not wanton, respondent's burden in showing that the actual shooting constituted the wanton and unnecessary infliction of pain is an extremely heavy one. Accepting that respondent could not have sought safety in a cell on the lower tier, the fact remains that, had respondent thrown himself to the floor, he would not have been shot at. Instead, after the warning shot was fired, he attempted to return to his cell by running up the stairs behind Whitley. That is equivocal conduct.

JUSTICE MARSHALL filed a dissenting opinion, joined by JUSTICES BRENNAN and BLACKMUN, and joined in all but note 2 by JUSTICE STEVENS.

I share the majority's concern that prison officials be permitted to respond reasonably to inmate disturbances without unwarranted fear of liability. I agree that the threshold for establishing a constitutional violation under these circumstances is high. I do not agree, however, that the contested existence of a "riot" in the prison lessens the constraints imposed on prison authorities by the Eighth Amendment.

The majority has erred, I believe, both in developing its legal analysis and in employing it. First, the especially onerous standard the Court has devised for determining whether a prisoner injured during a prison disturbance has been subjected to cruel and unusual punishment is incorrect, and not justified by precedent. That standard is particularly inappropriate because courts deciding whether to apply it must resolve a preliminary issue of fact that will often be disputed and properly left to the jury. Finally, the Court has applied its test improperly to the facts of this case. For these reasons, I must respectfully dissent.

The Court imposes its heightened version of the "unnecessary and wanton" standard only when the injury occurred in the course of a "disturbance" that "poses significant risks." But those very questions—whether a disturbance existed and whether it posed a risk—are likely to be hotly contested. It is inappropriate, to say the least, to condition the choice of a legal standard, the purpose of which is to determine whether to send a constitutional claim to the jury, upon the court's resolution of factual disputes that in many cases should themselves be resolved by the jury.

The correct standard for identifying a violation of the Eighth Amendment under our cases is clearly the "unnecessary and wanton" standard, which establishes a high hurdle to be overcome by a prisoner seeking relief for a constitutional violation. The full circumstances of the plaintiff's injury, including whether it was inflicted during an attempt to quell a riot and whether there was a reasonable apprehension of danger, should be considered by the fact finder in determining whether that standard is satisfied in a particular case. There is simply no justification for creating a distinct and more onerous burden for the plaintiff to meet merely because the judge believes that the injury at issue was caused during a disturbance that "pose[d] significant risks to the safety of inmates and prison staff." Determination of whether there was such a disturbance or risk, when disputed, should be made by the jury when it resolves disputed facts, not by the court in its role as arbiter of law.

[. . .]

The majority suggests that the existence of more appropriate alternative measures for controlling prison disturbances is irrelevant to the constitutional inquiry, but surely it cannot mean what it appears to say. For if prison officials were to drop a bomb on a cellblock in order to halt a fistfight between two inmates, for example, I feel confident that the Court would have difficulty concluding, as a matter of law, that such an action was not sufficiently wanton to present a jury question, even though concededly taken in an effort to restore order in the prison. Thus, the question of wantonness in the context of prison disorder, as with other claims of mistreatment under the Eighth Amendment, is a matter of degree. And it is precisely in cases like this one, when shading the facts one way or the other can result in different legal conclusions, that a jury should be permitted to do its job. Properly instructed, a jury would take into account the petitioners' legitimate need to protect security, the extent of the danger presented, and the reasonableness of force used, in assessing liability. Moreover, the jury would know that a prisoner's burden is a heavy one, if he is to establish an Eighth Amendment violation under these circumstances.

[Footnote 2]

The majority also rejects the pure Fourteenth Amendment due process claim asserted by respondent before the District Court. For the reasons stated in JUSTICE BLACKMUN's dissent in *Davidson v. Cannon*, 474 U. S. 344 (1986), which I joined, I believe that the evidence precluding a directed verdict under the "unnecessary and wanton" standard also precludes a directed verdict on respondent's due process claim. JUSTICE STEVENS does not join in this footnote.

WILSON v. SEITER, 501 U.S. 294 (1991)

JUSTICE SCALIA delivered the opinion of the Court, joined by CHIEF JUSTICE REHNQUIST, and JUSTICES O'CONNOR, KENNEDY, and SOUTER.

This case presents the questions whether a prisoner claiming that conditions of confinement constitute cruel and unusual punishment must show a culpable state of mind on the part of prison officials and, if so, what state of mind is required.

Petitioner Pearly L. Wilson is a felon incarcerated at the Hocking Correctional Facility (HCF) in Nelsonville, Ohio. Alleging that a number of the conditions of his confinement constituted cruel and unusual punishment in violation of the Eighth and Fourteenth Amendments, he brought this action under 42 U.S.C. § 1983 against respondents Richard P. Seiter, then Director of the Ohio Department of Rehabilitation and Correction, and Carl Humphreys, then warden of HCF. The complaint alleged overcrowding, excessive noise, insufficient locker storage space, inadequate heating and cooling, improper ventilation, unclean and inadequate restrooms, unsanitary dining facilities and food preparation, and housing with mentally and physically ill inmates. Petitioner sought declaratory and injunctive relief, as well as $900,000 in compensatory and punitive damages.

The parties filed cross-motions for summary judgment with supporting affidavits. Petitioner's affidavits described the challenged conditions and charged that the authorities, after notification, had failed to take remedial action. Respondents' affidavits denied that some of the alleged conditions existed, and described efforts by prison officials to improve the others

[. . .]

Having determined that Eighth Amendment claims based on official conduct that does not purport to be the penalty formally imposed for a crime require inquiry into state of mind, it remains for us to consider what state of mind applies in cases challenging prison conditions. As described above, our cases say that the offending conduct must be *wanton*. *Whitley* makes clear, however, that, in this context, wantonness does not have a fixed meaning, but must be determined with "due regard for differences in the kind of conduct against which an Eighth Amendment objection is lodged." Where (as in *Whitley*) officials act in response to a prison disturbance, their actions are necessarily taken "in haste, under pressure," and balanced against "competing institutional concerns for the safety of prison staff or other inmates." In such an emergency situation, we found that wantonness consisted of acting "*maliciously and sadistically for the very purpose of causing harm*." In contrast, "the State's responsibility to attend to the medical needs of prisoners does not ordinarily clash with other equally important governmental responsibilities," so that, in that context, as *Estelle* held, "deliberate indifference" would constitute wantonness.

Whitley does not apply to prison conditions cases. Petitioner argues that, to the extent officials' state of mind is relevant at all, there is no justification for a standard more demanding than *Estelle*'s "deliberate indifference." Respondents counter that "deliberate indifference" is appropriate only in "cases involving personal injury of a physical nature," and that a malice standard should be applied in cases such as this, which "do not involve . . . detriment to bodily integrity, pain, injury, or loss of life."

We do not agree with respondents' suggestion that the "wantonness" of conduct depends upon its effect upon the prisoner. *Whitley* teaches that, assuming the conduct is harmful enough to satisfy the objective component of an Eighth Amendment claim, whether it can be characterized as "wanton" depends upon the constraints facing the *official*. From that standpoint, we see no significant distinction between claims alleging inadequate medical care and those alleging inadequate "conditions of confinement." Indeed, the medical care a prisoner receives is just as much a "condition" of his confinement as the food he is fed, the clothes he is issued, the temperature he is subjected to in his cell, and the protection he is afforded against other inmates. There is no indication that, as a general matter, the actions of prison officials with respect to these nonmedical conditions are taken under materially different constraints than their actions with respect to medical conditions.

[. . .]

As other courts besides the Court of Appeals here have understood, our statement in *Rhodes* was not meant to establish the broad proposition that petitioner asserts. Some conditions of confinement may establish an Eighth Amendment violation "in combination" when each would not do so alone, but only when they have a mutually enforcing effect that produces the deprivation of a single, identifiable human need such as food, warmth, or exercise—for example, a low cell temperature at night combined with a failure to issue blankets. *Compare Spain v. Procunier*, 600 F.2d 189, 199 (CA9 1979) (outdoor exercise required when prisoners otherwise confined in small cells almost 24 hours per day) *with Clay v. Miller*, 626 F.2d 345, 347 (CA4 1980) (outdoor exercise not required when prisoners otherwise had access to day room 18 hours per day). To say that some prison conditions may interact in this fashion is a far cry from saying that all prison conditions are a seamless web for Eighth Amendment purposes. Nothing so amorphous as "overall conditions" can rise to the level of cruel and unusual punishment when no specific deprivation of a single human need exists. While we express no opinion on the relative gravity of the various claims that the Sixth Circuit found to pass and fail the threshold test of serious deprivation, we reject the contention made here that no claim can be found to fail that test in isolation.

After disposing of the three claims on the basis of *Rhodes*, the Court of Appeals proceeded to uphold the District Court's dismissal of petitioner's remaining claims on the ground that his affidavits failed to establish the requisite culpable state of mind. The critical portion of its opinion reads as follows:

> "[T]he *Whitley* standard of obduracy and wantonness requires behavior marked by persistent malicious cruelty. The record before us simply fails to assert facts suggesting such behavior. At best, appellants' claim evidences negligence on appellees' parts in implementing standards for maintaining conditions. Negligence, clearly, is inadequate to support an eighth amendment claim."

It appears from this, and from the consistent reference to "the *Whitley* standard" elsewhere in the opinion, that the court believed that the criterion of liability was whether the respondents acted "maliciously and sadistically for the very purpose of causing harm." To be sure, mere negligence would satisfy neither that nor the more lenient "deliberate indifference" standard, so that any error on the point may have been harmless. Conceivably, however, the court would have given further thought to its finding of "[a]t best . . . negligence" if it realized that that was not merely an argument *a fortiori*, but a determination almost essential to the judgment. Out of an abundance of caution, we vacate the judgment of the Sixth Circuit and remand the case for reconsideration under the appropriate standard.

JUSTICE WHITE filed an opinion concurring in the judgment, joined by JUSTICES MARSHALL, BLACKMUN, and STEVENS.

The majority holds that prisoners challenging the conditions of their confinement under the Eighth Amendment must show "deliberate indifference" by the responsible officials. Because that requirement is inconsistent with our prior decisions, I concur only in the judgment.

It is well established, and the majority does not dispute, that pain or other suffering that is part of the punishment imposed on convicted criminals is subject to Eighth Amendment scrutiny without regard to an intent requirement.

Not only is the majority's intent requirement a departure from precedent, it likely will prove impossible to apply in many cases. Inhumane prison conditions often are the result of cumulative actions and inactions by numerous officials inside and outside a prison, sometimes over a long period of time. In those circumstances, it is far from clear whose intent should be examined, and the majority offers no real guidance on this issue. In truth, intent simply is not very meaningful when considering a challenge to an institution, such as a prison system.

The majority's approach also is unwise. It leaves open the possibility, for example, that prison officials will be able to defeat a § 1983 action challenging inhumane prison conditions simply by showing that the conditions are caused by insufficient funding from the state legislature, rather than by any deliberate indifference on the part of the prison officials.

HUDSON v. McMILLIAN, 503 U.S. 1 (1992)

JUSTICE O'CONNOR delivered the opinion of the Court, joined by CHIEF JUSTICE REHNQUIST, and JUSTICES WHITE, KENNEDY, and SOUTER, and joined by JUSTICE STEVENS as to Parts I, II-A, II-B, and II-C.

This case requires us to decide whether the use of excessive physical force against a prisoner may constitute cruel and unusual punishment when the inmate does not suffer serious injury. We answer that question in the affirmative.

I

At the time of the incident that is the subject of this suit, petitioner Keith Hudson was an inmate at the state penitentiary in Angola, Louisiana. Respondents Jack McMillian, Marvin Woods, and Arthur Mezo served as corrections security officers at the Angola facility. During the early morning hours of October 30, 1983, Hudson and McMillian argued. Assisted by Woods, McMillian then placed Hudson in handcuffs and shackles, took the prisoner out of his cell, and walked him toward the penitentiary's "administrative lockdown" area. Hudson testified that, on the way there, McMillian punched Hudson in the mouth, eyes, chest, and stomach while Woods held the inmate in place and kicked and punched him from behind. He further testified that Mezo, the supervisor on duty, watched the beating but merely told the officers "not to have too much fun." As a result of this episode, Hudson suffered minor bruises and swelling of his face, mouth, and lip. The blows also loosened Hudson's teeth and cracked his partial dental plate, rendering it unusable for several months.

Hudson sued the three corrections officers [. . .] alleging a violation of the Eighth Amendment's prohibition on cruel and unusual punishments and seeking compensatory damages.

We granted certiorari to determine whether the "significant injury" requirement applied by the Court of Appeals accords with the Constitution's dictate that cruel and unusual punishment shall not be inflicted.

II

[. . .] the appropriate inquiry when an inmate alleges that prison officials failed to attend to serious medical needs is whether the officials exhibited "deliberate indifference." This standard is appropriate because the State's responsibility to provide inmates with medical care ordinarily does not conflict with competing administrative concerns.

By contrast, officials confronted with a prison disturbance must balance the threat unrest poses to inmates, prison workers, administrators, and visitors against the harm inmates may suffer if guards use force. Despite the weight of these competing concerns, corrections officials must make their decisions "in haste, under pressure, and frequently without the luxury of a second chance."

Many of the concerns underlying our holding in *Whitley* arise whenever guards use force to keep order. Whether the prison disturbance is a riot or a lesser disruption, corrections officers must balance the need "to maintain or restore discipline" through force against the risk of injury to inmates. Both situations may require prison officials to act quickly and decisively. Likewise, both implicate the principle that '[p]rison administrators . . . should be accorded wide-ranging deference in the adoption and execution of policies and practices that in their judgment are needed to preserve internal order and discipline and to maintain institutional security.' In recognition of these similarities, we hold that whenever prison officials stand accused of using excessive physical force in violation of the Cruel and Unusual Punishments Clause, the core judicial inquiry is that set out in *Whitley:* whether force was applied in a good-faith effort to maintain or restore discipline, or maliciously and sadistically to cause harm.

Extending *Whitley's* application of the "unnecessary and wanton infliction of pain" standard to all allegations of excessive force works no innovation.

A

Under the *Whitley* approach, the extent of injury suffered by an inmate is one factor that may suggest "whether the use of force could plausibly have been thought necessary" in a particular situation, "or instead evinced such wantonness with respect to the unjustified infliction of harm as is tantamount to a knowing willingness that it occur." In determining whether the use of force was wanton and unnecessary, it may also be proper to evaluate the need for application of force, the relationship between that need and the amount of force used, the threat "reasonably perceived by the responsible officials," and "any efforts made to temper the severity of a forceful response." The absence of serious injury is therefore relevant to the Eighth Amendment inquiry, but does not end it.

Respondents nonetheless assert that a significant injury requirement of the sort imposed by the Fifth Circuit is mandated by what we have termed the "objective component" of Eighth Amendment analysis. *Wilson* extended the deliberate indifference standard applied to Eighth Amendment claims involving medical care to claims about conditions of confinement. In taking this step, we suggested that the subjective aspect of an Eighth Amendment claim (with which the Court was concerned) can be distinguished from the objective facet of the same claim. Thus, courts considering a prisoner's claim must ask both if "the officials act[ed] with a sufficiently culpable state of mind" and if the alleged wrongdoing was objectively "harmful enough" to establish a constitutional violation.

With respect to the objective component of an Eighth Amendment violation, *Wilson* announced no new rule. Instead, that decision suggested a relationship between the requirements applicable to different types of Eighth Amendment claims. What is necessary to show sufficient harm for purposes of the Cruel and Unusual Punishments Clause depends upon the claim at issue, for two reasons. First, "[t]he general requirement that an Eighth Amendment claimant allege and prove the unnecessary and wanton infliction of pain should . . . be applied with due regard for differences in the kind of conduct against which an Eighth Amendment objection is lodged." Second, the Eighth Amendment's prohibition of cruel and unusual punishments " 'draw[s] its meaning from the evolving standards of decency that mark the progress of a maturing society,' " and so admits of few absolute limitations.

The objective component of an Eighth Amendment claim is therefore contextual and responsive to "contemporary standards of decency."

Because society does not expect that prisoners will have unqualified access to health care, deliberate indifference to medical needs amounts to an Eighth Amendment violation only if those needs are "serious."

In the excessive force context, society's expectations are different. When prison officials maliciously and sadistically use force to cause harm, contemporary standards of decency always are violated. Otherwise, the Eighth Amendment would permit any physical punishment, no matter how diabolic or inhuman, inflicting less than some arbitrary quantity of injury. Such a result would have been as unacceptable to the drafters of the Eighth Amendment as it is today.

That is not to say that every malevolent touch by a prison guard gives rise to a federal cause of action.

In this case, the Fifth Circuit found Hudson's claim untenable because his injuries were "minor." Yet the blows directed at Hudson, which caused bruises, swelling, loosened teeth, and a cracked dental plate, are not *de minimis* for Eighth Amendment purposes. The extent of Hudson's injuries thus provides no basis for dismissal of his § 1983 claim.

B

The dissent's theory that *Wilson* requires an inmate who alleges excessive use of force to show serious injury *in addition to* the unnecessary and wanton infliction of pain misapplies *Wilson* and ignores the body of our Eighth Amendment jurisprudence.

C

Respondents argue that, aside from the significant injury test applied by the Fifth Circuit, their conduct cannot constitute an Eighth Amendment violation because it was "isolated and unauthorized." The beating of Hudson, they contend, arose from "a personal dispute between correctional security officers and a prisoner," and was against prison policy. Respondents invoke the reasoning of courts that have held the use of force by prison officers under such circumstances beyond the scope of "punishment" prohibited by the Eighth Amendment.

We take no position on respondents' legal argument because we find it inapposite on this record.

JUSTICE STEVENS filed an opinion concurring in part and concurring in the judgment.

JUSTICE BLACKMUN filed an opinion concurring in the judgment.

The Court today appropriately puts to rest a seriously misguided view that pain inflicted by an excessive use of force is actionable under the Eighth Amendment only when coupled with "significant injury," *e.g.*, injury that requires medical attention or leaves permanent marks. Indeed, were we to hold to the contrary, we might place various kinds of state-sponsored torture and abuse-of the kind ingeniously designed to cause pain but without a telltale "significant injury" entirely beyond the pale of the Constitution. In other words, the constitutional prohibition of "cruel and unusual punishments" then might not constrain prison officials from lashing prisoners with leather straps, whipping them with rubber hoses, beating them with naked fists, shocking them with electric currents, asphyxiating them short of death, intentionally exposing them to undue heat or cold, or forcibly injecting them with psychosis-inducing drugs. These techniques, commonly thought to be practiced only outside this Nation's borders, are hardly unknown within this Nation's prisons.

JUSTICE THOMAS filed a dissenting opinion, joined by JUSTICE SCALIA.

Today's expansion of the Cruel and Unusual Punishments Clause beyond all bounds of history and precedent is, I suspect, yet another manifestation of the pervasive view that the Federal Constitution must address all ills in our society. Abusive behavior by prison guards is deplorable conduct that properly evokes outrage and contempt. But that does not mean that it is invariably unconstitutional. The Eighth Amendment is not, and should not be turned into, a National Code of Prison Regulation. To reject the notion that the infliction of concededly "minor" injuries can be considered either "cruel" or "unusual" punishment (much less cruel *and* unusual punishment) is not to say that it amounts to acceptable conduct. Rather, it is to recognize that primary responsibility for preventing and punishing such conduct rests not with the Federal Constitution but with the laws and regulations of the various States.

HELLING v. McKINNEY, 509 U.S. 25 (1993)

JUSTICE WHITE delivered the opinion of the Court, joined by CHIEF JUSTICE REHNQUIST, and JUSTICES BLACKMUN, STEVENS, O'CONNOR, KENNEDY, and SOUTER.

This case requires us to decide whether the health risk posed by involuntary exposure of a prison inmate to environ mental tobacco smoke (ETS) can form the basis of a claim for relief under the Eighth Amendment.

Respondent is serving a sentence of imprisonment in the Nevada prison system. At the time that this case arose, respondent was an inmate in the Nevada State Prison in Carson City, Nevada. The complaint, dated December 18, 1986, alleged that respondent was assigned to a cell with another inmate who smoked five packs of cigarettes a day. The complaint also stated that cigarettes were sold to inmates without properly informing of the health hazards a nonsmoking inmate would encounter by sharing a room with an inmate who smoked and that certain cigarettes burned continuously, releasing some type of chemical. Respondent complained of certain health problems allegedly caused by exposure to cigarette smoke. Respondent sought injunctive relief and damages for, *inter alia*, subjecting him to cruel and unusual punishment by jeopardizing his health.

[. . .]

It is undisputed that the treatment a prisoner receives in prison and the conditions under which he is confined are subject to scrutiny under the Eighth Amendment.

We have great difficulty agreeing that prison authorities may not be deliberately indifferent to an inmate's current health problems but may ignore a condition of confinement that is sure or very likely to cause serious illness and needless suffering the next week or month or year.

We would think that a prison inmate also could successfully complain about demonstrably unsafe drinking water without waiting for an attack of dysentery. Nor can we hold that prison officials may be deliberately indifferent to the exposure of inmates to a serious, communicable disease on the ground that the complaining inmate shows no serious current symptoms.

That the Eighth Amendment protects against future harm to inmates is not a novel proposition. The Amendment, as we have said, requires that inmates be furnished with the basic human needs, one of which is "reasonable safety."

The Court of Appeals has ruled that McKinney's claim is that the level of ETS to which he has been involuntarily exposed is such that his future health is unreasonably endangered and has remanded to permit McKinney to attempt to prove his case. In the course of such proof, he must also establish that it is contrary to current standards of decency for anyone to be so exposed against his will and that prison officials are deliberately indifferent to his plight. We cannot rule at this juncture that it will be impossible for McKinney, on remand, to prove an Eighth Amendment violation based on exposure to ETS.

We affirm the holding of the Court of Appeals that McKinney states a cause of action under the Eighth Amendment by alleging that petitioners have, with deliberate indifference, exposed him to levels of ETS that pose an unreasonable risk of serious damage to his future health. We also affirm the remand to the District Court to provide an opportunity for McKinney to prove his allegations, which will require him to prove both the subjective and objective elements necessary to prove an Eighth Amendment violation. The District Court will have the usual authority to control the order of proof, and if there is a failure of proof on the first element that it chooses to consider, it would not be an abuse of discretion to give judgment for petitioners without taking further evidence. McKinney must also prove that he is entitled to the remedy of an injunction.

With respect to the objective factor, McKinney must show that he himself is being exposed to unreasonably high levels of ETS.

[. . .]

Also with respect to the objective factor, determining whether McKinney's conditions of confinement violate the Eighth Amendment requires more than a scientific and statistical inquiry into the seriousness of the potential harm and the likelihood that such injury to health will actually be caused by exposure to ETS. It also requires a court to assess whether society considers the risk that the prisoner complains of to be so grave that it violates contemporary standards of decency to expose *anyone* unwillingly to such a risk. In other words, the prisoner must show that the risk of which he complains is not one that today's society chooses to tolerate.

On remand, the subjective factor, deliberate indifference, should be determined in light of the prison authorities' current attitudes and conduct, which may have changed considerably since the judgment of the Court of Appeals. Indeed, the adoption of the smoking policy mentioned above will bear heavily on the inquiry into deliberate indifference. In this respect we note that at oral argument McKinney's counsel was of the view that depending on how the new policy was administered, it could be very difficult to demonstrate that prison authorities are ignoring the possible dangers posed by exposure to ETS. The inquiry into this factor also would be an appropriate vehicle to consider arguments regarding the realities of prison administration.

JUSTICE THOMAS filed a dissenting opinion, joined by JUSTICE SCALIA.

To state a claim under the Cruel and Unusual Punishments Clause, a party must prove not only that the challenged conduct was both cruel and unusual, but also that it constitutes punishment. The text and history of the Eighth Amendment, together with pre-*Estelle* precedent, raise substantial doubts in my mind that the Eighth Amendment proscribes a prison deprivation that is not inflicted as part of a sentence. And *Estelle* itself has not dispelled these doubts. Were the issue squarely presented, therefore, I might vote to overrule *Estelle*. I need not make that decision today, however, because this case is not a straightforward application of *Estelle*. It is, instead, an extension.

In *Hudson*, the Court extended *Estelle* to cases in which the prisoner has suffered only minor injuries; here, it extends *Estelle* to cases in which there has been no injury at all. Because I seriously doubt that *Estelle* was correctly decided, I decline to join the Court's holding. *Stare decisis* may call for hesitation in overruling a dubious precedent, but it does not demand that such a precedent be expanded to its outer limits. I would draw the line at actual, serious injuries and reject the claim that exposure to the risk of injury can violate the Eighth Amendment.

FARMER v. BRENNAN, 511 U.S. 825 (1994)

JUSTICE SOUTER delivered the opinion of the Court, joined by CHIEF JUSTICE REHNQUIST, and JUSTICES BLACKMUN, STEVENS, O'CONNOR, SCALIA, KENNEDY, and GINSBURG.

This case requires us to define the term "deliberate indifference," as we do by requiring a showing that the official was subjectively aware of the risk.

The dispute before us stems from a civil suit brought by petitioner, Dee Farmer, alleging that respondents, federal prison officials, violated the Eighth Amendment by their deliberate indifference to petitioner's safety. Petitioner, who is serving a federal sentence for credit card fraud, has been diagnosed by medical personnel of the Bureau of Prisons as a transsexual, one who has "[a] rare psychiatric disorder in which a person feels persistently uncomfortable about his or her anatomical sex," and who typically seeks medical treatment, including hormonal therapy and surgery, to bring about a permanent sex change. For several years before being convicted and sentenced in 1986 at the age of 18, petitioner, who is biologically male, wore women's clothing (as petitioner did at the 1986 trial), underwent estrogen therapy, received silicone breast implants, and submitted to unsuccessful "black market" testicle-removal surgery. Petitioner's precise appearance in prison is unclear from the record before us, but petitioner claims to have continued hormonal treatment while incarcerated by using drugs smuggled into prison, and apparently wears clothing in a feminine manner, as by displaying a shirt "off one shoulder." The parties agree that petitioner "projects feminine characteristics."

The practice of federal prison authorities is to incarcerate preoperative transsexuals with prisoners of like biological sex, and over time authorities housed petitioner in several federal facilities, sometimes in the general male prison population but more often in segregation. While there is no dispute that petitioner was segregated at least several times because of violations of prison rules, neither is it disputed that in at least one penitentiary petitioner was segregated because of safety concerns.

On March 9, 1989, petitioner was transferred for disciplinary reasons from the Federal Correctional Institute in Oxford, Wisconsin (FCI-Oxford), to the United States Penitentiary in Terre Haute, Indiana (USP-Terre Haute). Though the record before us is unclear about the security designations of the two prisons in 1989, penitentiaries are typically higher security facilities that house more troublesome prisoners than federal correctional institutes. See generally Federal Bureau of Prisons, Facilities 1990. After an initial stay in administrative segregation, petitioner was placed in the USP-Terre Haute general population. Petitioner voiced no objection to any prison official about the transfer to the penitentiary or to placement in its general population. Within two weeks, according to petitioner's allegations, petitioner was beaten and raped by another inmate in petitioner's cell. Several days later, after petitioner claims to have reported the incident, officials returned petitioner to segregation to await, according to respondents, a hearing about petitioner's HIV-positive status.

The Constitution "does not mandate comfortable prisons," but neither does it permit inhumane ones, and it is now settled that "the treatment a prisoner receives in prison and the conditions under which he is confined are subject to scrutiny under the Eighth Amendment." In its prohibition of "cruel and unusual punishments," the Eighth Amendment places restraints on prison officials, who may not, for example, use excessive physical force against prisoners. The Amendment also imposes duties on these officials, who must provide humane conditions of confinement; prison officials must ensure that inmates receive adequate food, clothing, shelter, and medical care, and must "take reasonable measures to guarantee the safety of the inmates."

It is not, however, every injury suffered by one prisoner at the hands of another that translates into constitutional liability for prison officials responsible for the victim's safety. Our cases have held that a prison official violates the Eighth Amendment only when two requirements are met. First, the deprivation alleged must be, objectively, "sufficiently serious"; a prison official's act or omission must result in the denial of "the minimal civilized measure of life's necessities." For a claim (like the one here) based on a failure to prevent harm, the inmate must show that he is incarcerated under conditions posing a substantial risk of serious harm.

The second requirement follows from the principle that "only the unnecessary and wanton infliction of pain implicates the Eighth Amendment." To violate the Cruel and Unusual Punishments Clause, a prison official must have a "sufficiently culpable state of mind." In prison-conditions cases that state of mind is one of "deliberate indifference" to inmate health or safety.

At what point a risk of inmate assault becomes sufficiently substantial for Eighth Amendment purposes is a question this case does not present, and we do not address it. Although we have never paused to explain the meaning of the term "deliberate indifference," the case law is instructive.

While *Estelle* establishes that deliberate indifference entails something more than mere negligence, the cases are also clear that it is satisfied by something less than acts or omissions for the very purpose of causing harm or with knowledge that harm will result. That point underlies the ruling that "application of the deliberate indifference standard is inappropriate" in one class of prison cases: when "officials stand accused of using excessive physical force."

We reject petitioner's invitation to adopt an objective test for deliberate indifference. We hold instead that a prison official cannot be found liable under the Eighth Amendment for denying an inmate humane conditions of confinement unless the official knows of and disregards an excessive risk to inmate health or safety; the official must both be aware of facts from which the inference could be drawn that a substantial risk of serious harm exists, and he must also draw the inference. This approach comports best with the text of the Amendment as our cases have interpreted it.

Our decision that Eighth Amendment liability requires consciousness of a risk is thus based on the Constitution and our cases, not merely on a parsing of the phrase "deliberate indifference." And we do not reject petitioner's arguments for a thoroughly objective approach to deliberate indifference without recognizing that on the crucial point (whether a prison official must know of a risk, or whether it suffices that he should know) the term does not speak with certainty. Use of "deliberate," for example, arguably requires nothing more than an act (or omission) of indifference to a serious risk that is voluntary, not accidental.

We are no more persuaded by petitioner's argument that, without an objective test for deliberate indifference, prison officials will be free to ignore obvious dangers to inmates. Under the test we adopt today, an Eighth Amendment claimant need not show that a prison official acted or failed to act believing that harm actually would befall an inmate; it is enough that the official acted or failed to act despite his knowledge of a substantial risk of serious harm.

While the obviousness of a risk is not conclusive and a prison official may show that the obvious escaped him, he would not escape liability if the evidence showed that he merely refused to verify underlying facts that he strongly suspected to be true, or declined to confirm inferences of risk that he strongly suspected to exist (as when a prison official is aware of a high probability of facts indicating that one prisoner has planned an attack on another but resists opportunities to obtain final confirmation; or when a prison official knows that some diseases are communicable and that a single needle is being used to administer flu shots to prisoners but refuses to listen to a subordinate who he strongly suspects will attempt to explain the associated risk of transmitting disease). When instructing juries in deliberate indifference cases with such issues of proof, courts should be careful to ensure that the requirement of subjective culpability is not lost. It is not enough merely to find that a reasonable person would have known, or that the defendant should have known, and juries should be instructed accordingly.

Because, however, prison officials who lacked knowledge of a risk cannot be said to have inflicted punishment, it remains open to the officials to prove that they were unaware even of an obvious risk to inmate health or safety. That a trier of fact may infer knowledge from the obvious, in other words, does not mean that it must do so. Prison officials charged with deliberate indifference might show, for example, that they did not know of the underlying facts indicating a sufficiently substantial danger and that they were therefore unaware of a danger, or that they knew the underlying facts but believed (albeit unsoundly) that the risk to which the facts gave rise was insubstantial or nonexistent.

In addition, prison officials who actually knew of a substantial risk to inmate health or safety may be found free from liability if they responded reasonably to the risk, even if the harm ultimately was not averted. A prison official's duty under the Eighth Amendment is to ensure " 'reasonable safety,' "

[. . .]

Accordingly, we reject petitioner's arguments and hold that a prison official may be held liable under the Eighth Amendment for denying humane conditions of confinement only if he knows that inmates face a substantial risk of serious harm and disregards that risk by failing to take reasonable measures to abate it.

JUSTICE BLACKMUN filed a concurring opinion.

JUSTICE STEVENS filed a concurring opinion.

JUSTICE THOMAS filed an opinion concurring in the judgment.

HOPE v. PELZER, 536 U.S. 730 (2002)

JUSTICE STEVENS delivered the opinion of the Court, joined by JUSTICES O'CONNOR, KENNEDY, SOUTER, GINSBURG, and BREYER.

In 1995, Alabama was the only State that followed the practice of chaining inmates to one another in work squads. It was also the only State that handcuffed prisoners to "hitching posts" if they either refused to work or otherwise disrupted work squads. Hope was handcuffed to a hitching post on two occasions. On May 11, 1995, while Hope was working in a chain gang near an interstate highway, he got into an argument with another inmate. Both men were taken back to the Limestone prison and handcuffed to a hitching post. Hope was released two hours later, after the guard captain determined that the altercation had been caused by the other inmate. During his two hours on the post, Hope was offered drinking water and a bathroom break every 15 minutes, and his responses to these offers were recorded on an activity log. Because he was only slightly taller than the hitching post, his arms were above shoulder height and grew tired from being handcuffed so high. Whenever he tried moving his arms to improve his circulation, the handcuffs cut into his wrists, causing pain and discomfort.

On June 7, 1995, Hope was punished more severely. He took a nap during the morning bus ride to the chain gang's worksite, and when it arrived he was less than prompt in responding to an order to get off the bus. An exchange of vulgar remarks led to a wrestling match with a guard. Four other guards intervened, subdued Hope, handcuffed him, placed him in leg irons and transported him back to the prison where he was put on the hitching post. The guards made him take off his shirt, and he remained shirtless all day while the sun burned his skin. He remained attached to the post for approximately seven hours. During this 7-hour period, he was given water only once or twice and was given no bathroom breaks. At one point, a guard taunted Hope about his thirst.

The Court of Appeals held that "the policy and practice of cuffing an inmate to a hitching post or similar stationary object for a period of time that surpasses that necessary to quell a threat or restore order is a violation of the Eighth Amendment." The court rejected respondents' submission that Hope could have ended his shackling by offering to return to work, finding instead that the purpose of the practice was punitive, and that the circumstances of his confinement create a substantial risk of harm of which the officers were aware. Moreover, the court relied on Circuit precedent condemning similar practices and the results of a United States Department of Justice (DOJ) report that found Alabama's systematic use of the hitching post to be improper corporal punishment. We agree with the Court of Appeals that the attachment of Hope to the hitching post under the circumstances alleged in this case violated the Eighth Amendment.

As the facts are alleged by Hope, the Eighth Amendment violation is obvious. Any safety concerns had long since abated by the time petitioner was handcuffed to the hitching post because Hope had already been subdued, handcuffed, placed in leg irons, and transported back to the prison. He was separated from his work squad and not given the opportunity to return to work. Despite the clear lack of an emergency situation, the respondents knowingly subjected him to a substantial risk of physical harm, to unnecessary pain caused by the handcuffs and the restricted position of confinement for a 7-hour period, to unnecessary exposure to the heat of the sun, to prolonged thirst and taunting, and to a deprivation of bathroom breaks that created a risk of particular discomfort and humiliation. The use of the hitching post under these circumstances violated the "basic concept underlying the Eighth Amendment[, which] is nothing less than the dignity of man." This punitive treatment amounts to gratuitous infliction of "wanton and unnecessary" pain that our precedent clearly prohibits.

JUSTICE THOMAS filed a dissenting opinion, joined by CHIEF JUSTICE REHNQUIST and JUSTICE SCALIA.

BROWN v. PLATA, 563 U.S. 493 (2011)

JUSTICE KENNEDY delivered the opinion of the Court, joined by JUSTICES GINSBURG, BREYER, SOTOMAYOR, and KAGAN.

This case arises from serious constitutional violations in California's prison system. The violations have persisted for years. They remain uncorrected. The appeal comes to this Court from a three-judge District Court order directing California to remedy two ongoing violations of the Cruel and Unusual Punishments Clause, a guarantee binding on the States by the Due Process Clause of the Fourteenth Amendment. The violations are the subject of two class actions in two Federal District Courts. The first involves the class of prisoners with serious mental disorders. That case is *Coleman v. Brown*. The second involves prisoners with serious medical conditions. That case is *Plata v. Brown*. The order of the three-judge District Court is applicable to both cases.

I

A

The degree of overcrowding in California's prisons is exceptional. California's prisons are designed to house a population just under 80,000, but at the time of the three-judge court's decision the population was almost double that. The State's prisons had operated at around 200% of design capacity for at least 11 years. Prisoners are crammed into spaces neither designed nor intended to house inmates. As many as 200 prisoners may live in a gymnasium, monitored by as few as two or three correctional officers. As many as 54 prisoners may share a single toilet.

In 2006, then-Governor Schwarzenegger declared a state of emergency in the prisons, as "'immediate action is necessary to prevent death and harm caused by California's severe prison overcrowding.'" The consequences of overcrowding identified by the Governor include "'increased, substantial risk for transmission of infectious illness'" and a suicide rate "'approaching an average of one per week.'"

Prisoners in California with serious mental illness do not receive minimal, adequate care. Because of a shortage of treatment beds, suicidal inmates may be held for prolonged periods in telephone-booth sized cages without toilets. A psychiatric expert reported observing an inmate who had been held in such a cage for nearly 24 hours, standing in a pool of his own urine, unresponsive and nearly catatonic.

Prisoners suffering from physical illness also receive severely deficient care. California's prisons were designed to meet the medical needs of a population at 100% of design capacity and so have only half the clinical space needed to treat the current population. A correctional officer testified that, in one prison, up to 50 sick inmates may be held together in a 12- by 20-foot cage for up to five hours awaiting treatment. The number of staff is inadequate, and prisoners face significant delays in access to care. A prisoner with severe abdominal pain died after a 5-week delay in referral to a specialist; a prisoner with "constant and extreme" chest pain died after an 8-hour delay in evaluation by a doctor; and a prisoner died of testicular cancer after a "failure of MDs to work up for cancer in a young man with 17 months of testicular pain."

Many more prisoners, suffering from severe but not life-threatening conditions, experience prolonged illness and unnecessary pain.

B

These conditions are the subject of two federal cases. The first to commence, *Coleman v. Brown*, was filed in 1990. *Coleman* involves the class of seriously mentally ill persons in California prisons. Over 15 years ago, in 1995, after a 39-day trial, the *Coleman* District Court found "overwhelming evidence of the systematic failure to deliver necessary care to mentally ill inmates" in California prisons. The prisons were "seriously and chronically understaffed." Mentally ill inmates "languished for months, or even years, without access to necessary care."

In 2007, 12 years after his appointment, the Special Master in *Coleman* filed a report stating that, after years of slow improvement, the state of mental health care in California's prisons was deteriorating. The Special Master ascribed this change to increased overcrowding. The rise in population had led to greater demand for care, and existing programming space and staffing levels were inadequate to keep pace. Prisons had retained more mental health staff, but the "growth of the resource [had] not matched the rise in demand."

C

The second action, *Plata v. Brown*, involves the class of state prisoners with serious medical conditions. After this action commenced in 2001, the State conceded that deficiencies in prison medical care violated prisoners' Eighth Amendment rights. The State stipulated to a remedial injunction. The State failed to comply with that injunction, and in 2005 the court appointed a

Receiver to oversee remedial efforts. The court found that "the California prison medical care system is broken beyond repair," resulting in an "unconscionable degree of suffering and death." The court found: "[I]t is an uncontested fact that, on average, an inmate in one of California's prisons needlessly dies every six to seven days due to constitutional deficiencies in the [California prisons'] medical delivery system."

A report by the Receiver detailed the impact of overcrowding on efforts to remedy the violation. The Receiver explained that "overcrowding, combined with staffing shortages, has created a culture of cynicism, fear, and despair which makes hiring and retaining competent clinicians extremely difficult."

D

The *Coleman* and *Plata* plaintiffs, believing that a remedy for unconstitutional medical and mental health care could not be achieved without reducing overcrowding, moved their respective District Courts to convene a three-judge court empowered under the PLRA to order reductions in the prison population. The judges in both actions granted the request, and the cases were consolidated before a single three-judge court. The State has not challenged the validity of the consolidation in proceedings before this Court, so its propriety is not presented by this appeal.

The three-judge court heard 14 days of testimony and issued a 184-page opinion, making extensive findings of fact. The court ordered California to reduce its prison population to 137.5% of the prisons' design capacity within two years. Assuming the State does not increase capacity through new construction, the order requires a population reduction of 38,000 to 46,000 persons. Because it appears all but certain that the State cannot complete sufficient construction to comply fully with the order, the prison population will have to be reduced to at least some extent. The court did not order the State to achieve this reduction in any particular manner. Instead, the court ordered the State to formulate a plan for compliance and submit its plan for approval by the court.

II

As a consequence of their own actions, prisoners may be deprived of rights that are fundamental to liberty. Yet the law and the Constitution demand recognition of certain other rights. Prisoners retain the essence of human dignity inherent in all persons. Respect for that dignity animates the Eighth Amendment prohibition against cruel and unusual punishment. "'The basic concept underlying the Eighth Amendment is nothing less than the dignity of man.' "

To incarcerate, society takes from prisoners the means to provide for their own needs. Prisoners are dependent on the State for food, clothing, and necessary medical care. A prison's failure to provide sustenance for inmates "may actually produce physical 'torture or a lingering death.' " Just as a prisoner may starve if not fed, he or she may suffer or die if not provided adequate medical care. A prison that deprives prisoners of basic sustenance, including adequate medical care, is incompatible with the concept of human dignity and has no place in civilized society.

A

The State contends that it was error to convene the three-judge court without affording it more time to comply with the prior orders in *Coleman* and *Plata*.

1

The parties dispute this Court's jurisdiction to review the determinations of the *Coleman* and *Plata* District Courts that a three-judge court should be convened. Plaintiffs claim the State was required to raise this issue first in the Court of Appeals by appealing the orders of the District Courts. When exercising jurisdiction under 28 U. S. C. §1253, however, this Court "has not hesitated to exercise jurisdiction 'to determine the authority of the court below,' " including whether the three-judge court was properly constituted. *Gonzalez* v. *Automatic Employees Credit Union*, 419 U. S. 90, 95, n. 12 (1974) (quoting *Bailey* v. *Patterson*, 369 U. S. 31, 34 (1962) (*per curiam*)); see also *Gully* v. *Interstate Natural Gas Co.*, 292 U. S. 16, 18 (1934) *(per curiam)* ("The case is analogous to those in which this Court, finding that the court below has acted without jurisdiction, exercises its appellate jurisdiction to correct the improper action".) The merits of the decision to convene the three-judge court, therefore, are properly before this Court.

2

Before a three-judge court may be convened to consider whether to enter a population limit, the PLRA requires that the court have "previously entered an order for less intrusive relief that has failed to remedy the deprivation of the Federal right sought to be remedied." 18 U. S. C. § 3626(a)(3)(A)(i). This provision refers to "an order." It is satisfied if the court has entered one order, and this single order has "failed to remedy" the constitutional violation. The defendant must also have had "a reasonable amount of time to comply with the previous court orders." § 3626(a)(3)(A)(ii). This provision refers to the court's "orders." It requires that the defendant have been given a reasonable time to comply with all of the court's orders. Together, these requirements ensure that the " 'last resort remedy' " of a population limit is not imposed " 'as a first step.' " *Inmates of Occoquan* v. *Barry*, 844 F.2d 828, 843.

The first of these conditions, the previous order requirement of § 3626(a)(3)(A)(i), was satisfied in *Coleman* by appointment of a Special Master in 1995, and it was satisfied in *Plata* by approval of a consent decree and stipulated injunction in 2002. Both orders were intended to remedy the constitutional violations. Both were given ample time to succeed. When the three-judge court was convened, 12 years had passed since the appointment of the *Coleman* Special Master, and 5 years had passed since the approval of the *Plata* consent decree. The State does not claim that either order achieved a remedy. Although the PLRA entitles a State to terminate remedial orders such as these after two years unless the district court finds that the relief "remains necessary to correct a current and ongoing violation of the Federal right," § 3626(b)(3), California has not attempted to obtain relief on this basis.

The State claims instead that the second condition, the reasonable time requirement of § 3626(a)(3)(A)(ii), was not met because other, later remedial efforts should have been given more time to succeed. In 2006, the *Coleman* District Judge approved a revised plan of action calling for construction of new facilities, hiring of new staff, and implementation of new procedures. That same year, the *Plata* District Judge selected and appointed a Receiver to oversee the State's ongoing remedial efforts. When the three-judge court was convened, the Receiver had filed a preliminary plan of action calling for new construction, hiring of additional staff, and other procedural reforms.

Although both the revised plan of action in *Coleman* and the appointment of the Receiver in *Plata* were new developments in the courts' remedial efforts, the basic plan to solve the crisis through construction, hiring, and procedural reforms remained unchanged. These efforts had been ongoing for years; the failed consent decree in *Plata* had called for implementation of new procedures and hiring of additional staff; and the *Coleman* Special Master had issued over 70 orders directed at achieving a remedy through construction, hiring, and procedural reforms.

[. . .]

The State argues that the violation could have been remedied through a combination of new construction, transfers of prisoners out of State, hiring of medical personnel, and continued efforts by the *Plata* Receiver and *Coleman* Special Master. The order in fact permits the State to comply with the population limit by transferring prisoners to county facilities or facilities in other States, or by constructing new facilities to raise the prisons' design capacity. And the three-judge court's order does not bar the State from undertaking any other remedial efforts. If the State does find an adequate remedy other than a population limit, it may seek modification or termination of the three-judge court's order on that basis. The evidence at trial, however, supports the three-judge court's conclusion that an order limited to other remedies would not provide effective relief.

Even if out-of-state transfers could be regarded as a less restrictive alternative, the three-judge court found no evidence of plans for transfers in numbers sufficient to relieve overcrowding. The State complains that the *Coleman* District Court slowed the rate of transfer by requiring inspections to assure that the receiving institutions were in compliance with the Eighth Amendment, but the State has made no effort to show that it has the resources and the capacity to transfer significantly larger numbers of prisoners absent that condition.

Construction of new facilities, in theory, could alleviate overcrowding, but the three-judge court found no realistic possibility that California would be able to build itself out of this crisis. At the time of the court's decision the State had plans to build new medical and housing facilities, but funding for some plans had not been secured and funding for other plans had been delayed by the legislature for years.

[. . .]

The State has already made significant progress toward reducing its prison population, including reforms that will result in shifting "thousands" of prisoners to county jails. As the State makes further progress, the three-judge court should evaluate whether its order remains appropriate. If significant progress is made toward remedying the underlying constitutional violations, that progress may demonstrate that further population reductions are not necessary or are less urgent than previously believed. Were the State to make this showing, the three-judge court in the exercise of its discretion could consider whether it is appropriate to extend or modify this timeline.

Experience with the three-judge court's order may also lead the State to suggest other modifications. The three-judge court should give any such requests serious consideration. The three-judge court should also formulate its orders to allow the State and its officials the authority necessary to address contingencies that may arise during the remedial process.

These observations reflect the fact that the three-judge court's order, like all continuing equitable decrees, must remain open to appropriate modification. They are not intended to cast doubt on the validity of the basic premise of the existing order. The medical and mental health care provided by California's prisons falls below the standard of decency that inheres in the Eighth Amendment. This extensive and ongoing constitutional violation requires a remedy, and a remedy will not be achieved without a reduction in overcrowding. The relief ordered by the three-judge court is required by the Constitution and was authorized by Congress in the PLRA. The State shall implement the order without further delay.

JUSTICE SCALIA filed a dissenting opinion, joined by JUSTICE THOMAS.

JUSTICE ALITO filed a dissenting opinion, joined by CHIEF JUSTICE ROBERTS.

12

CONCLUSION

Thomas Jefferson wrote in 1816 that we "might as well require a man to wear still the coat which fitted him when a boy, as civilized society to remain ever under the regimen of their barbarous ancestors" (Jefferson, 1816). Until the mid-20th century, the Eighth Amendment's three clauses provided mere "parchment barriers against the encroaching spirit of power," as warned in *Federalist 48* (Madison, 1788). For the first 170 years of the Union, federal prisoners were deprived of access to constitutional rights, with the picture no better at state-level, where local courts left matters of sentencing to the legislature and the imposition of fines and punishments to the executive. For the past several decades, however, the Supreme Court has taken the Eighth on a journey of evolution. This book has sought to outline the most important steps along that voyage.

Any bail imposed above necessity is unconstitutional; excessive conditions of release—taking into account the perceived evil—are likewise proscribed. Similarly, fines and forfeitures (including civil, where property is confiscated by the government without a criminal conviction) are subject to the limitations of the Eighth Amendment, and such fines or forfeitures must not be grossly disproportional to the gravity of a defendant's offense. The method, extent, and scale of the death penalty have shrunk close to the point of vanishing. Subjective assessments such as mitigating evidence must be reviewed and weighed, and only adult offenders who commit aggravated murders can be executed. Juveniles have a special status in the eyes of Eighth Amendment review, as do those offenders who are less culpable either through their acts or their individualized characteristics, such as their character and record. Life without parole sentencing has been limited,

DOI: 10.4324/9780429398780-13

particularly insofar as it concerns younger defendants, and mandatory minimums have met short shrift for their disparate impact, including on mass incarceration. Prisoners retain the essence of human dignity inherent in all persons, and while the Constitution does not mandate comfortable prisons, neither does it permit inhumane ones. The treatment a prisoner receives while confined (and the conditions of imprisonment) are subject to Eighth Amendment scrutiny.

One scholar has written that "the Eighth Amendment is on the road to extinction" owing to the Court's dramatic turn toward originalism and away from the evolving standards of decency test (Ryan, 2023). Perhaps such evolution has paused, at least for the current generation of Justices, but what is clear is that significant constitutional checks have been created, balancing governmental power to punish its citizens. The Eighth Amendment has not stood still for long, although there have been periods of several years where judicial "hands-off" doctrines have limited the Court's innovation. Whenever an individual-rights-leaning majority has sat, the interpretation of the Eighth has not been fastened to the obsolete but has acquired meaning as the Court's opinions have become enlightened by a humane justice. With the current composition of the Court relatively recently renewing its commit to originalist doctrine and favoring discretion in such cases, the Eighth Amendment's next moment of evolution might wait a while longer.

References

Jefferson, T. (1816) *Letter to Samuel Kercheval*, 12 June. Available at: https://tinyurl.com/o33bvrr

Madison, J. (1788) 'Federalist no. 48: these departments should not be so far separated as to have no constitutional control over each other', in *The federalist papers*. The New York Packet.

Ryan, M. (2024) 'The death of the evolving standards of decency', *Florida State University Law Review*, 51, 2023.

INDEX

For Product Safety Concerns and Information please contact our EU
representative GPSR@taylorandfrancis.com
Taylor & Francis Verlag GmbH, Kaufingerstraße 24, 80331 München, Germany

www.ingramcontent.com/pod-product-compliance
Ingram Content Group UK Ltd.
Pitfield, Milton Keynes, MK11 3LW, UK
UKHW022347190926
475702UK00015B/2157

* 9 7 8 0 3 6 7 0 2 6 0 1 1 *